A GLORIOUS AND TERRIBLE LIFE WITH YOU

Selected Correspondence of Northrop Frye and Helen Kemp, 1932–1939

Selected and edited by Margaret Burgess
from the edition prepared by Robert D. Denham

Northrop Frye's status as one of the most influential critics and intellectuals of the twentieth century makes it difficult to gauge the personal qualities of the man behind the work. However, an intimate picture is revealed through the correspondence Frye exchanged with his first wife, Helen Kemp, and which he bequeathed to Victoria University at the time of his death. In *A Glorious and Terrible Life with You*, Margaret Burgess presents the essential narrative at the heart of the correspondence, focusing on the thoughts, feelings, and formative experiences of the two central protagonists as they chronicle both their own intertwined voyages of growth and discovery and the central events of their time.

Bringing to life their interactions with families and friends, their educational milieu, and the significant cultural and historical currents of the 1930s, these letters show both Frye and Kemp engaging with and contributing to the unique cultural climate of the period. Rich and compelling, they exemplify the wonderful eloquence and vitality of spirit that is evident throughout the correspondence. *A Glorious and Terrible Life with You* is a touching and highly revealing account of the relationship between two kindred spirits and remarkable minds.

Lavishly illustrated, this new edition includes family photographs and original graphics by both Helen Kemp and her father, S.H.F. Kemp, mostly dating from his own student days at the University of Toronto.

MARGARET BURGESS taught the mythology half of Frye's "Bible" course, "The Mythological Framework of Western Culture," before his death in 1991. She is currently editorial assistant for the Collected Works of Northrop Frye at Victoria University in the University of Toronto.

A Glorious and Terrible Life with You

Selected Correspondence of Northrop Frye and Helen Kemp 1932–1939

Selected and edited by Margaret Burgess
from the edition prepared by Robert D. Denham

UNIVERSITY OF TORONTO PRESS
Toronto Buffalo London

Printed in Canada

ISBN 978-0-8020-9765-1 (cloth)
ISBN 978-0-8020-9476-6 (paper)

Printed on acid-free paper

Library and Archives Canada Cataloguing in Publication

Frye, Northrop, 1912–1991.
A glorious and terrible life with you : selected correspondence of Northrop Frye and Helen Kemp, 1932–1939 / selected and edited by Margaret Burgess from the edition prepared by Robert D. Denham.

ISBN 978-0-8020-9765-1 (bound)
ISBN 978-0-8020-9476-6 (pbk.)

1. Frye, Northrop, 1912–1991 – Correspondence.
2. Frye, Helen Kemp, 1910–1986 – Correspondence.
3. Critics – Canada – Correspondence. I. Frye, Helen Kemp, 1910–1986. II. Burgess, Margaret, 1949– III. Title.

PN75.F7A4 2007 801′.95092 C2007-903008-4

This book has been published with the help of a grant from the DeGroote Trust for the Collected Works of Northrop Frye at McMaster University.

University of Toronto Press acknowledges the financial assistance to its publishing program of the Canada Council for the Arts and the Ontario Arts Council.

University of Toronto Press acknowledges the financial support for its publishing activities of the Government of Canada through the Book Publishing Development Program (BPIDP).

For Bob Denham
—the greatest decipherer
of the "original hieratic"

and

for the relatives and descendants
of the Fryes and the Kemps

and

of the Victoria and Emmanuel
classes of 3T3 and 3E6

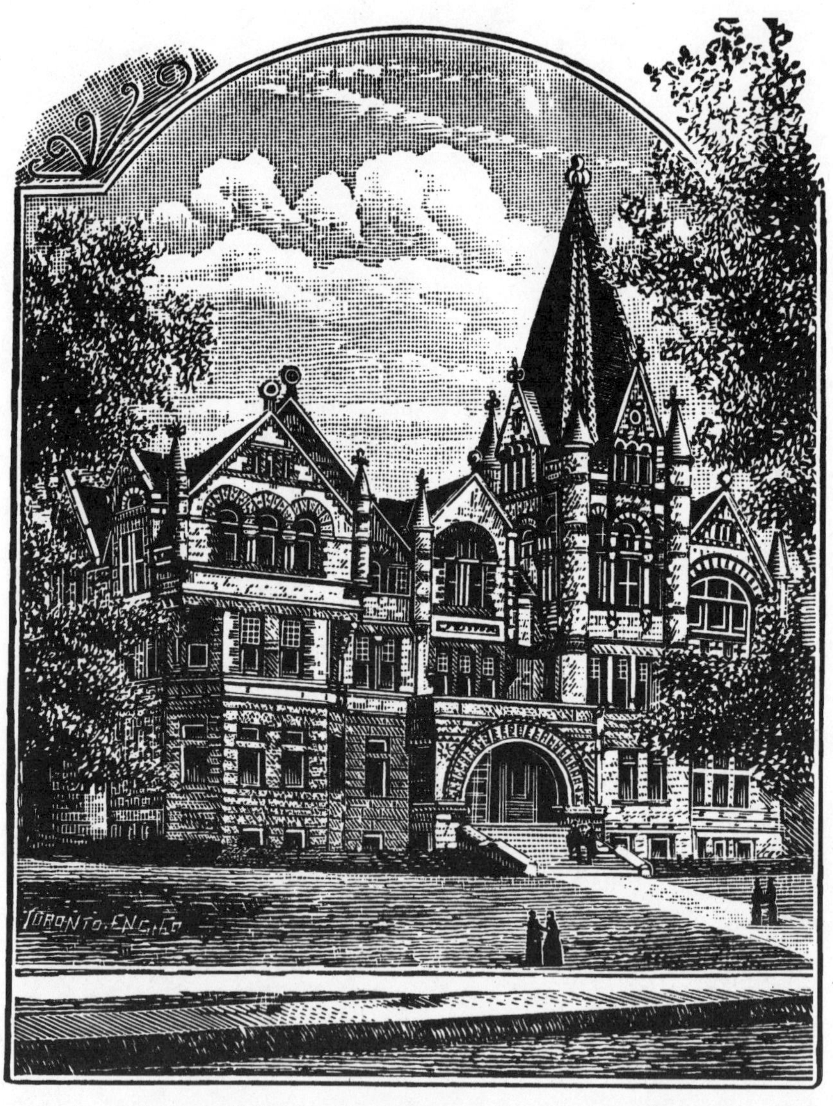

Victoria College, reproduced from *Torontonensis*, 1906
(courtesy of Victoria University Library, Toronto)

Contents

Preface
ix

Introduction
xv

Summer of 1932
1

Summer of 1933
52

Summer of 1934
98

1934–1935
168

1936–1937
254

1938–1939
345

Abbreviations
407

Directory of People Mentioned in the Correspondence
409

Preface

It is a modest understatement to say that the present edition of the selected correspondence of Northrop Frye and Helen Kemp, together with all of the Collected Works editions of Frye's previously unpublished papers, could simply not exist without the painstaking labours and tireless dedication of Robert D. Denham. Not only has Denham toiled unceasingly to provide the extensive annotation and introductions required by this enormous body of new material; he has also gifted the Frye readership with the transcription of hundreds upon hundreds of pages of the most difficult handwriting imaginable, deciphering with a prescience nothing short of uncanny words that are run together, misspelled, ill-formed, unfamiliar, smudged, blurred, run off the page, or otherwise illegible and unintelligible to other would-be transcribers.

Beyond this phenomenal feat of the original transcription of the letters, however, Denham's definitive (or as nearly so as is humanly possible) two-volume edition of the complete Frye–Kemp correspondence in the Collected Works has also benefited the present edition immeasurably by liberating it to be a purely *popular* edition. For the fact that such a complete and meticulously reproduced and annotated edition already exists has made it possible to dispense here with all but the most rudimentary scholarly apparatus, to cut and paste at will with a clear conscience, and generally to resort to every trick in the proverbial book in order to compress the greatest amount of material into the least amount of space.

This being said, it has still been a task of the utmost difficulty to cut the 905 pages of the original correspondence to the strict 464-page limit set by the publisher for the selected edition without sacrificing either the continuity of the narrative or any of its most essential components.

The selection has necessarily focused on the two central characters themselves, their developing relationship, the major events in their lives, and their thoughts and feelings as they experience them, set against the background of their families and innermost circle of friends, their educational milieu, and the most important of the cultural and historical currents and events that swirled around them and shaped them, and in which they in their turn were to become significant actors and contributors. Gossip, peripheral references to other people and events, and explanatory notes have for the most part had to be ruthlessly eliminated, and readers wishing to look into any of these more closely are directed to the complete and annotated Collected Works edition.

Without cataloguing in detail the numerous space-saving devices employed here, I must emphasize that at no time have words of any substance been put into the mouths of the writers that they have not themselves written. On rare occasions a connective "and" or "but" has been supplied, or a substitution along the lines of "a doleful letter" made for "one of my most doleful letters"; and in one instance the word "better" was inserted at the end of a sentence in place of a much longer clause for which the antecedent material had already been deleted ("I've got the stuff of an unusually good writer in me, and the sooner I get established as one the *better*"). Otherwise, the wording, however much condensed, cut, and pasted, is *always* that of the original letters.

The time period covered by the letters spans from the end of the correspondents' third year at Victoria College in 1932 until the completion of Frye's second and final year at Merton College in 1939. The letters are divided into six "chapters" chronicling their separations during this time.

The narrative begins in May of 1932, just as the academic year is drawing to a close. Frye's first letter appears to have been written while both correspondents were still in Toronto. However, they have already said their goodbyes, and Frye's next letter is from Moncton, where he remains, working in the local public library and practising his piano, until his return to Toronto in mid-September for their final undergraduate year at Victoria. Kemp's first letters document visits in June with an aunt and uncle in Forest, Ontario, and with the family of classmate Jean Elder at their cottage on Georgian Bay. Then she returns to Toronto to her music and her art (it is during this period that she creates her inspired map of the University of Toronto campus), and to jobs at the college library and, towards the end of the summer, at the Canadian National Exhibition.

The last two letters in this sequence were written after Frye's return to Toronto, and are included here primarily to showcase Kemp's artwork.

The series for the summer of 1933 begins with a letter sent by Frye in mid-June from Chicago, where he has gone to visit his sister Vera and to see the World's Fair. In August he returns to Ontario to spend some time at the Kemp family cottage in Gordon Bay before going home to Moncton for the month of September. Kemp has in the meantime divided her summer between the cottage and a stint as camp counsellor at Lake Onawa, near Huntsville, Ontario. After two weeks or so at the cottage they travel together as far as Toronto. Frye then continues on to Moncton and Kemp again goes to work at the CNE and at the college library, and also attends a Student Christian Movement conference at Lake Couchiching, Ontario. In her last letter to him before his return to Toronto at the beginning of October to enrol in Emmanuel College as a theology student, Kemp announces that she is to be given a job at the Art Gallery of Toronto (later renamed the Art Gallery of Ontario) as part of a new program for art education that is being created by Arthur Lismer.

In April of 1934 Kemp travels to Ottawa to continue her training in gallery work at the National Gallery of Ottawa, and at the end of the month Frye leaves for Saskatchewan to take on his first and last student summer mission field. While she is in Ottawa Kemp's mentors persuade her to apply for a scholarship to study art history at the Courtauld Institute in the University of London the following year. When her application is successful it looks for a while as though she is going to have to leave for England before Frye returns from Saskatchewan. However, Frye manages to extricate himself from his commitments to his mission field a week early and the two are able to come together for a weekend in Montreal before her departure on 21 September.

Continuing on almost immediately, the letters for 1934–35 show Kemp travelling by ocean liner to England and then getting settled and beginning her studies in London. Meanwhile, Frye resumes his theology course at Emmanuel College, enrols in graduate courses on Blake and Shelley, teaches two English courses at Victoria College, and assists with the preparation for publication of a new edition of the English textbook used by the affiliated colleges, *Representative Poetry*. While in England, Kemp travels to the Lake Country for Christmas and to Italy for six weeks at Easter, and then makes two additional excursions to Europe, to Brussels and Ghent in July and to Paris in September, before returning home in the middle of October.

The letters written during 1936–37—comprising by far the longest chapter of the correspondence—posed the greatest dilemma for the selection process, as it was here that the largest cuts had to be made, and consequently the most difficult editorial decisions as well. The block of letters that could be most easily sacrificed without disrupting the continuity of the whole was a sequence at the very beginning of the section. Reduced to thirty pages in the original version of the abridgment, the letters in this section show Frye travelling to Moncton in August to spend some time with his family and then sailing for London and Oxford in September, while back in Toronto Kemp searches for and moves into an apartment to be shared with friends. However, she is then invited to become a don at Wymilwood, one of Victoria College's women's residences, where she will live while continuing to work at the art gallery. Unfortunately for the present edition, this is also the time during which she underwent a secret and illegal abortion, and for readers who are familiar with the story this will undoubtedly be the most controversial omission from the abridgment. Hopefully, it will be clear that the cut was made purely for reasons of length and not out of any undue sense of delicacy with regard to the topic, and readers are reminded that the complete and unexpurgated story is readily available in the Collected Works edition (*NFHK*, 2:534–49). In the letters that have been retained Frye arrives in Oxford at the beginning of October and, with the exception of several brief trips back to London and five weeks spent in Italy in March and April, remains there until June, when he is forced to interrupt his studies and return home by his failure to make arrangements for his Royal Society grant to be renewed.

After spending the intervening year teaching English at Victoria, and having married Kemp in August of 1937, Frye returns to Oxford to complete his degree in September of 1938. There he shares a flat off campus with friends from his previous sojourn in Oxford, travels with them to London and Paris at Christmas, takes part in a performance of the Oxford University Drama Society, and then moves back into residence in order to prepare for his final exams. Meanwhile, Kemp continues to work at the AGT, lectures outside the gallery on various fine art topics, trains her voice for radio talks, and serves as art editor for the *Canadian Forum*. In June she joins Frye in England and they are able to make a hurried trip to the Continent before returning home in August of 1939, just in time to avoid the outbreak of war.

In conclusion, I would like to express my gratitude to the friends and colleagues who have made this endeavour possible: to Ron Schoeffel of the University of Toronto Press, who originally conceived the idea of a selected edition and then waited long and patiently for its manifestation; to Robert D. Denham, who decided that the project wouldn't fit into his busy schedule and passed it along to me; to Alvin A. Lee and Jean O'Grady, general and associate editors respectively of the Collected Works of Northrop Frye, who gave me time to work on the project and whose persistent proddings in the face of both internal resistance and external distractions eventually resulted in its completion; to Ward McBurney, my fellow editorial assistant on the Collected Works, who offered sage advice and moral support at times when my energies were flagging; and to Nicholas Graham, independent scholar and Frye aficionado, who has lent boundless enthusiasm and the luck of the Irish to countless small details related to the project. The latter five read all or parts of the manuscript and/or proofs and offered helpful suggestions for corrections and improvements, as did John Ayre, Michael Dolzani, Erin Reynolds, and Janet Ritch. Jean O'Grady paid for the high-resolution scan of the black-and-white version of Kemp's map, and Alvin Lee arranged for a subvention from the DeGroote trust to assist the publisher with the financing of the edition.

Heartfelt thanks are due also to the staff at the Victoria University Library at the University of Toronto: to chief librarian Robert Brandeis and his administrative assistant Ann Black; to Lisa Sherlock, quietly competent overseer of the Frye Special Collection, and Bradley Holstead, who scanned all of the photographs, graphics from the letters, and line drawings by S.H.F. Kemp from the 1906 *Torontonensis* used in the edition; and to David Brown (moved on and still missed), Bev Branton, Doug Fox, Alison Girling, Lynda Hayes, Halyna Kozar, Linda Oliver, Debra Ozima, Karen Wishart, and Gabbi Zaldin—all of whom have been a cheerful and never-failing source of assistance and support through every Frye project, not only this one. The library has also granted permission for the publication of the letters and for many of the illustrations, and Victoria University has authorized the reproduction of details of both the black-and-white and coloured versions of Kemp's map. Other illustrations were generously provided by Oxford University Press, the late Jean Elder, and Susan Sydenham, through the ever-gracious medium of Robert Denham, and Ian Price turned up opportunely at the last moment with the 1931 watercolour by S.H.F. Kemp.

Additionally, grateful acknowledgment is owed for the following out of copyright sources for illustrations of Oxford: *The Story of Oxford*, by Cecil Headlam (1926) for the lithographs by Herbert Railton of the Old Gateway, Merton College, and Kemp Hall used on pp. 254 and 345; *The Adventures of Mr. Verdant Green: An Oxford Freshman*, by Cuthbert Bede (pseudonym of Edward Bradley) (1853) for the woodcut depicting the freshman and his scout on p. 306; *Oxford: Its Buildings and Gardens*, by Ralph Durand (1909) for the watercolour by William A. Wildman showing the northwest corner of the Mob Quad (where Frye roomed during his first year at Oxford) on p. 309; and *An Inventory of the Historical Monuments in the City of Oxford*, The Royal Commission on Historical Monuments, England (1939) for the map of Merton College, Oxford on p. 344.

Noel S. McFerran, Head of Public Services at the Kelly Library at St. Michael's College, participated enthusiastically in the search for the illustration finally located in *The Adventures of Mr. Verdant Green*, noted above. At the United Church Archives, Alex Thomson and Julia Holland were very helpful in establishing life dates for graduates and faculty of Emmanuel and Victoria Colleges and for United Church ministers listed in the Directory.

At University of Toronto Press, production was overseen by production manager Ani Deyirmenjian and managing editor Anne Laughlin, both of whom have contributed massively to previous Frye-related projects, and who guided me through the progressively steeper learning curve associated with this one; designer John Beadle created the cover, lovingly hand-tinting the original black-and-white photograph of the Fryes to give a 1930s feel to the book; and typesetter Eric Mills was endlessly patient in what turned out to be an ideal collaborative partnership for transforming a technically demanding manuscript into its final camera-ready form.

Finally, and on a different level entirely from all of the practical considerations dealt with above, an immense debt of gratitude is owed by all of us to the two perpetrators and protagonists of the narrative, who, through the act of bequeathing their letters to Victoria University, so bravely exposed their innermost thoughts and dreams to publication and posterity. In so doing they have greatly enriched the lives of those who have been thus privileged to see the world through their eyes, and to experience their wonderful eloquence and vitality of spirit. Truly we are blessed to be the recipients of such an inheritance.

Introduction

"Oh, well, of course, *Frye*—" a thoroughly intimidated college chaplain is said to have remarked repeatedly "with a deprecatory smile" about the twenty-five-year-old prodigy during his year away from Oxford in 1937–38. The comment is reported in the context of references to the chaplain's reaction to Frye's "assaults on the citadel of Anglican smugness" in their discussions during Frye's first year at Merton College in 1936–37, but it could equally well have been made by his tutor Edmund Blunden, who was clearly no less overwhelmed by the formidable mental capacities of his remarkable young charge, and about whom Frye had written as early as November 1936, "I've scared the shit out of him, in the Burwash phrase, and I'm just beginning to realize it, and to comprehend why he gives me that dying-duck reproachful stare every time I finish reading a paper to him." For those of us who only knew Frye in his later years, when his position and reputation had long been firmly established, a major fascination of the "portrait of the critic as a young man" (as Robert D. Denham has dubbed it) presented in this early correspondence is the question as to just when this element of "of course" entered the picture, if it is indeed possible to pinpoint a precise moment when Frye's genius and his future role became discernibly clear, if not to himself, at least to those around him.

For Helen Kemp, who, granted, was in a position to know him more intimately than anyone else, the question seems to have been raised—and answered—relatively early. "I was so pleased to see you come out at the top once again—the point is, *are* you becoming infallible and inevitable?" she asks as early as June of 1932, when their final grades for their third year at Victoria had just been published. "In a very few years you are going to be known as one of the finest scholars on the continent," she has determined by May of 1934, and in December of the same year she writes from London: "I wish you wouldn't forget that you are a great man. The longer I am here the more I know it." In the meantime, there has been considerable external reinforcement of her own early suspicions. "Surely the college cannot ignore one of their best men (Auger: 'our best man') entirely," she writes in September 1933 when Frye says that he cannot afford to come back to Victoria for his final year as an undergraduate, replacing her initial tentative reading of the situation with the more authoritative opinion of the college registrar. And in April 1934, when she is working at the National Gallery in Ottawa, she reports overhearing a conversation between a visiting Pelham Edgar and Duncan Campbell Scott in which the former raved about "a *remarkable* youngster up at Victoria, yes a simply extraordinary chap—he had been doing some fine work on Blake .... Very clever youngster .... Well worth watching."

Frye himself, understandably, is a little less self-assured, particularly in the early stages of the correspondence. The first letter included here presents us with what is probably his only recorded panic attack, during which, under the combined pressure of end-of-the-year essays and exams and an *Acta Victoriana* editorial deadline, he starts to lose confidence in Kemp's affections for him. Indeed, the events of this first letter and their resolution seem to establish Kemp permanently in his psyche as a kind of touchstone or anchor that compensates for everything else that is in upheaval within and around him. "And now Helen is a pedal-point again," he writes:

> And all my thoughts go in the right direction, all my words say what they are meant to say, my gestures fall into their right places, and my whole nervous system goes humming and spinning along, easily and fluently, having found its essential harmonic base again. Tonight I feel strangely at peace—rested, for the first time in six weeks.

Subsequently he talks about having to "work myself blind and deaf over the weekend" to prepare a paper on Blake for the Graduate English Club at University College the following week, or he inscribes woeful laments such as, "I've got so damned much to do and I haven't been to a lecture for a month and my eyes hurt like hell and I've got to read anyhow and nobody loves me and I'm perpetually tired," or, "I'm only twenty-two, and I've been more or less sick all year, and I've got growing pains, and I feel maladjusted because you're not here, and depressed for more specific reasons like exams," but, despite what must have been the far greater pressures of later years, there is never again any published record of quite the same kind of total loss of perspective as afflicted him in the spring of 1932. "If anything happened to you," he writes in the same letter that contained this last outpouring, " I should be fit only for the distorted and broken minds of literature—Wycherley, for instance, or Hopkins; at the most Swift or Webster. That is, in case I survived at all."

Kemp, unfortunately, is far less confident of his love for her, and one feels enormous sympathy for her as Frye lapses in his letter-writing just when she most desperately needs his comfort and reassurance during her lonely year at the Courtauld Institute in the University of London. "My dear, if I don't find a letter from you shortly I shall feel very much the ex-wife," she writes plaintively, and she describes herself as "going about for weeks with a pinched little heart that felt like a stone." When he finally does get around to writing she reports that his letter has "more or less changed the world" for her, and she recovers her belief that "whatever happened I could not be cut off from you or you from me," but in the meantime much damage has been done—to her enthusiasm for and progress in her work, to her willingness to carry on on her own abroad, to her zest for life. "All I wanted to do was to throw it away somewhere in a garbage heap and bury myself with it," she writes of her constricted heart. "Week after week I hoped that something would be waiting from you, and there was nothing. And all I could do was to swallow my disappointment and arrange my face stiffly to meet the world as if my world were quite as usual."

Both Kemp and Frye are, of course, much happier on their own home territory, but the differences in their strategies for dealing with being in a new and unfamiliar place are highly telling. Kemp concentrates on meeting new people and establishing a circle of friends, moves from one rooming house to another, and, in typically female fashion, is generally unable to do much serious studying until she feels settled. "I can get to work now, which is what I could not do before," she comments after her move, "but I suppose two months fluttering about is not a dead loss and more or less inevitable in a new city and new course of study."

Frye, on the other hand, compensates for his intense social insecurities by retreating into what he knows best—books. On his first Sunday in Oxford he writes:

> I am completely surrounded by shell: I have no curiosity: don't want to go see anybody, or go for a walk: just want to sit in my room, devour books nervously and feverishly, and write to you. I'll get over that, of course. Becoming a freshman again has its temperamental difficulties. Repetition always calls up associations; so I feel the same awkward, coltish seventeen-year-old coming back again.

"I know where I am, working," he says; "then I have a certain amount of self-confidence, and there, until I am a little more at home in this grey, misty world of snuffling Englishmen, I shall remain." Unlike Kemp, who was deprived at the Courtauld of the kind of ready-made social community that a university normally has to offer, he would soon be befriended by other students in his residence, by classmates, and by fellow musicians who heard about the piano he had moved into his large and drafty room instead of a typewriter and came around to play trios with him. He would even be invited, on the recommendation of fellow Torontonian Douglas LePan, to become a member of the exclusive and prestigious Bodley Club. In the meantime, however, the reference to the return of the "awkward, coltish seventeen-year-old" calls up associations with the "little boy who suffered so intensely in school because of his yellow hair and spectacles and ability to beat the others hands down at work" who had plagued his school days, and who, along with his aging and self-absorbed parents, was undoubtedly a major contributing factor to his legendary dislike of his boyhood city of Moncton. Unable to throw off these associations, despite his initial assurances that he would "get over" them, Frye reports again at the end of November: "From a social point of view I have, in Dr. Spooner's words, tasted the whole worm, but there have been reasons for that, what with the paralysing effect of entering a new country, particularly this country, the work I've been doing, and an invincible shyness which is only gradually wearing off."

Kemp's announcement that she has failed her exams at the end of her year at the Courtauld Institute will be for many the most heart-wrenching moment in the correspondence, and yet there have been numerous telltale indications that circumstances are not adding up to a successful outcome for her. Apart from the amount of time it takes her to get acclimatized to her new living conditions, the organization of the Courtauld's program of studies seems to have been poorly designed to assist her. She reports, first of all, that she doesn't like the University of London's "scattered colleges and institutes and branches all over the city," and the "utter and absolute isolation of one small group from another." The Courtauld Institute "runs its own show, and there is hardly any social intercourse amongst the students. So that the picture and conception of university life is a mere mockery." She is also not very impressed or inspired by most of the people she encounters at the Institute. Of her instructors she writes, "I have not met anyone yet who has half as great an influence as Miss Ray, Dr. Locke, Lismer—and the Courtauld Institute is made up of dry specialists—on such things as 'arms and armour'!—dear old gentlemen like Constable, showy jokers like Webb—rude young gentlemen like Norris, and exasperated Germans like Freyhan. A good number can't lecture for beans although they are reputed to *know* a great deal." And of one of her more frequent companions and commiserators at the Institute, she remarks, "Certainly the sort of degree Gordon Snelgrove will get is not making a greater man of him—but he never will be a great man. Agreeable, pleasant, even useful, but not greatly so."

One raises a thoroughly sceptical eyebrow when she reports that she is "much more reconciled to the Institute now as Geoffrey Webb, my tutor, a Cambridge man, has told me to cut several courses of lectures and see things for myself"—a strategy that is shown to work for Frye, but surely not the best way for any ordinary student to find out what is going on and what is required of them in a new course of study. In fact, both her irresponsible tutor and the Institute in general seem to have let their students down in a major way. As late as February she writes that she is "still working away, all on my own—the idea here is to have supervision regularly and let students go their own way—but we haven't had any supervision all term and no essays to write as Webb is too busy or too lazy to read them and always postpones his session with us." And when she meets with the director of the Courtauld, William Constable, to discuss the possibility of her scholarship being renewed for a second year she finds he has been told that she is "doing excellent work(!)." "How the hell he found that out I don't know," she exclaims, "because Webb has no idea what I'm doing." So it is not at all surprising to read at the end of the year that "four people failed out of the nine who tried—the others had been at this two years," and that "after this the diploma course will be definitely for two years."

One also can't help but feel that Kemp personally has been let down by receiving bad advice from a number of quarters: from Arthur Lismer and the other authority figures in Canada who, afraid that she would miss her big opportunity and unable as yet to guarantee her a job at the Art Gallery of Toronto, rushed her into her year of studies abroad before she was ready; from her family; even from Frye himself. One wonders futilely what might have happened had she been allowed to postpone her trip, as McCurry alone of her advisers in Canada had seemed to think possible, in order to be in London at the same time as her beloved Norrie was in Oxford.

Frye was originally opposed to the idea of her applying to study abroad, noting with considerable foresight that she was "too green for intensive technical study—it took you all last year to get used to the idea of studying art. Nobody ever gets away with less than a year of mooning around." True as this may have been, probably the most important factor for Kemp was her reluctance to be separated for so long from the man she so loved and whom she had her heart set on marrying. Even before the decision to award her initial scholarship had been made, she recorded in a letter written in Ottawa the major quandary that the opportunity to study abroad created for her:

> But you are so far away, and sometimes I feel like a little girl lost, and I want you so badly. It's all very well having a job that is thrilling as a job can be— Perhaps I should be satisfied with that. Lots of women have had to make a job their only object in life. But I need you too. Sometimes I think that perhaps I should be content to be a meek little wife to you and not run the risk of losing you by dashing half way across the world and leaving you. On the other hand, I'd lose you probably anyhow if I did become an echo of yourself. . . . Oh my dear, whatever happens you *will* take a chance with me, won't you?

But Frye had also placed repeated emphasis throughout his letters on the importance of "growing up" and attaining "maturity": "I assure you that I am not trying to direct your career. I merely have a certain kind of interest in you—quite apart from friendship in general—and I consider that your one duty to God and man is to grow up." Travel for the purposes of personal and professional development was obviously perfectly consistent with this goal, and it therefore became increasingly difficult for him to sustain his initial objections, which, reinforced as they were by his own reluctance to be parted from her, began to feel to him to be more purely selfish. And so he had offered, somewhat hypocritically given his own frenetic work habits, various kinds of advice on how to remain cool and self-assured in the process, including the following highly revealing strategy:

> Keep your chin up with the people you meet. If you know anything at all about what's being talked about, spill it; if not, pretend you do, bluff through and change the subject as soon as possible. If you can't say anything, look interested, as though you could if you wanted to. Whatever you do, remember that speech is better than silence, and if silence is necessary, never allow yourself to look stupid or sheepish. Avoid making obvious remarks, particularly the accepted generalizations concerning the subject of conversation. Above all, strive to cultivate a sort of immense calmness, which implies, without your speaking, that you are just a bit better than your interlocutor, and are quite ready to tear him apart if he makes a fool of himself. You'll have all England, or any country, eating out of your hand in no time.

"All year I've followed your Chesterfieldian tactics more or less, and seem to get away with something or other," Kemp reports after receiving her exam results, referring to the brave exterior she is managing to present to the outside world despite her internal state of upheaval. As far as her actual studies were concerned, however, clearly the strategy has backfired on her.

On numerous occasions while she is in London it becomes abundantly clear that, whatever the transient pleasures of travel and exposure to some of the greatest art of the world, her heart simply isn't in the endeavour, and her ambivalence with regard to both her existing situation and the possibility of her scholarship being renewed for a second year erupts in statements along the lines of: "My dearest—what can I do for you, away so far from you here in London? You break my heart with longing for you and I want to run and comfort my man who is all that I care about, really"; "Snelgrove had word from McCurry to go ahead with his Ph.D. and a hint that his scholarship might be renewed next year.... He hoped that mine would be renewed. Just now I don't give a damn"; and (when she learns that a possibility of Frye's joining her in London with a scholarship of his own that summer has fallen through) "I don't know what to say about the summer. What *can* I say? I was counting on it so much, and now I must take a deep breath and go on. For my work I hope I get the renewal of money, for I'm terribly raw—but there is a pretty violent pull against my desire to stay."

She also records a remarkable meditation on a photograph of Carlyle as an old man in the house that had become his museum, in which the grandfatherly figure looking out at her from the image supports exactly her own sentiments about the question of whether or not to continue her studies in London for another year. "The eyes looked straight into your eyes," she writes, and "He seemed to tell me that to love someone was given to very few!"

> There are so many lonely people . . . and to some the same glorious thing happens, and to many others, it doesn't. Why then do you wish to live apart from the man who will be, who is, your husband? What can you gain of spiritual worth, away from him? You meet many new people and see many things in London, but are you getting your roots in the ground, on strange soil? Go home after this year and begin to work, there is enough to be done at home. You will create something there. Do not stay here amongst a crowd of agreeable fools who have no idea what life is to give them, spending your youth for a couple of letters tacked after your name. That is evading the issue. Do you realize that you are nearly twenty-five, and time is as relentless as ever— I stopped talking to myself long enough to look again at old uncle Thomas and he still seemed of the same opinion.

She does care about her studies, of course—enormously—as she discovers broken-heartedly when it is no longer a matter of her own free choice. But it is as though the failure of her final exams, aided and abetted by a severe attack of PMS just at the most critical moment ("If the stars in their courses didn't fight against you, the moon did"), was necessary to release her from the steamroller of external pressure to continue on a path that would have prevented her from doing what she knew in her heart she both wanted and had to do. "I can't argue my particular fate with everyone who wants to tug me this way or that," she had written in the summer of 1932, when various people—though, no doubt more influentially, not Frye—were advising her to go to art school or study music rather than complete her degree at Victoria. Here, however, Frye is unwilling to stand in the way of the advancement of either her personal development or her career, and her own desire to be "fitted not only for [her] job, but also to be [his] wife," and the need of her Depression-struck family for the financial benefits that could potentially accrue, are too great to ignore. And so, already ambivalent herself, and overpowered by the "combined weight of opinion" that is pushing for her to stay on, Kemp is rendered incapable of taking a firm stand in favour of her own genuine preference, which is to return home, leaving circumstances to conspire to find a way of making the decision for her.

There is a very definite sense in the correspondence—to this reader, at least—that Kemp is being groomed for a role that will complement, rather than emulate, Frye's. Part of this, it is true, is a matter of conventional and stereotypical roles for women. A look at any edition of the *Toronto Daily Star* contemporary with the correspondence, for example, shows an inordinate preponderance of society pages, with an emphasis on garden parties, debutante balls, and society marriages. And Kemp's father and Frye both write to her with advice about not allowing herself to be too much of a bookworm at the expense of her social life, and of the dangers of becoming a "bluestocking." "You'll go a long way without me, darling, but it won't be worth doing," Frye warns. "Remember that a bluestocking, a pedant, is a female who has sublimated all her sex instinct in her work. *Don't* wander off in that direction—that's the chief reason I want to be near you." But there seems to me to be something more to this as well, something that has more to do with the cooperative team effort required in face of the extraordinary circumstances of living and collaborating with genius (the word occurs numerous times in the correspondence) than with a mere acting out of social stereotypes. Kemp demonstrates her awareness of the precarious balancing act involved in utterances such as

> I know that you are great and will do great things, and I feel so scared sometimes. Scared and worried because perhaps the greatest thing and the most valuable work for the wife of a genius is to look after him. And then I think I should run home and marry you and study cookbooks and diets and chase microbes frantically and practically put you in a glass cage and dust it off every hour. But I'm afraid that if I did, I'd feel rather an ass, trying to echo your ideas, and nothing else.

She is also aware, though, that scholarly work is neither her passion nor her forte, and that she could never be happy with an academic career alone: "I haven't quite worked out yet what I can best do at home, but at home it must be. I am not made for the altogether contemplative existence, and to spend two years the way Gordon is, on his chasing after Richardson's portraits—I can't see it." For Kemp there is a powerful attraction of something beyond the strictly academic life, as recorded during her visit to Paris as her year abroad was drawing to a close: "I was just thinking of the great swirling throbbing stream of life outside the cloister walls, joyous and magic and terrible," she muses. "Perhaps I am not sufficiently over-awed at the life of the mind," she admits, "but I am learning many things that are not set down in books."

In fact, a large part of Kemp's strength in dealing with the phenomenon that was Frye was precisely in her refusal, difficult though it became for her at times, to allow herself to become too overwhelmed by his forceful personality and mind, or too impressed by his status and reputation. "As an institution you are exhibiting that very admirable quality of stability," she observes. But then she adds, "As a person—I'm not going to eulogize, even if it should seem the proper thing to do along with the rest of my enthusiasm." She also resists his efforts to draw her too closely into his personal obsessions. "And what if I don't read Spengler?" she defends herself. "You know, I shall not be able to follow you in many places—but then I am wandering by myself in others." When he plans to base a talk to the Moncton CCF on "The Historical Background of Socialistic Thought," she warns him that he will have a difficult time if he imagines "that your average inhabitant of Moncton will be less unable to understand Spengler than I was." "Try to remember to speak simply to them," she advises, "For after all this time I am used to what you are apt to say—but you overwhelm me even yet pretty often. It is hard, being a genius. It is also hard being the friend of a genius." And when he tries to persuade her to undertake a study of Blake's art, arguing that very little work has been done on the subject, but also that "you happen to have a husband who knows as much about him as any man living," she retreats from the idea, quipping warily that she is "now contemplating hooking the bright boy of 3T3 and living with him until Blake do us part." "I think that there are a few little problems with regard to art and the artist's public which could be dealt with to greater advantage than a study of Blake by me . . . the trouble is that I haven't thought much about Blake, I suppose," she demurs, and then adds:

> But darling, you do frighten me sometimes, and you might as well know it. Just sometimes when I feel tired and depressed and you are not near me to make me see you as a human being, very much alive. At those times I can only think of you as one of the great men of our time, someone so far above me, who will reach his goal in spite of everything. Whereas I diddle about—and find it hard to realize that I *have* actually pulled your

> ears and will do so a good many times yet. I always feel so damned uncomfortable when I get tired and sleepy and sentimental and put anyone on a pedestal. Because I don't feel it my role exactly, to stand round with my ears flapping and admire what you do—and yet I've got so proud of you, and so anxious to know that everything is right with you.

An even more revealing exposé of her misgivings occurs in Kemp's description of her relationship with Millicent Rose, a young Cambridge graduate and fellow student at the Courtauld Institute who travelled to Italy with her in the spring of 1935. "I have come to Italy for six weeks with Millicent who, besides being one of the most delightful people I know, is also one of the most arrogant," Kemp writes dolefully from Rome in her first letter to Frye after he has broken his long silence.

> And in my grim moments she reminds me of you. Sometimes I can't bear to be with her any longer, sometimes I run away to find a tattered remnant of myself, some bit that has not succumbed to her domination, for she is strong, and unconsciously takes the lead, and speaks loudly and dogmatically whether she is right or wrong.... I mean that in her brilliance and her self assurance and her dogmatic way of crushing all beneath her, she reminds me of the Frye who came to see me at Easter so long ago. Millicent has her glorious side, and thank God, so have you. But it is part of my general nightmare to identify certain crushed, hang-dog feelings with what I have felt sometimes because of my inability to cope with you. And then I think, because I would never try to live with Millicent for any length of time, how can I dare to live with you? What a nightmare that is when the fit is on!

Whatever the justifications for Kemp's anxieties about his intellectual arrogance and domineering personality, however, and aggravated as they might have been by the temporary falling off in his letter-writing, there were obviously other factors to be taken into consideration as well. Among these were Frye's social awkwardness—a by-product of his "customary shell of reserve and shyness"—and his ineptitude in practical matters, and consequently of his need for someone to act as an interface with the world, which would grow far greater in later years as he himself became increasingly more remote from it. Even at this early stage, Kemp's brother Roy provides the following amusing assessment after spending some time with Frye at the family's cottage in June 1935:

> I am not in the least perturbed at the man but after living with him for a week I find that the ordinary tasks and necessities of life do not seem to cross his consciousness until the actual moment of their performance.... He is a good lad and I like him, but oh how woefully does he need to do a little shifting for himself! He is so utterly useless when it becomes a question of doing anything practical that he shies from it and leaves somebody else to worry about it.... He is destined to live the academic life absolutely out of touch with the actual mechanics of our civilization. He is not concerned with "what makes the wheels go round." All he has is a highly developed critical sense of the finished product, be it in art, music, or literature. In a sense his whole relation to this society of ours is parasitical. And I say that quite dispassionately without envy, malice, jealousy or all the other motives which cause words of invective to be spoken. It is too bad, but I think Helen and he are going to have a good bit of adjusting to do to get used to each other's mode of existence.

Fortunately, both Kemp and Frye are well aware of these potentially problematic aspects of his nature. "If you are not careful you may become a prophet singing in the wilderness—especially if you follow Blake a great deal—however, if it does come to pass, I'll send you a crate or a cage full of carefully trained locusts and a jar or so of wild honey like a bubbling old Martha," she jokes early in their relationship, evincing her own brand of prophecy. And later on she begins to wonder whether she might perhaps do best to "become a social creature, and help you that way." Frye affirms this disconsolately at the end of his first year at Oxford: "Darling, it's perhaps as well that somebody has some idea of how to manage my affairs," he berates himself, "as I obviously haven't much idea of it myself."

If it is possible to say so here without being unkind, poor old Norrie's lack of—or unwillingness to condescend to the mundanities of—ordinary social and conversational skills, recounted in countless merciless anecdotes told at his expense, was to become the stuff of later legend. For this reason it is all the more striking to compare the vivaciousness and sparkle of Kemp in this regard with the reserved and prickly manner in social situations of Elizabeth Fraser. Fraser's art, poetry, and personality undoubtedly intrigued him, and it is interesting to speculate that he could conceivably have ended up with her had he not been forced home in the summer of 1937 by his own variation of Kemp's earlier crisis at the Courtauld, brought on by his failure to maintain regular communications with the individuals who would have been in a position to assist him with the renewal of his Royal Society grant for another year. In February 1937 he reports having had both Fraser and Blunden in for tea, during which "Elizabeth did just what I thought she'd do: shut up like a clam, and Blunden and I talked shop. It was simply another tutorial." However, as Frye himself had written in the spring of 1934, "There are some people in the world, like you and me, who have certain definite things to get done, and for them things open out and all the hopeless obstructions are cleared away, one after the other, by some unseen process that knows all about it beforehand." And one of the things that this "unseen process" seems to have been determined upon was preventing the destruction of their relationship by unduly long separations, whatever temporary hardships it might have called into play for the purpose in the realization of their—and also its own—other objectives.

This sense of an invisible process directing and guiding their lives is alluded to by Frye more than once in the correspondence. In the summer of 1932, in the midst of a hilarious discussion of the as yet unresolved question as to whether he should become a minister or a professor, Frye had written: "I wonder what those writers who talk about relentless and inexorable Fate would say to a man who had two Fates, pulling in opposite directions. The trouble is that I can't quite figure out which one is God." And in answer to Kemp's reply, written under the influence of a recent reading of Sinclair Lewis's *Elmer Gantry*, that she "could not see you performing with satisfaction to yourself the duties of a minister," he had elaborated: "My difficulty is not that of Frank Shallard, who was a weak-kneed prig, but that of an Ancient Mariner hounded on by a force at least as strange as himself to deliver his message to bored and uneasy Wedding Guests. For I have got a definite message to give, right now, which will develop but not essentially change as I grow older." Referring to the workings of this process or force again in 1937, he states—in marked contrast to his youthful protestations about feeling called to become a minister of the United Church of Canada, and whatever refinements may have evolved in his understanding of it later—that "This is about my only working religious belief, and it's one I've always had with me, though I've sometimes wondered what direction I was going. It's my idea of predestination."

In the context of their relationship, both Frye and Kemp identify their understanding of the guiding impetus behind the process or force much more explicitly. "I am never sure why such a wonderful thing could happen, or how," muses Kemp. "When I get that far, I wonder about God." And Frye counters in a similar vein that "around my love there is always a mystery: why, in a world that seems to make so little sense otherwise, did something so inevitably right happen apparently by accident?" "Because it's all right," he concludes, "even the wrongs. I know that now. My religion was, I think, the last thing to centre itself around you." With the result for their relationship that "things dovetail together so that what we are both cut out to do we can do together," because "that seems to be the way God works."

What they were to do together was to emerge only gradually, but their sense of being united in a common purpose is evident almost from the very beginning. "We have a tough hill to climb, and the worst of it is that we don't know its name—it's probably not Olympus, and it doesn't seem to be Parnassus or even the Mount of Olives. But it's there, and we've got to climb it," Frye writes from Moncton in the summer of 1932, and the theme is echoed by Kemp in a letter written from Ottawa in June of 1934: "You said once that you and I had a long way to go, a tough hill to climb—and sometimes I know it isn't any molehill!" The part of their journey that we are privileged to be given a glimpse of here takes them through the Depression period and the advent of war, and shows them bearing witness to the abdication of King Edward VIII, the growing influence of Communism and Fascism, and the rise to power of Hitler and Mussolini on the world stage, and, closer to home, to such milestones as the advent of the CCF on the political front, the growing influence of the Group of Seven in the art world, and the rise to prominence of ensembles such as the Hart House String Quartet in the local music community. It reveals some of their own friends leaning towards Communism ("It can't be the right religion"), the growing threat of war ("and Harold soon being old enough to be eligible for slaughter"), and the financial hardships of their families and those around them ("Daddy earned $8 last week"). And gradually, as they become involved with the editing of the *Canadian Forum*, attend meetings of groups such as the Picture Loan Society and the League of Social Reconstruction, and are asked to give more and more public lectures on subjects ranging from art and literature to various political and social topics, the increasing prominence of their own positions and roles becomes inescapably clear to them. By September of 1936, when Kemp is making tentative plans to travel with Frye in Europe the following summer, she is also becoming more and more aware of the implications for their privacy:

> You and I have a very innocent air, evidently. The prospect of next summer must be somewhat carefully considered I suppose. I'll no longer be able to act as I see fit without someone knowing what is going on. I'm not getting a fit of the Mrs. Grundy blues, but I'm just making allowances for the fact that I'll be making a good many new friends and acquaintances this year who will take an interest presumably in your and my affairs. There are so many people who know about you and there may be a few soon who'll have begun to be conscious of my existence—why the devil *do* we have to be prominent citizens?

And in April of 1939 she writes apprehensively, "I'm beginning to feel that you and I have got ourselves involved in a public career that we'll find hard to kick over."

In the meantime, Frye has progressed to the stage where he has been the one to draw up a course of lectures for his tutor Edmund Blunden instead of the reverse, he has submitted a first version of his book on Blake to Faber & Faber, and his future tenure-track position at Victoria is all but assured. Of the Blake, he has been able for some time to say, "I know Blake as no man has ever known him" and "what I have done is a masterpiece; finely written, well handled, and the best, clearest and most accurate exposition of Blake's thought yet written"; and he has made his now famous proclamation: "Read Blake or go to hell: that's my message to the modern world." His last "don rag" appears to have been a mere formality as his tutor in Anglo-Saxon, J.N. Bryson, passed him smoothly as "a very competent person doing things in [his] own way" and Blunden marked him as "Merton's No. 1 chance for an English first." And of his career in general, he seems entirely justified in his early assertion—made in August 1932(!)—that "From a purely academic point of view, I shall have things pretty well my own way, I should imagine."

Against the background of all of these developments, the letters chronicle a remarkable tale of mutual growth, understanding, and respect. Having been shown a sampling of them before her departure for London, Helen's father, S.H.F. Kemp, writes approvingly:

> I am inclined to think "that man Frye" has had a lot to do with steadying you. Since reading his letters I am convinced that he is rather wonderful. It is too soon to say whether his influence is all good, and whether he will be like the shadow of a rock in a weary land. The man is obviously such a genius, that his very ability carries with it its own question mark.

> He might turn out hard to live with. Yet there is nothing about him I can find fault with, and so I hasten to remove myself from the very suspicion of criticizing him. Apart from the illegible character of his handwriting, his letters are so away and beyond the ordinary that they are worthy of keeping for the rest of your life. The fact that they are so hard to read in the longhand in which they were written would be bar effectual enough against perusal by the ordinary busybody. . . . There is almost something inevitable about Norrie, isn't there?

And throughout the letters the theme of the writers' deepening love for each other sounds as a constant and steady refrain. Without being overly effusive or sweet—"You are precious, Norrie—you never embarrass me by being sentimental"—and despite mutual protestations regarding the inadequacy of the printed word to express their affection—"Don't you see, darling? I can't write you a sustained love letter, because when I try—and I have tried—the result sounds like a Chopin nocturne scored for brass"—the expressions of this profound love dedicated to a common purpose are on some occasions idealized, on others totally grounded, at times elevated, at others humorous, but they are never trivial, and occasionally they are even breathtaking in their eloquence. In his very first letter Frye reveals his side of the dynamic that Kemp had been so concerned about in her comparison of him with her friend Millicent Rose, explaining in part how Kemp was able to survive his powerful and frequently overpowering personality:

> A picture of you kept floating in and smashing things up. I kept trying to fight it down, but it recurred, and I finally discovered why. It was all that I worshipped in you and delighted in that I was fighting down and that kept recurring. I could hypnotize and fascinate you like a snake, I could crush your will under mine, I could do all sorts of strong-arm things with you, but there was something left, the something that makes you Helen, not my corporeal Helen that I like and am tickled by, but the inward esoteric Helen that I love and am swayed by.

It must have been rather daunting at times to be regarded as "the ideal lady at the other end of the postal service," yet Kemp does not appear—at least, not initially—to feel that she is being placed on a pedestal and trapped in a projection on the one hand, or manipulated and controlled on the other, whatever the inadvertently overpowering effect he may occasionally have on her. "You are different," she writes in August 1932; "you stimulate me to more or less positive action along lines of which my little conscience approves. Other people wanted me to fit into their scheme of things, and be myself, yet at the same time dance around being the sort of girl they wanted. My self was incidental." It is a fine line to walk in a relationship, and what seems to be going on on the surface is rarely identical to the underlying process. Nevertheless, in December 1934 Frye is still insisting, admirably, and in defiance of what the peculiar circumstances of his career might threaten to force on them in the future, that

> the last thing I want to do is to possess you. I don't want a subservient female to wipe my nose and bring my slippers and tell me what a fine guy I am and give me beautifully balanced meals. If I required that of you, I should be debasing the subtle, cultured, refined woman I fell in love with. Doubtless there are men for whom the wife is merely a representative of an indiscriminate horde of womankind. But I love you, not because you are a woman, but because you are you. If you are going to be true to me you have to be true to yourself.

However he is also honest enough to admit that, although he doesn't want "to pose, show off, lay down the law or make fun of you," he will "probably do all four unconsciously."

Still, in a mode that is quite the opposite of either projection and idealization or control and domination, it is striking to observe how wonderfully forgiving they both are of each other's failures. When Kemp writes dejectedly after failing her Courtauld exams that "If this makes any difference to you I shall just fade out of the picture so far as you are concerned" because "I will not have you marrying a stupid woman," Frye responds with a truly remarkable declaration:

> Don't end any more letters with appeals to me to forget you . . . If love were what the Elizabethans called it, a quotidian fever, any trifling accident like this might make me cool off. But love isn't like that. Not mine anyway. Its real essence is a little diamond packed in ice away inside me, to keep it away from the heat, which would only injure it. It's cold, and it's hard, and it's got sharp edges, but it's unbreakable. Outside are all the emotions, shifting and variable, worked up over everything and ready to stampede without provocation. Inside is a perfectly dry, impersonal re-

> spect which has nothing to do with my feelings. A thing like this, of course, doesn't touch me anywhere: but then the worst thing you could do, the most shameful or horrible thing, while it might hurt on all the burning sensitive places, couldn't get through the ice; it couldn't really touch me.

And when Frye in his turn fails to arrange for the renewal of his Royal Society fellowship and is forced to return home in disgrace instead of having Kemp join him in Europe, Kemp handles the situation at home with the utmost tact and discretion. "So I'm having some important changes of plan which make it necessary that I stay here," she writes. "You don't need to feel afraid to see people—it is quite natural that you should come home this summer and it will be cheaper for both of us.... And I love you very very much, and want to sit in the sun and watch you get freckled. My dear."

Larger than either the roles they play for each other or their temporary setbacks and failures is the extent to which each pervades and shores up the other's very being. "It is queer, being in love with so many people all at once in so many different ways, with you at the back of me all the time as my end and my beginning," writes Kemp. "Everything I think about seems to come back some way to you." "The more I am enjoying what I see, the more I feel a part of you, as if you had quickened all life for me." "Thinking of you even is like coming to rest in a holy place." And, although it is an old and worn-out cliché to talk about the woman who stands behind every great man, Frye makes it absolutely clear that it is his love for Kemp that gives meaning to his work and to his entire existence. "I have never been able to regard you . . . as a help or inspiration to my career," he says,"you just won't fit into that niche. My career, whatever there is of it, can only be a help and inspiration toward loving you—because my whole life is dedicated to you."

> . . . the point is that a life to be any good has to mean something to the person who lives it as well as to other people, and I couldn't find anything that would give my capacities any value or meaning to *me* until I was sure of you. Now I'm all right—I can go ahead building and planning. You have the power to destroy that building at any time, if it pleases you, but until then at any rate I am secured by knowing that everything I can achieve in contributions to "culture" or "the intellectual life" or whatever abstraction you please, as long as I can keep pouring them out, has another name, and that name its real name, Helen.

But by far the most extraordinary outpouring occurs in a letter written in January of 1935, in which Frye expands spectacularly on imagery from Dante's *Divine Comedy*, and in which he epitomizes the whole impetus and momentum of the correspondence. "And so I get round again to the adoration of my own manifestation of Beatrice," he writes. "All the beauty and quiet fostering strength of Helen. All womanhood focused, for the personal reveals the infinite, in any object of love. . . ."

> What really pulls and tears at me is a compulsion to struggle to educate myself, to mature and grow serene and strong, to become too big for irritation and sulkiness, to prepare myself for a glorious and terrible life with you. My words sound inflated, but they are inadequate and not false. To live with another human being on equal terms must be by far the most difficult and subtle of the arts, and yet the most thrilling and satisfying. But love and friendship with you! . . . .
>
> We shall live a divine comedy together, our inferno a boiling torrent of sexual love, our purgatory the perfect peace of repose through the satisfaction of desire. We shall descend hell as lover and mistress, you as my monopolized hetaera, into the chambers of the virtuous heathen and the glib liars, talking, chattering and laughing endlessly of our ambitions, interests and studies. We shall be submerged in devouring flames of passion, swept into a delirium of touch. We shall sink to the depths of the universe and beyond, to the utter quiescent coma of union and surrender. Everything hot and troublesome and individual will fall away and leave us together. Then we shall gradually separate, and, immeasurably strengthened and purified, pass through love to the final paradise of friendship, when each will be in possession of an inward privacy of soul, to be respected because of the other.

In the *Late Notebooks* a grief-stricken Frye would return to the image of Beatrice as he tried to cope with his devastating sense of loss after Kemp's death. Aflame at the age of twenty-two with all the passion and anticipation of youth, however, his mood is, in his own words, "joyous and ecstatic," and it would appear that, in the presence of such love, life inside the "cloister walls" of academe, as Kemp had said of life outside them, can also be "joyous and magic and terrible."

Kemp, ca. 1934 (courtesy of Victoria University Library, Toronto)

Rome, March 31. 1935.

My dearest, your letter came here a few days ago, and more or less changed the world for me. I've been going about for weeks with a pinched little heart that felt like a stone. All I wanted to do was to throw it away somewhere in a garbage heap and bury myself with it. Week after week I hoped that something would be waiting from you, and there was nothing. And all I could do was to swallow my disappointment and arrange my face stiffly to meet the world as if my world were quite as usual. I wrote a horrid note to you. Left it for a day or so to cool off. Looked at it again, and knew I could never send it, for I knew that you must be working hard. and that whatever happened I could not be cut off from you or you from me. But oh, how hard it is to strain and try to be with you, off here in a strange land, where no one knows you and can talk to me about you. When Cameron mentioned you once I could have almost loved the man, for that much contact with you. And I had another worry up my sleeve. I have come to Italy for six weeks with Millicent who besides being one of the most delightful people I know, is also, one of the most arrogant. And in my grim moments she reminds me of you. Sometimes I can't bear to be with her any longer, sometimes I run away to find a tattered remnant of myself, some bit that has not succumbed to her domination for she is strong, and unconsciously takes the lead, and speaks loudly and dogmatically whether she is right or wrong. And of course, everything is Communism. Oh God! if she would only go to Russia, or get a job which would teach her the value and ~~the~~ need for painstaking careful work. Cambridge has given her a great deal, but no idea of doing consistent work at anything but what she wants to do at the moment. But her conversation is brilliant, and when she is good humoured she is so charming that I can't remember the horrid moments. ~~And this~~ Don't misunderstand what I mean. I mean that in her brilliance and her self assurance and her dogmatic way of crushing all beneath her, she reminds me of the Frye who came to see me at Easter so long ago. Millicent has her

Sample of Kemp's handwriting from letter of 31 March 1935 (courtesy of Victoria University Library, Toronto)

Frye, summer of 1933 (courtesy of Victoria University Library, Toronto)

Above all, it certainly doesn't mean that my friends ever imagine I'll be a minister. "Ministry?" says Ernie Gould. "Do you think your friends are going to stand by and see you waste your life and talents in that?" "Minister!" snorts the janitor of Gate House. "You'd make a damn' good hypocrite, that's what you'd make!" "My dear boy, you can't be a minister," says Norm Knight, "you've got brains." And so they go. They're absolutely and devastatingly right, of course. I wonder what those writers who talk about relentless and inexorable Fate would say to a man who had two Fates, pulling in opposite directions. The trouble is that I can't quite figure out which one is God.

I am still contemplating those results. They are bad this year, — the most dismal set I have seen by long odds. Fred Scotch failed — the only other man in Burwash Hall from a musical point of view. The Public Enema got a second. Life is like that.

Blair Laing failed. John Stinson failed. Rudy Eberhard failed. Jack Boland failed. Eye Armstrong failed. Oh, what the hell!

Well, I can't keep pouring out undiluted genius much longer when I am living the life of a misanthropic clam. I wish I wasn't quite so <u>DAMNED</u> lazy. That's another argument against the ministry — with my temperament I shall probably drift into writing or professoring or pugilism or some lazy man's profession instead.

No, you aren't a bread-&-water clam. You aren't artificial enough. I never said you were, anyway.

I have judiciously weighed the question of whether or not I should "mind very much" your saying that you love me and have decided that I do not. I find the statement even agreeable.

Sample of Frye's handwriting from letter of July 1932
(courtesy of Victoria University Library, Toronto)

Summer of 1932

[*Toronto?*]
Saturday night [*Spring, 1932?*]

Red Squirrel:

I've got all kinds of work I simply must get done, it's getting late, and I must catch up on my sleep. Consequently I am in bed writing to you. I guess I will never learn sense.

No, you have to be born with sense, and I wasn't. What a week I've spent! (This, I warn you, is going to be a very egotistical note.) I don't remember ever having been as thoroughly at loose ends before. Whenever I thought of you—which I did very often—I shivered, and whenever I thought of *Acta*—which I did the rest of the time—I felt malarial. Do you know, sweetheart, what I wanted to do? I would have given anything to have come to you. I wanted to spend about a day lying on the floor in front of you, with my arms around your ankles and my head on your feet, and to see if I really had forgotten how to cry. What an immense relief it would have been if I could have remembered!

But, of course, I didn't do anything so silly, or even try to. I had my institutional dignity to think of, and my duty to my public. What would English and History say if they saw their Norrie Frye making a fool of himself in front of a female?

So I tried to think of something else. But that didn't work. A picture of you kept floating in and smashing things up. I kept trying to fight it down, but it recurred, and I finally discovered why. It was all that I worshipped in you and delighted in that I was fighting down and that kept recurring. I could hypnotize and fascinate you like a snake, I could crush your will under mine, I could do all sorts of strong-arm things with you, but there was something left, the something that makes you Helen, not my corporeal Helen that I like and am tickled by, but the inward esoteric Helen that I love and am swayed by. And I knew that this something was beginning to despise me.

It was a hideous idea to face, but it was there. In my darker moments, of course, I began to see that if you did not, then I should end by despising you. I had lost touch with you, of course, because the more wretched I felt the more inferior I felt, and I was working out my inferiority complex by trying to force you into the status of the ex-girlfriend and slipping myself into the same treadmill. Then I suddenly felt very small and very lonely and utterly miserable.

Then *Acta* came out, but, relieved as I was, I wasn't able quite to realize the relief. But when I got talking to you Friday, though a bit frightened at first, I saw what had happened. There you were, the same Helen, there was I, the same Norrie. You had been waiting patiently and resignedly for me to come back, and I had come. And you showed very plainly that you knew that. "You're still mine," I said. I walked home with that ringing in my head.

And now Helen is a pedal-point again. And all my thoughts go in the right direction, all my words say what they are meant to say, my gestures fall into their right places, and my whole nervous system goes humming and spinning along, easily and fluently, having found its essential harmonic base again. Tonight I feel strangely at peace—rested, for the first time in six weeks.

Or maybe I'm just sleepy. It's one o'clock. You are sleeping now. And my lips have brushed your forehead, and my hand has smoothed down your hair. But you don't know that—you're asleep.

Norrie

24 Pine St.
Moncton, N.B.
Tuesday [*31 May 1932*]

This is the first letter from Frye's family home in Moncton. He had to borrow money for the trip home from W.J. Little, the bursar of Victoria College.

My dear Helen:

Well, as I haven't got the typewriter yet, you are reduced to deciphering the original hieratic. As you have probably guessed, I am home. Wednesday morning I went over to Little and touched him, quite successfully. For some inexplicable reason, however, I did not get the cheque cashed that day. There are two trains leaving Toronto for Moncton a day, but one of them leaves late at night, takes two nights on the trip, and stops at about every back door; the other in the early morning. So it was Friday morning before I actually left. I didn't communicate with you in the meantime because, as I explained, I detest an anticlimax. My trip was completely devoid of interest—I got in Saturday afternoon, looking the picture of beauty in distress, and have been sleeping most of the time ever since.

You remember Charlie Krug, who was Don of Gate House last year and is now head of the Department of Philosophy and Psychology down here at Mount Allison. He was up yesterday. He told me that Joe Binning had died of an operation for appendicitis in Moose Jaw last Friday. The news knocked me cold, for it was not only so utterly unexpected, but Joe was one of the finest men I have ever met. I pity poor old Gordie [Romans] deeply. Joe was everything to him—you know how affectionate he is, and Joe has been his best friend nearly all his life. I am writing to him tonight, but I don't know what to say. It is best, of course, to say nothing, but a sympathetic silence is a hard thing to communicate by letter.

Prospects of a job here depend of course on the Public Library—Dad found one or two stenographic vacancies but they naturally want them permanently filled, and when I am no longer under the aegis of the Business College I can do no public stenography. Dad himself is getting rather fed up—he sells builder's supplies and not a building has gone into the air since the well-known Depression entered into the Maritime stream of consciousness.

Soon after arriving I discovered to my amazement and horror that the family had possessed themselves of a radio. Not only that, but mother is taking a positively insane delight in the kind of thing she hears over it and is now considerably more familiar than I with contemporary music as conceived by the oracles of that infernal instrument. However, the resurrection of the piano is providing the house with enough noise to permit of a considerable diminution of the ethereal kind, and after hearing Gertrude Huntley Sunday night I'm gradually getting reconciled.

I was up to see the ex-girlfriend [Evelyn Rogers] last night. She is looking well and has fallen hard for somebody else, praise be to Allah—a graduate in Forestry from the University of New Brunswick. She says she would marry him if it weren't for the Depression—his work is unsettled and her father is in the C.N.R., an institution which, as no doubt you know, is headed in the general direction of the ashcan—or Limbo of Vanities, if you prefer. Moncton, of course, is largely dependent on that railway, which is why the town is at present as dead as a reconstruction of Stonehenge. I shall probably stay away from the kid this year, as the influence I have over her seems to be well-nigh hypnotic—at least always has been. So another problem has solved itself.

Work on Bach has not yet started. I was looking over some of Howard's (my brother's) music and discovered Czerny's Op. 740—the book you have. The discovery is little short of providential, as it is exactly what I need at present. Czerny I always thought a unique character. He had no more creative originality or inspiration than a manure spreader, but he is immortal simply because he came along when the pianoforte was developing and realized so clearly what fun it is to play one. I have not quite decided what to do first in Bach—probably the Prelude & Fugue in B flat from the second book of what must be by now a decidedly ill-tempered clavichord.

Well, I have already sprained a couple of convolutions trying to produce a poem and the damned Muse is still too stuck-up to come. I keep kidding myself I have too strong a sense of humor to write poetry. Which is true in a way—it certainly is too strong for my kind of poetry.

(Remark to the effect that I should shut up to follow here.)

Norrie

Box 186, Forest, Ontario
Thursday night [2? *June 1932*]

Kemp was visiting her paternal aunt and uncle, Clara and W.W. (Well) Kemp.

My dear Norrie—

I am writing in a somewhat difficult position. I have adopted your custom and am propped up in bed. It is nearly midnight and there was a fly buzzing noisily around the electric light. I turned it off, and Mr. Fly has retired into a corner somewhere. If he comes near the bed lamp, I shall have to pull the covers over my ears like a youngster and squall.

I've just finished getting my face all stuck up with grease from a half-pound chicken drumstick. I wouldn't be at all surprised if I turned out quite fat—I believe I might have it in me. I actually think I'm developing hips, shoulders, and everything. But maybe it's just a fond delusion. I was weighed today (with the aid of George Case, who lives here, and is a nice boy etc.). Weight 94 pounds + 14 ounces. Wouldn't bring much in the hog market, but it's the best I can do.

I'm glad you have a piano. I am doing my best with Aunt Clara's. You probably know what I would be doing—Scarlatti, Schumann, Czerny, a couple of Chopin Études. I haven't played for more than two hours any day, for when I get started George comes in and plays radio, or Aunt Clara starts talking to me. Aunt Clara has quite definite views on love, marriage, funerals, illegitimate babies, preachers, the United Church of Canada, Roman Catholics, the younger generation (lazy and not like when we were young) etc. When I find we disagree on the illegitimate child business—and she talks about the young mother and her "shame," I soft-pedal, and let it go at that. I have been talked at quite a bit. Aunt Clara spent yesterday afternoon talking about their troubles when they had to care for my grandparents—grandma especially who grew terribly intolerant, jealous and insanely spiteful before she died. However, I fumigated my soul by lying out in the sun for the rest of the afternoon—the garden is lovely.

Darn it all, I could tell you a lot of things about this place but I'm too lazy. The more I stay here, the more I'm glad about you. Everything is so much fun. I like you so much, and so many thrilling things happen because of you, that I should tell you all about it. But the fly is buzzing in a very determined fashion, and you are a sympathetic soul anyway, and probably know what I mean. Since I am getting sleepier and just had to brush the fly off my nose, I'll say goodnight my dear—and I've had a hunch that I *may* have passed in economics after all.

Helen

c/o Mr. & Mrs. A.B. Elder
Honey Harbour, Georgian Bay
[*Early June 1932*]

Written from the summer cottage of Kemp's friend and classmate Jean Elder.

Dear Norrie—

Your letter arrived very opportunely fifteen minutes before I started off with Jean's people for three weeks of swimming and black flies and tall trees and sunsets and general all-round heaven. If you were here I would certainly push you off the dock, my dear Illustrious Student.

Jean's father decamped yesterday for he couldn't stand the flies and mosquitoes. There is something about the Elder epidermis which is peculiarly sensitive to sunburn and fly bites. Jean is swollen up in odd places. My hide, resembling the younger rhinoceros, is not so sensitive.

Jean and I have been swimming twice—before breakfast. It is a matter of principle. As the moths have found a nest and haven in Jean's bathing suit and as I have none with me, we are glad of the excuse to take "nature's way" and streak in before we have time to think. It is so cold that we gasp and sputter and insist that it is quite warm. But this morning I had a regular bath and came out feeling buxom and pleased with myself for staying in so long—but had to duck rather hurriedly into a raincoat because of a boatload of Sunday worshippers coming up the channel.

I am sorry to hear about your friend Joe Binning. Of course I did not know him, but merely gazed from afar at one of the great minds who then seemed so far removed from such a foolish little wretch as myself. Do write to Gord Romans, and send him my deepest sympathy.

We also have acquired a radio. A wretched contrivance, especially as I have not yet heard anything except *In a Persian Market* and *Naughty Marietta* issue forth between announcements.

My dear man—and this time I am the grandmother—if your influence over "the ex-girlfriend" is as you say "well-nigh hypnotic" you certainly had better "stay away from the kid" or your problem will not have solved itself by any manner of means. Ask grandma, she knows—from the ex-girlfriend's standpoint.

Having decided that I will not *improve my mind* or do anything in the least uplifting or educational, I have spent the day reading Jean parts of W.J. Turner, and listening to the absurd notions of that uplifting female in *Main Street*. I shall be very interested in seeing how your muse develops. I have a hunch that at present you would probably produce something more on the flavour of Pope than Keats or Blake—but as I have told you, I know nothing about poetry, and while I am gradually becoming interested, I am not yet intelligent on the subject, and probably would wrong you, Feathertop.

I spent the Friday afternoon that you left town with Miss Ray. We had a long long talk about this and that—the Frye being mentioned, whereupon I achieved one of the reddest and most prolonged blushes of my career while she sat and laughed and watched me suffer *and* suffer. I am certainly going to get over that habit.

Say—I'm going to stop right here. I suppose you head the course again, Illustrious Student—I shan't know until Thursday so I send my very best wishes, condolences or congratulations.

Helen

Moncton, N.B.
Saturday [*11 June 1932*]

My dear Helen:

Well, the Bach has stopped due to the arrival of a visitor (to be presently explained) and (prospectively) of a baby to the lady downstairs, so I am taking this opportunity afforded by enforced leisure and unemployment to catch up on my not very heavy correspondence. No one except yourself has written me yet—presumably they are all waiting for the results to come out.

Monday morning I spent forcing my surprised and indignant fingers into the C major scale. Monday afternoon R.G. [Pete] Colgrove arrived, looking as though he had made himself up for a vaudeville act. I said little, but pointed to the bathroom, whence he emerged about ninety minutes later fairly respectable, except for a collar that looked like a Toronto movie censor's mind, and told me that he had boarded the Ocean Limited at Lévis opposite Quebec and ridden to Moncton in the tool chest back of the tender, wearing a pair of overalls over his suit. Well, anyway, Pete stayed until Wednesday noon.

The Muse is still stubborn. I have a good idea but no technique. I have a conception for a really good poem, I am pretty sure, but what I put down is as flat and dry as the Great Sahara. I guess I'm essentially prosaic. I can work myself up into a state of maudlin sentimentality, put down about ten lines of the most villainous doggerel imaginable, and then kick myself and tear the filthy stuff up. However, I got a book of twentieth-century American poetry out of the library and that cheered me up. There are bigger fools in the world. I think your experiment in literary criticism a rather unfortunate one in some ways. You say I should produce something more of the flavor of Pope than of Blake or Keats. But knowing me as you do, do you think I should be more likely to produce this sort of thing from Pope's *Messiah*:

The Saviour comes! by ancient bards foretold:
Hear him, ye deaf, and all ye blind, behold!
He from thick films shall purge the visual ray
And on its sightless eyeball pour the day.

'Tis He th' obstructed paths of sound shall clear,
And bid new music charm th' unfolding ear.
The dumb shall sing, the lame his crutch forego
And leap exulting like the bounding roe.

—or this sort of thing, from Blake's *Ideas of Good and Evil*:

I asked a thief to steal me a peach.
He turned up his eyes.
I asked a lithe lady to lie her down,
Holy and meek, she cries.

As soon as I went
An angel came.
He winked at the thief
And smiled at the dame.

And without one word spoke
Had a peach from the tree,
And 'twixt earnest and joke
Enjoyed the lady.

Of course Pope would have made a better poet than either Blake or Keats if his soul had not been as small as a weasel's.

Yes, I think you should cure yourself of blushing. Mother tells me of a sister of hers [Mary Howard] who was entertaining a young man in the parlor when another sister entered and made one of those innuendoes common in late Victorian humor. My aunt blushed furiously, kept on blushing; the young man cast an alarmed glance at her and did not call again. The said aunt died two years ago an old maid of 56—in the very bed, incidentally, on which I am now reclining.

Monday. Well, here comes a most tantalizing and exasperating missive in the mail from Ruth [Dingman]. It begins: "All hail to the victor once more!" which is a sufficiently energetic start, and then continues, "Naturally, my mood ranges from disgust to horror when I think of my brilliant standing. However I at least didn't get a sup. Of course, you can imagine my opinion regarding that. As I've often said before, these people who care only . . . well, I won't say any more"—and, damn her, she doesn't, but passes serenely on to other matters leaving me gasping like a fish out of water. She remarks later "It's too bad about Art [Cragg] not getting a first." It certainly is too bad. But I should like to have my information more didactic and less rhapsodic, more categorical and less esoteric, that is, if you get what I mean. It sounds as though I had led my course, presumably with a first or at least a second, with my thoroughly deserved and confidently expected sup. in R.K. But I don't know how you made out, and I think Art might have let me know more definitely—that is, if he's in town—I haven't heard a word from him.

So I guess I had better let it rest at that. My regards to Jean.

Norrie

Honey Harbour, Georgian Bay
Monday [*13 June 1932*]

Dear Norrie—

This is a very warm and enthusiastic note of congratulation. I was so pleased to see you come out at the top once again—the point is, *are* you becoming infallible and inevitable? If you are not careful you may become a prophet singing in the wilderness—especially if you follow Blake a great deal—however, if it does come to pass, I'll send you a crate or a cage full of carefully trained locusts and a jar or so of wild honey like a bubbling old Martha—

You are getting ahead of me by leaps and bounds, I can see that, you lucky beggar, with a piano and the fugues. Reading so far has been *John Brown's Body*, *Main Street*, three short stories of D.H. Lawrence, ending up this morning with a bit of sentimentalizing with J.M. Barrie over the *Little Minister*—women sent to smooth the ragged ignoble brow of mankind to peace and a sense of their own utter depravity, angels of God pointing the way to celestial realms etc. One of those saccharine fictions one would love to be ass enough to believe—

Well anyhow, I meant this to be, as I said before, a note of congratulation. And if I seem to meander, you know that I am tremendously glad for you. As an institution you are exhibiting that very admirable quality of stability. As a person—I'm not going to eulogize, even if it should seem the proper thing to do along with the rest of my enthusiasm.

Yours—on the crest of the wave,
Helen

Moncton, N.B.
Sunday [*19 June 1932*]

My dear Helen:

Thanks for your congratulations. I am not particularly elated, as a matter of fact I am rather sick about Art's not getting a first. I should like to have seen him lead the course this year. I know how that sounds, but it's true. As long as I get my standing in first class I don't care where I come in the list. I don't compete for things, except incidentally; all competition is fundamentally a scramble, which is undignified. I told the boys on the chain that the moral to be deduced from my standing was, "Go to the grasshopper, thou slugger, consider his ways and be worldly wise." I don't know if they'll appreciate it or not but let's hope for indulgence.

Your talk about cabbages and twelve hours of sleep makes me think that you are getting fat. I warn you that if I come back and find you looking like the cornerstone of Stonehenge I will pinch you all colors of the rainbow. Reading J.M. Barrie too, just like any buxom matron.

Read *Babbitt* and *Arrowsmith* as well as *Main Street*. [Sinclair] Lewis is a diabolically clever writer and does the cleverest things so easily that he is too often underrated. His execrable style, which clanks along like a surveyor's chain, is annoying but necessary to the kind of thing he is doing. However, he is a pure technician and was consequently spoiled by recognition. *Elmer Gantry* and *Dodsworth*, his later works, are far too self-conscious.

Bach is still in the air. Damn neighbors, especially pregnant ones. Oh well, give my regards to Jean again, and write whenever you happen to be awake. Thanks again for them kind words.

Norrie

Moncton, N.B.
Tuesday [5 *July 1932*]

Dear Helen:

Well, you've been a pretty good girl—I was very glad to see you get through so well. Sorry you didn't get an A, but, in spite of my exhortations, I hardly expected it. As it is, I think you can consider yourself well out of reach of my avuncular hairbrush. Convey my sincerest congratulations to Jean on her standing. By the way (this should have come earlier, of course) thanks a lot for sending the clipping. It relieved me considerably, though the results are rather depressing. Nearly every Junior in Gate House has a sup. The official confirmation of mine came the other day. I discovered to my vast disgust that the weak-kneed sons of indiscretion had let me through the exam and plucked me because I didn't write their silly term test. They gave me 50 on the paper and 00 for my term mark, and called the aforementioned marks "approximate," though I fail to see anything approximate about that double goose egg. I have no intention of writing it this fall, of course. And yet I don't know—the prof is retiring this year, which means that the subject will go to some misguided young enthusiast who will insist on our working at it, so perhaps—oh, to hell with it.

Vera (my sister) has her salary at last, but can't come home this summer as she has an apartment lease to keep up. Mother is disappointed, but she doesn't want to come home anyway and I don't blame her. She doesn't like Moncton—neither do I, though for a different reason. One of my professors told me last year that although he liked Handel he could never endure the *Messiah* and similarly he could never read the Bible because he had been brought up on both compulsorily and grew to dislike them. That's the way I feel about Moncton. Why? Well, everyone who ever amounts to anything has to get out of his system an enormous heap of painfully silly trash in his adolescence—stuff he would regard going back to like a dog's returning (but I mustn't get scriptural) and the decade I spent in this town, as regards living, was just as tentative and experimental. At least, however, it's a focal point for me. But Vera never lived here, and coming "home" would bore her stiff. Her last letter talks of an uprising in Chicago as possible. She writes: "There has been a panic this last week. About twenty more banks suddenly closed, including two of the oldest and strongest on the South Side . . . La Salle St. (Chicago's Wall St.) was almost impassable for days, and there were riots in many places. The newspapers suppressed all mention of the disturbances . . . Many insurance companies have gone under . . . The other day I passed one of the big banks which had just closed. There was a crowd standing in front of it—not talking—just standing. It was awful."

I have got letters from four of the chain gang—Ross Crosby, Art Cragg, Bob Bates and Doug Gordon. They are all happy but Art. Art is in Toronto with his father, writing his Lincoln Hutton—subject, primitivism. It means pre-Romanticism—Rousseau back-to-acorns stuff, but, as you know, it means a movement in modern art as well—a thing he won't believe. He is very rueful about his second.

Have you really got this far? By all means let me have all of your wanderings, logical and illogical. Wandering is the secret of successful letter-writing—and by successful I mean, of course, readable.

Well, this morning the baby came. The place has been shut up like a tomb all day and we don't even know the sex of the child yet.

I suppose I should gas away forever if something didn't stop me, according to Newton's laws of motion. So here goes.

Norrie

[*Toronto*]
Sunday [*10 July 1932*]

My dear Norrie—

I am perhaps indulging in a most unhealthy fit of sentimentality and ill-temper—I am so damned lonesome just this minute. I have just heard one of those Hungarian Rhapsodies perpetrated by a drunken little orchestra from Jasper Park. Heck, it's as full of slush—the way they play it—as a mid-March thaw in Toronto.

Roy [Kemp] is here and Bill Pike and Fred Heather—his cronies. Daddy checked out yesterday for the north country, and we are alone. I like the idea very much, but life does seem a rush, getting meals and keeping the house and oneself clean—as a civilized being should, I suppose, since Anatole France's Paphnutius is not a pleasant ideal to follow. Have you read *Thais*? It is very like the American play *Rain* (dramatized under title *Sadie Thompson* with Gloria Swanson) in which a stern old evangelist with a cross between a stone wall and an Alpine glacier for a wife becomes interested in the immortal soul of Sadie—a San Francisco prostitute. Under the neurotic pressure of a six-day tropic storm the preacher "saves" Sadie's soul, seduces her (no alliteration intended) and then shoots himself, leaving Sadie to conclude all men are beasts etc. and go on as before. The difference being, Thais manages to die as a saint I believe (I haven't finished yet). Why is it that so many sincerely earnest men manage to look ridiculous? Is it merely because the scoffers find it easier to ridicule than to weigh the truth in the evangelist's message? Or does an evangelist, to be successful, necessarily lack a sense of humour? Judging by some of the books that we are discarding, that is, consigning to the lower regions until a few die-hards finally do kick off—the latter is true.

Ida [Clare] and Pat Lipsett and I are in the library now. I have been lettering, and sorting periodicals—the latter being a sort of glorified house-cleaning bee. I am growing so methodical that I very nearly file away the dishes when I wash them. F. Louis Barber arrived unexpectedly today. The man is priceless—such dignity! You should see the important air with which he transacts the most trivial business. But then he is a man, and can afford to be somewhat pompous in carrying out routine which we women would do as a matter of course.

Tonight we went to Marcus Adeney's for dinner. Marcus has turned musician temporarily—the novel is given a rest I suppose. He has some odd books—the most surprising being a translation of Ovid's *Art of Love*. He has a copy of James Joyce's *Dubliners* and an early book of short stories which he will loan me.

I was at Old Mill the other night with George [Clarke]—I talked like a blooming suffragette but we had a lot of fun. You should go there sometime. It is one of the most charming places in Toronto—the old-world atmosphere was the dream of Home Smith who was one of the big men behind the scheme for improving Toronto's downtown streets a few years ago. The scheme fell through, partly through the efforts of the *Telegram* which appealed to the suburban penny-pinchers. Oh well, what if we do go through life surrounded by ugliness—

By the way, I meant to mention this long ago. Of course I understand how you feel about R.K. but I advise you to be like Mr. Golightly for the simple reason that Miss Ray remarked that Prof. Auger and the R.K. prof and even Edgar were somewhat annoyed because you didn't work at the subject. Something to do with the Trick scholarship, I imagine. I don't know whether she told me thinking that I might pass on the idea to you—but anyhow, you get the idea. You can't afford to pull their beards too much—in the form of *Acta* articles and so on.

I think I have said about enough for this siege.

H.G.K.

Moncton, N.B.
July 15 [*1932*]

My dear Helen:

I have recently completed another decade of my alleged career and feel quite old-fashioned. My birthday, which is the same as that of France, has been signalized by a pouring rain on the last sixteen occasions of its celebration. This time the day dawned clear as a mirror; no vestige of a cloud anywhere. It stayed that way until eight o'clock at night, when suddenly and without warning a horrible-looking black thundercloud leered up over the horizon, like the devil coming for the soul of Faust, and for an hour the world was a stringy mass of water. I have just received your letter. Yeah, I know they're sore about the R.K. They wrote me a letter telling me I could have a hundred dollars if I wanted it, so I think they're going to hang the Trick upon me. They practically promised one to Cragg, and if they give one to him and not to me it's deliberate discrimination against me, for which, however, I could hardly blame them. I hope they don't hold my article in *Acta* ["The Case against Examinations"] against me—it would be a piece of petty spite quite beneath them if they did. It will be interesting to see just what effect the R.K. sup. will have on the Trick awards, though.

George Birtch's letter is here now. He holds three services on Sunday and six "Sunday" Schools throughout the week—covering an area of

120 square miles. Lives in a tent. No women. Got tossed off a horse. Plays on 3 men's softball teams and coaches two women's teams. Is getting up a play and directs it himself. After reading a letter like that I sometimes wonder what right I have to exist anyway.

I'm so glad you're not going to get fat. I shall greatly prefer a Helen of Troy to a Helen of Avoirdupois. Launch a thousand ships and you're all right, but overbalance a single canoe and you're done for.

It rains all the time, so about all I do is remain indoors and think very clogged thoughts about uninspiring subjects. I guess I'm going to be a professor after all. Which is a horrible thought. I seem to be anchored to my chair by my guts. A symptom of pedantry, probably. Or sedentry. (For which I apologize.)

Yes, I think you are right in ascribing the failure of so many earnest men to a lack of humour. Humour arises from the perception of incongruities and discrepancies in human nature. The reformer is impatient of these discrepancies; he calls them the result of cynicism and scepticism. His outlook is too exclusive and narrow for them, because he wants to apply a few formulas to the world which, universally accepted, would cure all of that world's evils. Now a man who has a panacea in any sphere is a quack. And a quack is always a nuisance, generally a menace. Whether he makes himself ridiculous or not depends on the amount of humour possessed by his portrayer or auditor, not on his own. (This is the sample of the workings of a mind with mould clinging to it, as aforesaid.)

I have shelved the Temperamental Clavichord for a week or so in favor of the Three-Part Inventions—those in E minor, A major, B-flat major and C minor—four of the loveliest pieces I know.

I guess I must be getting lonesome for you, pet. There is a seventeenth-century ballad which begins:

I wish I were where Helen lies
Night and day on me she cries.

Does she? I doubt it, and if she did she wouldn't admit it, certainly. The Helen of this particular poem was dead, which factor made the couplet considerably more respectable than plausible. As for the first line, you being very much alive, there would probably be a scandal which would ruin both of us. But even with these reservations, the quotation expresses my state of mind in general.

[*July*] 17

Well, I've covered two days in the course of writing this letter, and it's Sunday now. Mother has just dragged me out to church. Our church has gone in with a Baptist one for the summer and it's their choir and organist. The anguish I suffered listening to the latter is not easy to imagine. They plunged into a fairly difficult *durchkomponiert* setting of "Dear Lord and Father of Mankind" and when they finished—or at least when they stopped—I was leaving grooves in the pew. The minister was apparently not a Baptist, as he made a reference to his University career. He told us that the Bible was historically quite accurate. I forget his text—so did he, for that matter. Towards the end he wanted to know indignantly if the world were played out. I anticipated a discussion of *The Decline of the West* thesis of Spengler—a book that I am hoping against hope that you will read this summer—and came to life. But he remained as innocent as H.G.K. of the said volumes. He decided, however, that the world was not played out, as there was to be an Imperial Conference at Ottawa soon.

Thank God for Bach and Mozart, anyway. They are a sort of common denominator in music, the two you can't argue about. Beethoven, Chopin, Wagner—they give you an interpretation of music which you can accept or not as you like. But Bach and Mozart give you music, not an attitude toward it. If a man tells me that Beethoven or Brahms leaves him cold, I can still talk with him. But if he calls Bach dull and Mozart trivial I can't, not so much because I think he is a fool as because his idea of music is so remote from mine that we have nothing in common. This is the difference between—oh God, shut up. I guess I'm going to be a professor after all. Damn it, I *won't* be a professor. Wanna be a minister and join the Rotary Club. I wouldn't mind writing these exegeses if they (a) edified you (b) didn't sound so damned pontifical. But I guess I can't help talking down to people that feel down—can I, varlet?

Well, having nothing to say I think I did fairly well to stretch it out this far. My letters will brighten up a bit, perhaps, when I get at the library.

Norrie
XXX—

205 Fulton Ave., Toronto
July 26 [*1932*]

My dear Norrie—

I have been trying to write to you for several days and something turned up every time to prevent it. Last night I was so mad at people in general that a letter would not have been a very sanctimonious occupation—I can't seem to get away from *people*—young people, stupid people, people who come in and sit and talk about nothing and whose conversations are just a series of trivial questions. Lord! I never can be alone it seems. After your last letter I bought a copy of Mozart and have been worshipping at the shrine of pure music—when I get the chance. So you may imagine my annoyance last night when I had played two movements of the C major no. 3 and in walked Mrs. Smith in a kindly mood, to cheer me in my loneliness etc. The trouble is, my time at home is so infinitely precious just now, when I must be at the library presumably helping on the world's work, and then keep house besides, and in the odd moment attend to my own little soul.

I have not written to you these last few days for another reason. I will not send you another protracted groan and toothache like my last missive. I *am* a varlet. I have discovered that my besetting sin is a morbid introspection and a periodic melancholy for which there is no particular excuse except that I have inherited it from my father. Diet and lack of exercise and so on are other factors, so I am waging war against melancholy.

But I must tell you the highlight of the last few days. Aside from interruptions in the direction of midnight visits from Ernie Harrison and George Clarke, and Dick Smith and Harry Walker and Hans Lincke, there have been a few good turnips. For instance, Roy and I went to Chapmans' again, and listened to Joyce Hornyansky and Mrs. [Evlyn] Howard-Jones, Marcus Adeney, Miss Dennison, and Geoffrey Waddington (director of CKCN) play a Brahms Quintette and, with the aid of Arthur Mulliner, play Schubert Sextette (Op. 36). Joyce is beautiful—when she plays she seems like the prophetess in the grip of Apollo—she is so intense and so passionate. It was a strenuous evening—the Brahms tired me out completely, so through the Schubert I gazed at the graceful line of throat and neck and ear of Joyce Hornyansky. I think that I have never seen such a beautiful woman.

On Saturday night Jack Cumberland and Dorothy [Darling] and George Clarke were here, and at the last moment Hans Lincke came with his cello. We played some trios, and a little bit of the jazz Jack brought with him. Next day Hans came back and we spent a day as human beings should—we played the C minor Beethoven trio in the morning and then walked by the Don in the afternoon sunshine, and Hans and I sat on a log bent across the road while Roy feasted his photographer's soul on the surrounding scenery. Hans told me about his troubles (his father is ill, neurotic and so on). And he says he is in love, and he is happy and proud and doesn't care who knows it, and it is no one's business—if anybody teased him he would tell them to mind their own affairs. (This in answer to my telling him of the teasing I get at the library by that fool of a Robert.) So then Hans asks me, have I been, am I, in love. I try evasions of various sorts, that I used to think so and so on—well, I did mention you Norrie. Do you mind, very much? (My dear girl, where *is* your Victorian reticence?)

Have you thought that my two extra (possibly fruitless) years make much difference—my hastily assumed Victorian reticence steps in so that I do not here go into detail. And what if I don't read Spengler? As I say, I shall have one precious month before the exhibition—shall I spend it reading Spengler? You know, I shall not be able to follow you in many places—but then I am wandering by myself in others.

I am improving my acquaintance with Mr. Thornhill and his wife, two of the most intelligent and delightful people I know. We went sketching one afternoon—I was busy in the thick of deciding whether or not to come back to college next year—the question has been vexing me of late—but I suppose I shall return.

I am working on a map of the university buildings—it is the most interesting thing I have had to draw yet and I think it is good. I have had to park myself on street corners—to draw the buildings of which I had no photographs—Mary John's for one. You remember, you were there one night. I had Chinamen and paper boys looking over my shoulder.

(Do you know yet that I think of you very much, and I am so glad to be alive that sometimes I could dance—or even sing if my opinion of singers were more favorable.)

Norrie, you must not let the rain get you.

Probably by now you are feeling much better—I hope so. I have had so many low moments that I don't want to see you catching the disease. And I am lonesome for you—but that must be fought off as best I can. As for your being a professor—do you think you need to be a stuffy pedant? My conception of that type of mind is of an antique soul who has lost contact with people and living beauty and with enthusiasm—distinctly not a social being. There is too much of the fighter or of the controversialist about you to remain passively letting the world go by—and I think you may develop a broad human sympathy—you have changed a good deal within the last year in that regard.

By the way, it is rather amusing to discover some of the remarks you have made in your time regarding the deadly sex in general, and the dire fate awaiting the man who so far forgets his manhood as to fall for the spell of Eve and all her daughters.

I am getting sleepy—I'll be making my towers all crooked tomorrow if I'm not careful. One word more. I would suggest that you do some walking—a lot of walking—if you will not swim. Fresh air being an excellent thing for cobwebs, and rainy atmosphere, and "a mind with mould clinging to it."

Helen

Moncton, N.B.
July [*1932*]
(The nearest calendar is 2 rooms away.)

My dear Helen:

Well, it's still wet and my brains are still water-soaked. So should I do some walking, take some exercise, get some fresh air, hey? This, to one who has ground the length and breadth of Toronto under his heels! You *are* reasonable. How the hell can I walk when it's raining all the time? And if it does happen to be a "fine" day, it's so much hotter and stuffier than hell that that overworked simile can be left off duty for once. I can walk all over this infernal city in half an hour, and if I venture outside it, whiz comes a car that honks me into the ditch. And the natives stare at me, wherever I go, as though I really were the combination of owl and bird-of-paradise that I resemble.

The results have just come. They're not giving me a Trick, apparently, and they did give one to Cragg. I can't imagine who the other one is. I can't quite understand their attitude towards me altogether, but that isn't what's worrying me. I shall not know definitely for a month yet whether I am going back or not. I simply will not face my final year with inadequate financial backing, and if I can help it I am not going into debt. I've come to college before without any money, of course, but this is my senior year. Well, I shall leave it to God—or circumstances, I should say, being a church student.

I'm still unrepentant about my R.K.—it's a nuisance, but it *does* fit in so beautifully with what I said in *Acta*! Ernie Gould has just written. He's bitterly opposed to my going into the ministry and says it's a divine judgment on me. I thought the powers that are in Vic were too big to notice my *Acta* article—will I *never* get over my freshman verdancies? I have been disillusioned like that once before. I was at chapel in the beginning of my first year. Chancellor Bowles was speaking. He said that the truth would make us free. He said that we would find as we went along that many things we thought very fine would eventually appear as sham. He spoke of the way his literary, artistic, musical tastes had developed in separating the true from the free—I mean the trivial. Then he said, "Let us join in singing Hymn No. 403—'Will Your Anchor Hold in the Storm of Life?'"

Mme. Hornyansky *is* magnificent, isn't she? I shall never recover from the stupor into which she plunges me every time I see her, no matter how distantly. There is something distilled and refulgent, almost mathematical, about her. She expresses what those grim celibates of the Middle Ages were trying to say when they painted their Madonnas. A woman to them was merely evil in herself and in her sexuality; she was of use only as a symbol of something higher. That is what is back of the "Virgin Birth" idea. It is also what is back of the remarks I have made about women that you find so amusing. I am not a misogynist, but I represent, in my twentieth-century, late-Victorian, decadent way, the same monastic-Puritan attitude.

I am not going to church any more. The Baptist preacher is at our church now. I put both feet down and told Mother I wouldn't go and hear that man if he had been commissioned to open the Seventh Seal, a remark that scandalized the parent at first, but as she can't hear a word anyway, she gave in.

I am reading *Don Quixote* now. It's immensely long, brutal and at times nauseating, but, oh, boy, what a book! The translation I have is 18th-century by a man who knew what concrete nouns were. *He* didn't say "insides" when he meant "guts," or "perspiration" when he meant "sweat," or "side" when he meant "belly." That is the one thing that proves our alleged "reaction" from "Midvictorianism" a fraud and a lie—the way we steer around realities with polysyllables and elliptical statements.

No, I don't want to be a professor. Theoretically. In practice I should like it well enough. But there is something about such an eminently cultured occupation that would make me feel as though I were shirking something. A professor is, as I think I have said before, an orchid—highly cultivated, but no roots in the ground. He deals with a crowd of half-tamed little savages who get no good out of him except intellectual training and, in some cases, the radiation of his personality. He is not a vital and essential force in a community of live people. He is not a worker in the elemental sense of that word. Most professors, to gain a reputation, specialize so intensely in their work that they are cut off even from the undergraduate. These are the pedants. The rest are not so cut off from reality, but they are cut off from life. Oh, well, you get the idea. The ministry is my "vocation," etymologically. I have been "called" to it just as much as any blaspheming fool of an evangelist that ever bragged about what a sinner he was before he was converted. But that doesn't mean that I am fitted for it, necessarily. It doesn't mean that I am not deadly afraid of it and would rather do a hundred other things. Above all, it certainly doesn't mean that my friends ever imagine I'll be a minister. "Ministry?" says Ernie Gould. "Do you think your friends are going to stand by and see you waste your life and talents in that?" "Minister?" snorts the janitor at Gate House. "You'd make a damn good hypocrite, that's what you'd make!" "My dear boy, you can't be a minister," says Norm Knight, "you've got brains." And so they go. They're absolutely and devastatingly right, of course. I wonder what those writers who talk about relentless and inexorable Fate would say to a man who had two Fates, pulling in opposite directions. The trouble is that I can't quite figure out which one is God.

Well, I can't keep pouring out undiluted genius much longer when I am living the life of a misanthropic clam. I wish I wasn't quite so *DAMNED* lazy. That's another argument against the ministry—with my temperament I shall probably drift into writing or professoring or pugilism or some lazy man's profession instead.

I have judiciously weighed the question of whether or not I should "mind very much" your saying that you love me and have decided that I do not. I find the statement even agreeable. But you frighten me a little, you sweet child. "Love" may mean anything from a quiet friendship to an overwhelming passion. It may be anything from a purely sexual impulse to a declaration of honorable intentions based on a close survey of the economic field. In the sense that I like you better than anyone else of your sex, I love you. I love you in the sense that I would do anything for you. In the sense that no revelation of weakness in your character would diminish my respect for you. In the sense that I think of you a great deal, and always affectionately. And so on. But if I were to go into poetic ramifications of the subject, and tell you that you filled my days with sunshine and my nights with longing, I should be merely a liar, and you would be well advised to regard me as an insidious and designing villain. Don't you see, darling? I can't write you a sustained love letter, because when I try—and I have tried—the result sounds like a Chopin nocturne scored for brass. It acts like a tonic on me to hear you say that you love me, certainly. But it does make me rather nervous to be carrying such a warm and pulsating little heart around in my pockets. I'm afraid it might drop out and break.

Your two years make no difference to me, whatever they make to you. I have always associated with women older than myself—and besides, if I patronize you, what would I do to a sixteen-year-old? Dose her with castor oil, probably.

Well, having got this far, I find my mind an absolute blank. Whenever I get jolted out of my customary shell of reserve and shyness, I feel very uncomfortable and naked, and so the sooner I shut up the better.

Norrie

[*Toronto*]
Friday. August 5 [*1932*]

My dear Norrie—

Your letter came a couple of days ago. I have been thinking about you a great deal since then. I have told you before this that I could not see you performing with satisfaction to yourself the duties of a minister. The average church congregation seems to me to be a community of bustling Marthas held together by a weekly sewing meeting and another meeting devoted to purging one's soul by communion with the unknown, expressing one's soul by singing third-rate tunes, and edifying one's consciousness in general by listening to a few ethical principles half hidden by quotations from the Hebrews, followed by a plea for more substantial collections. The women gossip, the men quarrel, the soprano soloist with an eye to matrimony ogles and attempts to seduce the young minister. The young minister himself is inevitably (if he is intelligent) assailed by grave doubts about the infallibility of his doctrine, and the right of the Christian church to attempt to evangelize the world. If he comes through all this struggle he will have attained a deeper spirituality and a broader sympathy with toiling sweating humanity. If he never arrives at a solution, and still remains in the ministry, he is forced to pour forth his weekly platitudes as usual, to live a life at which his inner being revolts. He is forced to live a lie, stunting his own growth, still blindly hoping that he *must* be doing some good. How can a man at war with himself be a leader of other men?

No work of art—and a spiritual life is a work of art—is attained without a certain amount of purification, and forgetfulness of individual pettiness. Possibly I am picturing an ideal unattainable to most, and reached by a few men of genius—a sort of nirvana. But what is a man of genius if not one who has struggled and tapped the hidden spring of beauty and truth and has imprisoned a little of it for thirsty men?

If you have anything of value to preach to humanity, it will come in spite of yourself—and at a much later date than now. This sounds hopelessly conservative I know, but it arises from my suspicion of the child prodigy. It is a good thing that croakers like myself did not dam up the enthusiasm of a Keats or a Mozart. To any great extent, that is.

You told me once that you thought some biting satire would be a good thing for the church, or for religion, I forget which. But, tell me, can you get a child to feel the awe of the idea of infinity by bullying him into learning every dot, comma and fly-speck on two dusty pages of an old algebra disclosing the binomial theorem? Can you make him enjoy the *Aeneid* by bewildering him with the ablative absolute and all the legions of participles which join together in one scraggy skeleton? Can you drive men to the love of God or the love of the good life by writing a *Tale of a Tub* or *The Christian* or *Elmer Gantry*? I mean, has satire ever any positive value other than laughing to shame certain follies? Iconoclasm seems to be one of the chief sports of this age—and the best paid, for that matter.

I cannot say anything about the church in general—I have not thought much about religion. As I told you before, church services bore me (and I am accustomed to the Church of England service which is fairly active) and I never go to hear people who amount to a great deal. So I can not say that I am a Christian particularly—or even an intelligent pagan. The first church I went to was Westminster, when John Neil, a kindly venerable old gentleman, was alive. But we moved to this district shortly afterwards, and Roy and I were sent to an Anglican church where the minister gave marks for bringing more collection than the other children, gave interminable sermons on the evils of putting big nickels on the collection plate and bawled most ferociously at people who stayed away from church to wash the family automobile. He took great pride in the number of children he had prepared semi-annually for confirmation by the bishop. Of the catechism I remember several useful things such as Q: "What is your name?" Ans. "M or N." Q. "Who gave you this name?" Ans. "My godfathers and my godmothers at my baptism wherein I was made a member of Christ, a child of God, and an inheritor of the Kingdom of Heaven." And so on.

August 11

Did I say I wouldn't write you another indigo effusion? Well, I won't, but I certainly could at this moment. I went to get Thorny's advice last night and I find that I have to change the map around—do all the buildings over again from a bird's-eye view instead of straight front view. Like this:—

instead of this:—

So I'll be parked here for another two weeks, I suppose. Of course, it is fun making the thing, but a wee bit discouraging to undo what has taken quite a lot of time to get this far with.

I left off in the middle of weighing the pros and cons of a minister's career. For one thing I am too deeply impressed with *Elmer Gantry* to be unbiased. I had gotten so far in my thinking when I came upon Frank Shallard's difficulties and find that Lewis anticipates H.G.K. I can't agree with you entirely about your orchid professor. How are you going to tame your little savages if you don't hold their interest in some line or other—I mean awaken an interest. And is not the enthusiastic teacher going to have a tremendous influence in that way? To be sure, an unawakened dictaphone with the faculty of retaining facts and strutting them forth is not going to spell life to the little savages who have probably really felt and experienced more than she has. The function of a teacher seems to me essentially the same as that of a minister—to bring colour into a drab life. But have you noticed very many inspired teachers? Can you blame children altogether for being the savages which you so unsympathetically dub them? Most people don't know how to enjoy life—why blame their children for not being divinely inspired?

You are precious, Norrie—you never embarrass me by being sentimental. Sentimentalism is one thing that makes me ill—from the sobbing saxophone player to that female who sang yesterday "Luv made a Buh-a-aby of Muh-ee."

Still, I have my moments—you know about that. I must get back to work and start on Emmanuel—see how skittish I can make it.

Helen

205 Fulton Ave., Toronto
Monday [*15 August 1932*]

Norrie my dear—

What *are* you doing? I've been watching the postman like a hawk, for days, and there is no word from you. Are you dead, or sick, or disgusted, or lazy, or worried or blue or frightened or bored stiff, or immersed in books? Are you coming back, or do you know yet?

As to that, I have been thinking that Victoria College will not likely allow one of its most brilliant students (and incidentally a showpiece in every publication like the *Victoria College Bulletin*—see how bright our students are, etc.) to stay away for lack of money. You see, I heard [C.E.] Auger talking about "our showing in scholarship," and at another time about "young Frye who seems to be cleaning up on everything."

I still am on the fence about coming back myself—money, this time. But Daddy says "yes, why not?" In spite of the fact that he has been making a weekly amount of money equivalent to the earnings of a Toronto scavenger, all summer. I start in at the Exhibition in a few days now. Cooking beans this time. I am working like fury trying to finish the map, which is a work of art, to my way of thinking. I *can* draw, boy.

We are going to Miss Dennison's again to play a trio I fancy—perhaps a piano quartette or a quintette if Hans and Lucy [Cox] can come. So I am on the way out.

But I should like to know something about you—you are rather far away, you know. I've still got the habit of taking an extra long look at every male platinum blond—and then I remember, of course, you are several provinces away.

I must go—

Love,
Helen

Moncton, N.B.
[*?–25 August 1932*]

My dear little girl (or does that sound sentimental?):
Respected Madame (a euphemism for Respectable Female):

I have just received your letter with its polemic re the priesthood. It is very clever, sincere and well expressed, but as I read *Elmer Gantry* about five years ago and went over the ground you survey quite thoroughly at that time it misses the difficulty I am in at present. As your criticism has obviously been strongly influenced by that book, I may as well tell you what I think of it. Sinclair Lewis, as I remarked before, was spoiled by success—if you ever attack *The Man Who Knew Coolidge* you will realize that—while in *Dodsworth* he drops all his claims to distinction and returns to the rank and file of scribblers. The era of postwar tolerance and disillusionment made the production inevitable of a kind of satire for which a trick of imitation and a technical gift—which Lewis certainly has—even *Elmer Gantry* is a technical triumph—would suffice. But Lewis obviously has a commonplace mind and one as thoroughly Philistine as Babbitt himself, and when he was hailed as a prophet and genius lost his head. Imagine what a farce *Main Street* would have been had Lewis taken sides with Carol!—yet he does that in *Elmer Gantry*. Lewis' critical faculties seem to have been suspended when he wrote the book—partly because, no doubt, of the grim associations of religion with his childhood, but partly too because he has no adequate weapons except the bludgeons of an antiquated materialism with which to meet contemporary religion. So *Elmer Gantry* fails both as a satire and as a polemic. Again, while *Main Street*, etc., were inevitable to the 1920s, *Elmer Gantry* is obviously an out-of-date product the proper place for which belongs midway between *Uncle Tom's Cabin* and the beginning of pragmatism. As it is, I am faced with the United Church of Canada, anno domini 1936 or thereabouts—surely a very different matter. As you say, I think some biting satire is essential to the church, but the satire must bite, not bark. I do not quite understand your identification of satire with dusty pedantry. Surely the one is the best cure for the other. Lewis passed up an opportunity to write a great novel here. Think of what he overlooked!—Protestant individualism clashing with Protestant bigotry, Catholic anti-intellectualism cloaked by Catholic urbanity, mysticism in its last ditch, the clergy slowly retreating from their hell-fire vindictiveness to a vague and emasculated ethical sentiment, the slight but apparent rise of superstition and occultism, to mention the barest outlines of some of the themes.

My difficulty is not that of Frank Shallard, who was a weak-kneed prig, but that of an Ancient Mariner hounded on by a force at least as strange as himself to deliver his message to bored and uneasy Wedding Guests. For I have got a definite message to give, right now, which will develop but not essentially change as I grow older, and I am not an infant prodigy. Nor am I worried about the infallibility of my doctrines—there is no commonsense doctrine in existence that cannot be harmonized into a consistent interpretation of Christianity. What I am worried about is my own personal cowardice. I am easily disheartened by failure, badly upset by slights, retiring and sensitive—a sissy, in short. Sissies are very harmless and usually agreeable people, but they are not leaders or fighters. I would make a very graceful shadow boxer, but little more. I haven't the grit to look the Wedding Guest in the eye. "Put on the armour of God," said a minister unctuously to me when I told him this. Good advice, but without wishing to seem flippant, I don't want armour, divine or otherwise—snails and mud-turtles are encased in armour—what I want is a thick skin. You don't need to worry over me. I am not a deep or interesting problem, except perhaps to an entomologist. At present I am merely a poltroon on the outskirts of a battle, armed with one or two powerful weapons I may or may not get a chance to use, and trying to make my teeth stop chattering long enough to decide whether to go forward or crawl back to where the generals are and accept a position with them of great dignity and opulence. If I do the latter, you can cut my acquaintance any time, if you like, though of course I hope you won't. The only thing is, "None but the brave," etc.

Your description of the local Anglican church is accurate enough. All churches are more or less like that. Yet everybody has a soul, however shabby, cheap and fly-specked a one it may be. Incidentally, I hate to seem intolerant, but I do not approve of Anglicanism. There are two possible approaches to Christianity, or any religion—the Protestant or individual approach, and the Catholic or collective one. Anglicanism never made up its mind which it was going to be, and did not much want to, as it was based on the useful but muddle-headed English idea of pleasing everybody. If you look at the first article of the Elizabethan Six, you will see that it supports transubstantiation—the second denies it. Not that that matters, but it shows the Anglican point of view—religion itself is in bad taste—it is only the observance of it that is in good taste. I think that in England now it is beginning to break up into its two constituents under pressure of the necessity of defining its religious attitude now that the support of The Crown, The Nobility, The Nation, The Army, The Fleet, and a lot more "The's," including the Oxford and Cambridge Accents and Poses, genuine or aped, which has bolstered it up heretofore, is beginning to weaken. Here, of course, it is a fish out of water—the Established—that is, the Representative Church is the United Church of Canada. This is an inevitable product of Canadianism—its counterpart would be inconceivable in the U.S.A.—and it is representative of all that Canada means in history—in its good nature, in its tolerance, in its conscientiousness, in its vague and sentimental combination of Socialism, Imperialism and Nationalism all at once—a very appealing mixture, unpalatable though each individual constituent may be—above all in its determination to apply old traditions to new surroundings which makes Canada sturdier than England and more coherent in its perspective than the United States.

Whew! What a harangue to make to a harmless child, who hasn't done anything even to deserve being spanked, or shut up in a closet with her conscience, let alone having to spend an hour or two trying to get interested in the workings of mine.

Well, I'm hideously sick at my stomach today. I'm not going to eat any more of whatever it was I ate. I was working in the library today from twelve to six and at about four I left ten taxpayers who wanted to find Ethel M. Dell and Edgar Wallace and went outside and gave up the ghosts of the last ten meals I had eaten. When I got home I promptly took a chill and swallowed about three quarts of lemonade, hot. I'm still a sick gazelle, to express it poetically, but convalescent.

I dreamed about you last night, sweetheart. I dreamed I was back at Toronto seeing you again for the first time in four months. And I held you *very* close to me, to be exact, at a pressure of 20.3786 recurring pounds to the square inch. But you were afraid of being strangled, and bit a large piece out of my neck, so I let you go, and kissed the tip of your nose, the dimples on your knees, and a small pink toe projecting from your shoe (which was rude of you, my dear—you should have been better dressed for the occasion)—and woke up quite happy.

Which is the silliest trash, and quite unworthy of my dignity. That damned library of yours is making me send back Windelband's *History of Philosophy* before I had finished it. I didn't figure there was much point in reading it too long before the term opened. Maybe Ruth [Dingman] had something to do with its recall, or Art [Cragg]. They're getting alarmed. Ernie [Gould] says if I don't get some competition next year I'll *never* get out of bed. I don't expect much. From a purely academic point of view, I shall have things pretty well my own way, I should imagine.

Later. Tomorrow has come, and with it your last letter. I'm frightfully sorry, lotus-blossom—I didn't realize what an unconscionable amount of time had elapsed between the first two sentences of this letter. Not that I am offering an excuse, of course. I'm an ill-mannered cur and I shall not attempt to gloss the fact.

Your letter is comforting as regards my going back, but Victoria College does not seem to my mind so much interested in my welfare. I was of all the church students the most eligible for the Trick scholarships—I cannot forget that. I think I shall attempt the return. I should rather starve in Toronto than feed in luxury here. I think I shall go in for a less erratic source of income than scholarships, in any case.

Norm Knight has written. He's got in with the Trotskyite section of the Canadian Communist Party and is Secretary of it. His antics are beginning to worry me a little. I sometimes wonder if he is ever going to grow up. His sense of humor may redeem him, or he may fall in love. Humor and virility are not allies of Communism.

I hope I shall be able to see your map sometime. Your statement that "you can draw" is an agreeable surprise to me, as, not having seen much of your work and not being able to judge of it if I had, I had accepted your former statements to the effect that you couldn't.

I trust this new nightmare about *your* not going back to college will prove to be as completely rooted in indigestion as the former ones. It *is* a nightmare, and a horrible one—though at least the financial reason is more acceptable than your asinine impulse to pack your brain and soul in ice and go to Art School. Not that Art School is a bad place for a college graduate or an ignoramus. You being neither, I object. But surely you should be able to manage college all right, living in town. And your father ought to know whether you can go or not, though of course fathers occasionally err on the side of optimism. I am certainly not relying on the confidence of my own Wilkins Micawber of a progenitor. If you cannot actually afford to go back next year, and I figure I can, I should not lose interest in you, however, as I might do if you had deliberately thrown up your college course. In the little reading I did for my Aesthetics last year I saw where Edmund Burke made a remark to the general effect that beauty in distress was more enticing than beauty in a smock. You see, to me you are essentially an amateur, a developing amateur, in the literal sense of a lover. You are just beginning to love music, you are just touching the outskirts of literature, you are beginning to love art, and you are beginning to love me. To take all this amateurishness—that is, loveliness—away from you and immerse you in an atmosphere of professionalism would spoil you.

Well, ducklet, I hate to stop talking to you, but there's a limit to every thing.

Star Cloud, Brown Mouse,
Wind Ripple, Little Grace-Note,
Wren Nest, and Sweetest of all Sweets,
Good Night.

Norrie

205 Fulton Ave., Toronto
Tuesday [*23 August 1932*]

My dear Norrie—

Another day has gone past—I was thinking of you tonight, and so I write to you for a little while, because I should like to be talking to you.

I have been working very hard all day long—practising a little, but mostly accomplishing wonders on the masterpiece. I gave up at nine o'clock finally, almost in a state of exhaustion—and got out Bach again. And the F major Mozart sonata, and good Czerny who is such fun. Especially since I have him almost under control here and there.

I feel somewhat serious tonight. I have been reading a book *War Letters of Fallen Englishmen*—actual letters of young men for the most part under the age of twenty-five. Well-educated Englishmen—some schoolboys straight from the classroom, some schoolmasters, some doctors, some fellows of Cambridge. The prevailing note is one of reverence for a God, of loving and democratic fellowship, of hatred of the stupid bungles of politicians who were, they felt, the cause of the mess, and a constantly recurring belief that only by fighting it out to the finish will they be able to establish peace and the ideals of the pacifists. In the midst of it all they felt they must go on to the finish. One man hoped to be there on the last day, when men of either side would rush together in friendship, exchanging souvenirs, and now no longer feigning a hatred which neither actually felt.

I have lately been wondering what makes human beings cling together so—parents and children, husbands and wives, lovers, brothers and sisters, strangers—overlooking the sex attraction, is it merely a matter of habit, a lack of initiative in seeking distant fields? And then, in the matter of religion, surely a God is not entirely a figment of the imagination—"man's hopes and desires projected on the world about him." Throughout these letters of the war generation there flowed a faith in God, and a sincere hope of ultimately achieving peace and friendship. I wonder whether this generation would write with the same faith and sincerity—when the youngsters with brains are busy debunking and writing flashy criticisms of the work of others. A generation is growing now which must feel that there is no place for it in the world. To the serious-minded this is ruinous. To the frivolous, equally so, but in a different way.

Oh well, one must not worry. I have looked up a very nice copy of *Don Quixote*—translated by Motteux (also 18th century, with delightful etchings by Lalauze). You are not reading Smollett's translation are you? I gather that it is slightly coarser than need be—I have just reached the middle of the second volume (there are four in this edition) and have not had my Puritan modesty startled terribly yet. It is a delightful book, isn't it?

Goodnight, dear,
Helen

205 Fulton Ave., Toronto
Sunday [*28 August 1932*]

Dear Man—

When I came home yesterday night your letter was here. Roy was also here, but he bicycled out to camp with Fred Heather after midnight.

So I have been, and am now, alone. I have no idea what I shall do today—I am quite content. If it had not been for your letter I should have had to do something about my loneliness—but not now. You are different—you stimulate me to more or less positive action along lines of which my little conscience approves. Other people wanted me to fit into their scheme of things, and be myself, yet at the same time dance around being the sort of girl they wanted. My self was incidental. And so, unsuccessful as a sport model and Typical Girl, after a somewhat lonely summer, I feel very peaceful.

Monday afternoon. Today is children's day at the Exhibition—hordes, mobs—O Lord! I have the afternoon off.

I was extremely edified by your lecture—no I'll not tease you, you're not boring me. And do you not think I am interested? You may talk down to me all you like—because I am extremely tolerant where you are concerned. But I *should* like you to overcome your habit of squelching people who haven't interested themselves in Scott at the tender age you did, or people who aren't interested in Bach. Mainly my reason is this. I am growing suspicious of people who try to hold the floor entirely (don't be annoyed, I am speaking generally. This only applies to you somewhat—for you do enjoy "bringing up young ladies in the way they should go"). For while I like Marcus Adeney, I find him still plunging radically into ideas and conclusions and spouting as dogmatically about subjects with which he is relatively unacquainted as would a college sophomore who has just discovered Communism or women's suffrage or birth control or (a few years ago) evolution. Charles Comfort, who is a very clever and much talked of artist in town, does the same thing. Hans Lincke, who is a fair musician, knows nothing except making fiddles (he does that well). Yet in a group of people he talks louder than anyone else, boasts of how *he* tells people exactly what he thinks and, in short, acts with extreme boorishness. But he has an extremely kind and generous heart. (I finally put a stop to his arguments about university—he insists that I am wasting my time. Now, I can't argue my particular fate with everyone who wants to tug me this way or that, for I've been told I should go to art school, and I should study music, and what good was this doing me anyhow, for so long that the subject grows tedious.)

I am so sorry to hear that you have been sick—you must be careful. But you make me slightly curious. You say you dreamed about me "last night," and then you are "hideously sick today." You make me nervous, man. If I have such an effect, you'd better devote yourself to the ex-girlfriend and continue to write brilliant essays on Blake. Other slight errors: I am not afraid of being strangled, and my knees resemble those of a knotty, tree-climbing little urchin, more than any pink-toed, soft-fleshed, soft-eyed damoiselle. Too bad, isn't it. Still, my general physique is quite serviceable though it would never inspire ten thousand ships.

11:10 P.M. My Dearest Uncle! I have seen the map of Quebec that was exhibited last year at the gallery, and is now at the Ex—just before the building closed. Beautiful, beautiful things there—I shall spend much time looking—I am fairly breathless, I am so excited. I am *sure* I can do something good—I am going to work, dear man, and show you!

Am I writing too much, am I bothering you? Darling I'm head over heels tonight—so happy that I should be capering over the moon—you know? Percy Grainger plays the A minor fugue—Garbo says "As You Desire Me," Hornyansky plays Haydn, the D minor Toccata and Fugue, a bit of glorious paint, and you are there, near or far, it doesn't matter. A thousand delights rolled into one. I kiss you goodnight.

Helen

Moncton, N.B.
[2 *September* 1932]

My dear Helen:

I have just received your last letter.

No, there is nothing terribly shocking about *Don Quixote*. I said "brutal and disgusting" because of the relish Cervantes seems to take in physical violence. I have Motteux' translation. Smollett's is not really a translation at all, as Smollett did not know any Spanish.

I assure you that I am not trying to direct your career. I merely have a certain kind of interest in you, and I consider that your one duty to God and man is to grow up. People like myself are determined to be adults, and not all the clangor of brazen-throated folly can stop me from civilizing myself. Others prefer to remain infants. Still others have the right idea, but need help from friends—and I think you belong here.

Our fine arts training in Canada is so childish, and the general background of culture provided by our schooling so negligible, that it is rare to find a professional in one of them of broad outlook and culture. And when I see the beautiful and good things of life entrusted to a crowd of chattering jackals I see red. I don't care whether they have good hearts or not—a great artist is necessarily *sans peur et sans reproche*. As a custodian of beauty he has a great tradition to sustain—if he ignores that tradition he is a nuisance. Of course, a city with cheap and smug culture will harbor cheap and smug purveyors of it. Now don't impute my motives in saying this. I have no desire to hold the centre of any stage except on my own merits. But I am determined to do all I can to "squelch" ignorance and blatherskiting no matter where I find it. My love for Bach is not a personal idiosyncrasy, for God's sake. There is only one refuge in Toronto for an ambitious adolescent, and that is the university. This applies equally to both of us.

I am sorry about the unfortunate association of ideas concerning the dream and the resulting sickness. I noticed the break, but decided to let it go. The dream did not actually take place, of course—it was merely a passing fantasy. I am sorry too that you should have taken my innocent nonsense about your knees in the spirit of Shakespeare's 128th sonnet. I am quite familiar with your personal appearance. But may I not pay you the compliment of blinding my eyes to your ugliness occasionally?

No, little Chinese Lady, you are not writing too much nor are you bothering me. Your script is a joy to read and you don't gush.

I am sure that you can "do something good" too, dear. I shall, for your own good, continue to sneer for a while, however. Only remember that I am quite sincere when I say I want to help you—I don't want to pose, show off, lay down the law or make fun of you, though I shall probably do all four unconsciously. We have a tough hill to climb, and the worst of it is that we don't know its name—it's probably not Olympus, and it doesn't seem to be Parnassus or even the Mount of Olives. But it's there, and we've got to climb it.

There are so surprisingly few things that really matter. Music matters, and babies matter—so do poetry, sunsets over marshes, plain food, and people's flea-bitten souls. But that's about all. So why bother about anything else? People who laugh at dreamers and stargazers merely can't distinguish what's necessary from what's important. These practical-minded people are also necessary but not important, which is why they hate to feel slighted.

Well, two weeks more and I'll be out of this infernal place and back to civilization.

Norrie

205 Fulton Ave., Toronto
Wednesday [*7 September 1932*]

My dear Norrie,

I have just come from the art gallery—I shall go again just for the purpose of hearing people's reaction to John Russell's beautiful nude—a girl of fifteen, surrounded by small puppets and Dresden dolls. Such a lovely chaste and graceful thing. There was another nude—a warm-blooded, passionate woman from the south, with the face of a sophisticated, but not a great, soul. And a painting of an old man with the eyes of a mystic—blue-shadowed, white-beard with amber light bringing out the silkiness of it. Violet, jade and indigo colours for his robe. His hands were long and nervous, and his eyes gazed beyond the world, yet followed after one. I am a little disappointed in Will Ogilvie's work, showing there. He's one of the men I mentioned before—comes from South

Africa, paints negroes, and plays Bach on the Orthophonic Victrola. Charlie Comfort I suspect of playing to the gallery.

I came home with Will Auger the other night, and went in for coffee with his father and mother. I had quite a chat—about music and Professor Currelly's disgust with the university life—thinks students never talk about their work, are crammers for the most part—students in general are not intellectual and so on. I had to agree for the most part, in fact I did quite a bit of talking on the subject. I needn't go into that here, for it doesn't matter much yet what I think—to anyone but myself.

But Norrie dear, you mustn't be vexed if I am prickly and prudish sometimes—for I loved your "innocent nonsense"—and if I withdraw into my shell it is from pure shyness, or wonder that anything so lovely could be happening to me. For the shell, which is not a real shell, is rapidly dissolving in the sun. And then what else shall I do? But please remember to wield the razor strap, right lustily—for Miss Ray told me I needed discipline, therefore I applied myself to that dull library with such a zest for routine and with so little imagination that I thought I was dead. If *your* discipline is Bach and Mozart—why, Lazarus revives!

I came home last night and worked on the map. Hans and Bill Pike and Ernie [Harrison] came in, each telling me some trouble—one has a busted love affair, and the other had a quarrel with the woman who is his boss, and Ernie devoted himself to Marion [Kemp]. Marion is home again, thank God. She cleaned the house, and washed the dishes, and is taking full charge. Home is now home again somehow. I do seem to be a hopeless incompetent—when it comes to housework—I can *do* it, and do it well, but Lord! I can't get interested enough to keep it up. Did you say a woman naturally fitted into routine?

Helen

Moncton, N.B.
Sunday [*11 September 1932*]

My dear Helen:

This is the last letter that I shall write to you, and you need not answer this one, as I shall be leaving sometime next week.

I have hardly touched a piano this last month. I read music quite a bit, but I am afraid my touch and technique are beyond hope—at least for what I want to play—and when I get an irresistible urge to regular practice I think of the common room at Gate House, Burwash Hall. Our piano is in a ghastly shape, anyway, and delicacy of touch is wasted on it. Henceforth I shall listen only to you.

Your apology was very pretty and of course acceptable. You may have noticed that I belong to the mollusca myself.

I want Romanticism as my topic for my Philosophy thesis and Browning for Edgar, and I want to get to headquarters and make sure of getting them. I have already done quite a bit of work on Browning—I suppose, take him all in all, he's my favorite poet. I have very definite heroisms in literature—Donne, Milton, Bunyan, Swift, Blake, Dickens, Browning, and Shaw—and I like writing about them. So you see that the war-horse already sniffs battle. I sincerely hoped that Cragg would lead the course last year—I sincerely hope I shall next year.

There is very little to write this time. But then, I usually say that, and turn out a screed a couple of quires long. But I'm worn out and tired of summer. I get more and more tired all the time I stay here. The change back to Toronto will get me up again. I came here to rest, of course, only to find that four months of it was a little too much of a good thing. I am fairly itching to get back to work, and back to a city where nobody cares what color your hair is. I don't know of another city that deserves being cursed and kicked more than Toronto, nor of any city that is so well worth it. And I'm in a hurry to grow up. My mind develops in jumps, corresponding to the college terms.

Well, I told you you needn't answer this letter, but if you get an answer off in time by all means send it.

Norrie

Only a week or so now, sweetheart
sweetheart
sweetheart
sweet
sweet
sweet

205 Fulton Ave., Toronto
October 10, '32

This and the following letter were written after the correspondents returned to campus for their final undergraduate year at Victoria College.

My Dear Norrie
Sunday:—

The gist of all this is that I am trying not to be such an ass—I can see that what I am heading for is a liver-complex—if you see me doing so much again (I will be often, because my judgment is a mere infant!) will you please paddle me well! For I should die if I became one of these dames "Oh be sorry for me, it's my nerves, you know!" Ugh!

I've got to cut down on something, I can see that. Shall it be you, or the library or *Acta* or Sigma Phi, or college or music or drawing pictures? In this state I am certainly not much use to *Acta*, and you won't find me very interesting either pretty soon. College, music, you, and the library are necessary—I need not pick out which ones are *most* necessary to me. But I'll have to have you in smaller doses.

I'm getting back to the signs—solving such problems as this

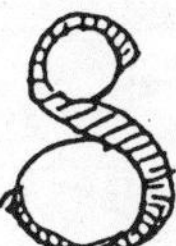 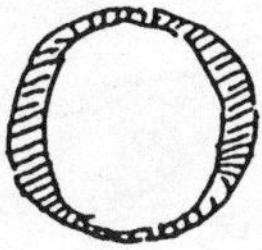

I think perhaps I'll desert Mr. Thornhill this afternoon.

Yours, with a bigger sense of humour

Cabbagehead

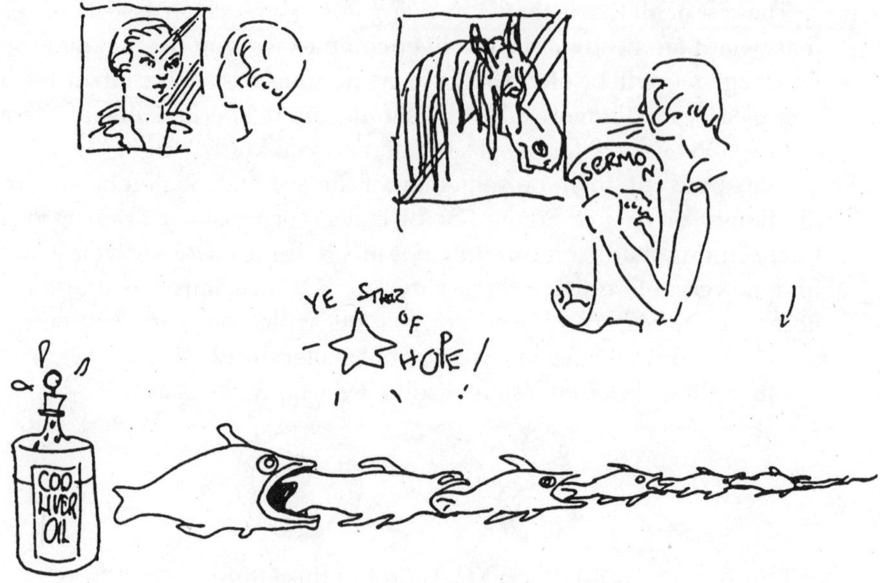

P.S. This is still later. I *did* desert Thorny and I'm not going around with my head in a tub. Jean [Evans] is about to arrive any minute now for that practice I told you about. My lettering is doing nicely, thank you, such fine curves on the "O's," and as for the "S's"!

They look like nicely corseted mid-Victorian chorus girls, although more chaste perhaps in their general character.

Spirits are up again!!

Oh h——Norrie, my dearish man!

Turnip

Tuesday [*11 October 1932*]

Brown Mouse:

Even if I *was* born an old hen, why did I have to have such a brood of temperamental young ducks? Barely have I got Jean Cameron quieted down and Romans more or less reconciled to existence when another pitiful little wail strikes up in Fulton Ave. Never you mind, honey, mamma's coming! And don't sniffle, darling; here's a handkerchief. I wonder if the direct methods employed by the old woman who lived in a shoe really were effective. But in any case, I can understand her feelings. I think I should join the pan-Hellenists.

Little Chin-Rest:

But what an exquisite little letter! It is one of my permanent possessions. I never saw anything quite like it. What an attractive child you are, Pierrette! Sentiments resembling the above was what I was trying to get through over the phone. Now it is true that you on a phone are literally a *dea ex machina*. But a phone is so damnably diluted a way of communicating. Oh well—

"I'll have to have you in smaller doses." "You are something far too precious ever to lose—" Saturday. "See if you can restore my morale by going home and letting me sleep—" Sunday. These last two are easy to harmonize. But now you want me in small doses. Oh, very well, Miss Kemp.

Go soak your head.
Go suck a turnip.
Go to hell.
Sweet, sweet, Little pomegranate.

But just where do I stand anyway.

Am I an angel of light or do I belong to the rapture and roses of vice?

You see, I'm a bit foozled. I haven't yet made out my chart tabulating the periodicity of your risings and fallings, ups and downs. If I thought the roller-coaster effect you present was entirely physiological I might get myself a marked calendar, like Lorne Campbell used to have. But I don't know. . . . According to the Dow-Jones theory in economics, when certain business factors correlate, business is on the upgrade; when they disintegrate, depression sets in. So I suppose that when you find octaves and so on slipping— Oh, you're only a cracked little hazelnut. Why should I bother about you?

But where do I come in? You say I am necessary to your existence. Does that mean:

(a) That I am 135 pounds of mashed turnip; something necessary in the way of companionship—someone to tell one's troubles to—someone who will pet you and spoil you and cuddle up when things go wrong?

(b) That I am a condiment, bringing a sharp tang and new zest to existence—reminding you of the world, the flesh and the devil and so humanizing you?

(c) That I am a stimulant, helping to correlate your activities, encouraging your talents and spanking you for your weaknesses?

(d) Or, that I am a narcotic, a drug, very powerful, to be taken, as you say, in small doses, temporarily relieving you, like a headache powder, from your ethereal worries by plunging you into an orgy of physical excitements which leaves you exhausted and silenced?

(e) Or that I am an insufferable bore who stays too late?

(f) Or a combination of the above?

You see, being a man, I'm so densely stupid. I haven't any sort of intuitive tact. I am your typical male—whenever you get depressed I don't know anything except what I personally want to do—that is, take you in my arms and strike solicitous and protective attitudes. If there's any crying to be done, I want it done on my shoulder. I want to be present and look helpful whenever you are in difficulties.

Little white-throated sparrow:

But, of course, that won't do (always, at any rate). There will be times when to the callous and cataracted eye of Madame Kemp Norrie would look very attractive decorating a South Sea Island or the Great Desert of Arabia.

Still, this will have to be explained. I won't get it otherwise. You're such a volatile youngster, you know. In other words, if all is not going well in the soul supposed to be captained by you I want to have a fairly good idea of what it's all about, and what I'm supposed to do. And in telling me don't spare either my feelings or your blushes.

Silly as it sounds, it is quite simply and literally true that I would rather die than deliberately hurt you. So while you may find me insensitive and stupid, you will not find me brutal.

Having got that off my chest, I feel so exalted and noble that I really think I'd better close on that note.

Good night, little hedgehog,
Paris

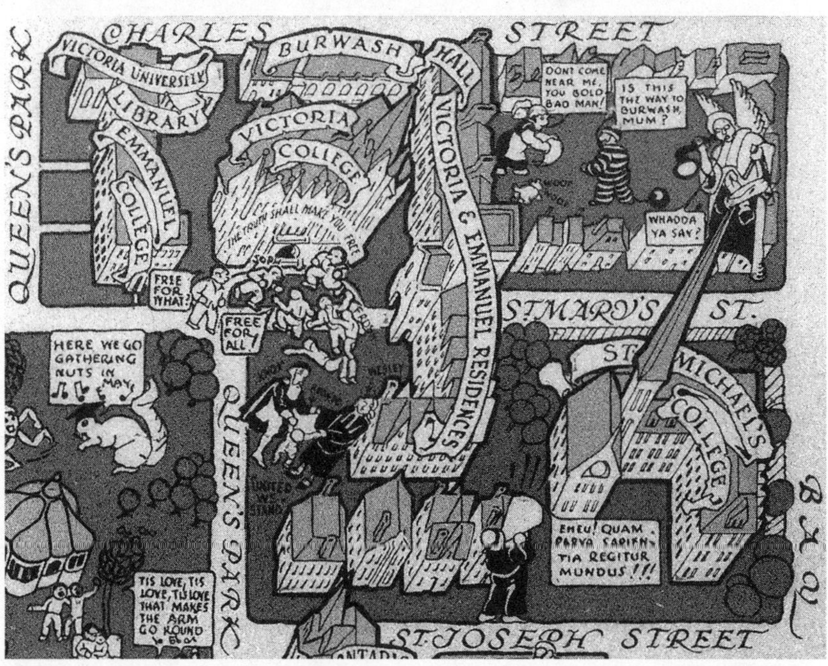

Details from the coloured (*above*) and black-and-white (*over*) versions of Kemp's map of the U of T campus, 1932 (courtesy of Victoria University, Toronto)

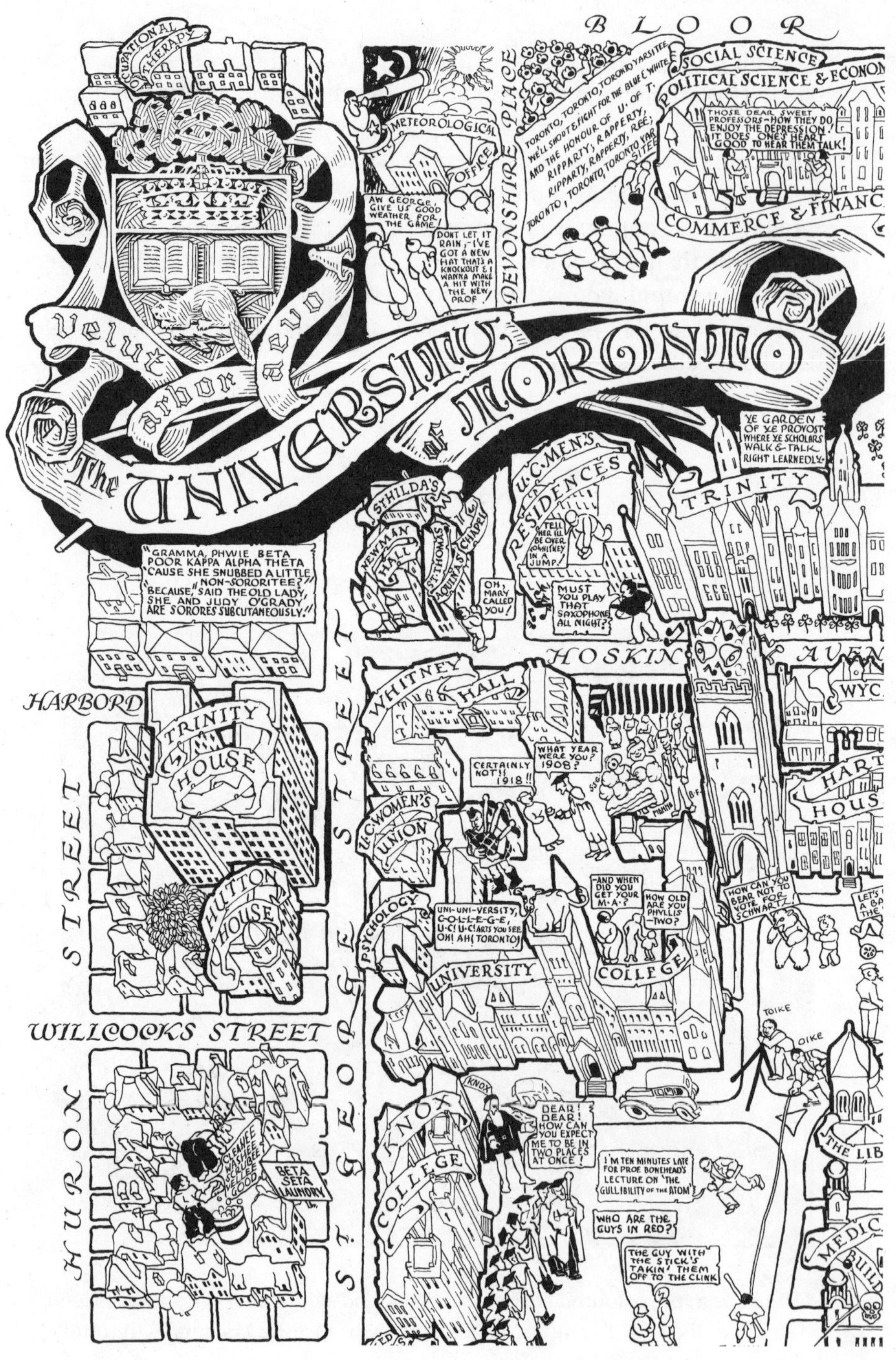

BLOOR
OCCUPATIONAL THERAPY
METEOROLOGICAL OFFICE
AW GEORGE, GIVE US GOOD WEATHER FOR THE GAME!
DONT LET IT RAIN, - I'VE GOT A NEW HAT THAT'S A KNOCKOUT & I WANNA MAKE A HIT WITH THE NEW PROF!
DEVONSHIRE PLACE
TORONTO, TORONTO, TORONTO YARSITEE WE'LL SHOUT & FIGHT FOR THE BLUE & WHITE AND THE HONOUR OF U. OF T. RIPPARTY; RAPPERTY, RIPPARTY, RAPPERTY, REE; TORONTO, TORONTO, TORONTO YARSITEE
SOCIAL SCIENCE
POLITICAL SCIENCE & ECONON
THOSE DEAR SWEET PROFESSORS - HOW THEY DO ENJOY THE DEPRESSION! IT DOES ONE'S HEART GOOD TO HEAR THEM TALK!
COMMERCE & FINANC
velut arbor aevo
The UNIVERSITY of TORONTO
YE GARDEN OF YE PROVOST WHERE YE SCHOLARS WALK & TALK RIGHT LEARNEDLY.
TRINITY
ST. HILDA'S
NEWMAN HALL
ST. THOMAS AQUINAS CHAPEL
U.C. MEN'S RESIDENCES
TELL HER I'LL BE OVER TO WHITNEY IN A JUMP!
OH, MARY CALLED YOU!
MUST YOU PLAY THAT SAXOPHONE ALL NIGHT?
"GRAMMA, PHWIE BETA POOR KAPPA ALPHA THETA 'CAUSE SHE SNUBBED A LITTLE NON-SORORITEE?" "BECAUSE," SAID THE OLD LADY, "SHE AND JUDY O'GRADY ARE SORORES SUBCUTANEOUSLY."
HOSKIN AVEN
HARBORD
TRINITY HOUSE
HUTTON HOUSE
WHITNEY HALL
CERTAINLY NOT!! 1918!!
WHAT YEAR WERE YOU? 1908?
WYC
HART HOUS
U.C. WOMEN'S UNION
PSYCHOLOGY
UNI-UNI-VERSITY, C-O-L-L-E-G-E, U-C! U-C! ARTS YOU SEE, OH! AH! TORONTO!
-AND WHEN DID YOU GET YOUR M.A.?
HOW OLD ARE YOU PHYLLIS -TWO?
HOW CAN YOU BEAR NOT TO VOTE FOR SCHWARTZ!
UNIVERSITY COLLEGE
HURON STREET
ST. GEORGE STREET
WILLCOCKS STREET
BETA SETA LAUNDRY
TOIKE
OIKE
KNOX
KNOX COLLEGE
DEAR! DEAR! HOW CAN YOU EXPECT ME TO BE IN TWO PLACES AT ONCE!
I'M TEN MINUTES LATE FOR PROF. BONEHEAD'S LECTURE ON 'THE GULLIBILITY OF THE ATOM'
WHO ARE THE GUYS IN RED?
THE GUY WITH THE STICK'S TAKIN' THEM OFF TO THE CLINK
THE LIB
MEDIC BUILD

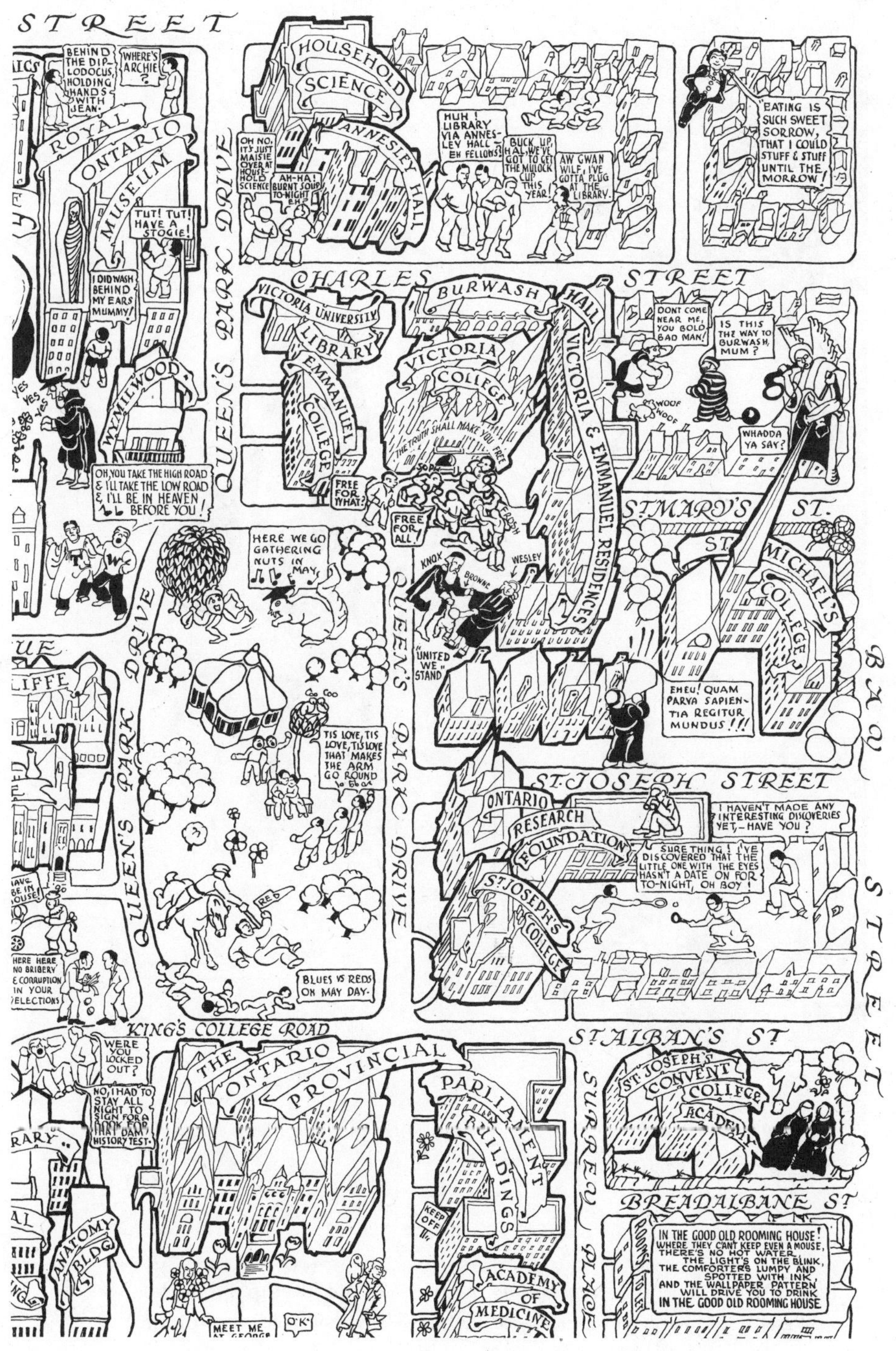

STREET
BEHIND THE DIP-LODOCUS, HOLDING HANDS WITH JEAN.
WHERE'S ARCHIE?
ROYAL ONTARIO MUSEUM
TUT! TUT! HAVE A STOGIE!
I DID WASH BEHIND MY EARS MUMMY!
WYMILWOOD
OH, YOU TAKE THE HIGH ROAD & I'LL TAKE THE LOW ROAD & I'LL BE IN HEAVEN BEFORE YOU!
QUEEN'S PARK DRIVE
HOUSEHOLD SCIENCE
ANNESLEY HALL
OH NO, IT'S JUST MAISIE OVER AT HOUSE-HOLD SCIENCE
AH-HA! BURNT SOUP TO-NIGHT EH?
HUH! LIBRARY VIA ANNES-LEY HALL — EH FELLOWS!
BUCK UP, HAL, WE'VE GOT TO GET THE MULOCK CUP THIS YEAR!
AW GWAN WILF, I'VE GOTTA PLUG AT THE LIBRARY.
"EATING IS SUCH SWEET SORROW, THAT I COULD STUFF & STUFF UNTIL THE MORROW!"
CHARLES STREET
VICTORIA UNIVERSITY LIBRARY
EMMANUEL COLLEGE
BURWASH HALL
VICTORIA COLLEGE
THE TRUTH SHALL MAKE YOU FREE
VICTORIA & EMMANUEL RESIDENCES
FREE FOR WHAT?
SOPH
FREE FOR ALL!
FROSH
DONT COME NEAR ME, YOU BOLD BAD MAN!
IS THIS THE WAY TO BURWASH, MUM?
WOOF WOOF
WHADDA YA SAY?
ST. MARY'S ST.
HERE WE GO GATHERING NUTS IN MAY,
KNOX
BROWNE
WESLEY
"UNITED WE STAND"
QUEEN'S PARK DRIVE
ST. MICHAEL'S COLLEGE
EHEU! QUAM PARVA SAPIEN-TIA REGITUR MUNDUS!!!
BAY STREET
COO COO
TIS LOVE, TIS LOVE, TIS LOVE THAT MAKES THE ARM GO ROUND
REDS
BLUES VS REDS ON MAY DAY.
QUEEN'S PARK DRIVE
ST. JOSEPH STREET
ONTARIO RESEARCH FOUNDATION
I HAVEN'T MADE ANY INTERESTING DISCOVERIES YET, — HAVE YOU?
SURE THING! I'VE DISCOVERED THAT THE LITTLE ONE WITH THE EYES HASN'T A DATE ON FOR TO-NIGHT, OH BOY!
ST. JOSEPH'S COLLEGE
HERE HERE NO BRIBERY & CORRUPTION IN YOUR ELECTIONS
KING'S COLLEGE ROAD
WERE YOU LOCKED OUT?
NO, I HAD TO STAY ALL NIGHT TO SIGN FOR A BOOK FOR THAT DAM HISTORY TEST.
THE ONTARIO PROVINCIAL PARLIAMENT BUILDINGS
ANATOMY BLDG
KEEP OFF
ACADEMY OF MEDICINE
O.K.
ST. ALBAN'S ST
SURREY PLACE
ST. JOSEPH'S CONVENT COLLEGE ACADEMY
BREADALBANE ST
ROOMS TO LET
IN THE GOOD OLD ROOMING HOUSE! WHERE THEY CAN'T KEEP EVEN A MOUSE, THERE'S NO HOT WATER, THE LIGHT'S ON THE BLINK, THE COMFORTERS LUMPY AND SPOTTED WITH INK, AND THE WALLPAPER PATTERN WILL DRIVE YOU TO DRINK IN THE GOOD OLD ROOMING HOUSE.

Drawings of Marion Kemp (*top and right*) and Harold Kemp. From Helen's sketchbook, 1927–31 (courtesy of Victoria University Library, Toronto)

Young Northrop, pictured with his mother (*above*), ca. 1919 (courtesy of Victoria University Library, Toronto)

Vera Frye, Vera and Howard Frye, and Howard Frye in uniform (courtesy of Victoria University Library, Toronto)

Housemates at Frye's Charles House residence and detail of Frye, 1929
(courtesy of Victoria University Library, Toronto)

Summer of 1933

c/o V.V. Frye
6104 Woodlawn Ave.
Chicago, Ill.
[*17 June 1933*]

This letter was written by Frye at the beginning of a six-week visit to his sister Vera in Chicago.

Sweet:

Well, I hope you don't feel funny inside anymore. Not having seen anything of you more tangible than a snapshot for forty-eight hours, I am beginning to feel like an ascetic. However, I thought I'd better hurry and write before the novelty of being here wore off and I really started to miss you.

When your palpitating little orange sweater had been lost to view—I like you to wear orange sweaters because anything so close to your heart should be of a warm color—I stumbled into a railway carriage half full of smoke and nearly strangled during most of the night. I pulled in here at nine and boarded a bus for Vera's domicile. The bus was full of frightened, noisy, curious and perplexed tourists, and I seemed to be the only one who had any idea where I was going. There don't seem to be *any* native Chicagoans left. I suppose that's because they kicked all the gangsters out of the city for the Fair.

I haven't seen the fair yet, but expectations run high. What buildings I have seen are magnificent. Peggy Craig showed me one, restored from the 1893 Fair and erected at a cost of two billion dollars. When I gasped that the Panama canal had been dug at half the cost, Peggy said: "Well, do you imagine that the Panama canal is as pretty as this?"

Chicago is an ideal place to hold a World's Fair. It *has* washed its face *so* hard. There is a poem on Chicago by Sandburg in that book of Untermeyer's. To a casual visitor who does not see the dreary side of things Chicago looks far more naive than Sandburg presents it. It is such a cheerful, hospitable, adolescent city. They tell me that the clothing advertisers urge Chicagoans to get a metropolitan cut to their clothes to impress the hick visitors. That is typical Chicago. The silly city is far too young to have any of the traditions of a real metropolis, like London, Paris or New York—everybody has grown up with Chicago from a small town or come into it from smaller towns. Everybody looks at you as if they wanted to speak to you, but then you might be a gangster or pick-pocket or cut-throat or something, so they don't, but merely look shy. Like all youngsters, Chicago makes far too much noise; like all youngsters, it spends far too much money on pretty and expensive toys; like all youngsters, it can look disarmingly clean when it cleans up; like all youngsters, it is impulsively generous and hospitable, but with the main eye to its own advantage; like all youngsters, it grows appallingly fast but keeps well-proportioned. No other city in the world is half so perfectly adapted to a World's Fair.

Well, I haven't done much yet. Vera's school doesn't close till next week and for the present I'm suspending operations. Vera says that if she gets the rest of her salary she's gonna buy a car and we'll go places, starting with Toronto and ending at Moncton. Marvellous girl, this sister of mine. I shall be at Chicago longer than I expected—six weeks, Vera said.

I'm staying here until a room opens up for me opposite Vera's apartment. They have a piano in the hallway—locked. Musical people somehow always manage to lose the keys of their pianos. Now don't get funny—you know what keys I mean.

Well, darling, I'll write again when I have something to write about. Good night. This letter is harder to read than usual, but it says nothing of importance. Six weeks! God! But it's not four months.

XXXXX
Norrie

Chicago, Ill.
Sunday [*18 June 1933*]

Helen dear:

Well, now I've seen the World's Fair, I'd better write again as I have something more to write about. Yes, I've seen it. It's a World's Fair all right, and very like the world—huge, pretentious, artificial, mostly vulgar, partly beautiful, and, in spite of everything, magnificent. It isn't noble, or sublime, or awe-inspiring, and, what's far better, it doesn't, unlike the '93 Fair, try to be. Whoever got it ready had, certainly, vast executive powers and almost infinite ingenuity. But they must have known that people at a Fair aim primarily at irresponsible enjoyment.

Frye's graduation photograph, 1933
(courtesy of Victoria University Library, Toronto)

The whole show is put on with an exuberant and boisterous, and yet a curiously subtle, humor, and although its motto is "A Century of Progress" it isn't bombastic about it. As I say, it isn't grandiose, but it's all kinds of fun. I'm glad it came in a Depression period.

The thing is breathtakingly huge—seven or eight square miles of grounds—and the important buildings are all in vivid colors. The Electrical Building is red and yellow, the Hall of Science blue and white, Social Science purple, white and black, another is a vivid green, another a yellow. The colors are very intense, but they have a dull finish and as each building has only one or at most two colors, it doesn't seem loud, and, as nothing glitters in the daytime, it doesn't seem vulgar. The only thing that does seem vulgar is the Midway, which is chiefly a magnification of Toronto's. Yet even there, you can find something amusing—the barkers announcing the cheap side shows are entertaining. One was proclaiming the virtues of some alleged "Oriental dancing," watching his audience narrowly and adjusting to it the right degree of naughtiness. (He looked like Prof. Martin of the History department.) "This show has passed all the censors, ladies and gentlemen—there is nothing objectionable about it—nothing filthy. Of course, there is that voluptuous—er—*something*" (he waved his hips in illustration) "which has always affected people of susceptible—er—visibilities. But everyone is agreed that this show is quite clean, if, perhaps, a little—uh—*risqué*."

There is the famous Chinese Temple of Jehol—brought over here bodily, so I understand. The temple is a gorgeous thing which defies description. The roof, outside and inside, is gold. If in another forty years they have another World's Fair here, they will probably bring over the Great Pyramid and the Sphinx and set those up.

There is a horticultural exhibit—twenty-odd varieties of gardens—rose gardens, rock gardens, formal gardens, Italian Renaissance gardens, Versailles gardens—perhaps altogether the Horticultural exhibit is the most beautiful thing in the Fair. All these gardens are outdoors, of course. Indoors, there are exhibits of all kinds of trees and flowers—mostly from California.

I don't like the general run of the people at this place. They all seem to be tired, hot, and stupid. Endless processions of petty bourgeoisie with fat bums and their wives with fatter ones. The remarks one overhears almost never have any relation to what they are supposed to be looking at except an occasional aggrieved—"Here I've been all day and haven't seen a third of it yet!" Hysterical transient visitors trying to cover the whole Fair in a day, dragging along protesting youngsters who want to stop and look at something with "Come on, dear, we've got *so much* to see!" All this sounds as though I were crabbing, but I'm not. I can't tell you much about what I've seen and liked—things such as the Jehol temple can't be described. But what is really communicable are the oddities, the foibles and weaknesses.

I've been getting some idea of the schoolteacher racket from Vera. Normal School here is four years, and free. Once hired, the Normal Association *has* to find a place for you. You're in for life—if you quit teaching for ten years and then go back to it they still have to find you a job. You can't be dismissed without a deliberate court martial and jury trial—in practice it is impossible to fire a teacher. My sympathy for Chicago school teachers is cooling slightly, though they certainly are having a pretty rotten deal, even if they don't earn their unpaid salaries.

I haven't much leisure to make this a coherent epistle—you'll understand—the situation, I mean, not the letter. Good night, sweet. And I shall bring you something *very* nice from the Fair. The heat is fearful, but I have got rid of the mockery of clothing. The only trouble is Vera's radio. Peggy unfortunately likes radios. In this city I guess you have to have an opiate for harassed ears.

XXXXX and so on

The Temple of Jehol wasn't brought over bodily—but a replica was made in China and *that* was brought over. 20,000 pieces—if it matters.

205 Fulton Ave., Toronto
Thursday night [22 *June 1933*]

DAISIES WON'T TELL, SO THE POOR FISH WILL NEVER KNOW THAT THEY ALL BUY FLOWERS FOR MARY AT THE VARSITY FLOWER SHOP

My dear Norrie,

I am so sorry that I have waited all this while to write to you—I feel a little strange. I shall have to look at the *Acta* picture and read your last two letters first. I'm just a bit lonely of course.

Tonight Jean Evans had a party for the library crowd. Dot Darling, and Miss Ray, Miss Hand and Miss Glaves, and Doris Livingston etc. Doris

Livingston *is* a cold woman. Working on Dora Russell's theory that the children reflect the love life of their parents, I should say that the Livingston-senior alliance was purely and stiffly platonic, and a dyspeptic stork must have deposited the disgruntled infant among the cabbages. Oh well, she can't help it. I *am* afraid, however, that when Doris grows older she is going to be a *very* virtuous woman. We played a lot of crazy games, and had a splendid time. Dot Darling is priceless, the way she says things—and does things. I've got Kenneth Johnstone's address from Doris Livingston but I have not written to Norm Knight yet. Miss Ray leaves for England next Tuesday.

There is no use trying to tell you everything that has happened since you left—most of it would be dull by now. I have fairly well decided upon a piano—$50—a Hardman, very old, good action, good innards etc. Miss Ray is giving me enough for the initial payment. The worst thing that has happened is that Miss Ray has been too rushed to work out the wording of the signs she wanted me to make. Consequently I shall have very little of her work to do, and will have to do it in the fall. Of course I shall have the piano, and I am working away—Bach Preludes and Fugues, Schumann and Czerny are the diet at present.

I went to Thornhill's on Sunday night and listened to Beethoven's Ninth Symphony, which was quite a consolation. Kay Coburn was coming with me, but she lost her way. However, I had lunch with her next day—Maysie Roger was with us too. I am beginning to understand what you mean by the Oxford affectations—Kay is interesting, and I like being with her—but she is a snob. She talks about Canadian low standards and systems and preachers with fearful smugness. I suppose I am a bit touchy about snobbishness in other people, because I am a snob myself. And in some cases I suppose it is a form of self-protection. But I don't have much fun *being* a snob, that's why I don't think it is such a good idea.

I have had all sorts of hare-brained schemes lately, but I am settling down to practise the piano, and enjoy life. I think I can do it—except that I do get up in the air when I wonder what is to happen next year, and when I haven't got the hairbrush to keep the silly youngster in order. But really, I am being quite good on the whole. Dr. Edgar suggested that I try illustrating some of the more dramatic Canadian poems. I thought, and thought. Then I decided that his idea was to do the purely obvious thing. And I don't think I am ready yet. If I tried to get a book ready for next Christmas (which was his suggestion) I would need to stay around town for most of the summer for material. So I have just about decided to be a quiet citizen with a purpose that will come out later.

It was awfully good of you to tell me so much of the great parade. Most people would be too busy running round about to write anything longer than a ten-word telegram or a postcard. And of course I should love to be there with you. But I am enjoying things by proxy anyhow.

If you are driving through here—do you think you could manage to come to Gordon Bay? You and Vera? I should like it very much.

It is three o'clock, and I like you very much, and (my goodness, I tell you that every time! But I mean it, just the same). Well, anyway—

Goodnight,
Helen

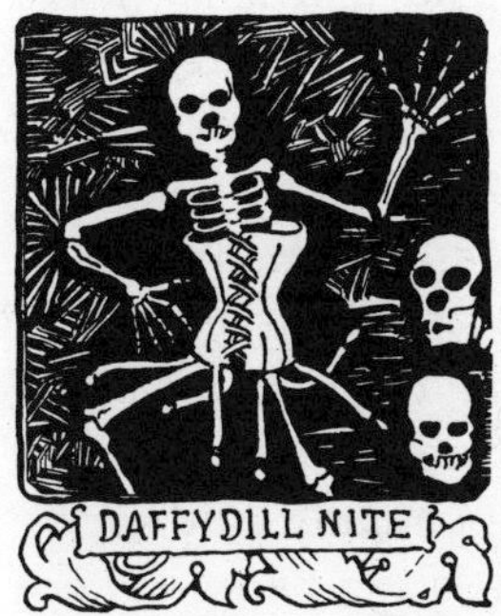

6104 Woodlawn Ave., Apt. 208
Chicago, Illinois
Wednesday–Thursday [*21–22 June 1933*]

Jenny Wren:

The reason for the hybrid date is that dawn is just breaking. My sister got me a room here just across the street from her. The landlady was a rather nice-looking little woman, there was a piano in the hallway, and the two nights I spent here were O.K. But earlier this evening I was peacefully writing when I saw a sinister brick-red insect climbing over my pillow. After he had suffered a comminated fracture in every part of his anatomy, I went on writing, and saw another one at the foot of the bed. Well, said I, I guess I'm in for it. And I was. I turned in and slept about an hour, waking up to ask myself why I should be feeling so fearfully hot and uncomfortable on an otherwise normal night. I turned on the light and found a couple more. Then I examined myself and counted eighteen bites. So I got up and dressed. I was feeling a bit sore, and I am sorry to relate that when I went to the bathroom to wash my face I wantonly killed two perfectly innocent cockroaches I found sitting on the window sill. I know now what that musty smell was I had put down to bad ventilation. So now you will understand why I have come to be writing you letters at such hours.

I have seen some more of the Fair. The Italian exhibit is typical of a Fascist government. You go into a big round hall with nothing in it but posters around the walls, commemorating various aspects of modern Italian industrialism. Below the posters are some enormous snapshots of the Forum and similar views in Rome. Roma Caput Mundi, as one of their own posters said! The Italian building is arranged roughly in the shape of an aeroplane because Il Duce is sending his air fleet over later in the summer to show Chicago how strong it is.

The Swedish exhibit is tolerable—the best thing is some woodwork. The Danish is good too—some very fine lace and beautifully carved silver. But easily the best foreign exhibit is the Irish Free State one. The walls are covered with paintings by Irish artists—many of them very fine. There's a fairly full exhibit of a Society of Arts in Dublin—leatherwork, pottery, and so forth—all of it beautiful. The most gorgeous things are Roman Catholic vestments and altar vessels—chasubles embroidered in gold, chalices set with amethysts in gold, and so on. There are one or two medieval uncial MSS you would have pored over. Everything was beautiful and artistic. Apart from the inconvenience caused by getting my rear end pushed all over the block by impatient transients who took one uncomprehending gawk and hurried on, I felt as though there were some hope for the world.

The Canadian exhibit is disappointing. I could have arranged a better one myself. All the other countries concentrate on the beautiful workmanship done in the country. But ours is apparently paid for by the C.P.R., and is merely the usual tripe about hotels and parks and opportunities for American investors. The exhibit consists of a few stuffed animals, specimens of wheat, chunks of ore-bearing rocks and the largest map in the world on the walls, whose size did not impress me. Taking a hint from the Irish, the odd Lawren Harris or A.Y. Jackson would be a good idea, and what with all the wonder of carved totem poles, the hooked rugs of Labrador, the spinning wheels and window blinds of old Quebec, Ukrainian costumes, Indian moccasins and baskets, examples of minerals instead of pieces of rock, exhibits from Art Schools, pictures of Norma Shearer, Mary Pickford and Marie Dressler, miniature models, such as Alaska had, of picturesque spots along the railways—I think even I could do better than to stuff a wildcat and label it "Canada Lynx." There was one Mountie there, bored and hot.

So you can see that I am more or less getting down to business about this Fair, now that the surge of general impressions has subsided. The first time I was there my head was in too much of a whirl to see much beyond generalities—

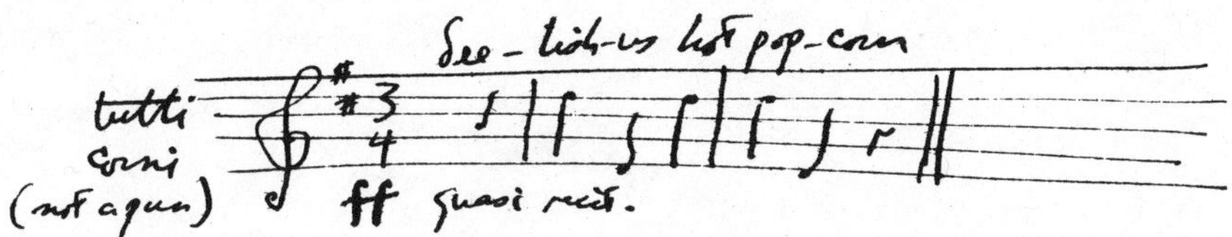

—and the like. I like the look of the Fair more and more all the time. I like the blazing buildings and like even more their straight, cool, slim lines. It gave me a shock to read on one of their own circulars the frank statement that when they started it was intended to overdecorate the buildings, load them down with detail, and achieve the loudest color combinations, but that the lack of finances cooled their enthusiasm. They simply couldn't afford to be tasteless. When I said I was glad it came in a Depression all I meant was that a period of overstuffed prosperity would mean solemn blasphemies about progress and the benignance of God and this wonderful America of ours. The Depression, by drawing away the reality from the ideal, brought out the incongruity between them which makes for humor. But this is another reason for thankfulness.

The landlady—it is now eight o'clock and I have been reading in the interim—just came in to make the bed, seeing that I was up. "Madam, I was nearly devoured by bedbugs last night. I hope you can see your way clear to their eradication before I sleep in that bed again." Her lower jaw sagged against her knees. "But—why—you—you—*couldn't* have!" "I assure you I was, madam—do you think I don't know when I've been eaten by a regiment of confounded beetles?" "But—I sprayed the bed and the walls with gasoline!" "I have been smelling that gasoline for three nights now, madam—it asphyxiated me, but not the bedbugs. Please see to it at once." "Well" (doubtfully) "I'll see what I can do." She retired without the honors of war and without making the bed.

But as I was saying, there is something epic and transcendent about American vulgarity. It scorns to paint a lily, but it delights to whitewash an iceberg. And yet the vulgarity does not go much deeper than the pockets. It is the over-stuffed belly and the lethargic brain of a Sybarite that engenders it. Put an American on a more ascetic diet, and there emerges, not the pompous, heavy portentousness of the '93 imitation Parthenons, but a light, easy, colorful, shapely miniature of skyscrapers, full of sunshine and humor.

But I have said quite enough for one instalment.

Norrie

205 Fulton Ave., Toronto
Monday [*26 June 1933*]

My dear Norrie,

Since life goes on much as usual I suppose there is nothing to tell you. On the other hand, being a female, I can gabble along quite well under those circumstances. It is hot, terribly hot. We have been expecting a thunderstorm all day. The house is in a turmoil since we are gathering our clothes together to pack them off to Muskoka. We are leaving this week, probably motoring with Cronins.

Tuesday. 9 P.M. Let's begin again. It is *still* terribly hot. (I may have to keep this up for a week, starting and stopping and remarking feebly about the weather. I'll try to do better.)

I am trying your experiment—that is, in regards to the mockery of clothing. Miss Ray's step-ins (the pink ones) are quite a comfort just now, since even a chorus girl could hardly boast less clothing. As I said before, some of us expect to get out of here on Thursday or Friday, and the rest on Monday. I sometimes have my doubts about it though, judging from the amount of fuss there is about getting off the piano. I have been playing Bach quite faithfully—his new preludes and fugues are on the way, five and six in the first volume—D major and D minor.

Tomorrow I go to see the great Perkins Bull. True Davidson suggested that he get me to design the endpapers for the celebrated opus—in the form of an animated map of each township. Something may turn out, but I am not cherishing sanguine hopes until I see it in print, and perhaps not even then. For my experience with animated maps has not left me as verdantly exuberant as I used to be, and reports of Mr. Bull—well you know. He got Dr. Pratt to recommend several girls lately, promising them fifteen dollars a week. So Pratt sent over some. When he discovered later that they were given only five dollars a week, you can imagine what he would say! I am also seeing Dr. Locke at 11:30, about that job for one of the branch libraries. That is my news up to date.

I have been waiting for your next letter to see whether there is anything to answer or not. I needn't bother I suppose, because your letters sound like an intelligently conducted travel tour, and I have no comeback. You must be kept busy writing to everybody about Chicago—why don't you put me on the end of the chain gang and save effort? Of course if you did how I should howl! Just like an illogical female.

I am reading *Le Morte Darthur*. It is a lovely thing, and yet, every so often Mark Twain and Cervantes poke up their heads and grin ludicrously. So that I find it difficult to really get the spirit of the thing and feel the glory of all this jousting and saving fair ladies, and waiting for men to come along a road so that you may fight with them on some trivial pretext. The book I have has no introduction. And since I have not looked elsewhere, I am a little at sea about some aspects of it. I shall stop writing to you now for a while and go back to fifteenth-century ideas of dwarfs and wizards and ladies fair and noble knights.

Wednesday afternoon. What a disjointed affair this is getting to be! Weather broadcast: "Is Hell like this?" I don't see how you will survive for another month of this in Chicago. I think you should come north with me. I'll leave the arranging to you and Vera. Just let me know when you will be there and I'll do the rest. You could stay a week, couldn't you? Mother says she is still expecting you to pay the long put-off visit.

I am somewhat bothered just now and if I should tell you what about, I might feel better, on the confession principle. Today I saw Dr. Locke and his job is all right. He *is* a good old scout. (Miss Ray said he is most like God of anyone she knows.) Then I saw Perkins Bull in his horrid old house, dark and full of carved antiques and florid decoration, with effigies of bulls strewn about. And the old man himself—fat and huge, with a great stomach and fleshy lips, and a rough iron-grey beard, small ill-natured eyes, and high blood pressure. He is a eunuch, too, after an adventure with Chicago gangsters. I didn't like the man, and I did not want his job, especially after he asked whether I would work for nothing. I couldn't tell how much work there would be to do, so promised to phone True Davidson tonight. She suggested ten dollars for each map. I thought that that would be a fair price, but Daddy blew up and said twenty was more like it. He says he doesn't want me to take it on anyhow and his attitude toward Perkins Bull is with thumb on nose. And since I finally quoted 20 dollars as the price to True Davidson, I can't think why I'm still stewing about it. Lord, why was I born a worrier? And what *am* I worrying about? There, now that it looks so silly, and I know that I shan't starve in the streets because I may not make some extra money, I feel a little more comfortable. Just a little whining and sniffing seems to cheer some humans at times. And goodness knows, you have seen me do enough sniffing in your time! It must have been very comical at times—and I am so glad you don't laugh at me until it's all over. Like this.

I am reading Mr. Housser's book on the Group of Seven. It is well done, a nicely made book, and beautifully written. The man is so enthusiastic, and seems so thrilled with the work of the men of whom he writes. Naturally Canadians, and especially Torontonians, are interested acutely in a book that deals with a young movement, with men whom many know personally. When you read the book you feel that Canada has a definite art tradition, and has established herself as a cultured nation. Of course, when you consider that there are some five or seven men who gave the original impetus to the movement, your words about Victoria College being a seat of a Canadian culture—or the United Church of Canada being its mainstay—(I may have your theory a little twisted) at any rate do not seem terribly far-fetched. So that you and I and some of the rest of us may be more important than I, at least, had thought. That is one reason why I get so annoyed with myself when I allow such things as the Perkins Bull episode to disturb me from my own path. For I haven't practised at all today.

I shall go off to bed—I'm *on* the bed now but you know what I mean. Thanks so much for listening to my confession. Poor dear, I buttonholed you, and you had no choice, did you? I wonder how your bedbugs are now. What a terrible thing to have happen! Goodnight.

Thursday night. The girl is developing into a writer of memoirs! Today I went to a meeting of the east-end women's branch of the C.C.F. There were excellent speakers and an enthusiastic crowd of women there. I think that I shall have to take a definite share of this, next fall.

But are you all right? You haven't had a sun stroke have you? Because you should be careful in this heat. However, I suppose you are busy, and that is why I haven't heard from you. It is quite a good idea not to write to me every other day as Art [Cragg] does to Florence [Clare].

Because letter-writing is often a dissipation of energy. Still I do begin to wonder mildly whether you have been overwhelmed by the heat, the fair, gangsters, automobiles, bedbugs, or just general inertia.

We leave tomorrow morning at seven for Lake Joseph, so I must get the rest of my things ready. The next address is Gordon Bay, Lake Joseph, Ontario.

I shall send this off at last.

Helen

Chicago, Ill.
July 1 [*1933*]

My dear Helen:

I should think that, to put it mildly, it's about time I was writing again. The inordinate delay is due to several causes. One is the overpowering, stifling, enervating heat, which makes me feel so damn listless and lethargic I don't care whether you live or die, to say nothing of myself. Then this last week the cleaners have come. They are cheerful souls who paint the woodwork and repaper the walls. Every stitch of furniture has to be moved out into the centre of the floor and all covered with a canvas cloth—things generally were in a hell of a mess during the four days they were here. And one man living, or, strictly, tagging around after, four women gets some idea of the enormous resources of waiting, delaying, shuffling, hanging fire, dilly-dallying and general a—ing around of which womankind is capable. (I was about to say, in reference to the temperature, that since I wrote you last it has never dropped below ninety and usually hangs around a hundred. And of course I'm rather heat sensitive, being a heliophobic blond.) I suppose I should explain the four women. Peggy's mother and baby sister drooled around and live here half the time. Mother a fine and dignified woman—splendid nineteenth-century type. Baby sister nineteen. Eleanor. Shy, awkward duckling. Looks about fifteen. Just out of Business College. Gives an impression of being out of the shell but not quite dry. Very sweet girl.

Moved. No more bedbugs or cockroaches. The new place is full of nice people, I'm told—it's a University of Chicago boarding house. Piano. Got early Italian Piano Music, Bach Chorales arranged, two books by

Scriabin, Cuntry (the typewriter did that) Gardens and the MacDowell Keltic Sonata. Haven't played much yet.

The Art Institute has a special exhibit which I have visited twice. Renaissance painting—Tintoretto, Titian, two Leonardos—one called the *Madonna of the Yarn Spinners*, a magnificent Italian Madonna, with the same inscrutable Mona Lisa smile, and the freshest and rosiest youngster I have ever seen. Some of the representations of the Christ-Child are almost blasphemous—he looks sometimes like a manikin of forty, sometimes like a wizened old priest. One Raphael—very simple but breath-taking—a man dressed in black. Two Botticellis—one I could have sworn was modern French. The Renaissance pictures were all very soft and quiet in color. But the medieval ones were different. Nearly all of them had gold backgrounds, and the figures were splashes of brilliant reds and greens. The haloes were bewilderingly ornamented. Poses stiff and architectural, often notably Byzantine. But a sort of quaint childlike humor all through. One picture of the Last Supper shows a little spaniel in the foreground gnawing a bone. One Madonna and Child shows the latter with his fist stuck in a dish of candy. I liked these medieval pictures best of all, I think. Then the Dutch school. Some rare humor here too. One a young group of smokers trying to blow rings. A beautiful *Rembrandt—Girl at Half-open Door* and a portrait of his father. Several Franz Hals—all the *Laughing Cavalier* type. And so on. There is an English room—several graceful Gainsboroughs, a Romney, Reynolds, Raeburn, Zoffany, and Hogarth. American colonial painting, including the two famous Gilbert Stuart portraits of Washington. Whistler—the great portrait of his mother—one of the biggest attractions—a superb picture. And the Thames "nocturne"—the one that started the row with Ruskin. Modern French too—a room full of Matisse and Picasso. That man Matisse knew how to handle color. A picture of Picasso's of a youngster eating out of a bowl called *Le Gourmet* is very popular. Manet, Renoir, Gauguin, Van Gogh—oh, shut up.

I just got your second letter. This epic has been hanging fire for so long that I have almost dreaded to look at the mail box for fear of getting a reproachful letter. You poor child—you must be having rather an awful time. As for the Bull—charging too much is an undergraduate complaint, and in any case it is quite all right to charge twenty dollars. It's hardly necessary to add that you don't need to worry because you're afraid of overcharging Perkins. Worry still less about Cervantes and Mark Twain. Cervantes didn't say that all the medieval romances were rubbish—he went out of his way to prove that they were not. And Mark Twain was a damned fool anyway.

I know I must sound like a travel tour. But what would you do in my place? I'm going to send this letter off without further preamble and start it again in a day or so. I haven't said anything about the Fair yet, but it's time I quit for now.

Norrie

Gordon Bay, Lake Joseph, Ont.
July 5, 1933

Dear Norrie,

I have just had a letter from Norm Knight in reply to my invitation to stay with Roy during August. He is still in a state of insolvency, but as he says, hope springs eternal, and he may yet get a job. Except for the fact that he is unable to live anywhere else because Ken is financing him, he would like to stay with Roy. As I mentioned some of your Chicago experiences when I wrote him, he says that he would risk his eyesight in order to get some of your reactions to the century of progress. So would we all. You are probably risking your own eyesight at the present time, if you are still devoting yourself as wholeheartedly to the Fair as when you started out. Life in large cities and amongst a howling mob is far remote from anything I can think of here. It is twilight, and I am sitting at a desk planted firmly between pine trees that lean over the lake. Everything is quiet. Only the faint call of a whippoorwill, and the gentle movement of the water moves the stillness. That orbed maiden with white fire laden has been gazing down fondly upon a purple-green island and a lake of mauve and rose colour. These things are my confrères. How could I have stayed away so long? And how can I think of life in a city—just now?

The piano is here. I have been playing Bach and Scarlatti still. I have just finished memorizing the *Pastorale*, and the Schumann *Papillons*. I should be having a look at two Preludes tonight because I haven't done much today except write a letter to Mr. Perkins Bull who is coming round right courteously (ten dollars after all, and not twenty) and swim, and talk to the two girls next cottage, and lie in the sun. And of course I must let you know how I am progressing and how much I enjoy being a big girl now. That's what you said, you know.

I think I have told you a few things about the Davis family, the wealthy people next door. The Davises spend no end of money every year on cheap thrillers as they come off the press, and cheap dance music as it comes off the tin pans, and the kids ask Harold [Kemp] why I practise so much. Oh well!

The mosquitoes are getting busy here. And they call me to play bridge. Anyhow, I have given you the news, and can't think of anything else of importance. I hope you are still having fun.

Helen

Gordon Bay, Lake Joseph, Ont.
July 13, 1933. 10 P.M.

My dear Norrie,

Since today is your birthday, I have been wondering whether you were having any sort of celebration or not, or whether you were still more or less overcome with heat. I hope you have had a nice time.

Your last letter came after I had almost given up hope of seeing a Chicago postmark. Never mind—it is your birthday. I mustn't scold. Besides I write to you when I feel like it myself. If I kept a diary there might be too many sniffles scattered here and there. That last remark just means that I've had a spasm again—the day before yesterday—which was a kick below the belt in good style, and I had to stumble off toward the tall rocks and sniffle to myself and one squirrel and one rabbit, and wonder dismally why I was born, and review the ghosts of all my misdeeds, and everything that had worried me since my conception came past in a gibbering procession. But after that was over I remembered you, who would be sure to say "get it out of your system—and by my marked calendar, I suspect—" So you were right and I have spent today being quite miserable but happy in the knowledge that I'm a normal female—if that's anything to brag about. But it is terribly annoying to go half insane for an afternoon once every month. I burst forth in front of Daddy, who was quite bewildered as to the cause of all the fireworks, but said later he supposed it was just the moon in its course. Trouble is, I never remember these things at the time and lose control altogether. I used to think that women who acted that way were disgusting—and now I'm taking to emotional sprees myself! I really don't know what to do about it.

Incidentally, I didn't thank you for the silk handkerchief you sent. It is very pretty. I had a little difficulty growing accustomed to pink being combined with rust colour, but the general effect is quite charming. And you are rather nice to think of it.

I forget now whether I told you about Mrs. Turkington's invitation to go to camp or not. Jean Evans and Dorothy Bishop are there, and she wanted me to go for the summer—20 bucks a month. But I turned it down because I thought I should be in the hole rather than any the richer, financially. Besides how could I get away from camp to wave a flag at a man passing through on a train from Chicago? But it was a very tempting offer, because Onawaw is a good camp, one of the best—and if I had known sooner I am sure that I would have gone. Still, I am quite peaceful lying in a hammock reading *Mozart*. I have at last got hold of a copy of Marcia Davenport's book.

The writer upon musical subjects is usually either so pedantic that no one save a trained musician can understand him, or else so high-flown and fanciful in his interpretation of compositions that no musician has the patience to listen to him. But Marcia Davenport has written a book that deserves the praise it has been given. She has steeped herself in the spirit of the time and has a great love for Mozart, and more than a dilettante's appreciation of his music. She allows characters to speak for themselves more than many biographers do. Partly because of the voluminous correspondence of Mozart is she able to do this, and partly through old Leopold's letters, and the reminiscences of Michael Kelly, Lorenzo Da Ponte, and even the wizened up old profligate, Casanova. At any rate I am enjoying the book very much.

When I had got to the point, last night, in Marcia Davenport's book, where she talks about Mozart's marriage to Constanze Weber, I was led off into a long train of thought on the subject of marriage. I thought I should have to sit right down and talk it over with you. However, I forget what it was all about now. Something about love being largely a matter of people being seen often, and what was love anyway. And could one have a romantic view of married life and still not be indulging in sentimental deception. Whether one should reduce things to a largely physical basis—as Dora Russell likes to write about—in a glorified sense of course. I'm not quite sure whether I think she is a very sensible woman. And if one does go about having these glorified friendships with men—which, in her latest book, she thinks will enhance one's social and emotional life so much—will one have any emotional energy left to devote to more ideal pursuits? And I, poor child, haven't time, or nerve enough to spend my life like Isadora Duncan, finding out. Or inclination. What a humdrum world it would be if everyone sat in a hammock, like me, and wondered. So you see, all I did was get into a muddle, and decide that until I got a better idea, I would be gently romantic. What else can I do being the product of numerous novels, the American movie, and reflecting the English ideal of the glorification of womanhood. But on the other hand the mixture of Sir Thomas Mallory's men who ask—"Will you have her as your paramour, or do you want her as your wife?" with the eighteenth-century freedom gets me somewhat confused. The court of Louis with his poor queen stowed off in a corner with her plain but kindly daughters, while Pompadour occupies a sumptuous suite downstairs, and filthy back stairways allow transient maids-for-the-night access to the royal bed chamber, must have been an interesting household. Mozart himself loved to have his fun while Constanze enjoyed a flirtation, too. One night he crawled into bed beside her at four in the morning, after being goodness knows where. And Constanze only teased him and said "Ach Wolfi, you have a very guilty conscience!"

I must stop at this point for Ghent Davis is taking the mail off (it being morning of the next day).

Helen

Chicago, Ill.
[*14 July 1933*]

My dear:

In case you're beginning to wonder what the hell, I'm still alive. I got another letter from you, written apparently before you had received mine. Oh, sweet! I'm homesick enough to compose a set of variations on *Rule Britannia*. Not that I haven't a good time, especially when I'm with Vera. Went to the aquarium today and came away with a profound sense of the beauty and dignity of trout and the ugliness of salamanders. The tropical fish were gorgeous. Went to a show the night before. *The Gold Diggers of 1933*. Their last number called "Forgotten Man" was rather fine. For once, jazz singing was put to its right use. It was about soldiers returned from the war, standing in breadlines, widows, and so on.

Took a chance and bought half of Haydn's sonatas. Played for a while in the landlady's parlor. Several people usually drift in to listen. I don't mind—they're not critical. The most frequent remark is, "My, it's a relief to get that instead of the radio!" Then why in hell—Oh, well.

I've seen quite a bit of the Fair, though not so much after all. I've been down more often to the Art Institute. I have seen part of Marshall Field's exhibit of the various accessories of the Russian Royal Family—ikons, vanity cases, objets d'art, dishes, jewellery, carpets, and so forth. There was an 18th-century snuff box with a little bird inside who would come out and sing a song. There were Easter eggs—rather significant, that Russian emphasis on Easter!—in gold and precious stones. Everything was bewilderingly ornate—barbarically so, but gorgeous none the less.

And so on. The Japanese Pavilion at the Fair was splendid. I sent you a handkerchief I got there, didn't I? Their exhibition left nothing out, but was always in the best of taste—screens of some dark wood inlaid with ivory, jade carvings, and so forth. I liked too the Ukrainian Pavilion, where I got the little lace handkerchief I am sending.

And then there was an A & P carnival (chain grocery store) with a marionette show—Tony Sarg's, and splendidly handled. The last act introduced George Bernard Shaw. He encountered the master of ceremonies and was told he had no manners and was kicked in the pants to prove it. Shaw protested he fought with words, not physically, and so the master of ceremonies introduced the great American knocker, Babe Ruth, who terrified Shaw into silence with his bat. Curiously enough, the rhymed dialogue was clever and very adroitly handled, but I am afraid that whatever truth lies in Shaw's remark that the 100% American is 99% idiot is more confirmed than otherwise by the introduction of Babe Ruth.

A squadron of Italian flyers is coming here for the Fair. This Balbo, who is leading them, is the gorilla who thought up the castor oil treatment for Socialists.

I guess if I'm to write at all readably, I should write more often and in shorter dimensions. This is the first letter I have written to you that I haven't enjoyed writing, the reason being that I have been spending so much time gawking at things that I'm full of news and still haven't anything to say. I haven't the slightest idea when we're going home.

Sweets to the sweet, farewell, as Gertrude said to Ophelia's unresponsive tombstone.

Norrie

Chicago, Ill.
July 15 [*1933*]

Addressed to Kemp at Gordon Bay, Lake Joseph, Ont. *Forwarded on 25 July to* Camp Onawaw, via Huntsville, Ontario, *where she had gone for a few weeks as a camp counsellor.*

Dearest:

This whole city has gone wild over the arrival of General Balbo and his air fleet. They came roaring over the city this afternoon. Tremendous reception broadcasted. Balbo spoke. English not a Balbo accomplishment. Understood only the end of it: "Viva Italia! Viva Chicago!" A diabolically clever move, this. Feeling between United States and France is pretty strained, and just at the psychological moment up rolls Italy from across the Atlantic! The American speakers decided that Italy's contribution to American culture (e.g., Al Capone) was a valued treasure and that the bonds of union so closely knit between the two nations—blah, blah. When Italy attacks France in 1935, according to her programme, a friendly U.S.A. is going to help the situation.

Thank you for your card, sweet. It was lovely. Vera took Peggy [Craig] and me to dinner at a restaurant called "A Little Bit of Sweden." The food—well, the meals are like dramatic poems, a scene in each course. One helps oneself to an enormous plate of appetizers—smörgasborg they call it—and then goes for the meal itself. It rained from five o'clock till nine. However, I had a very happy birthday.

So you are joining the C.C.F. in the fall. I should have thought Canadian politics even more of a *cul de sac* than basketball, but of course you know best. At Confederation the Conservative and Liberal parties represented opposed urban and rural interests, but the Conservatives were in power so long that the Laurier Liberals adopted practically their platform. So that since 1906 or 1911 or whenever it was—or, for practical purposes, since 1867—there has been no real opposition in Canada, but only occasional shiftings of government due to scandals, slogans, bribery, disgust or the long-continued graft of one party, and so on. The C.C.F. means a genuine labor–agricultural opposition. Again, it should be the typical party of Canada and the political expression of the same movement of which the United Church is the religious expression.

I wish to hell you'd stop bawling. That is—I mean to say—oh, well, let it go. Around a college prices matter, and if Perkins Bull was satisfied, why worry? Your physical condition I do not worry about—I should hate to be in it in hot weather, but a little bundle of twisted nerves, and especially a young woman who is developing intellectually at the inevitable cost of her social poise, is bound to suffer a good deal. Poor child, I wish I were there, just the same. You're wrong—I don't mark your calendar—it isn't necessary.

Marriage, darling, is a physical contact, and any touch of the spiritual defiles it. Any sane philosopher knows that desires are to be gratified, but not dwelt upon. Everyone must eat frequently and choose food carefully, but anyone who has a spiritual kinship with food, that is, a glutton, epicure or gourmet, who spends hours in anticipation or reflection of eating, is of no use in the world. Similarly, the relations between men and women ought to be as much as possible those of men with men, or women with women—that is, social relations. When a man finds the right woman he has found the right social companion. But these vaguely sexual alliances are little more than sublimations of overt acts. "Platonic love," *as Plato conceived it*, was a rare spiritual kinship between men in which physical contact was disgusting. This is the precise reverse of heterosexual alliances, as Plato never imagined a woman capable of a "Platonic friendship." And Dora Russell is an ass. See? The pen is dry. Damn.

Norrie

There is just enough ink left to say that if you take your name of Helen too seriously you are going to be difficult to handle.

[*Gordon Bay, Lake Joseph, Ont.*]
Saturday afternoon [22 *July 1933*]

Dearest—

I do seem to be having some difficulty with my mail (or male) lately. Here I have been chasing your letters one after another for weeks! And I suppose the same thing is happening this time again. At any rate, since I can't tell when you may visit Ontario, and since you don't know either, I have decided to go to Mrs. Turkington's camp for two weeks starting next Monday and finishing on the seventh or eighth of August. And if you and Vera decide to come this way before that time, I suppose there will be nothing left for Elaine the fair to do but climb into her barge and wander downstream to something akin to Ophelia's unresponsive tomb. I don't know exactly what I am to do at camp—something in the way of talks on music and art, I gather. Jean [Evans] and Robin [Govan] and Dot Bishop seem to have a lot of plans, and Mrs. Turkington is paying my expenses. Her invitation this time was so urgent that I could not have turned it down even if I didn't want to go.

When her letter came, the dope from Perkins Bull arrived also, so I have had to work steadily at that this week. Pencil sketch is just about ready. I did not go to Toronto for copy as I thought I should do—for I found the things I needed in the oddest places. For instance I had been looking for a *Jersey Cow*—and there it was on a baking soda box. You'd laugh if you could see the garb I'm half in at present. I am getting a sunburn—bathing suit is half off, and the sunglasses are quite an aid to beauty. Like this: —

Fred Smith is in the same state. We have to observe which boats are passing to be sure our friends the Hamers don't come along. For there are limits to what they approve of. They are the natives, the Plymouth brethren—very nice people. Last Sunday I went to their meeting and listened to a three-quarters of an hour sermon—it was supposed to be a study group—from a mealy-mouthed Plym who insisted that man must live by *faith*—quoting the same text from Paul about seventeen times, totally ignoring Paul's interest in *works* also.

Saturday night. I stopped just there because Fred wanted to go swimming. So finally he rowed across the bay and I swam.

I see that the C.C.F. is having a grand pow-wow in Regina—the *Star* is giving it a lot of space. They are drawing up a formal programme, and debating quite hotly over some things. Agnes Macphail threatened to withdraw if they retained the plank in regard to confiscation of property without compensation. As a result, of course, they agreed to some compensation—thus displeasing the supporters of revolutionary methods. The people in the West seem to be ardently C.C.F., and one man from Quebec said that the Jesuit priests were just waiting for the results of this conference to proclaim their opinion—he implied that it was decidedly favorable. The other two parties will have to snap into it and dope out a definite policy or they will be left at the post. For there is the element of youthful enthusiasm, and of hope in the C.C.F. organization that is altogether lacking in the hardened machinery of the others. And of all things, people need hope and enthusiasm, or they die.

Your Ukrainian lace handkerchief was lovely. Sweet of you to send it to me. Do you know that I think you and I could have quite a bit of fun looking over an exhibition!

You will let me know what you are going to do, won't you? I don't want to bother you of course, but you *would* like it here, especially after Chicago's heat. And if you can come, why do so—come when you can and wait till I get here. I should like to see you—so much!

I suppose I shan't have much time when I am at camp. I have had to work on the drawing lately, and so have not prepared my "cultah" talk—or whatever pill I'm supposed to administer. But we shall see. The address is simply "Camp Onawaw, via Huntsville, Ontario."

Goodnight,
Helen

Chicago, Ill.
Tuesday [*25 July 1933*]

Pet:

Your letter just came, but the chaos in which the juxtaposition of Elaine's barge and Ophelia's tomb has plunged my feeble intellect—confound it all, you don't float into a tomb on a barge!—you might barge into a tomb or tomble into a barge, however, but the metamorphosis from Launcelot to Hamlet is too much for me on short notice—I can say with Prufrock, "No! I am not Prince Hamlet, nor was meant to be"—has made it impossible for me to fathom your position. If I come down to Toronto, can you get to that city?—a question to be asked.

You see, my visit here has more than an even chance of ending rather dismally. Just before I came, the President-elect of Evergreen Park School Board, accused by his opponent of not being able to get the teachers paid, said that the money to pay up the teachers in full was in the bank. "Then," said Vera, "can I plan my summer accordingly?" "Of course, my dear," said the President-elect unctuously. Well, Vera at present has two bucks, and no other resources except the money for my ticket home. The bank is arranging for a loan, and Vera is fairly sure of getting it soon, but how soon? If not soon, Norrie ambles off home by himself, feeling, foolishly but quite naturally, like a sponger and parasite.

I should have left yesterday but Vera wanted to wait. And Georgie Wall is a girl who graduated with Vera from Mt. Allison in '24 and roomed with her in her first year. And Georgie Wall is on the Latin teaching staff at Mt. A. And Georgie Wall is trying to persuade the University of Chicago to disgorge another M.A. And Georgie Wall has written a very long and very dull thesis to justify the disgorgement. And she wants that thesis typed. You may be able to guess the rest.

So from Saturday till Wednesday (tomorrow) we've worked steadily at that thesis. I do perhaps most of the typing and Vera checks the errors. I don't think it will get Georgie an M.A., but it may get us ten bucks. I don't think Georgie has any conception of the type of work required for graduate degrees. If the University of Chicago has no conception of it either, Georgie is safe; but the University of Chicago is not the University of Arkinsaw or Jawfish, not by a long sight.

So if, we'll be coming God knows when, and if not, I'll probably be leaving within a few days—before the end of the week, most likely. And now what about you? Suppose I wire you or something, and then if you can't get down you can wire back or phone back or something else to Burwash. Wiring is better—I might not get a phone call. I am not sure, of course, about the Gordon Bay visit, but wouldn't it perhaps be better if you came to Toronto anyway? Vera, of course, wants to come home soon, but due to this hitch we haven't seen much of the Fair & may want to wait a while if the salary leaks out.

Oh, darling, if I don't see you soon I'll choke or something. However, I rather like my present regimen—typing all day and reading a detective story—an excellent one—while Vera gets the meals or relieves me. I shouldn't care for it as a steady diet, but it isn't going to be.

Camp Onawaw
Huntsville, Ontario
Friday [*4? August 1933*]

My dear Norrie:

Your last letter came yesterday night (the one before that only reached me the night before) so the mail service is somewhat irregular.

I have thought and thought, and I think now that *if* you come to Toronto at all—and I want to see you—it would be a better idea all round for you to go directly to Gordon Bay. Several reasons:

1. Cheaper—you spend something like *$8.80 return* to go there which would soon be swallowed up if you stayed in Toronto, for meals & Burwash etc. And I would not need to scoot down from here—which would cost $9.10 return (which I haven't got!)

2. You can stay longer at Lake Joseph. It would be more fun than Toronto for as you know, Toronto isn't much fun in the summer.

There is a cheap fare to Gordon Bay sometime soon. Be sure to enquire. We are three miles from Gordon Bay. There is a farmhouse near the lake where the post office is also. People are Hatherleys—old man and wife, and his daughter Mrs. Weston. Mrs. Weston is a great friend of Marion's [Marion Kemp's] and you might ask her how to get to our place. This is of course in case our folks don't meet you. *Somebody* is certain to be there to meet the train or to get the mail. See Mrs. Weston and you are all right.

I do think this is a better idea. Mother said you were to come straight along—and she is expecting you. Incidentally, I hate to seem insistent on money matters but we're not as broke as we *were*—so you need not worry about the starving Kemps. Daddy has been very busy all summer.

I'll stop now—breakfast.

Helen

205 Fulton Ave., Toronto
Thursday [*31? August 1933*]

After spending two weeks at the cottage, Frye and Kemp took the train to Toronto, where he spent a long weekend before heading back to Moncton and she began work at the Canadian National Exhibition. The article referred to is "The Freshman and His Religion," The Canadian Student, *16 (October 1933): 6–9.*

My dear,

Since the Freshman is still here, if I ever want to see the completed version I should send the rough draft to you, shouldn't I? The magazine is to be in circulation by October 1st, which means that it goes to print two weeks before that. If you could dispose of the freshman within a week and send him to me, I should receive him gladly. I had a letter from Murray Brooks which was quite cheering. For they are paying all my expenses gladly, and seem full of enthusiasm about the conference. Murdock Keith drapes his length around the post above the steaming soup with great frequency, and tells me that there are some fifteen Toronto men and thirty Toronto women going to this affair. The leaders will be rather good, I believe. Jean Elder and Jean Cameron are going—I shall be rooming with them probably. So much for the S.C.M.

My letters to you will look like a diary very probably, for I want you to know what is happening to me—it is one way of amusing myself. I may make good-natured fun of your straw hat, or the way you plant your feet, or some of your small-boy tricks that make me gasp when I recall that you are the age of my brother's friends—but underneath all that is the fundamental trust in you. You know that.

Well, my dear, since you need the Freshman, I shall send this off and continue later. The article should run around thirteen hundred words I think. The Exhibition continues as usual. One grows very tired, but one sleeps a lot to make up for it. I am no longer attempting to do three things at once. I am going on the principle that you have reiterated so often—"There is lots of time." I do hope that you are not too used up after being jolted about for a day and a night, or maybe two nights.

Goodnight,
Helen

Moncton, N.B.
Sometime toward the end of the week
[*31 August 1933*]

Brown Agate:

Excuse the pencil, but you know how it is. I'm propped in a bed at last, thank God! the first since Sunday night I've had of my own. Trip uneventful but hellish. Got on the train feeling choked—thank the Lord my tears lie pretty deep—and decided to go to bed. So I simply turned the preceding seat over and shoved my feet across it. The connective tissue, from my ankles to my knees, decided that being hung upon nothing was too monstrous a miracle, and raised a howl. Finally I got a knee parked in each ear, my chin cushioned on my genitalia, my skull flattened against one board and my arches against another, and fell into a troubled sleep thinking how luxurious Goliath would have felt had he slept with Procrustes. Woke up in Quebec with enough pins and needles to start a factory. Got off at Montreal and ate breakfast—roll and coffee—bad coffee. Walked over Montreal. Got on the Maritime Express for the first and last time in my life. (The slow local train to the Maritimes.) Repeated the compression process with variations to Campbellton. Got here at half past ten this (Thursday) morning. Since then have done nothing but take a bath. Will start on your article tomorrow.

Conditions here are, of course, bad—we're away behind with rent and so on. I don't blame Dad—there isn't any conceivable way of getting money out of selling construction materials to three provinces who won't construct. Mother is rather broken up at present. There's Vera, still without her salary. However, one of her friends has promised to do his best to get her a job with reasonably honest employers.

Well, I shall start to work immediately. For music perhaps an attack on the Inventions. And no end of correspondence. But I feel like what H.G. Wells calls a Gawdsaker—one who is perpetually saying, "For Gawd's sake, let's *do* something." Perhaps some day I shall be a rich man with money, flocks and herds. But just now all the assets I have are one little ewe lamb. But how I love her!—even if I have been taken up and set down fifteen hundred miles from her.

Norrie

Moncton, N.B.
[*4 September 1933*]

Hazelnut:

I am sending your article. Or my article, if you like. It isn't a particularly good article. I had to rush it a bit, of course, and no one feels so inspired with the squalling of French brats in his ears, the thumping of an engine in his brain, and the odd lump of coal in his back teeth. Mark my words, the Maritime Express is going down in history as The Train Norrie Frye Didn't Like. Of course the opening of the article is on your desk, and I had to remember what I could of it. But I wouldn't get it now, at least, till Tuesday, and you should and, I think, will have the complete opus yourself by that time. I don't think you need to recopy it, but suit yourself. I can't get a typewriter just now.

The current issue of *Maclean's* (Sept. 1) has a very interesting catechism in it on Canadian problems and so forth that is supposed, after being related to a score, to show whether you are of a Conservative, Liberal, or C.C.F. temperament. It's pretty ingenious, and interested me chiefly because it placed me, with perfect accuracy, on the fence between the Liberal and C.C.F. battalions, exactly where a follower of Spengler and Mazzini ought to be. I think, with the C.C.F., that capitalism is crashing around our ears, and that any attempt to build it up again will bring it down with a bigger crash. I think with the Liberals that Socialism, as it is bound to develop historically, is an impracticable remedy, not because it is impracticable—it is inevitable—but because it is not a remedy. I think with the C.C.F. that a cooperative state is necessary to preserve us from chaos. I think with the Liberals that it is impossible to administer that state at present. I think with the C.C.F. that man is unable, in a laissez-faire system, to avoid running after false gods and destroying himself. I think with the Liberals that it is only by individual freedom and democratic development that any progress can be made. In short, any "way out" must of necessity be miraculous. We can save ourselves only through an established cooperative church, and if the church ever wakes up to that fact, that will constitute enough of a miracle to get us the rest of the way.

Sometime when your father comes home, ask him whom I should write for information about the C.C.F. Then he could put me in touch with the Maritime man to see.

There isn't much news yet, of course, and as I have too many letters to write now, I'll quit here. So long for a few days.

Lovingly,
Norrie

[*Toronto*]
Wednesday night [*6? September 1933*]

My dear—

I am too tired to write a decent letter tonight—and I feel very small and sleepy and rolled up in a ball downstairs. Everybody has gone to bed. Family seems fairly well busted—I have been listening to Depression talk all day at the booth and feel a little jaundiced.

I wasn't alone this weekend after all. For Jack Oughton got back on Thursday night and I met him Saturday as I was coming home. He came along and drank coffee while I had supper. Then we went paddling at the island and read *The Hunting of the Snark* and enjoyed moonlight and the willows and the water. Tuesday (last) night he and I went to the art gallery at the Ex. So, as a playmate, Jack is very agreeable. Regards me as the girl-down-the-street-that-he-knew-when-she-was-just-so-high. I miss you, Norrie, but not so much yet. The Exhibition is such a hellish grind. But one doesn't mope. Besides, I'm getting so tired of people asking me what I am going to do that I must find out soon. Anything might happen! And I'm ready to work, too!

I phoned the C.C.F. people here. Their address in Toronto is "Cooperative Commonwealth Federation, 3 Charles Street West, Toronto." The man told me that there *isn't* any headquarters in Moncton just now, but that the man who is organizing the Maritime provinces is Mr. A.B. MacDonald, Antigonish, Fredericton, New Brunswick.

And thanks so much for writing soon—please don't leave me too long in between. Whoa! Cheer up my girl! (I almost slipped that time. I'm going to bed now just to keep smiling.)

Bill [Conklin] and Ida [Clare] called on Dot Drever on their way to Conklins' cottage—both very happy. Bill going to Columbia. Oh my dear—everybody asks me if you are coming up here this year.

Damnation! The way I am talking one would think this the downfall of Carthage even. I am almost through *Salammbô*—really the diabolical way that man Flaubert describes gushing entrails and the last stages of leprosy and pits reeking with the rotting lower limbs of men not quite dead is enough to endanger a stomach not already weakened by the stench of soup. Ugh! I mean, I shudder when I think of soup. The battlefield is almost inevitable after being surrounded by the sight of bloody tomatoes. Ah well.

The article isn't here—you probably forgot to enclose it in your last letter. It's all right anyway. I am getting in touch with Rutherford—she can do what she pleases about it. I think I'm through with that magazine.

I'll probably rave on again tomorrow, but just now, goodnight. Ah Norrie, Norrie, Norrie—girl trails off—

Friday afternoon. Your article came yesterday, and you *are* an angel. Except for a few places where you talk of "once grasping this fundamental principle," etc., I enjoyed it very much. And that's saying something, just now.

I leave for the conference on Wednesday. But before that I have to get work done for Miss Ray, and expect to be pretty busy. She is working hard reading the proofs of Dr. Edgar's book.

Marion is taking these things, i.e. your pen, this letter, and your essay (mailed to Gertrude Rutherford) to the post office—so I shall stop now. I feel I am being dreadfully dull anyhow. It's probably just the soreness in the throat and the sneezly feeling in my nose and my eyes that want to drip heavily. Sneezles and wheezles.

Helen

P.S. I love you very much.

Moncton, N.B.
12 September 1933]

Chipmunk:

Your letter came some time ago, and—what's the matter with me?—it came this morning—and I wish I felt more like being cheerful. If your family's talking Depression or feels busted, you should—hush, I'll tell you that when I feel more like that too. The ex-girlfriend dropped in on Friday, having heard that I was home from a local gossip. She's supposed to be practically engaged to a Forestry and Civil Engineering graduate of U.N.B., but I don't think she cares much about him.

Poor little girl—you and your sanguinary surroundings. And Flaubert—of all men to read at such a time. You'll be tackling Zola in your childbed next. Thanks for all your information, though "Antigonish, Fredericton, New Brunswick" is a bit ambiguous, Antigonish being a town in the eastern part of Nova Scotia. Possibly the address symbolizes his ubiquitous organizing activity.

There being nothing in the way of news, I must tell you a story instead. Do you remember that I called you an agate in my first letter? This was why.

Parable of the Agate

When God made Adam out of the mud and clay, the precious stones were scornful, all but the moonstone, who was an art critic and thought the rest were Philistines. She said: "A brilliant technical *tour de force*, showing what can be done with the basest of materials, but it evinces an outlook essentially pedestrian." But when Eve was created, the precious stones began to whisper, and the bloodstone, a very old and wise stone, broke in upon the moonstone (who had got as far as "evincing a superior delicacy and sensitivity of outlook") to say:

"I think we are reappearing in the world."

"So do I," said the sapphire. "But why?"

"Do you not see," said the bloodstone, "how she delights and tantalizes him with an elusive brilliance? Do you not see how he goes mad to possess her, and when he has possessed her, how baffled and disappointed he is? He will go mad to possess us in the same way, and will get as little from us. And from whence does she derive her power? By leaving her whole being exposed and absorbent to him, so that she reflects his own soul, and to nature, so that she reflects nature's beauty as a frame for it."

"This is getting deep," said the amethyst.

"Be quiet, you minx," said the sapphire. "How long do you think Eve will last? These animals are ingenious things, but they aren't built to stand weather."

"She will last indefinitely," said the bloodstone. "She has all of our hardness."

"I don't see that," protested the amethyst.

"Adam's all squishy and gooey, and Eve's a lot softer than he is."

"Adam and Eve cannot last long," said the bloodstone, "but there will be others like them, and Eve will produce them. We call ourselves eternal, but only this is true immortality, and that is why, beautiful as we are, the animals are greater than we. No, in Eve God has completed an idea He only started with us. We take our measurement of importance in the world from them."

The amethyst said, "Oo!" the strident topaz yawned, the sapphire looked thoughtful, the carnelian started to raise a difficulty. But the diamond blazed with a great light, and said:

"If this be true, then how great is the diamond! For I am hardest and most eternal of all. And I am of all stones the brightest and the purest. I reflect every angle of light in a splendor that shames the sun, but interpose nothing of my own. I am a symbol of supreme greatness in woman. I am the empress of stones. I am the most precious thing in the world."

And the ruby glowed in splendid crimson, and said:

"If this be true, how great is the ruby! For in me men will see the love of passion, ending in death. Women who worship me will conquer heroes and their names will resound eternally through the world. I am a queen of stones."

And the sapphire gleamed in her intensity of blue, and said:

"If this be true, how great is the sapphire! For in me is the strange remoteness which renders woman true to herself. Women who worship me will govern empires through the force of their mysticism and cause all men to stagger in blindness to their feet. I am a queen of stones."

And the emerald kindled her green fire, and said:

"If this be true, how great is the emerald! For I am the symbol of fruitfulness. Women who worship me will rear strong children and may have what they like as a reward. I am a queen of stones."

And the opal burned every color of flame, and said:

"If this be true, how much greater the opal! For I am all of you, and more. I am every woman by turns. Women who worship me can wring the last ounce of either anguish or delight from men. I shall be hated, looked on with dread, but respected none the less, as the queen of stones."

And the pearl chuckled softly, and, diffusing a weird phosphorescence, said to herself:

"Even the pearl will be the queen of stones. The women who worship me will really rule, and let these other noisy ones do their agonizing. Men will struggle for riches, and for young women, and above all else for young daughters of rich men. And they will bow down to me, who am likewise an irritant made lustrous by a good-natured oyster."

Then the lesser stones declared their rank, and aligned themselves, but one. And the bloodstone looked keenly at the agate, and said:

"Do you expect to be great too?"

"How can she be?" broke in the turquoise. "She's dark brown. None of us are dark brown."

"The soil is brown," observed the agate mildly.

"Pah! That filthy stuff!" said the turquoise.

"God made Adam from it," said the agate. "There is sanity and intelligence in brown, a sympathy and understanding in it, at least, which cannot be found in brilliance of your glittering variety. Above all, there is self-reliance in it. I belong to myself, not to the whim of the sun."

"Gawd! Gimme a dicshnary, willya?" gibbered the topaz."Where'dya learn all that stuff?"

"It isn't your color but your cloudiness I object to," said the lapis lazuli. "I don't claim to be anybody great—I'm opaque, I admit it—but at least I've got nothing to hide."

"I dare say not," said the agate. "I prefer to keep my individuality and my soul to myself. You may have noticed that I alone have a pattern—I vary, but I am constant within myself."

"Say it slow," said the topaz. "Whats's in-the-which-uality?"

"It's a word she got from Adam," said the amethyst.

"Bah!" said the topaz. "What's a soul?"

"I think she got that from God," whispered the turquoise.

"Yah!" said the topaz.

"Your women will never rule the world," said the bloodstone.

"They will never make anyone suffer," said the agate.

"I like you," said the bloodstone.

"I thought you would," said the agate.

Keep cheerful, my dear, and remember I'm as close as I can be. I know that your love for me goes far deeper than the snivelling level. But you're in civilization at least. I suppose it won't be long before you go to the Conference of Coruscating Christians to defend my wretched article against the torrent of orthodox abuse, if printed. Speaking of playing hymns—oh, well, we almost were—the local organist gave a rendition of "Nearer, my God, to Thee" which certainly made me feel like edging nearer

—yesterday evening. At least it sounded like the foregoing—I may be unjust. I suppose you have heard this type of pounding, the left hand first. This creature may have been a supply. We met in the Baptist Church—a small building with the organ on the bum—the above improvisation was on the piano, which was why I noticed it. The preacher was an old man, and he recited his sermon as glibly and perfunctorily as a bribed witness—which I expect he is, in a sense. It sounded like a twentieth or thirtieth repetition of it. I have to go to church here—mother insists on going, although she doesn't hear, and I hate to see her go alone.

Well, I guess I'd better tune out for this time. Goodnight.

Me
HGK/NF

Y.M.C.A. Park
Lake Couchiching, Ont.
Sunday afternoon [*17 September 1933*]

My dear Norrie,

When I recalled that I hadn't written to you since the feverish caterwaul I sent over a week ago, I felt a little bit conscience-stricken. Weeping and sniffling are horrible things to convey in a letter, especially since you have several things to worry you at home. I really did get a cold that time, though, which kept me away from the last day of the Exhibition, in bed.

Monday and Tuesday I spent running around after Miss Ray, Dr. Locke, Mr. Lismer and so forth. Miss Ray has some work—enough to keep me going for a week or two. Mr. Lismer's scheme is quite indefinite as yet because he had not at that time seen his board of directors, who squeal every time he mentions a new idea. But he has already bought an old house which is being decorated now and will be opened as a centre for children's work in art. He has great plans for it—something like the Children's Library on St. George Street—and wants me to be one of the bright young things on the staff. But it won't bring in much money, because at best it can only be for a few hours a week, for some time to come. However, he says that he thinks it is a good thing, that eventually the work will expand, and that it will grow into a paying proposition. All well and good. See him when I get back. He wants me because of musical training. Marjorie Lismer is up here at the conference.

I had tea with Kay Coburn on Monday afternoon. She liked the Pass Course article very much, and was glad that the subject had been dealt with seriously, as it was a matter of some concern at present. She had been talking to Prof. Sissons about it and he, too, liked it very much. She wasn't sure that your conclusion, the abolition of the Pass Course, would solve the problem, but you put across some good arguments. We had a nice chat, about England, a job for me, and music in the college.

I am not going to tell you much about this conference, I think, because the atmosphere is, I suppose, something like the Chicago Fair, a little difficult to communicate except by superlatives. I am not rushing about from place to place in search of people's opinions, for oddly enough, I am beginning to get a vantage point of my own. You would like the conference, Norrie, I am sure you would. Last night Larry McKenzie and [John] Bickersteth motored up, bringing Noel Baker, secretary of Lord Cecil, graduate of Cambridge, many years' experience on the inside of the League of Nations. He spoke on the League, of course. All is not lost, stay with the ship, the League while only half a league since the Manchurian situation, will function again effectively. Cited cases of wars averted, with details. Great man.

Bishop Owen and F.J. Moore took the Sunday service today, with Jules LaPointe fiddling. Not as good as Roy, but plays quite well. Jim Endicott plays sometimes too—since he learned by himself in China, he is anxious for practice here. There are some 280-odd people here today. Dr. [Walter T.] Brown and Dr. [John] Line, and Dr. [Frederick W.] Langford are here. Etc. etc. J.D. Robins is coming tonight to give the usual talk on folk songs. Little Helen plays away and enjoys it all.

Now this is perhaps a little news. Art [Cragg] has been given a $300 fellowship in Philosophy. I think that Art has just recently heard of it. And it is rather splendid for him. I have wondered whether there might not be a little something in store for you, too. I remember last year you didn't know how you were to get back, and along came the Trick again. I haven't any suggestions to offer, except that you do a little writing around to Dr. Brown, or somebody else.

I had breakfast with Dr. Brown and Dr. Line this morning, at the same table that is. When Dr. Brown asked me what I was going to do next I couldn't tell him then and there that I should like a job at the library. Besides, when I think of the work that there is to be done there I am not keen about it. Very dull stuff on the Bell books.

It is time now almost to go off for the evening programme, so I shall mail this on the way. My dear, I hope there will be a letter from you tomorrow, and that some good things will have happened during the week. Vera may have landed a job, or your father sold some bricks or your mother recovered, or you may have some new idea. At any rate, I think that surely the college cannot ignore one of their best men ([C.E.] Auger: "our best man") entirely. And keep cheerful! By the way, I should like to know how you are getting on about the C.C.F. article. Dr. Line told me that Mr. MacDonald is a college man, quite a good man for the movement. (I casually asked about the Maritime organizer.)

Both Ida [Clare] and Florence [Clare] send you their best, and hope very much that you will be back. And as for me, you know that I am hoping and hoping.

Helen

Moncton, N.B.
[22 *September 1933*]

The ex-girlfriend's father is an ardent C.C.F. worker—almost a fanatic, in fact—why in hell should I get entangled with daughters of paid agents of Moscow and consequent emissaries of the devil?—and called here one night to take me down to an executive meeting of the C.C.F. here, of which he is chairman. Small, but active enough, with old man Rogers supplying most of the energy. Mother said when I was gone: "If he gets a chance to get up and speak, he's away for the evening!"—and I got my chance. They asked me to give the big pow-wow at their opening meeting. So I wrote to 3 Charles St. West Toronto and said Please send me some

My dear Helen:

	Well, here I am again.
2¢	There isn't any news, but here goes.
each	Sorry to be so long answering,
	but I've been desperately busy.
	It's still a bit chilly, with occasional showers.
slightly	
soiled	Here's mud in your eye.
reduced	
1¢	

or what have you, that will give me at least some idea of what in thunder I'm talking about, literature, pamphlets, S.O.S., R.S.V.P., P.D.Q. But when did I refuse to speak?—and I'd talk on syntactical difficulties of the *Rig-Veda* to have something to do, at least in the company of other people. I wish there were a copy of Spengler somewhere east of the Don Valley—I'm going to give them both barrels of him, in any case. And, being nothing if not versatile, I am to read my paper on French music to the local Thanatopsis club.

Your letter just came. Poor little darling—if my arms could only stretch to Ontario for a few minutes. I'm afraid you're not very well adapted to work like that. You'll just have to make up your mind to the fact that you're healthy enough, but not strong, and just aren't built along tomato soup lines.

I cannot come back this fall, sweetheart. Don't worry—I've canvassed the possibilities more thoroughly than you give me credit for. I'm very glad Art got his scholarship—I knew he had applied for it. And the situation here is not one that I feel I can leave, without being in a sure position, just yet. Sorry, but there it is. It hurts me to hear you say that you are hoping and hoping—I feel the same way, but there isn't anything I can do, just now, that will remedy the situation immediately. I am quite sure of that.

Dad is trying to get an agency, which he has a reasonable chance of getting, with a Montreal firm on a salary. The squad of letters from the West came also, finally. Ross [Crosby] has had two fights with inebriates, a night watch over a prospective suicide, funerals, and a lady who protested that she was wearing no underwear and wanted emergency relief in the way of clothing. "So," says Ross, "after careful investigation, I complied."

This man MacDonald is well known, but not as a C.C.F. organizer. The local club wanted him to come here and speak without having any idea of his political connections. He's assistant professor of economics at St. Francois Xavier College (Catholic), Antigonish, N.S.

More to follow sometime. My subject is "The Historical Background of Socialistic Thought."

Lovingly,
Norrie

205 Fulton Ave.
Monday night [*25? September 1933*]
(around midnight)

My dear Norrie—

Your letter came today. I am very glad that you are getting busy on the stump. I should think, however, that you might tackle a subject more nearly related to the present situation in the minds of your listeners than the historical background of socialistic thought. For if you are talking to a crowd of workers in factories, and ex-railroad men, you are dealing with people profoundly worried about their particular world, who are not particularly concerned with an intellectual or historical approach to the socialism position. People want to understand some of the major reasons for the present crisis, and some of the remedies. They do not have to go through the intellectual process which drove you to formulate the aims of your Sunday morning study group last winter. To be sure, I can imagine an address built upon the historical approach which stresses the present situation and aims of socialism, which would be of interest to the ordinary yahoo, but a discussion of Owenism and Fabianism and even of Marxism (perhaps especially the latter) will not hold your audience, I am afraid. You must not give them the impression that you are dealing with an academic question. Of course, you won't—with all the things that you see happening to your audience, you could not possibly ignore their need. Sorry to talk at this length, for you probably will see the right way to handle them as you go along, but then again, if you imagine that your average inhabitant of Moncton will be less unable to understand Spengler than I was, I am afraid that you will have a difficult time. Economics has been taught very little, only through the newspapers of late. Philosophy and a philosophy of historical development not at all. Talk of tariffs and taxes and trade alliances is intelligible, but to the ordinary citizen a dying culture means nothing and is of no interest except to raise resentment against the highbrow who thinks that our Main Street isn't the greatest spot on God's earth. So, if you say the same old things, in a new and vigorous way, you can lead your people as you will. But do be careful.

I was not going to talk long tonight because I have been out walking miles (Jack Oughton again), and I feel a bit sleepy. I helped shunt freshies about yesterday afternoon, and introduced Miss Ray, and so forth. Miss Ray is in the process of creating a part-time job for me. And I am working on Albion Township for Mr. P. Bull.

I am sorry to have worried you, hoping that you would be back. Norrie my dearest, you know that I don't want to hurt you ever, or be a nuisance. I am getting to work with a will, for I have several ideas revolving round in my dome. So that when you do come I shall have things to show you. And in the meantime you will be doing great things in New Brunswick—you've no idea how tickled Daddy was with the idea of your spreading the socialist gospel.

Thursday morning. Stayed home this morning to practise—Scarlatti, two Chopin Études. We are coming on very well, thank you.

Yesterday I did some lettering at the library and saw lots of people. In fact I was pretty fed up by noon, after answering fifty million who asked "And what are you doing this year?" I gave up when that ass Heathcock brayed in my direction, and I told him I had no idea whatever, I wasn't going to library school and I wasn't going to O.C.E.

No, this family isn't doing much worrying or talking about Depression, thank God. It gets one sometimes, of course—when the mortgage man comes round to inquire into our financial status or when we wonder what in hell Roy expects to use for college expenses. But you never can tell with this family. The Lord evidently does provide. Roy is starting in full of pep, in Modern History and says Ted Avison and Harold Fair and Cec Wilson were asking for you.

You may laugh at this, but I have been roped in, too. I am going to speak to the Riverdale C.C.F. club tomorrow night on women's duty to be intelligent about politics or something like that. They'll never know how little I know about it. It's a gift. Half an hour. And I'll write my speech myself this time, thank you!

Spent an hour yesterday with Gertrude Rutherford trying to figure out what was the epitome of the freshman's relation toward his fellows, and toward God. She decided to make a few changes, and I told her to go ahead, because there wasn't time to let you rewrite your opening paragraph. You should have seen your poor article, as typed by the secretary! She did her best with your writing but I had a great deal of corrections to make. They liked it (Howard Alexander has revised his whole opinion of you, he tells me, since reading that) but thought the opening was a little uninspired (my own word. It was.).

Fred Skitch is giving a recital in Burwash on Sunday. Cec Wilson said Burwash and the College would miss you. Ida said they would miss you. (My inaudible reply was something like "And you're telling *me*!?!")

Are you enjoying the free finger movement of this writing? Evidently comes from practising double sixths. I'm going sketching this afternoon. Courage, mon ami, le diable est mort (darn near).

Friday. My dearest—Since I have forgotten to post your letter again, I may as well tell you some more of what has happened today.

This morning I worked at the library, and had lunch with Jean Evans at Diana Sweets. While we were there, Lois [Hampson] and Joby [Freeland] walked in—the crazy kids are at O.C.E. and are fearfully perturbed about the Pass Course and what good college has done them anyway etc. They agreed with your article, but the silly idiots didn't do anything but take everything you said personally and conclude that they hadn't learned a thing from college. I did not have sufficient time to try to cheer up Joby much, but I did say a few good words for the Pass Course, and told her that we didn't expect to get vocational training when we entered upon it in the first place. That article of yours has been a darn good thing—evidently you have vocalized a lot of

Pass Course dissatisfaction. Joby is going to O.C.E. because her mother thinks it will be something to fall back on. Her four years of college have not fitted her for anything, and she will at least have something after this, although she doesn't ever expect to get a job. Hell! Why don't people take a chance and do what they want to do!

From Diana's I went to see Perkins Bull, who was fairly affable, liked the drawing, found a lot of little corrections to make, and sent me off telling me to come back again, with a smile on that sweet little face of mine. Wasted practically my whole afternoon.

Came home and rested up, and delivered a pretty fair speech tonight —to over a hundred people, mostly hard-faced and blank-faced, and water-eyed men, with one in the front seat who chawed gum, and another who cleaned his teeth with his tongue. A fair sprinkling of women in the audience also. I talked for nineteen minutes (by Daddy's watch. Daddy and Ernie [Harrison] sat in the front row for moral support.) Just a general pep talk about the duty of women to use their role and vote intelligently—with a reference to the Oxford Group, Karl Marx and the passive way some people accept the Depression (by way of explaining some people's reaction to Depression and their idea of curing social ills). Oh well, I can't tell you all I said, a great deal of it was what Agnes Macphail said in a magazine article—I mean I used her partly—and the time was filled creditably anyhow. Point is, I'm not so interested in those people, as in the practice I get in speaking. Mamma said I halted a bit too much, but I think myself that it was the best speech I ever made—taking into account stops and everything.

When I got home, Lismer had phoned. He told me to chuck the library in the morning and come to see him. It was important. So that's another reason for being a little excited.

I met Del Martin and George Morrison on the street today. Del was asking for you—he said he wouldn't be at all surprised to see you land in here before Christmas. Your friends have great faith in your miraculous powers.

When I think of the concerts there are to go to this year, I get as homesick as the devil, for you. But it's all right, you know. At least you know that I'm not sniffling. And while I can enjoy friendships with other people—I can't get over loving you.

Helen

[*Toronto*]
[*1? October 1933*]

This is the last letter written to Frye in Moncton during 1933; shortly after receiving this letter he returned to Toronto to enrol at Emmanuel College.

My dearest Norrie,

You are reading a letter written by a very excited little person! I hope you will rejoice with me. I just found out yesterday that

I'VE GOT A JOB ! ! !

and this is how it is:—

What Lismer had to say *was* important. He has just come back from Ottawa where he had been making arrangements with the National Gallery, and things are soon to be settled. They have had two new grants of money this year, with which to carry on a new type of art education in the country, and they are planning to send people to England for study. And little Helen is one of the first to be there on the spot. I am to work at the art gallery (and perhaps at the National Gallery in Ottawa for some months, too) this year, doing all sorts of things in order to get experience and show my ability, etc. They are to pay me around $500, more or less—keep me, at any rate, and next year send me to the Courtauld Institute in London, with expenses paid, which will include a trip or so to European art galleries. Pinch me! am I dreaming!

Lismer was quite tickled himself, said he urged them to settle it quickly before I made plans for the winter. He took me through the underground places of the gallery, where they store children's work, and frame pictures, and get them ready for exhibition, and where they have collections of lantern slides and prints to be loaned to schools. He took me through the new children's house where a carpenter was busy making bookcases for the library, and showed me the room for woodblocks, and the classrooms, and so on, not furnished completely yet.

And he told me some of the things I am to do. He said the only danger might be that he would work me too hard. I must get acquainted with the slides, to send out collections when needed. When they send picture collections I am to write short summaries of the collection with enough details of interest to make them more interesting. I may try my hand at writing biographies of artists for the monthly catalogue of the exhibition. He said he wanted someone with literary ability and university training. (Miss Ray says I have literary ability.) Then he mentioned music, he said Gallery people thought that was going to be needed too, and he said I might give talks to the kids in the new house, and help arrange the programmes for the monthly musicale in the Grange. And that I would have to study the odd thing he would suggest—history of art. And get practice in lecturing. It sounds like a lot of work, and no end of fun. What a break! If you were here just now you could help me be enthusiastic. And you would, wouldn't you? I hurried to the library just a minute before it closed, and told Miss Ray, and she was so *pleased*—more so than I was, because I can't realize it is going to happen, and that I'm getting in on the ground floor of a good job.

I have been reading Elizabeth Drew's *Discovering Poetry*—the one you read up north. It is the best thing I have ever seen on the subject, for one at my stage of appreciation.

Mamma and Daddy send you their kind regards, and Ernie will post the letter.

Good night,
Helen

Watercolour of the family cottage by S.F.H. Kemp, 1931
(courtesy of Ian Price)

Friends from the Victoria College class of 3T3 (courtesy of Jean Elder).
Back row from left: Jean Evans, Ruth Dingman, Marg Torrance,
Robert (custodian), Lois Hampson, Jean Elder, Berna Langford.
Front row: Dot Darling, Dot Drever, Jean Cameron.

Helen Kemp, Jean Elder,and Dot Drever, 1933 (courtesy of Jean Elder)

Florence and Ida Clare, 1933 (courtesy of Jean Elder)

Summer of 1934

152 Argyle Ave., Ottawa
Wednesday night [*11? April 1934*]

The letters from this period begin with Kemp at the National Gallery in Ottawa, where she had embarked on a training program for museum work. Frye was initially in Toronto, continuing his degree studies at Emmanuel College, and then left for his summer student mission field in Saskatchewan.

My dear Norrie,

I am settled at last, in the place I told you of, at Miss [Winifred] Smith's—and it is just the *very* best place I could have gone to. After a few doubts Miss Smith let me come here for ten dollars a week, so long as I did not tell the other people, because she charges twelve regularly. Miss Fenwick is two doors away, and the other people are a lot older mostly, but all doing something and all interesting in one way or another. One woman is a Ph.D. in geology, I think, at least she does work in that department of the museum. She is the one who owns the piano which is in a room all by itself and I can practise on it anytime. And someone else in the house has studied for a Mus. Bach. degree and has left a whole pile of music on top of the piano—Beethoven Sonatas, a large collection of Chopin, Debussy, and the Forty-eight Preludes and Fugues in one volume. There are books all over the house. It used to be a girls' school, you know, and Miss Winifred always leaves a shelf-full of books in each bedroom. Next door are two sweet old ladies. I mean living in the rooms on either side of me. One is Mrs. Macoun, who I find is an aunt of Maureen Macoun of Sigma Phi fame. Tonight after dinner we had a fire downstairs in a sitting room, and a cigarette, and a lot of talk. Miss Fenwick who improves greatly upon acquaintance, Miss [Esmé] Moonie, a lovely Scottish woman who came out to do work with the Radio Commission and somehow got side-tracked into social service work, the two old ladies, and Miss [Alice] Wilson (who owns piano) and myself were the cronies. I don't mind in the least being with older people—in fact it is quite a relief. You should see the place I *almost* got into—two radios and a player piano, loud curtains and bridge-playing roomers. Whew! What an escape.

The McCurry's are very good to me, too. Really I am terribly fortunate. And I am working. Practised yesterday and today half an hour twice in the day. Then in the morning I am arranging reproductions of drawings of French, German, Dutch, English, Italian etc. painters—not with a view to getting a job *done* but to grow familiar with their work. Time off to read anytime I like—but I must keep definite hours.

It is late, so I shall say goodnight—in the chaste maidenly way belonging to a woman living in a female residence, and liking it!

Love,
Helen

152 Argyle Ave.
Ottawa, Ontario
Saturday night [*14 April 1934*]

My dear Norrie,

So many things happened to me today that I am almost overwhelmed, but I must tell you all about it just the same. After all, it *is* Saturday night, and I usually spend it with you—so here we are.

This morning I went off to the gallery and I settled down to finish this article I was writing on educational work at the Vancouver Art Gallery. I was working all by myself in the print gallery which is a marvellously quiet place, with a collection of Blake's drawings on the walls at present—when—who should walk in but Pelham Edgar with Duncan Campbell Scott! He didn't notice me of course—my brown sweater tones in well with the furniture and I was only a little mite of no account anyway, surrounded with paper and ink. And he looked rapidly at each drawing, paying very little attention to them because he was so busy talking about a *remarkable* youngster up at Victoria, yes a simply extraordinary chap—he had been doing some fine work on Blake, post-graduate. He had written a paper on Blake's *Milton* which was very fine. Remarkable breadth of interest too. He loved music. He had his philosophy. Very clever youngster. At present studying theology at Emmanuel. Well worth watching. (All during this I was whirling around like the man in the barrel at Niagara, hot, cold, red, white and green and shivering like a first recital. Why wouldn't I? If he'd known what a special interest that waif by the window had in that remarkable young man. Oh my dear!) Well, anyway, I gathered my papers together, walked over and said "Good morning, Doctor Edgar" and he *was* surprised. So I told him I had just come here last Sunday and was very glad to see him and hoped he would enjoy his trip very much. And he asked me what I was doing. So I inquired whether he had heard of my fortunes and he said "no, but I hope they are commensurate with your abilities, my dear." Whereupon I thought, and said, that was very sweet of him, and told him about the scholarship and how much I was enjoying everything. Later Mr. McCurry said Doctor Edgar was talking about me, and was very glad I was getting on so well. Mr. McCurry it was told him I was getting on so well.

This afternoon I went hiking with Mr. and Mrs. McCurry and Mrs. Jenkins and Margot McCurry. We went three miles away to the Sugar Bush to a place called the Holy Ghost which is a Roman Catholic training school for young boys who will be priests. And we saw them tapping the maple trees and running the sap into pails. I am sending you some. We walked back. Mr. McCurry talked to me all the way back and boy oh boy—*am* I getting the national viewpoint! and *am* I working Toronto out of my system! Just give me time. And Mrs. McCurry is going to give me lessons in voice production for nothing because she says that I couldn't afford to pay what she charges, and that probably I can do something for her sometime in return. Am I dreaming? Last night I had dinner with Mary Carman at her home. I had a grand time.

I am getting a cramp from scrawling. I think I should stop and go to the post office to mail your maple sugar. Give Roy [Kemp] my blessing and keep on taking care of him, and give the family as much news as you like from this.

Love,
Helen

Toronto, Ont.
[*15 April 1934*]

My little girl:

I got your letter Friday morning, and have been sleeping off and on ever since. The more sleep I get, the sleepier I feel. I'm so glad you are happy and in the right place. You can't think how your letter bucked me up. I mean, it just settled things for me, though I knew all along you would be all right. There are some people in the world, like you and me, who have certain definite things to get done, and for them things open out and all the hopeless obstructions are cleared away, one after the other, by some unseen process that knows all about it beforehand. This is about my only working religious belief, and it's one I've always had with me, though I've sometimes wondered what direction I was going. It's my idea of predestination.

I've just been out (Sunday night) to your place. I slept till noon, went to Sunday School, which I'm going to close up next Sunday, and then went out. I had dinner and played through about everything in the catalogue with Roy. We played Tartini, Bach, Corelli (the Folio), the Handel Sonata, the Mozart Sonata in A, the Bruch, Mendelssohn, a squad of early music arranged by Kreisler, finishing with the Handel Lament I always go for. Your mother invited out Edna Hough and her sister for dinner. Edna told Mr. Kemp I was a big improvement on [Al] Sedgwick—a sentiment I believe I have heard you echo. I should like to meet this bird Sedgwick. I had a pretty good time, though the ghosts walked a little. Oh, my dearest! Is it only a week?

I'm getting intensely interested in Blake again—it's damned near a monomania. We had our group Friday and I read another paper on Blake and Romantic Philosophy. I combined what I knew of Blake with my Romanticism epic and gave them the works. I'd been up all the preceding night. They were pretty badly overwhelmed. Our exam is the 26th and we can take our texts into it. I think the Blake thesis will be a book, all right. I've got some ideas on the subject of Blake, as you know, and if this university has any money I'll publish it, and if I have a book out at this age they'll give me a job, and if they give me a job I'll marry you, and if I don't drop my milk pails.

Wednesday Ida [Clare] sent an S.O.S. call. She had a paper to do for Sanderson on the modern novel, and wanted some ideas straightened out. I think I was some help, and next day I offered to type her paper. We went walking all afternoon at Summerhill Park, and I backed her into Murray's at tea—she was on duty at the library. I think I'll take her to the B minor Mass if I can get the tickets. Now that I haven't a crush on her I don't need to make a fool of myself, and now that Bill [Conklin] isn't around she won't make a fool of me, so we get along very well. She's a sweet girl, if she is a bit insipid beside you.

This being now Monday night, I may say I got first-class honors in theology. They don't rank them; they just classify, so I don't know how

I stood in the course. I understand I got (I didn't see my marks) four firsts, two seconds and a third, the third emanating from Mr. George McMullen of Public Squeaking fame. It's fifty bucks automatically for getting a first. Hugh [Moorhouse] tells me I got the Church History scholarship—thirty bucks.

I've been talking to Jim Lawson, telling him hesitantly that I *might* cop the Travelling Fellowship two years from now. He laughed and said "You silly ass!" which sounded as though there were no one else in sight. Then he went on to tell me what I should do *when* I went to Edinburgh or Cambridge. He did his B.D. thesis on Christian art and its relation to dogma, and I spoke of doing one on music. He was very urgent that I should do it, and laid big plans for graduate work, etc. I wanted to do Spengler and St. Augustine. But there are two things which are absolutely unique about the Christian religion and which guarantee its truth—one is music, the other a philosophy of history, and, though I'll do them both eventually, I don't care which I start on. They're intimately connected, of course, and it may be better to get a solid musical background first. We'll see how things turn out. I was glad to get that push from Lawson. He told me that there might not be another student in generations with my combination of background that could do the job. Tell me what you think of this.

Work steadily, sweetheart, but not hard. When you sweat you're not absorbing. I leave on April 30—Monday. Goodnight, my pet, and don't let anything bother you.

Norrie,
Who is Very Sincerely Yours.

Toronto, Ont.
Wednesday [*18 April 1934*]

Well, I'm in the middle of music Centennial Week, wishing and wishing that my little invisible brownie were here too. I heard the ninth symphony last night. I enjoyed the symphony, though that *Ode to Joy* bothered me as usual. I would like to hear the 9th as the only thing on the programme, with the *Ode* sung in some language I didn't understand. The translation was execrable. The singing was all right, or would have been if it had been possible to sing that infernal orgy at all—most of it is simply sopranos screaming on an A flat, a sound which fairly pulls my own vocal chords apart in pure sympathy.

Tonight was the Hart House Quartet and Ossip Gabrilowitsch, son-in-law of Mark Twain, guest of Toronto, excellent pianist, and conductor of the Detroit Orchestra, in the order named, according to the newspaper. First was the Mozart Quartet. Not the best Mozart, but very fine—performance impeccable but a bit stiff. Then the Beethoven C sharp minor. *What* the devil Beethoven was getting at in those last quartets I can't imagine. Just to follow, the writing is masterly, but considered as a unified work of art, it's hopeless. When you listen to music, what's gone before subconsciously piles up, like Bergson's cosmic memory, and works out its own form if it's got any. And this thing was just a thin thread of beautiful sound all through—no taking on of form. I feel similarly helpless with all the Wagner I have heard—that's one reason why I think Wagner a tonic for lazy minds. There are people whose judgment one is bound to respect who think these quartets are absolutely the last word in music. I'd like to get hold of one and pin him down with a few questions. *When* does one movement stop and another one start? Does the thing finish logically, or does it just get tired and quit, with a coda of two measures? *Why* does Beethoven repeat exactly the same subject eight times without taking it anywhere? And so on. Beethoven surely must have known that the thing had no form—was it just romantic egoism, or is the whole idea of absolute formal perfection to be given up as pedantic? It isn't pure music, like a fugue or a sonata, working out its own self-directed laws, nor programme music, depending on the shape of something externally obtruded for its form. It seems to be something intermediate, taking its form from itself, or the mind of its composer, or God knows what, and so falls between the stools. Performance mechanically perfect, a bit uninspired. Then a glorious performance of a glorious work—the Brahms quintet in F minor. Excuse my raving like this, but you understand. I can't talk to you much about music, but I can write.

I was walking past the Vic Library when Gordon Webber hailed me from the depths of a very luxurious car—Isabel McLaughlin's. I gave your regards to him and to Norah McCullough, and he reciprocated. Then he told me all about a friend of his who was quite a bright chap but studied theology and got his mind hermetically sealed as a result—Union Seminary, New York, where Fosdick is. Wanted to know how I reconcile the undisputed possession of a brain with my entry into the realms of dogmatic benightenment, or words to that effect. I was about to commence a four-hour oration on the place of dogma in thought when Isabel came back and I was introduced to her. I asked her if she wanted to hear it, as I was quite sure it was going to be a good speech, but she had to rush away to an engagement.

I got a second in New Testament after all, and one in Field Work. If I'd gone to all my lectures this year I'd have collected seven firsts in a row. I guess that's the most painless way of getting through theology—unlike Arts. I should come out floating next year—no McMullen.

Goodbye for now, but I shall return and haunt you with another monologue. Got to get to work now on Blake.

Norrie

[*Ottawa, Ont.*]
[*22 April 1934*]

The essay referred to in the second part of this letter is "Robert Cowton to Thomas Rondel," Northrop Frye's Student Essays, *235–56.*

Norrie, my darling,

If there's anytime I've missed you terribly, it's been today. Sunday—and I'm sick and a little lonely because I can't read, my eyes are too sore, and my head aches and my stomach aches and my nervous system is in a hell of a female mix-up. Last Wednesday I had a splurge and Miss Fenwick, bless her soul, alternately scolded and petted me and took me into her room and bucked me up.

Now I'm cheered up, and I'll tell you what made me mad.

Everyone but a few old maids was out for supper tonight. And they started talking about Miss Moonie who left for the South to help take care of a widower's family—an old friend of hers. And she has had the place in a great stir all week about going. She has two or three beaux, and the old girls can't see what men see in her. She is really a beautiful middle-aged Scottish woman with a lovely voice and no end of problems which must be solved by someone protective. These women talked about love, and couldn't see what men see in women—as they say "Lots of men come to me for advice professionally but they're never interested in me any other way! I wonder what those women do to attract them. I wish I weren't so fat. I wish I weren't so thin. I wish a man would look at me and not be bored . . ."

Daddy told me the old maid's repressions and prickles were more truth than poetry. I always thought that old maids were that way from choice and that they didn't want any men. Evidently not. May God—and you—prevent me from such a state! If that's the price a woman pays for a little learning, I'm ashamed and sorry for the sex. Perhaps my generation need not. Naturally I don't think I will.

My dear, this side of the line is all cheerful. I'd tear up the rest except that it shows what I am finding out about the female of the species. Ernie [Gould] studied other things besides History when he was away, and restricted as I am, I may as well too. For I am not to be here forever—I mean among such bitter chastity.

I wrote to Norah and to the family last night and I'm afraid I haven't much energy to say everything that I want to tonight. I'll tell you the outlines and you can ask Roy about the rest—that *is* a mean way to treat you, darling, isn't it? But the point is:—Mr. McCurry liked my article—900 words—modern principles of education grafted onto Vancouver. He doesn't like Sherman Wright who may lose his scholarship. He evidently likes me and wants me to hurry with my thesis for it is to be submitted to a committee who will give me a Gunther award. He thinks still that I might better postpone my trip for another year. He might keep me here next year. Says there is great need for someone who can write on art—all the papers in the country would publish articles which he would supply them—if he had someone to write them. I told him I wanted to try writing a bit after I finish the thesis. I can't possibly get the thesis done this week as I haven't started to write it. Someone here can type it for me, but perhaps I should let you look it over first. If I send it out west to you, registered, later on, could you read it there for me? The typing of it isn't important, but I want your criticism beforehand.

I am so terribly glad that you got your first, and the Church History Prize. That essay probably did the trick. They are sending it to me, Daddy said. Jim Lawson was very nice to you—and of course what he says is true. I am not clear about the implications of the travelling scholarship. Does it mean that you must confine yourself to a theological basis of study, or would you do it from choice? I understand what you want to do in a way perhaps. (Darn it, this having to *write* everything is an awful nuisance.) Do you mean you would work out the extent to which music reflects the changing religious spirit of different ages? I can understand that. And I'd like to see you do it. Of course you're the man for the job. The Travelling Fellowship seems to be your chance to get away, and you *must* do that. You'll be coming as I am leaving, perhaps. Maybe I can make a date with you for five years from now in Murray's. Oh darling, darling—but of course, I can come home for holidays and things if I've got this much money. I understand that Chicago is having another fine exhibition this summer. I wondered whether I might go, instead of to camp.

Monday noon. Have spent the morning reading the *Encyclopaedia Britannica* on Italian painting. I am having a little trouble getting people straightened out in their proper places, but if I keep pegging away I've no doubt it will clear up in time. I can tell Italian drawings now when I see them, as different from German. That's one step. I can usually recognize a Dürer, and a Cranach. Naturally Leonardo and Michelangelo drawings are quite easily distinguishable from a mass of stuff.

Daddy sent your essay and I've just read the first few pages, but it is *good*. I love the way you have written it. Your Franciscan speaks with the tenderness—sometimes—and the simplicity of Giotto. May I have it with me for a while? I think it is one of the best things you have done.

I am beginning to think that perhaps two months or even one at camp would be a waste of time at my present stage. Mr. McCurry suggests that I stay here all summer. I could live in a cottage up the Gatineau and do as I please about study and working at the gallery. He has a lovely cottage there at Kingsmere and Professor [Hubert] Kemp and his wife come up from Toronto and are there all summer. If I study all summer perhaps I could take a few weeks off later and do nothing. I have had the camp experience. At present I need to soak in some sound information. I am beginning to know what I want to do, and so I might just as well make up my mind to do it. What do you think?

Do forgive my little squawk at the first, I am never quite sure whether to complain about the stomach aches, or to wait and write something cheerful. But invariably I take the risk of having you think me a spluttering infant, and get it off my chest. If you just take it for that and don't worry, you will know that I feel better afterwards. And deep underneath I am so happy about everything—you, and my work, and a few friends—that I feel on the right track at last.

Brown Owl

P.S. Good luck with the Blake exam.

Toronto, Ont.
April 24 [*1934*]

Now, my dear, never mind the women—surely you know that old maids have repressions and that every unmarried woman is either repressed or suppressed when she has any sex at all. It's just one of those little facts of life we've all heard so much about. No, my pet, let me have all your troubles and miseries along with your ecstasies and raptures—I'm used to both, associate you with both, and I want to make sure it's all of you writing to me.

I'm tired today—slept all morning, being up the night before, listened to Cragg's phonograph—the Smetana G minor trio—very well developed and thoroughly enjoyable. Saturday—I forget when I wrote last—I went to Eaton's for lunch, figuring I couldn't face Burwash anyway, and I wanted to hear the concert there. Then I came home, and called for Ida. We walked down, by ourselves, met Pete Colgrove, Nora [Conklin] and Florence [Clare] at Massey Hall. The Mass itself was, of course, a new tone-world—another St. Matthew Passion, perhaps more concentrated, scholarly and austere. An annual B minor Mass for another four years, and it would be part of my life like the Passion. The choral singing was marvellous, and the orchestral response better, I think, than MacMillan gets in choral works, but the conducting as a whole, though fine and sensitive, was not as vital as MacMillan's.

Sunday I slept, of course, got up and dismissed my Sunday School class. I talked, and I think I talked quite eloquently and sincerely, for about half an hour, and then gave them some idea of how much I liked them. About three of them instantly said in chorus, "You'll be back in the fall, won't you?" If they feel that way about it, I certainly will. Then I went out to your place, and, being all shot in the nervous system from being up all night, didn't do so well with Roy.

I'm sorry you won't be able to send your thesis in time for me to type it. Better wait till you hear from me from the West before sending it, as it may not be such a good idea, depending on the mail service. If I forget to mention it, send it anyway, if you're in no immediate hurry. It'll take at least two weeks. I'm so glad that you get along so well—by all means do all the writing you can, and God watch over every word you set down. You've got genius in you, critical rather than creative. You can't paint like Matisse—thank the Lord!—but you can write better than Ruskin or Pater, and with sounder ideas, when you are mature. You aren't affected, hysterical, sloppy or sentimental, which raises you automatically above nine-tenths of art critics. You understand music, and that is absolutely indispensable to a critic of the fine arts who wants balance and completeness—Ruskin and Pater didn't have music any more than they had balance or completeness, remember. You're educated, you know how to write, and can learn more. You are developing an attitude to literature. You are not a shallow-pated mouther of glib phrases picked up from arty conversation, and consequently you are getting your roots deep into the rich soil of art tradition. A woman who can tell Dürer from Cranach, to say nothing of a woman who has heard of both, can write about Canadian art and wither all the mountebanks and self-advertisers in the country, setting in their place enthusiastic and talented students. You will be feared and hated, you may sometimes feel that only one man still believes in you. But you will be respected and listened to. Now get busy on that thesis.

I'm glad you like the friar, and you can keep him as long as you like. The Fellowship is for graduate work in theology. Yes, that's about what I want to do with music. I want to show, since only the Christian Church has developed a systematic tradition in music, that music bears a peculiarly intimate relationship to Christian dogma, besides to the history of Christianity. In other words, I want to show—my old problem!—why Bach is greater than Chopin, Franck than Tschaikowsky. Of course, I don't expect to get as far as Palestrina before I go over, though I may make a general survey first. And I expect they'll renew your scholarship in England a year if somebody tactfully suggests it.

Friday night I go to Bertram Brooker's and hear the Hart House Quartet rehearse for their special concert. Next Sunday—well, never mind that. Write this week, for God's sake. Monday night I leave.

Chicago is a good idea, and the Gatineau cottage is an excellent idea. With those alternatives, I'd drop Onawaw like an anchor.

I'm too tired to write any more now. Goodnight, or morning, my dearest pet.

Norrie

[*Ottawa, Ont.*]
Wednesday night [*25 April 1934*]

My dear Norrie,

This is just a very little letter because it is midnight and my energy is almost all used up, what with talking to two crowds of people this morning—an hour each, and listening to Lismer give a darn good talk this afternoon—he took our class just to show us how—but we weren't far off the track anyhow. Then I went to a tea at Mr. McCurry's, where I met Marius Barbeau and his wife, and Mrs. McCurry and her mother who are both keen musicians. They insisted on my staying to dinner—just the two McCurrys, Lismer and myself.

Kathleen Fenwick and I have been talking to these Normal School students all week. Which means a straight lecture for about twenty minutes at the first, then a talk about various pictures, methods, and men as we come to them. Usually about thirty people in each group. I was quite amazed to find that I am really developing some sort of speaking ability. I can go on for twenty minutes quite comfortably now. By the end of the week I shall have developed some sort of lecture on the French painters. And the exhibition itself is simply thrilling! The National Gallery has some remarkable paintings upstairs which I have had little time to examine as yet. But it is a great place. Mr. McCurry wanted me to stay on just now, but I want to get back—to Dr. Locke's job, to Toronto, to music, and mostly, to you. But I *was* glad to see Lismer walk in today. I am terribly keen about him. I can appreciate the work he is doing in Toronto, when I see how there is absolutely *nothing* of the sort done anywhere else in Canada.

Tell me what you think of my attempting to write up this exhibition for the *Forum*. I am beginning to think I can do it very well. And when I come back, I think I shall have done a good job here. I've got so much to tell you. Good night, my dearest.

Friday [27 *April 1934*]

As usual, your letter came just as I was beginning to get the least bit annoyed. It is very inconsistent of course, on my part, but when I feel a week older I think there should also be a letter. And there usually is. Yesterday I journeyed upstairs doing a little mild cussing to myself, and when I got to my room your letter was there! And, you idiot, your writing has put my eyes out of gear for the time being. I'll have to make you type your letters soon.

But really, I can't see this writing except through a haze, and then there are three pens, three lines and many thumbs. I can begin to understand the idea of *Nude Descending a Staircase* if this is the way an artist feels at times. The reason, of course, is quite simple. This afternoon I had my eyes examined and had to stay all afternoon to have drops of something put into them. My old glasses are not bad, Dr. Patterson said, but they perhaps over-corrected the astigmatism. I may not need to buy new ones, if I take care not to face the light too much, etc. (You'd laugh if you could see me trying to write, for I can see best an object far away, and as there are limits to the distance at which one can hold a pen and function on paper, I must sit with my eyes popped open, straining to see. Like this—

—you see I can't even see clearly enough to make my lines go in their proper place.)

Last night I saw three plays of the Drama Festival. Mary [Carman] is writing up the whole affair for the *Forum* and took me with her. I was excited about it very much. After all, I feel the contrast between the small town and the larger small town life quite keenly sometimes. And this was such fun!

I was thinking of you tonight at Bertram Brooker's, hearing the Hart House Quartet. I am so glad for you. You are beginning to know people who value your friendship and your intellect, people who will not scoff at you for being the bright little fair-haired boy at the head of the class.

Your kind words were pretty damn welcome to me. You seem to combine a twinge of conscience with a beacon light that keeps me somewhat on the alert.

I am at this stage now so I shall try writing like this:

—I can hardly realize that you leave on Monday to go such a long way. But you have done it before, of course, and we still manage to keep smiling. (Broad grin just for practice.) I haven't your address, you know, so you might send it to me as soon as you can. For if it takes two weeks —two weeks!!—to get a letter to you, I had better start in on the next instalment.

Well, my dear, it is one o'clock and your cross-eyed Susan is about to turn in for the night. I hope you have a pleasant journey out to Barebones. And do make sure about the mails. *And do take care of yourself.*

Darling, goodnight,
Helen

Toronto, Ont.
[*30 April 1934*]

I leave tomorrow night instead of tonight. The stagecoach, which is the mailcart—I ride on the mail sacks for about sixty miles—leaves Tompkins Friday and Friday only. Consequently I have to spend an extra day at either Toronto or Tompkins. My address out there is Stone, Saskatchewan—and I asked for bread. It's quite easy to remember. I get off the train in the middle of the night, of course, it will be pouring rain for the only time during the summer, and the supervising pastor will have to bury somebody and won't be there to meet me. And I'll get off the train and bay at the moon all night. I go with George Birtch as far as Winnipeg.

The Brooker affair was gorgeous. The Quartet was in good form—a Prokofiev—diabolically clever, a Weiner, whoever he is, sound and very interesting, and a Castelnuovo-Tedesco, enjoyable but not up to the others. I talked a good deal with the Brookers and I think they wanted me to stay longer, but I was sleepy. They asked me to call them in the fall.

Sorry about your eyes, but if you're having them seen to I'm glad. Get somebody to read you the letter, now that you've got this far. The drama festival must have been fun—I saw accounts of it here.

Well, darling, it just struck three—suppose I continue this later? I'll be desperately rushed tomorrow, but as soon as I can, on the train.

Norrie

Tor. & Ft. Wm. R.P.O.
May 2 [*1934*]

Written while Frye was on his way to his mission field in Saskatchewan.

My dearest-gug-gug-girl:

The train is pitching and tossing like a maniac in a nightmare, and my nerves are none too good anyhow. I'm in a hell of a bad temper right now, and I don't care who knows it. Tuesday morning I got up, finished packing, went shopping, got my ticket, had lunch at Eaton's. Then I came back, packed my trunk, went over to talk to Lane and take him back his essays, one of which had a big question mark on it in place of an A, meaning that the wretched girl (second year Household Ec.) had turned in an essay taken word for word from Kant. Then I got a phone call from Ida telling me that that little girl had packed a box of fruit for me, and would I call for it. So I went over, and went for dinner with her. She was on duty at the Library at six, and left in the middle of it. That was another hour, and I went back home and finished various odd jobs. By this time I was thoroughly tired out and at ten I took Ida over to Murray's for coffee. We came back, met Art [Cragg] and Florence, talked for a while, and said goodnight to Ida. This was at the Bell House. Then I tried to short cut to Charles St., and was assaulted by a half-drunken egg who was apparently a plainclothesman—it never even occurred to me to ask if he had a badge—who accused me of prowling, loitering, window-peeping and general vagrancy. He marched me into the house, dragged Ida downstairs, got a water-tight alibi from her, and finally went away very sulky. I don't know yet what he thought I was trying to do—

apparently waiting for an opportunity to sneak in and rape somebody. He swore there had been two calls to the police station about window-peepers from that house, which of course could not have been true. He was not simply a policeman making routine inquiries; he was a vulgar and abusive lout who got more so after he realized he had no case. The whole affair was as irritating as it was ridiculous—on any other night it would have been funny. As it was, I took a taxi and just made the train, so damned rattled I forgot to check my trunk. I slept with George in a lower berth—hot as hell. I didn't sleep much. So I'm sore.

But I still love you, and that's about all I've got the energy to say. I'll write later, of course, when I arrive.

Lovingly,
Norrie

Tompkins, Sask.
Friday [*4 May 1934*]

There's nothing much to say about the trip, pet, except that I made it—or most of it. There was a big oaf on board who got on my nerves a bit. He's in theology in Queen's, his father's a country minister, and his field is north of Tompkins, so that he has the same supervising pastor. I didn't sleep much the two nights, sharing a bunk with George, though better the second night than the first, and was out of temper anyhow, as you realize, no doubt. George sent his regards in the last letter, which I think I forgot to enclose. We docked in Winnipeg, where George left me, and I had to travel alone with the yokel, whose conversation was terrible—dislike of socialism, athletics, militarism, and so on. He sort of wore me down. We got here at eleven and our supervisory pastor met us—Kerley—a good head. Wife a lovely soft-spoken Scotch woman. Seven kids—oldest boy at college, ministry. Oldest girl a music teacher—piano—what I did to that piano, after not touching one for ten weeks, all morning! I have to rush this off, sweetheart, and I'll write tomorrow more fully.

Norrie

Gull Lake, Sask.
Saturday [*5 May 1934*]

Oh, darling:

If I were a mystic, this last week would register as my dark night of the soul. I'm as miserable as I can be, which is saying a good deal. I don't know why exactly—it's probably physiological, though less obviously so than some of your relapses. Nothing very bad has happened to me, but I'm in one of my spasms of mental and moral hypochondria, and nothing but talking to you will relieve it.

First of all, what's happened, which is routine stuff. The drive was uneventful. Then I was dropped off at Walter Meyer's, who is responsible for generally looking after me. I went into the garden and found Mrs. Meyer, a shrewd, cynical, reserved sort of woman, and tried to make small talk for three everlasting hours. I was told that Harold Anderson and Ralph Williams had set the precedent of moving week by week to a new place. I hinted that I didn't care for that idea, and felt her stiffen up and freeze in a kind of sullen hostility. This field is supposed to look after paying for my board, but if I spend a week in each place I get boarded for nothing, and the field gains accordingly. The local school teacher, Mrs. Meyer's sister, works for nothing—ten dollars a month to be exact—teaching eight or nine out of twelve grades, and boards around a month at a time. I revived a bit when she came in—lively and ugly—typical country school teacher—helped dry the dishes, and managed to begin to feel more or less at home. Then I was shipped over here to Mrs. McCrae, mother of Mrs. Meyer. Walter Meyer is a good head. Mrs. McCrae is probably the nearest approach to your motherly soul, and isn't so near at that—she won't coddle me, and I want to be coddled, badly. Then I went to bed, and the whole pent up force of irregular eating, uncomfortable living, unspeakable sleeping, nervousness, terror, exasperation, nostalgia, constipation, over-ripe cherries (don't tell Ida), that officious fool of a plainclothesman, worry over my trunk, which hasn't arrived, etc. lodged a humiliating and undignified but very explicit protest—hives. I was sure it was bugs at first, but it wasn't. There wasn't an inch on my body that didn't itch. So I spent a hell of a night again, getting some sleep toward morning. But I've been resting all day, thank God, and tomorrow I take two of my three appointments, getting around in a car. Monday the fun starts, along with the horse and the visiting. Worst of it is I can't figure out this damn country—the farms are infernally big—you look over the horizon and all you can see is your own farm. I don't know who will help with the horse. I take Stone here at three and Stonepile, eight miles east, at seven, and stay at Stonepile where the animal is. He's quite a gentle animal, I gather; they've got a wilder one in store for me as soon as I get used to the idea. I'm not fussy about changing, but didn't tell them that. I'm scared to death of Stonepile—Williams had some kind of row there—three places shut their doors in his face and the people used to congregate in the schoolhouse (or church) after he got through preaching to raise hell. But they've made all kinds of good resolutions to "treat the new student white," Mrs. McCrae says. Christ, I hope so.

I'm really all right, you know, but I do feel depressed. I daren't think of four months and a half, or I'd fly into a panic, and I daren't think of anything in Toronto, or I'd go insane. I had a horrible spell of claustrophobia in looking over the prairies this afternoon—no trees much, no chance of rain. It isn't exactly a rolling country here, it's more like a fretful, tossing country. The grasshoppers just began to raise hell last year, and are starting in in earnest this year, and everyone is feeling depressed, so I have to cheer up soon. The shock is abrupt—too abrupt—but I shouldn't have been in such a state in the first place. But sometimes I almost feel that if you have serenely strolled off to England before September 27 or so I'll be running around in circles—but, of course, I won't. Go ahead if duty calls, but that's a long way away.

You'll get a flood of letters from me, some passionate, some bored and bothered, some mere calf-bawling and self-pity, some purely sexual—I can feel the need for you as a general Slough of Despond fairly obviously. Take them all, but not seriously. I don't want to distress you. I don't think I shall be particularly energetic this first week, and if I have to endure riding stiffness and scratch hives at the same time I'll go nuts. The hives alone have pretty well sent me off. Goodbye, for now, pet—oh, my dear.

Tuesday. They left me off at Stonepile over Sunday and for the following week, which means that the letter can't possibly leave on Tuesday, as it would over in Stone. I'm sorry, but I didn't invent the mail service. I wrote this on Saturday night. I spent the rest of that night scratching myself when asleep until I woke up, and then setting my teeth and trying not to scratch until morning. Sunday I spent getting up my sermon in the morning, then walked to church at Stone and attended Sunday School. This is run all winter by two old people called the Bonfoys, and has three classes. The adult one asked me to do the lesson, and on such short notice I didn't do much with it. Mrs. Bonfoy is an oppressive and slightly irascible old lady, and knew more about the lesson than I did, although I made quite a display, as it was one of the passages [John H.] Michael dwelt on last year, thank goodness—Christ's entry into Jerusalem. Then I took the service and got through it all right—preached on the first commandment: "Thou shalt have no other gods before me." (Pardon me a minute: the two front legs have just fallen out of my chair.) I said that the worship of idols was a worship of spirits, some good, some evil: that it took more effort and energy to try to get the latter on the side of the worshippers: that interesting an evil spirit could only be done by making evil actions: hence idolatry ended up in the worship of the worst things one could imagine; e.g., Moloch and child-sacrifice. That with the collapse of superstition there returned a new kind of idolatry—the worship of men instead of God. The present trend to dictatorships is therefore idolatry, and there is nothing to save us from the same progression toward the evil, which is why Hitler & Co. appeal to the worst and cruellest instincts of mankind. Then they took me in a car out to Stonepile, about ten miles of the most complicated trail one could imagine, all of which I am supposed to remember. Mostly younger people over at Stonepile—evening services, I'm told, are poorly attended. Two dismal schoolhouses, one wheezy organ and one dropsical piano, both badly played. I haven't seen the field's pianos yet. This week I am staying with the [Hugh] Mackintoshes—the man the typical dour Scotchman, the wife attractive in an early middle-aged sort of way, and quite friendly. I change boarding houses week by week. This one is comfortable, probably one of the best I'll be getting. Yesterday morning I walked 2 miles to Stewarts', had lunch there and got the horse—an absurd doddering twenty-year-old mare named Kate. She's quiet all right—in fact she's practically motionless, when I'm on her. I made a call on another Stewart family, and with the aid of the hired man managed to persuade her to stumble off home. This morning Mrs. Mackintosh and I chased her all around the yard—there's no feed, they have to be turned loose—and got the brute saddled. I'm not at all stiff today: perhaps I didn't ride far enough.

I'm in for a tough summer, what with boarding around in such a huge area. Twenty more Sundays. I don't quite know how I'll survive—I get horrible twinges still, but I'm more resigned. Don't be surprised if I don't answer your letters sometimes, as I may not get them (as in this case) for some days after I've written. Once I get settled time will go faster, as I've lived through a couple of years in the last week.

Very lovingly,
Norrie

Ottawa, Ont.
Monday night (May 7 [*1934*])

My dear—

I have just realized with a shock how long it is since I wrote to you last. And I don't know how long it takes to get a letter to your stone pile. Let me know how long this one is on the way, then perhaps I can time things a little better.

Poor Norrie—imagine you being mistaken for a ravager of women in boarding houses. I am inclined to doubt that that man was a genuine member of the police force. What he could have been up to I have no idea. But just when you were on edge about your trip and nearly missing your train was certainly no time for such delay. Sleeping two in a lower berth into the bargain. I don't see how there could be room for a man of George's size and you in one of those little cages.

I am just a little fed up tonight. I would like some quietness, and time to talk to you, and not listen to Kathleen Fenwick's English italics for a while. Thinking of you even is like coming to rest in a holy place.

Went to Kingsmere for supper tonight with the McCurrys, Marius Barbeau, K.F. [Kathleen Fenwick], A.Y. Jackson and Ruth Elliott who is a young painter. Just got home. The party was fun, but I was not feeling like talking much. I rode out in the back of the car with Mr. Barbeau and tried to talk to him but he is a bit difficult at times. Quite a susceptible Frenchman—and the source of endless amusement on the part of Mr. and Mrs. McCurry. Quite kindly of course for they couldn't be anything else. But Marius doesn't treat his wife very well. He has almost completed a book on Krieghoff.

I have been side-tracked again on the damned thesis, although what I am doing is interesting. I am writing a 5,000 word report on the national and international loan exhibition service offered by the National Gallery. This is to go to the International Museums Conference under the auspices of the League of Nations, which will be held in Madrid in October. They invited us to send a delegate and a report on any problems or unique service rendered by us. We're not sending a delegate but we are sending a report as you see.

Had a marvellous letter from Norah [McCullough] last week. She is going to England this summer on Carnegie money—it is a big secret as yet. Bless her! She cheered me up immensely with a good word here and there. The only thing Baldwin is worrying about is whether she will come back to the Gallery. He seems to think she may get married and never return. And he wants to make her sign a promise to return. So she is quite pleased to feel herself so indispensable. I was telling Mr. McCurry all this about Baldwin and he laughed. He is entirely in sympathy with the woman who wants a home and married life and a job. Says it is a problem that a woman must work out, and that—oh well I needn't tell you exactly what he said because he put into words what I feel and know to be true. And he has tried it. He and his wife are two of the finest people I shall ever know. I told him that Norah would never let anyone down. That I wanted to do the same thing myself, not of course going into detail. But I did mention you before to them. They will know fairly well how I stand in most ways. Living this way is all very well for the purpose of study and development, and because of the peculiar arrangements of fate, but it won't do for ever, you know.

The last two nights I have wakened up after horrible dreams. Sunday morning I was in a cold sweat, not knowing exactly where I was since I dreamt (don't laugh, it wasn't at all funny) that I was just about raped by a gorilla who had me naked except for some pink silk shorts (true to the feminine instinct for being suitably clad even in emergencies!) and as I got away from the ghastly brute and walked up a main street of a town he kept poking and pawing at me, and then some men looked on and did the same thing (not at all in a gentlemanly way) and nobody offered me an overcoat or anything. God! was I scared!

Next night I dreamt that George [Clarke] came back and that I was hypnotized into being crazy about him. That idea took such a firm hold that I thought when half awake that I would write to him or see him some way and see what the reaction would be. Of course I knew even in that state what the result would be and decided something along the same lines as what you remarked about taking Ida out. But this blasted dreaming is beginning to make me a little sore because it takes me off guard. Now for heaven's sake don't tell me I'm getting neurotic. After all you had a dream once yourself about a tiger woman. But those are just some of the things I should like to talk about quietly if you were here, grandfather.

I was talking to a nurse who has just come from the west and tells me of some of the terrible conditions there, of people on relief, dried-out areas, shifting sand, children without clothes to go to school, Regina College closed down. Heaven help you. Have you got into a community like that? And are you stiff and tired from unaccustomed exercise?

I had a letter from Mrs. Turkington who offers me 80 bucks to go to camp. I am beginning to weaken about staying here all summer and using up all my money. I have to help see Roy [Kemp] through next year, you know, and this recent heat wave just about wilted me as far as studying goes. But having written you what may sound like a doleful letter, I shall be up and at 'em tomorrow. I am not doleful at all really. You know how it is. I just feel like howling at the moon. I am really surprised at my ability to adapt myself to circumstances in general and have such a good time altogether.

I'll get to bed now. My honour, respect, friendship, love, desire—what else? Take what you wish, you have everything now in your keeping. Goodnight, my dearest.

H.

152 Argyle Ave., Ottawa
Wednesday [*9 May 1934*]

My dear,

Your letter came on Monday and I was a little depressed and didn't have enough cheerfulness to write to you then. I didn't want to add to your troubles. My poor darling, I was afraid you wouldn't be having much fun when I began to hear what conditions are out west. And that episode with the policeman was a little too much. If your trunk hasn't arrived yet, you might write to Roy to look after it. You were bound to feel physically on the rocks when you got there. After all, you've just been through another set of exams and that's no joke. You've done a lot of work this year, and don't forget that either. And don't you dare call yourself a narrow and secluded pedant, for you're not. You get physically on your feet, and take care of your health—it is *so* important—and in a very few years you are going to be known as one of the finest scholars on the continent. I *know* that now, just as much as I know that if you wanted me to, I should probably travel after you to the ends of the earth with a hot-water bottle and a spoon full of medicine to administer at regular intervals. But apart from the tediousness of the journey and the weariness resulting from practically a week's loss of sleep and the extreme heat which latter is the cause of hives when you have eaten much fruit—you will be all right, won't you?

As for the people, you will probably find them more congenial after a while. Helping with the dishes is a very good thing to do—and try to remember to speak simply to them. For after all this time I am used to what you are apt to say—but you overwhelm me even yet pretty often. It is hard, being a genius. It is also hard being the friend of a genius.

Having waited this long, I'll not keep you in suspense any more. I'm not going to England in September. I've talked to H.O. [McCurry] about it, and he will arrange definitely to give me the scholarship a year from now, so that I will not lose it by waiting, as Lismer feared. He tells me privately that he is well satisfied with my work and will recommend me to the committee. They will pass me on the strength of my thesis. I began work on it today, as I have been working on this loan collection report which is now in rough shape but almost finished. There are times when I wish I could write as quickly and as well as you do, but I'm doing as well as I can, and my brain is working a lot better than it did. There is a lot in keeping to regular hours, and getting into a steady routine, as you say. But I have never been able to do it—before now.

I'm going to write to Baldwin and Lismer to be sure that they will offer me a job next year, and I think I will have the thing cinched. I am asking to be allowed to work next year either in Toronto or Ottawa, preferably Toronto in order to do some work in history at the University. H.O. is asking Constable how long it takes to get an M.A. from the Courtauld Institute.

H.O. has given me a pretty confidential job—making a summary of all the requests for grants and scholarships. They are to be discussed at the next meeting of the Canadian Committee for Carnegie Grants on May 29th when my fate along with others will be gone into. It has just about given me the willies, reading the begging letters for museum grants, and all the qualifications some students have. (I may say, though, that I think, when all is said and done, that I am just as promising and worthy as any, considering age, training, experience, inclination, etc.) Makes me feel rather an ass to be making out applications of my own competitors—except that they all want what I've already got.

I have written to accept Mrs. Turkington's offer of $80 for two months at camp. Everyone advises me to go, so I'm going. Evidently I'll have the rest of my life to study in. So that's that.

Your sermon sounded awfully well, from the outline you gave me. I think those people in Stone, and Stonepile, and Cactus Plant, and Parched Throat will be hearing the best sermons this summer that they have had from a student for a long time. And if you get busy and call on them all, they'll be your friends in no time. But the boarding about each week is a God-awful arrangement and I think they might realize it.

I have done my best to be a little Pollyanna—I am trying all the time to keep on an even sort of temper these days, for if I once get down in the mouth it's quite a process to snap out of it. I am hoping and hoping that you will be successful on your field, because if you are this time you won't need to do *that* again. And always remember I am fairly bursting with pride—being proud of you, and loving you, and wishing to comfort you. I had a queer thing happen last Monday night around twelve. I had gone to bed, and I thought you were with me. Your presence and—almost—your touch were so real to me that I very nearly spoke to you. I miss you dreadfully.

Roy [Kemp] has been doing quite well on his exams. Latest report was that he was considering three summer jobs: (1) gold mining/digging —in Keith MacIver's mine. (2) Y.M.C.A. camp at Couchiching. (3) Camp Franklin on Georgian Bay—I think he will go there. Photography & play fiddle all summer. Develops photographs and takes study groups in photography. Roy last year cleared $150. I am awfully glad because then I may not have to help him with his fees quite so much. Rest of family will probably go to Gordon Bay.

I can't think of anything else much to tell you—Marion [Kemp] says Ernie [Harrison] now on the high seas on his way to Africa.

Goodnight,
Helen

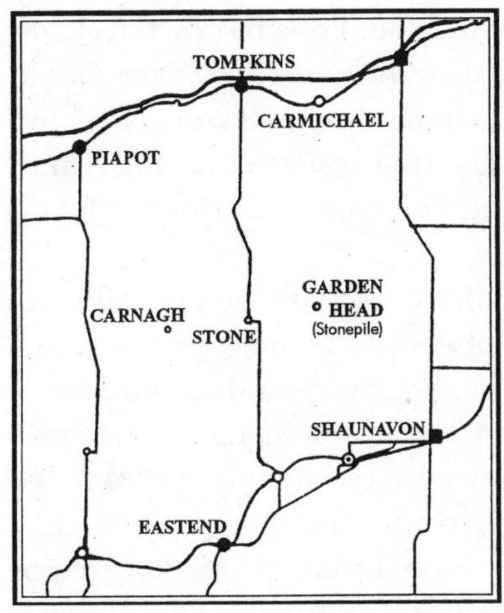

Stone, Sask.
Saturday. May 12 [*1934*]

Dearest:

No news much except about the horse. She's a lazy old strumpet, and if I haven't got a switch handy she'll hardly go at all, except when a road crosses, when she gets the idea that both of the ways I am not going would be infinitely preferable to the one I *am* going. She looks around just to one side and then to the other in an injured sort of way to see if maybe I won't take her home and turn her loose. Wednesday I didn't go out much, but very early Thursday morning the family I was staying with decided to go to town and I saddled the old Windstorm and rode over to Stone. I got through a fairly steep and difficult coulee (valley with a dried-up stream running through) but coming up the infernal bridle fell off, and try as I would she would have nothing to do with taking the bit in her mouth. So I turned her into the next farmhouse and stayed there three hours. Then I came over here to McCraes' and have been lying in, so to speak, ever since. I have been waiting for some time for Meyer to show up with the car, and am trying to write this and listen to Mrs. McCrae at the same time. Mrs. McCrae talks the most God-awful English—I am almost picking up a dialect—but she's a good old soul, with an obsession against drinking and smoking: I understand against dances too. More later—have to rush this off as Meyer has come.

Lovingly,
Norrie

Garden Head, Sask.
[*14 May 1934*]

I am beginning to get a bit more cheerful now, sweetheart, particularly since your last letter came. It seems almost too good to be true that you are actually going to be in Toronto next fall. All my good resolves about wanting you to develop yourself and stand on your own feet and see the world are fast beginning to weaken in front of my four-month sentence. Oh, darling! —and if you *are* taking graduate work, couldn't you manage the Blake course? Blake is about my only devouring enthusiasm. I don't share much with you. And you could contribute a lot on the art side. Think it over, anyway.

I'm sorry about the dreams, but I'm afraid they are the inevitable result of celibacy. No, of course you're not getting neurotic: those things are quite normal, unpleasant as they are. Your conscious mind knows you can't have me for four months (Oh God!); your subconscious mind offers George—something like that, anyway. No, I shouldn't care to see you reopening communications—obsolete attachments never die: they only become disorganized, and can always be stirred up again in a stumbling, awkward and painful revived existence. This from one who knows. The parallel with Ida and me is not exact, as I never went with Ida. But for over a month you have had no sexual life at all, hence the protest represented by the gorilla. September 23 I have to hold services here: September 24 I shall be starting east; in two days (sooner if the train will move faster with me pushing it) I shall be in Toronto, and if you are in town my arms will be around you, and you will find yourself with even fewer clothes than the gorilla left you.

I am horribly homesick and thoroughly miserable, yet I can't think I made a mistake in coming out here. It isn't that everything—horse, country life, standards of living, moral attitudes, social position in the community, conversation, interests—are so absolutely different from anything I've been accustomed to. I can never get accustomed to them. I would commit suicide without the slightest hesitation if I thought I should have to stay out here all my life. Some things about the country are absolutely and irrevocably false, and they make me squirm under them. For instance, if old Mrs. McCrae knew that a young lady of whom I was most inordinately proud and fully intended to marry danced, smoked, swore and had no moral objections to playing cards she would be scandalized, and in being her minister I sometimes cannot help but feeling that I am tacitly assenting, through a lack of courage, to a monstrous and absurd scale of values. Of course, I know that outspokenness on such a topic would be quixotic; that one must work from the inside, in their own language and sets of ideas, but the revulsion remains. But the cheapness and superficiality of their living! one would think that people living so close to nature and the soil would have a better idea of the difference between the simple and the inane, whether in music, art, literature, education, amusement or morals. The artificial culture of the city has its faults, but what these wretched farmers use for culture is more false and hollow than the most glittering and vacuous display of sophistication, as it does not even imitate anything that is good. I am quite sure that I shall not come out a second summer; if I can show this year that I can get through something that I am totally unfitted to do, that should satisfy Drs. [Walter T.] Brown and Lane.

And yet, I don't despise the *people*, I love and respect them. I am very grateful for the way in which they have helped me out and been good to me time and again. I admire the cheerful, quiet, uncomplaining way they get through their long and hard routine. I like the way they joke about the grasshoppers, and then silently set their shoulders to fight them. No, there's nothing wrong with the people themselves. What's so damnably evil are all these things foisted upon them which they are deceived into thinking good: trash for the arts, shibboleths and fetishes for religion. And it's precisely here that I'm helpless. Oh, well.

But naturally, being jerked out of my own element into another has left me struggling and gasping, with no really earnest thoughts about anyone except myself and my own welfare. The stiffness from horseback riding is largely over, but the other difficulties are still there. The brute won't go without a switch, and she has a fearfully rough trot—I give that on the authority of an expert, not my own. Then there's catching her in the morning—she runs all over the field to get away from me. And if her infernal bridle falls off I can't make her take the bit in her mouth and have to tow her in to the next farm. Last Sunday I couldn't get the big chimera out of McCrae's yard: she'd run out of one gate and into the other. So I persuaded the hired man to go over to Stonepile with me, and then changed horses with Chester Stewart going to church—my new horse trotted and galloped all the way to church and I didn't mind it a bit. But I have nothing but pity for the poor half-starved brute when I'm not on it.

No, this isn't that dried-out area—that's around Regina, and we're to the west of it. There has never been a total crop failure here, though last year's was badly damaged by grasshoppers. This year they are anticipating devastation and destruction from the insects. They're worried too because there has been no rain all spring. The grass is withering and the soil is sandy and crumbling. Today it's about a hundred in the shade—or would be if there were any shade—Saturday it was freezing.

The Sunday services get my goat at times, but I'll get along with them, I suppose. Yesterday morning there were thirteen people out, and at that we practically filled the school, which has eleven pupils. I talked on motherhood, trying to show that just as the concept of Fatherhood is contained in God, so is that of motherhood contained in nature, or our environment. That nature presents a moral order working, in spite of everything, toward the good; it is not indifferent or negative, let alone hostile or malicious. That many of our present troubles were brought by waste, extravagance and carelessness; that if we treated the world with the respect our mother is entitled to, nothing she could send would be too hard to handle, and an active cooperation would be possible. That would need a reference or two to emergent evolution to pull it out of the platitudinous state, and it didn't go over so well, so at the other two places I just talked about the loyalty and affection of Jesus and Mary for each other, and how the Christian religion alone had brought the idea of the sacredness of motherhood, as was evidenced by all the Madonna pictures, as compared to the mere goddess of fertility ideas of the world before Jesus. I have to talk about the Christian religion in fairly broad terms, as Catholics, Anglicans, Christian Scientists, Adventists and Lutherans all come to hear me.

Oh, dearest, I love you so. You seemed so fearfully far away until I got your letter. I'll probably bore you a good deal this summer, but please be patient, as it won't be so long, and if I ever get my arms around you again there will be no long periods of misery and heartache in between. If you are doing interesting work, and I am too, it won't hurt being away from each other, perhaps, for a few months at a time, as we can devote ourselves to other enthusiasms, or, in the abominable jargon, there could be an active sublimation. That would be temporarily satisfactory, I think. But I do want you so badly! right beside me, where I can see you and touch you and talk to you and live with you. I can't see you; I can only stretch my imagination till it's dead, like a worn-out elastic; I can only touch you in a dream; I can only talk to myself on this hideous cold paper, remembering that you will be reading it a week or two later, when I'm doing something else. As for living with you, all I do is wonder a hundred times a day what you are doing. "Out of sight, out of mind"—if that were only true! Marriage with the right woman, living together till we are dead—how utterly right and sane that idea is! I don't just want to love you; I want companionship and friendship—real friendship of constant contact. If there is one point where the modern world stands condemned, it is in balking and wincing at marriage—at postponing it till our youth, when all our generous and sociable impulses are highest, is over, and a premature middle-aged complacency is forced on us in our middle or later twenties. At trying to make a man do practically everything before it grants the one thing that gives balance and security to all the rest. At making a virtue of waiting and suspense and sneering at our strainings at the leash. God himself seems to fade away on these grim prairies: not that He is far away—I never felt that; but He seems curiously impersonal. That, of course, is largely because I left Blake at Stone, the nearest piano a mile away, and you in Ottawa. I am getting a sound and accurate knowledge of the Bible; the Bible is magnificent, but, in spite of what everyone says, it is a book for admiration rather than intimacy, like the natural world. Besides, its associations are not all favorable in this environment.

Please write fairly often—once a week anyway—and tell me occasionally that you love me.

Friday night. I haven't been exerting myself particularly this week. Wednesday I rode over to a family of Americans, the Clarkes. They were kind and congenial, but staying there overnight was a bad mistake—bugs. And it was bugs at McCraes' too, not hives. God! how these infernal things do torture me! They don't bother the thick louts who live here, apparently, but fasten on strangers.

I am not happy, but the only things worrying me now are the grasshoppers, shyness, bugs, horses that run away and are stupid old fools anyway with trots like earthquakes, vulgarity, no pianos, no Helen, homesickness, four months, etc.

Lovingly,
Norrie

[*Ottawa*]
Tuesday night. 10:30 [22 *May* 1934]

My dearest,

Your letter came at noon today, and I waited until after lunch to read it, for it looked so thick and full of news and when I have to store up my eagerness for so long between times I like to visit you quietly.

I wanted to write to you this weekend but several things prevented it. For one—I have been writing almost steadily for so long that sometimes my hand and arm are so stiff that they just won't function. And you know how much I enjoy filling up pages just for the exercise and to see the black marks put on thus and so. And if I can't enjoy the exercise I can't seem to think anyway.

Saturday I worked some more on the Loan Collection effort. In the afternoon I went to Kingsmere with McCurrys and Fenwick again. We had tea on the lawn and Mrs. Jenkins (Mrs. McCurry's mother) came over from *her* cottage and had tea with us. Dorothy McCurry sang and I played for her—Bach, and two Blake songs written by a young Englishman who was in Toronto last winter, whose name I've forgotten. They were lovely. Dorothy has a bamboo flute that she plays well—I am learning on one of hers which she loaned me. Professor [Hubert] Kemp is a disciple of Alan Sly and makes marvellous flutes, and I am about to consult him about making them for I am billed to do something of the sort at Camp this summer. I told the Turk [Mrs. Turkington] I would do that, talk on music, play the piano, take sketching classes and give talks on pictures (reproductions from the National Gallery, talks à la Lismer's picture-study stuff). That pleased her immensely and so she heartily agreed I needed time for quietness and she would arrange to let me live with Margaret Govan. At any rate, I am not going to be tucking youngsters in bed at all. For which heaven be praised. The rest will all be very good experience for me. The Turk is giving me an absolutely free hand. She seemed fearfully impressed with my humble abilities from the first last year, and I still don't understand why.

Last night I went to Mrs. Jenkins' annual recital. Vocal pupils. The best song recital I've ever been to—of pupils that is. Mrs. Jenkins played all the accompaniments herself and almost stole the show. I must tell you more about that family later. I want you to know them. They are among the few finest people I know. I mean, I keep the inner circle very select and exclusive. My most precious ones.

I am very tired by now. I am sorry to have written in jerks but it seems so hard to write fast enough. I find letters more unsatisfactory than I ever could have imagined—by way of trying to talk to you. It all seems so hanged one-sided—all this deferred reply, long-distance sort of thing. And I can't tell you tonight how I love you because I want to show you and have you read me a story and put me to bed. And there it is. All I can do is look at your picture, and the twinkling eye mocks me sometimes and the serious eye is sweet and kindly. Sometimes it almost seems to change expression and assumes a much graver expression. For you have grown much more mature in the last two years, and your face shows a man's look. You are mine and I am yours and I love to think of it. I am never sure why such a wonderful thing could happen, or how. When I get that far, I wonder about God.

Goodnight,
Helen

Carnagh, Sask.
[*23 May 1934*]

My dear:

I'm over at Carnagh for this week. Sunday morning there was a wind blowing from the west. It wasn't exactly a cyclone, nor exactly a hurricane, but it was a wind. It could lift three tons of soil at once and hurl it straight in your eyes. The soil wasn't so bad: it was dodging rocks and chickens and little children and back-houses that got me nervous. I got to Stonepile Church all right, past an old fool who has a spite against the church and turns out every Sunday to put seed in his ground, where everyone going to church can see him. He didn't gain a great deal by his gesture, as the wind blew all his seed into the road. I started for Stone, and got about three miles and collapsed at a farmhouse. That was Chester Stewart's, where I got my horse in the first place. Stewart rode over to Stone with me, leading both horses. I just made it, and spent about a quarter of an hour combing my hair out when I got there. I refused flatly to try to make Carnagh—it blew up a rain, of course. They tell me I'll get this kind of weather every Sunday, as they always have. Monday afternoon I set out for Carnagh and got there all right, though when the trail stopped and the open prairie started I lost my way and roamed around for the longest time, trying to find [Donald] Neely's, the postmaster. I am staying here this week, which is not particularly a good idea, in some ways. The young chap who is head of the household is friendly and better educated than the average, but the wife has a tendency to sing and the children (two) to make a great deal of noise, besides a radio. There is a kitchen, a dining-living room, and a bedroom. In the last named the four in the family sleep. The old man who owns the farm, however, sleeps on a cot with me in the dining-living room. His idea of disrobing for the night is to remove his socks, shoes and trousers. As they eat breakfast in my bedroom, rising is more or less called for. As I write, the wife, the radio, the kids, and the cream separator are all going at once, which accounts for the slightly befuddled tone of this epistle. I am getting more used to that infernal horse—we have had several arguments lately about where we are going and I've won them all. And I'm gradually getting able to trot on the beast without wondering if I can shut my mouth in time to save my kidneys.

This is going emphatically to be a week in which very little will get done. By the time things are quiet my room-mate goes to bed, and from the above remarks about space accommodations you can see there isn't much else for me to do either. Goodnight for now.

[*Ottawa, Ont.*]
Friday noon [*25 May 1934*]

My darling—

I'm so sorry—it is a week since I wrote to you last and I have been waiting for another letter from you in order to answer it. Your letter on Monday was so perfect—and so like you—I could have cried. Except for the fact that it was too fine for any such childish tricks.

I've had a blue time the last few days. It has rained and rained and rained. Mrs. McCurry has been away, Fenwick left for England last Friday, for two days Miss Scott and Mrs. Macoun were away—and altogether I was pretty lonely. Then that report on loan collections had to be rewritten because I made it so dull and so completely a rehash of annual reports and the Canada Year Book that Brownie [Eric Brown] said to do it over again. Perfectly right of course, and on reading it over I feel so annoyed at having turned in such an undigested mass of facts. Of course, I had an idea that a report should be a lot of generalities, and it was. But now I understand that a report should be written as well as any other project, with the same care and attention to making it readable. So I've been two and a half days doing that and feeling rather useless and stupid and a dull little person with no right to think she could produce anything in the literary way at all. But that is the way I have to write anything—with grunts and toil and sweat—and it sometimes turns out to be half-interesting by the time I've written it six times. I can't seem to do a thing spontaneously the way Mary [Carman] can—she sat down and wrote her drama festival criticism in a couple of afternoons, and it had a dash and sparkle that I'm not sure of ever being able to achieve. Brownie is a good scout—he said "you have a lot of valuable material there, but you should pay some attention to organizing it into a readable story." That is really a gentleman—for an article isn't anything without unity and solidity—and mine hadn't either.

Well, my dear, I'm going to pocket my spleen and get back to work—it's the only way to keep sane in this weather, what with this and that, and most of all, you being where you are. But you can't keep me down long. Oh my dearest!

H.

Ottawa, Ont.
Saturday [*26 May 1934*]

Darling, I'm afraid I'm in another stew, and I need to talk to you about it. It's about the scholarship and next year. The committee meets on the 29th (next Tuesday) to consider grants and scholarships. I have to submit a report of my year's work and a plan for future work & a request regarding next year. I wrote to Lismer and Baldwin asking them to put in a good word for me with regard to a job when I return from London, and also one for next year. I said that renewal of the scholarship depends partly on my having a job in view. So Baldwin wrote back, very kind letter, these being the main points:

"I will do all I can to help you along.

"For your consolation I may say that Mr. McCurry is extraordinarily pleased with your work since you went to Ottawa and has been asking me about jobs in the same way as your letter does.

"Now about the question of next year—I feel that it would not be a good idea for you to delay in getting over to London. Your present degree is all that you really need in the way of decorations and I think that it is of the utmost importance that you should take advantage of any opportunity which is offered to proceed with Art Education in the best possible place. My advice is therefore to direct your efforts to get over to London as soon as possible.

"With regard to the job after you return from the Courtauld—I cannot promise so far ahead but I feel that we need an extra person on the staff and if I can arrange to employ one, and much can be done in the space of a year, the job, if there is one, will be offered to you. If you do not go to London next winter however I will promise to see what can be done in the same connection here."

You see, I said that I wished to enrol at the university for graduate work which would definitely bear upon the work for the next year at London. If possible with a view to getting an M.A. I have been looking up the requirements for entrance to the M.A. course and I'll enclose one little note I made of it. But there are requirements which I'm not sure can be gotten over—I'd have to try an examination equivalent to the standard of the U. of London, in seven different subjects taken in the B.A. course. Things like:

General History of Art in Europe

History of Architecture

One of following special periods —Byzantine etc. (6 of them)

Two of " " " —Painting, Drawing, Engraving in Italy; in France & Spain; Sculpture in Italy etc. etc. (11 to choose from.)

Technical methods in Painting, Drawing, Engraving & Sculpture & their history.

History of Aesthetic Theories and of the criticism of art, *or* Iconography & The History of Costume.

Subsidiary subject: European History (either A.D. 395–1500 or A.D. 1500–1914)

Now I'm not sure whether I could register first in the one year course—there are two courses. One is called the Academic Diploma Course in The History of Art and is the one that scholarship students are evidently supposed to take. Subjects are exactly the same as these in the B.A. Honours Degree in The History of Art which takes two or three years, but one takes four of them instead of seven + subsidiary subject. Naturally in a shorter time one wouldn't learn as much.

I talked to Mr. McCurry about it yesterday and he said not to pay any attention to Baldwin's letter as it was just echoing Lismer, and he hadn't thought anything beyond what Lismer says. I told him that I could see a need in Toronto for a well-trained lecturer at the gallery if they ever get their faculty of fine arts going. For they will need to use the gallery. And the day of sloppy lecturing on art in Canada is about over. I am not a professional lecture goer or a chaser after cultah or any of those creatures. But on the other hand I can't get the necessary academic background in no time. H.O. said that I was to do what I like about it. I can't count on the Carnegie money for more than one year's support in London. But an M.A. would be invaluable. He thinks I should take another year here before I go to London to consolidate my ideas and to take some history at the university. He says that I've got all my life ahead of me yet. (You see Lismer is afraid they'll change their mind about me and I'll be left in the cold. Hence the urgency of shooting me across the pond in such a hurry.) H.O. on the other hand has promised to arrange that. Eric Brown is back now from England and he will back me up to the committee. E.B. said today that I had some interesting plans, and they'd all work out—just in casual conversation of course.

Then I got a letter from Norah today—

"I think I am to leave about the 20th of June. I am more thrilled about escaping than the thought of the new experience but expect that will come. If you get a chance to get away in September, *take it*! All the routine of galleries here will be unchanged when you return. Also, what you will get away is a thousand times more valuable. There is really very little to learn here in comparison. There may be change of government, a change of policy, a war, who knows what else and little Helen will miss her chance. Helen, if they are keen enough to send you once, you will probably have another chance to go after the special things—and a salary sooner to finance your own private ventures. For heaven's sake don't be timid about going. I really think *that* is what is worrying you—"

I have to make out my application before Monday for a renewal of the scholarship, so I am just doing my thinking on paper— It doesn't need to be decided this minute but certainly fairly soon. McCurry knows fairly well what I'm after and he'll try to keep me here next year if the Toronto scheme doesn't work. He says "You'll get a job all right, so don't worry!" But am I fussing too much about an M.A.? After all does it matter much?

Dearest, I've been pondering so long about the whole silly question that I've made it far more puzzling than it need be. Being on the job here in Ottawa at the centre of things I can keep a wary eye out for developments. But you are so far away, and sometimes I feel like a little girl lost, and I want you so badly. It's all very well having a job that is thrilling as a job can be— Perhaps I should be satisfied with that. Lots of women have had to make a job their only object in life. But I need you too. Sometimes I think that perhaps I should be content to be a meek little wife to you and not run the risk of losing you by dashing half way across the world and leaving you. On the other hand, I'd lose you probably anyhow if I did become an echo of yourself.

If you just weren't several provinces away I could get all this nonsense straightened out right now. But as it is I'm just giving my best pajamas a saltwater bath like any homesick schoolgirl. I love you desperately—oh Norrie—I must stop. I'm afraid I'm not behaving very well. But I need you so. I started out my stay in Ottawa by thinking that perhaps I should be quite reasonable, but there are times when it seems almost unbearable without you. This is just a very blue night and I'll cheer up tomorrow and tell you something interesting.

Goodnight my darling.

Monday. Weekend continued cloudy with slight showers. But here we are again bright and smiling.

The committee meeting is tomorrow. I had a talk with Eric Brown today and he is quite favorable with regard to my scheme, but suggested that I might go in the fall and plan to stay two years. Lismer wrote to me on the 24th of May on two filing cards, in an awful rush. Very kind letter. Says he doesn't really think there is much chance of his being able to squeeze out a job for the next year, but there definitely is after I get back. Further, he doesn't want me to come looking for a job, he wants me to go over and come back fully qualified enough to impress the powers that be. Fairly good reasoning there. But I told H.O. and he said if they won't have one for you, I'll arrange it myself. In the meantime we must get over the first step, just one thing at a time is important. And the main thing is to get your application past the committee. So I made out a report of what I've done during the past year and ended with a strong plea for a thorough training, saying that I desired to acquire as sound an academic training as I could and that I would do everything possible toward becoming a well-informed and experienced gallery worker. H.O. asked me to be present at the meeting to take notes of everything—everything else but my own case, of course. I'd call that decidedly unconventional myself, but it will be very interesting, especially since I've been over all the correspondence of all the cases in hand. Vincent Massey will be there, and [Robert] Wallace, and Judah from McGill, and somebody from Halifax, and Kermode from Quebec, Southam and Eric Brown and H.O. McCurry from Ottawa—I don't know who all is on the committee. So I shall sit in a corner and take my well-known very complete little sets of notes.

The meeting will last all morning, and then—guess what happens! Eric Brown and H.O. McCurry and I (maybe) will be going to Toronto to attend the American Museums Conference. All the people from big museums in the States will be there and some from Great Britain. H.O. suggested sending me—expenses paid!! So it is all quite exciting and I can go home until next Monday then come back here for a few weeks and then go home again. I wish I were going home to you.

Sunday afternoon I went driving with Bill and Anna [Fretz] and two friends of theirs—very nice people, but the conversation was all on operations and headaches and permanent waves and I made no effort to join in. I hoped for a little sympathy when I told Anna I was debating about a trip to London, but got no further because she said it all depended on how long I expect to be doing this work. I stopped right there, remembering her long talk to me last winter on how impossible it was for a woman to keep a job and keep her husband's affection and bring up a family at the same time. But I also recall how different the circumstances are in this case. I am not like her—I have very good health, a job that fascinates me, and the biggest opportunities I could ever wish for in the way of carrying on. I am going to marry a man who is everything I've ever longed for, and if I fail to make him happy my world will go up in smoke pretty badly. I'm taking a long chance on the job and the man. We'll be all right, you and I. If there is anything I'm sure of in every inch of me, it is that I shall marry you, and be so proud and happy. In the meantime I am anyway, just thinking about you.

I shall be back here on Monday, so I suppose you might address a letter to me here, same as usual.

H.

Toronto, Ont.
[*30 May 1934*]

My dear,

It is now 12:30 of the 30th of May 1934. I am on the train bound for Toronto, all settled down in a lower berth with the soot and cinders pouring in from somewhere and the atmosphere laden with that combination smell of stale egg and unhealthy living which is produced by train smoke or gas or something. I don't know how you and George could have stood it—with both of you in one lower berth on such a hot night. And as for the bed I understand you were sleeping in last week—!! At any rate you won't be having the gentleman in his underwear as bedfellow at present when I am writing this.

I thought I should send on a note as soon as I could about today. For I've got my scholarship reviewed—committee passed my application, I believe, without any fuss. So that is one thing over with. Next thing is to decide what I'll really do next year. But don't you worry my dear, everything will come out all right for us.

I was up early and over to work—the meeting was to start at 9:30. I sat through the whole meeting except the part dealing with scholarships, and wrote down everything. I've got a great respect for Massey and Brown, Wallace and McCurry. Southam is an astute gentleman, Webster is a loquacious fiery old Tory, Kermode and Brock are nice enough, and Judah is a queer duck from Montreal, not at all poised or sure of himself, and apt to splutter and look foolish. Snelgrove gets sent to Europe. The other scholarships were referred to the executive Committee—Southam, McCurry, Massey & Brown.

One step nearer—and I love you very much. Oh my dear, whatever happens you *will* take a chance with me, won't you?

H.

Stone, Sask.
[*30 May 1934*]

Darling:

I'm afraid there isn't much escape from the mail service. The mail is delivered Tuesdays and Fridays, and last Tuesday, or rather yesterday, your letter was among those present. The preceding Sunday finished up a week in Carnagh, and when I came roaring through on Katy I picked it up, so now I have two of the world's loveliest letters in front of me.

I didn't have a bad time at Neelys' (Carnagh) in spite of my grousing. I am feeling a great deal better. My trunk got here all right, eventually. Sunday I made the circuit for the first time myself. This week I am with [Frank] McCraes in Stone. Mrs. McCrae is kindly, though her ideas are obsolete. I think she respects me—she was raised in a tradition of ministerial authority. I think the people are ready to like me, and I am more than ready to like them. After one sleepless night here, I wrapped myself in a dressing gown, tied handkerchiefs around my head, inserted my hands into socks and slept peacefully, though a handkerchief slipped and I got a bite in the opening left. They must be desperately hungry.

Today I called on Mrs. Hickman. Now the Hickmans are more or less beacon lights, as I soon recognized when I first met them. They are lovely people, and they have a lovely piano. I was there nine hours, of which about seven and a quarter were spent at the piano. They were both intensely enthusiastic. I am to stay there next week, and am certainly looking forward to it. They are both well educated. I have spoken before of the dignity and courtesy there is even among the comparatively innocent here, and when there is a certain background of culture, the result is very pleasant.

I think perhaps you are wiser to take the camp this summer. I thought at the time that the old girl would eat out of your hand if you wanted her to, and if so you could make rather a good thing out of it. But I hardly thought you would have backbone enough to dictate your own terms, and your doing so is an agreeable surprise.

The local M.P.P. (C.C.F.) was much impressed by last Sunday's sermon and wants to talk politics. I think I'll go down and see him today. The sermon was on original sin, explaining why Christianity had to work with personalities rather than systems. Jeremiah 17:9.

O, my pet, it's hard for me to write a decent letter, apart from the interruptions caused by trying to answer Mrs. McCrae when she is sounding me about hell. But I love your letters so. I suppose I have read them each a dozen times. I read the earlier one seated on Katy, who waddled along quite peacefully, as though to say, "I know how it is." I'm beginning to like the old fool, and she's beginning to like me. She goes where she's told now, anyway. She's been abused, and she's still nervous, and soon responded when she found I wasn't a sadist.

You seem to be having a great time in Ottawa, dear, and I'm glad. If you're in Toronto, what fun we'll have.

Norrie

Toronto, Ont.
Monday. 5 P.M. [*4 June 1934*]

My dear,

I've had a very busy time and I am going back tonight on the train. Two weeks more in Ottawa, then I return to Toronto, then go to camp for two months. I haven't had the nerve to tell you—that's why I haven't written a day or so sooner. But everyone has advised me not to put off going to England in the fall—

But I was about to tell you that I've been overpowered finally by the combined weight of opinion—Miss Ray was really the one I heeded most. McCurry and Eric Brown veered round suddenly and now they think England is the only place for me to go next fall. Miss Ray thinks I'll have a better chance of getting the thing renewed if I've already got some good work put in next year, instead of fiddling about for a year. Since being at this conference I believe that I would be much further ahead if I go now, for the museum game is still in its infancy, and there is nothing of importance in regard to museum technique I could learn from an extra year here. I still think graduate work would be valuable, but the argument for London is that there are so many more things to see right from one's doorstep almost. So I'm afraid I'll have to go, darling, and I didn't know how to tell you but I've done it now.

I have thought that perhaps you will have a much pleasanter year next year—you are making some good friends in Toronto, you will have the Blake crowd and more time to get acquainted with them without me to take your time. Art [Cragg] will be here, and Ernie [Gould] probably, and Miss Ray, and perhaps Ida. (Although Bill [Conklin] is home again now.) But the worst part is really this summer. Everything will be all right when you get back to Toronto and your work—I mean work that you enjoy. And a year soon slips by. It probably won't be so bad for me because I shall be busy seeing new people and new places and grasping a whole new set of values (or enlarging my old ones) but it might be just a little dull to leave you— But darling, I *can't* do anything else now. Write to me quickly and tell me you will still love me across an ocean. Or at least that you will keep a small corner set aside for me when I do come back. I would have very little faith in your love if I thought that I had to camp on your doorstep to see that you didn't leave home with anyone else. But it *is* a bit hard sometimes, isn't it? There is one thing about it, though. When this same small parcel of humanity is delivered from London some months hence, it will be an improved article in lots of ways. I've learned a good deal in the last two months. What another year will do to me I don't know. But I am quite sure that I've got my mature skin and won't be shedding it for a while.

I saw Ida and Art—Florence [Clare] was studying—and enjoyed seeing them ever so much. Art was just reading a letter you had written to either George or Del [Martin]. He thinks you have a very tough field.

This business of commuting to Ottawa isn't so hot. I read a remark made by some prominent club woman who said that although she had got to the top of her career she'd rather have stayed home and kept house. Well, I'm not sniffling yet, I'm damned if I will—being one of the luckiest girls in Canada—but *stick by me* ! Oh my dear, I want you so.

H.

Piapot, Sask.
[*6 June 1934*]

O my child, I don't know what to tell you to do. It looks like you're going across this fall, and if you are, you will have a good time, and will be back all the sooner. If I am not to see you when I return this fall, well, then, I am not to see you. That is about all I can think of out here; I'm frightfully selfish, of course, but things look different on the prairie. But if you are endangering your chances of getting over by not leaving this year, then *start*, and stay as long as you can. You are perfectly right in wanting graduate training over here before you commence. You know all my reasons for wanting you to stay in Toronto this fall—too green for intensive technical study—it took you all last year to get used to the idea of studying art. Nobody ever gets away with less than a year of mooning around.

If you go over there full of what Canada can give you, and arrive self-possessed, well-trained, and with your background developed, Eng land will be of incalculable benefit to you. As you know, it isn't the training or study, it's the atmosphere of an older civilization that counts. If you are a finished New World product when you arrive, England—the essence of England—is waiting for you. The raw, impressionable rookies that rush over without getting a proper education just find that the atmosphere is too much for them. It makes them drunk, and they come back with nothing more tangible than a vague sense of superciliousness and the cheap superiority of having been somewhere. It is these who tell us that the North American continent is still living in the Old Stone Age—an idea they never got from England, but from the innocents back home who have taken their predecessors at their face value. Not that you are in any danger of being that kind of fool, but don't underestimate this education you are getting here. That is why I feel that I can conscientiously recommend staying here. But things will work out somehow, so don't worry about it.

I have to dash this letter off in a big hurry to get it to you some time this spring, so please don't fret and stew so much about it. You are getting marvellous opportunities, no matter what happens. And don't worry about seeing me—when we do finally come together, there will be no further separations. I'll write soon again.

Dearest, there will never be any choice between me and a career. If you love me and love your work, both are necessary expressions of your character, and you must have both. You will have both, too. You see, things dovetail together so that what we are both cut out to do we can do together. That seems to be the way God works. I am not going into the ministry because (a) I am not fitted for it and (b) because by doing so I should either have to give you up or wreck your career. Don't you see, darling, the two reasons are really the same?

Lovingly,
Norrie

[*Stonepile, Sask.*]
[*13 June 1934*]

Then I am not to see you when I return, sweetheart, not even once? —well, be it so, then. I don't want you even to run the risk of missing your chance. It seems a bit awful to me out here on these ghastly prairies, but four months will pass just as quickly—or as slowly—with Helen not there to meet me in Toronto. Oh, yes, I'll manage next year. The only thing is, I do feel so profoundly irritated. Irritated because all this rushing around doing things thousands of miles away from each other does seem so futile and such an utter waste of time. Surely if I am to have you, it should be in the full vigor of your youth, not our doddering old age. And out here things look gloomier—if the West ever produces any great thinkers, they will be pessimists. In Toronto I could see that we were born for each other and were ready to rush into each other's arms: out here I'm continually tormented by a sordid, blasphemous idea that because of that very fact, something might come up—some accident—to prevent us from being so deliriously happy. As neither of us can ever weaken in love, I am nervous and fidgety like some old granny, "afraid something will happen to you," and I keep fretting because I'm so helplessly broke on this wilderness. I want to get hold of you and make sure that nothing *does* happen to you. And that is the only fear I have. I am not in the least afraid, no matter where you go or what you see or whom you meet, that you will ever forget that you are a married woman. Mrs. H.N. Frye, spiritually, at least, which is all that matters. You do not seem to have a similar confidence in me—do you imagine that I'm going to marry the school teacher and settle down here on a farm? No, my dear, I am afraid you are a pretty firmly established institution.

I am at Stonepile this week, at McPhees'. The Mrs. is a genial soul, with a laugh that sounds like something stopping short in a hurry. I sleep with the hired man, a lumpish youth with a homosexual strain in him. Last week I was perfectly and serenely contented and happy. I was at Hickmans', in Stone. They have the best piano in the field, loads of music, and a comfortable and entirely bugless bed. *And* it poured rain all week, so I stayed in and slammed that piano black in the face. I got your letter on Saturday. Thanks very much for your father's letter. No, the people are all right, and they soon showed me how to prop the animal's face open with thumb as per instructions and insert the bit. I'm getting positively affectionate with the old girl—she has never been kindly or indulgently treated, I don't think, and she's as meek as a lamb now—and she goes where she's told as a rule. She always tries to kiss me whenever I put her halter on. Oh, she has her stubborn mulish moments, all right, but I can hang on better. In short, for practical purposes I have learned to ride.

I have to get this letter off tomorrow, so I'd better close now. A thunderstorm is coming up; I can see the lightning, so I know it's not the hired man snoring. Goodnight, my dearest pet. I guess my last letter is a bit obsolete.

Norrie

Stone, Sask.
[*19 June 1934*]

My pet:

I had started a letter to you last night, and laid it on a table, but one of our Western tornadoes started up and ruined it. I got up at half-past six this morning, after the hired man had barged into my room three times, slamming the door each time. However, he was entitled to some revenge. He breezed in from a dance about three and commenced to sublimate his libido, so I braced one foot against his diaphragm and the other against his belly and straightened out my legs. He hit the floor on the other side—I had no idea he would travel so far—but was too sleepy to challenge my remark that he had fallen out of bed of his own accord. From which you may gather I am still at McPhees'. I had a rather good time this week, from Wednesday on. Monday I held Sunday School and tried to teach a bunch of adolescent girls, who did nothing but grin and look self-conscious. Tuesday I called on the MacCallums. They are good church supporters, but they hated Ralph Williams and pulled him all to pieces. Williams used to read his sermons haltingly and nervously from the manuscript and go visiting at very tactless hours. It is not a good idea, for instance, to call on a mother of six or seven small children at eight o'clock at night. I told them to shut up, as Williams was a friend of mine, so they did. They told me that the more a preacher looked and acted like a cowboy, the better he went over in Stonepile. I went away feeling depressed. Wednesday I went over to Stone to see the Hickmans and stayed overnight. Thursday I went back to Stonepile in the evening, dropping in on Mrs. Geordie Mackintosh for supper. That's the local centre for the mixing and distributing of grasshopper poisoning. I watched them mix it—bran, sawdust, arsenic and water is the bill of fare. I don't know how much harm it does the hoppers, but it's laid out several dogs. We don't know anything about grasshoppers in this country yet. In South Dakota a sixteen-hundred acre field of wheat was cut to the ground in ten minutes. A man from Regina told me that chickens and hens on the farms there had nothing to eat but grasshoppers, and the eggs were all a sickly green. They are only hopping yet; when they start flying the farmers will be quite helpless. [Egerton] McKechnie in Stone says there will not be a single crop harvested here this fall. How would you like to be mistress of a homestead out here, pet? You would be expected to run the house, bring up the children, raise the poultry, tend the garden, help with the milking and the grasshopper poisoning, and belong to the women's club.

I think I'll get a new horse next week. I'll be at the Bonfoys', the people who run the Sunday School. The parents celebrate a golden wedding in July. It's the best house on the field, and is where the preceding students (before Williams) used to board. My new horse is a sorrel mare—a five-year-old. I haven't been on her yet, but she looks lively.

I've been trying to find out why I feel so infernally lonely out here. I think one reason is the anomalous position in which I find myself. Religion out here is not an inward individual experience. It is a set of social conventions; mostly taboos. Naturally, the taboos, being largely on things the youngsters want most to do, such as dancing and smoking, get more unpopular every year, and while I see their point of view, I have to insist that the church is the only medium for a genuine inward consolidation of spirit, the possibility of which becomes steadily more remote. Hence I am supporting the social convention, and, in doing so, my duties are discharged on Sunday. The other six days I am a nonpaying guest, even paid in fact, just to go around and make myself agreeable. Of using me as a bond to hold together the spiritual life of the community there is no question. At the same time I have the official position of spiritual adviser. At college, I am exactly that to a good many people without any official position at all. Yet Jean [Cameron] and Ernie [Gould] and Norm [Knight] and Art [Cragg] would never think of going to a minister with their troubles. The sudden reversal of fortunes makes me intellectually lonely, I think. The minister is in an excruciating dilemma, charged with the awful responsibility of bearing the only possible touchstone of all truth and trying to blast it through a moribund institution with complacent and totally misunderstanding allies. No wonder he weakens in the vast majority of cases. The Christian doctrine is complete and well-nigh anarchic revolution, and the only way to conquer that is to make it respectable conservatism. This is all very commonplace, of course, and clearly or vaguely realized by practically everybody. But it helps me understand why my isolation is so complete. The poor kids! They go to school as long as they have to, dance till they meet somebody that gives them an emotional spasm, get married. There's nothing peculiarly vicious about that progression, but there's certainly no room in it for serenity or beauty or anything else necessary to religion. And there seems to be no help for them.

It almost frightens me, sweetheart, the way standing on your own feet, just for three months, has helped you develop. Not that I didn't expect it—I knew that getting away from the family's and Miss Ray's and my apron strings would liberate an unlimited supply of mental energy and poise in your little body. I primed you as carefully as I could for a big explosion, and it's turning out just as I had hoped. But—there's always the paternal fear. I wish I was closer to fix up repairs and relapses and temporary attacks. Perhaps it was best, though, to have me clear away. But don't grow up away from me, darling. You'll go a long way without me, but it won't be worth doing. Remember that a bluestocking, a pedant, is a female who has sublimated all her sex instinct in her work. *Don't* wander off in that direction—that's the chief reason I want to be near you. And if such a female has refused to do the right thing by her inner essential vital self, what can she do in the way of writing except clatter ahead like the machine she is? It's so terribly easy to confuse suppression with control—that's one reason women are not as creative as they should be. It seems to be easy for a woman, anyhow, who shrinks and winces so easily, if she is sensitive and clever, from the physical contact of marriage. Don't look forward to being middle-aged. We will never be middle-aged—we won't have time.

This is a lot of wind, but I am merely setting down ideas. You see, out here, you are always with me. I never talk to myself—always to you. So sometimes I assume you know everything happening to me already, then I realize with a shock that you don't. I love writing letters to you—by the way—perhaps I should have told you earlier you don't need to read them, as I won't refer back to them, and it may get to be a sort of monomania. One thing, I am thoroughly cured of any desire to enter the active ministry. I was conceited enough to think I could be exempt from the brain-melting business of taking a sententious, didactic, goody-goody attitude toward everything and tearing everything I read apart for its homiletical possibilities, as a result of sermonizing. But I'm not. I guess nobody can be.

Oh, shut up. Goodnight, sweet. When do you leave for England?

Norrie

I've been strangling an impulse to tell my parishioners about the man who poisoned his grandmother with an axe, by giving her arsenic.

Toronto, Ont.
Wednesday [*20 June 1934*]

But my dear, do be practical. If I must go to England, I must go. If I waited another year it would just be delaying things longer. When I come home again—in a very short time, you know, I shall have a job—with some money, and you will get your lecturing job again, and—. Well damnit all, do I have to do the proposing?

Norrie do you suppose I am so keen about it? But I can't do anything else and so that is all there is to it. I shall be back in just one year and then probably you will be going away so it seems that you and I will not have much chance to settle down and grow moss for some little time to come. As for one year putting me into the doddering old stage—look here, Frye, I almost resent that! No darling, nothing is going to come between us. My going away is something that must be, for I *must* be fitted not only for my job, but also to be your wife. I can't forget that—my two ambitions in life are going to be fulfilled. Give me one year in which to grow and I shall come back to you.

In a way, I'm afraid that I am just a wee bit glad that you won't be here when I go. It is hard enough to do without you all this time, but to have you for one day or two and then to force myself to leave you seems almost more than I could stand. But don't you believe a word of it—if I thought you could possibly be here before September 20th—I should be so very happy and so glad to see you. I'd want to take something of you with me, if not you, at least your name. I'm afraid I can't write much to you tonight—cheerfulness is fast disappearing round the corner when I allow myself to wish what *might* be.

I came here Monday from Ottawa, feeling sorry to leave the place, for everyone was so kind to me and I liked the McCurrys so very much.

After my temporary setback (which was good for me) in the way of writing the loan collection report, I have been a little dubious about my ability to write. However, I got to work and polished off the report, much more to the point this time. But that left the thesis high and dry, so I am working on it now. Was at the Vic Library all day, had lunch with John Jones who is working at the Parliament buildings this summer and also studying honour Greek. He told me that his greatest ambition had been to win the Trick scholarship after you had held it. He said that he had often felt encouraged, imagining a few parallels between the two of you. At any rate, he is a very nice boy and admired you very much—and of course that is one of the quickest ways of making me like him. Not that I ever expand very much and grow really enthusiastic. Heavens, if I ever really started to show how much I cared about you I should start a monologue that wouldn't end soon. But I suppose it is my Scottish ancestry. I can't talk much about what is closest to me, except to you.

There's another thing. Everyone tells me how lucky I am, and expects me to keep in a state of being up in the air about going to England for a year. And I just can't afford them any excitement at all. All I can do is beam in a quiet way. But I think I know a darn sight more about where I'm going than some of the enthusiasts might. Too much of it is quite a waste of energy and detracts from the main issue. If you were on hand to keep me prodded in the writing line I should feel a bit more relieved. But I must see this through myself, and I will.

Next year I shall have quite a lot of writing to do, and after that I can perhaps tell whether there is any hope of my producing a style that is clear and graceful and worth developing. It has to be done anyway. I know that I'm not a genius, and that is perhaps one means of keeping clear of certain extravagances. I know that anything I ever do will have to be done with a great deal of grunting and snorting—and a good deal of inspiration from you. But I don't feel nearly as raw and green as I did two months ago, and I don't think England will go to my head. Because, for one thing, I am not out for fame and fortune particularly. That may come, but I have a stiff job to do and it is going to be done, and I'm going to enjoy every minute of it.

Will try to be on the job tomorrow with some good work. So I must get busy now.

Goodnight,
H.

Tompkins, Sask.
[22 *June* 1934]

Pet:

I'm at the Bonfoys this week. Say, do you realize this place actually has a bathroom? Not a greasy washtub in the middle of a sloppy floor, but a bathtub. Not a hideous foul-smelling fly-infested den with a hole cut out with an axe on a plank that leaves a circular scar on your a—se a foot in diameter, but quite what the likes of me and you has been accustomed to. Electric lights, too. I feel cosmopolitan again. I made the circuit on Sunday all right, but it was a fearfully hot day and I nearly died. Monday I managed to prod Katy over here, but the next day I was due for a tea-fight over at Stonepile and I decided to hoof it. I got as far as Jack Clarke's in the centre, had dinner there, and rode in their democrat to Mackintoshes. That was election day. The tea-fight was as noisy as thirty-five husky and hearty country females could make it, and that is saying a good deal. The same house served as polling booth, and the tea was charged for—advance toward preacher's salary being the idea. My parishioner was one of the five C.C.F.'s elected. The liberal landslide was a big disappointment to this community, who had hoped for a better C.C.F. opposition. Well, anyway, I rode back with Clarkes and stayed overnight. English family, ranchers, Anglicans, good books. I borrowed *The Fountain*—I'm going to read that book or bust, but I didn't think it would be out here. Then I walked back to Hickmans' and went through Haydn. Now I'm back home, this being the place where my pyjamas are, anyway.

Half of me is quite serene and happy. The other half is gnawing the leash. I thought I'd be more contented after I had got the idea of a Helenless Toronto, which gave me nothing to go back for, but I'm more impatient than ever, as the waiting, which God knows is long enough anyhow, is easier in Toronto. I'm going to spend a sizable portion of next year getting [Walter T.] Brown, Lane, Langford and the rest accustomed to the thought that I am not coming out again. Then perhaps you'll be coming back in a year from now, and if you do I may promise an apartment for you to stay in for a week or so. Damn it all, I'm entitled to that much of a break. Anyway, thank God we understood each other before we separated.

Morning. It's rather difficult doing anything for you, trying to cheer you up after a doleful letter at the time you are writing a cheerful one. But you do sound a bit depressed over the temporary failure of your report. It was a ghastly thing to get you to do. But do please remember that good writing is *not* a product of style. It always has style, but *style is the result of form* and organization. That is why trying to acquire a style is chasing a shadow and a waste of time, while trying to organize and arrange material is the chief job of every artist. From *Macbeth* down to a college calendar, the only job of every writer, of every creative mentality, is to compose, to bring out what is important and subordinate what is not, to utter in the most disciplined way possible something that increases the coordination and balance of the soul of the reader or listener. Now that applies just as much to your report as it does to the B minor Mass. When you write *anything*, don't try to make it clever or bright or stylish—that comes of itself if its presence is tactful—and don't aim at size or at passive absorption of material. But, always, strive for arrangement, balance, proportion, symmetry, soundness. And remember that that is your religion, and that all art rests on two purely moral qualities—sincerity and economy. This doesn't mean to take your work too solemnly or pretentiously, of course—*Alice in Wonderland* is a far better work of art than *East Lynne*—but for Christ's sake don't worry because a routine report doesn't move with the "dash and sparkle" that Mary's drama festival criticism did. If you and Mary were to exchange subjects you might change your view. Even at that, you haven't a brilliant mind, but perhaps you are better without it. A good many of the world's greatest writers, musicians and painters were by no means clever men. Don't go stale over your work—take it coolly, easily, quietly—take lots of time—don't fuss, don't splutter, don't cry—that all wastes time. But nothing should have the power to bore you, if you love your work. Think of Darius Milhaud with his musical setting of a gardener's seed catalogue, or Monet with his endless studies of one scene—those were challenges to boredom you have to take up too. So don't worry over your unpromising material, and don't try to make a saga of it either—just do it well.

I am sorry to have relapsed into platitudes, but that seems the best thing to say to a little girl who is tired and hot and sulky and out of sorts. As though the average college graduate wouldn't think an undigested mass of facts a very careful and conscientious piece of work, and be most astounded and aggrieved if anybody told her to rewrite it! You're perfectly all right and Mr. [Eric] Brown knows it. But don't waste any more energy doing things like that, will you, sweetheart? I'm sorry you got such a hard assignment, but you won't get easy things to do—they'll give those to other people.

Lovingly,
Norrie

Toronto, Ont.
Monday [25 *June 1934*]

My dear,

I shall have to write you a small letter tonight for I am busy with the education essay these days. It is coming along very well now, but I must finish it this week and I really got off to a good start today for the first time. I have been working at Vic Library ever since I came home.

Today I met George Clarke just as I was getting off the streetcar—I whistled and he came just the same as ever. (I don't mean that he came in the sense of "Here Fido!!") But anyhow, it was almost as if he felt a sort of proprietary interest in me, as we talked about what I was doing, and he was doing. (You see, he had called in here a week ago Sunday, just before I came home, and had a talk with Daddy.) I have been doing some thinking about him ever since I came home, and heard that he had called, and had said that he was sorry that he had gone into Dentistry instead of into an Arts course, or else the Ministry. Yesterday I was just telling mamma—on the way home from St. Paul's Church—that I should like to see him again, just to find out how the Dentists have changed the boy I knew, but that you had said old associations never die, and on the whole I thought that it would be better not to revive anything that might prove awkward. Of course, at present I am having a feeling of female triumph, in a way. Thinking that poor George should have stayed with me, and that he may not, could not, have found anyone—well, better—than me. But on the other hand, it is just there that one may make a mistake, by falling into a bathos of pity and perhaps finding soon that he has already got someone perfectly splendid who can play ball much better than I. The thing is, that now I feel that I am becoming an independent being, interesting in my own right, I have never expressed any desire to have him back. Will he want to come? Will any of his old feelings be revived etc? And on the other hand, I begin to feel quite mistress of any situation, almost motherly in fact. Viewed from the distance of my relationship with you—well, I almost feel like loving the rest of humanity out of pure joyfulness. For I love you so, darling, and I always will.

Does all this sound like a bluestocking or like the young authoress-philosopher in Linklater's *Juan in America* who sat in horned-rimmed spectacles and analysed her sensations and reactions to Juan? If it does, don't mind, my dear, for there is an explanation. I've been reading Murry's *Son of Woman* and am almost infected with the analytical habit. But I shall let you know how I get along Wednesday, when I have lunch with George. If my love for you can't stand talking to him for a little while, or if my physical being succumbs to his attractiveness—well I am still a bawling infant, and not worthy of you.

As I said, we went to St. Paul's on Sunday. Sermon on St. John the Baptist, wound up rather feebly I thought; but the choir sang "Jesu, Joy of Man's Desiring," and the stained-glass windows were enough to make me worship a great Creator. And I thought of having you, and was very humble. Tonight I went to St. Luke's, for it was the Confirmation Service and Harold was confirmed. Bishop Owen was there, a kindly man with a beautiful, soft, swishing voice like water running in a cool glade. But he had little of importance to say. He has all the presence and personality almost of the very voice of God Himself. And he has nothing to say.

I must write to Roy tonight, so perhaps I should cut this short. I never seem to be able to stop with a note when it comes to talking to you. There is so much to tell you, my dear, and as for being away from you for long, it is impossible. I feel you near me just the same, always. I think—Oh darling, I love you so! Please keep on talking to me. Of course I read all your letters, over and over again. Especially when I can't just imagine what you are like. Everything about you is beautiful to me—there will never be any shrinking from physical contact as far as we are concerned, surely? D.H. Lawrence is a particular case. Perhaps if he had not wished to be all-powerful so much, he could have been more at rest. But perhaps he never could be.

Goodnight,
H.

Toronto, Ont.
Wednesday [*27 June 1934*]

For all last week I was without any word from you, but of course two letters had gone to Ottawa and came to me here on Monday and on Tuesday. I am still working away on Educational Work, hell and damnation. I get absolutely bogged every so often and today was one of the times. (George postponed his lunch date because he was working on something that he couldn't leave, away down in the Dental Building, so I have that experience yet to go through with.)

Your last letter was in answer to my foggy wailing about the report. I think I told you in the next letter about having finished it before I left, considerably brightened up. But good heavens, the amount of growing pains before I give birth to a literary effort is something that should be looked into by modern science! Here I am again grinding away, discarding whole chunks of what I wrote the day before. I am beginning to see more and more what a hell of a big job I am tackling—in the implications of gallery work, I mean. Nobody really understands much about it but you and Miss Ray. To carry on the ideals which she has shown me into the field of art education—oh well, you know.

But there are times when it seems so stupid and hopeless and unbearable to have you far away from me like this. I couldn't do any good and sustained work for very long, going on like this. Besides I'm tired, and want a little comforting. I'm tired and nervous and need whipping into shape. And I just naturally want you anyhow. I'm afraid I am not very reasonable—but I don't want a week or two living with you. I want to stay with you all the time until you have to go away, as of course you must. And that would mean bringing about what Jane Carlyle called "the catastrophe of marriage." Darling, I am rather unkind to trouble you with all this when you can't do anything about it, and when everything seems enlarged to blacker and less natural proportions when we can't talk together except on paper. Besides, to take such a step might involve you in more difficulties later when you must go away. And if it prevented your chance of studying somewhere else I should never forgive myself for being a soppy clinging female. No, I'll just stow away the idea and keep on going—but the wicked little creature, it keeps popping up and demanding attention, and I can't do anything with it at all.

Norm Knight was having lunch today with Charlie Holmes for the purpose of coming to some conclusion about Herb Norman's state of mind. Herb is a Stalin supporter, which I gather from Norm is anathema to any Troskyite. Charlie is evidently a little shaken in his opinion of Herb's sanity, and is torn between that and his natural affection and admiration for him. So I expect Norm will have an interesting tale to tell tomorrow.

Dr. Pratt was in the library yesterday with his charming grin and his cheery greeting. "Well, and would you be doing a little work now?" he said, and beamed all over me. I told him I was writing a thesis to show the gallery people that I had a certain amount of native intelligence—and he remarked that that was hardly necessary, surely, by now. (Sweet and tactful men, these Victoria professors!) Prof. Auger greeted me with surprise the other day, with "Why I thought you were off making a grand tour of all the royal Galleries of Europe!" Told me that ten Vic students had gone off the deep end this spring—and two of them were not expected to recover sanity. God! It's pretty hideous to think of that happening to ten youngsters—and sixty-seven freshmen failed in their exams. He is seriously concerned about it all.

I think that I shall be leaving about September 20th from Montreal.

I thought you were being paid by the Mission Board. Haven't you any money? Do you have to depend on the proceeds of some bunfight? Could I send you some—or would there be any place to spend it if I did? You said once that you and I had a long way to go, a tough hill to climb—and sometimes I know it isn't any molehill! But after doing all this crabbing I feel better, and anyhow you're very dear to me even if you are stuck out on a farm with bedbugs and oceans of grasshoppers.

Goodnight,
H.

Stone, Sask.

Although this letter is postmarked 6 July, it was begun in late June.

My darling:

I didn't get this week's letter, if there is one—there wasn't last week—yet, as I'm in Carnagh, with the Pauls, a family from California. Very nice people and interesting to talk to, but with few intellectual interests.

I've got a new horse—a four-year-old mare, named Bessie. She's a strongly built little girl and trots like the wind, but very smoothly. She's a treat after Katy. I don't chase her in the pasture—she runs up to me, in fact, she's been petted so much that's she's a bit spoiled and a bit head-strong—I've had two big arguments with her over where we are to go, and the day of reckoning is not yet. Of course, she's not altogether used to me yet. She gets easily frightened and dashes away from tractors and bridges, so I have to watch her.

Last Sunday wasn't bad, though I got fearfully tired—in fact, I'm not over it yet. Sunday night I slept at Mrs. Steve Mellor's and got the god-awfullest dose of bugs since those first unspeakable nights at McCraes'. Monday I dropped in on a German Lutheran family who said grace after the meal and were enthusiastic about Hitler, and finally came to roost at the McKechnies', one of the more agreeable Stone families.

Stone is busy over the golden wedding celebrations for the Bonfoys so I have to propose a toast (in water) and I'll play if they drag in a piano. It's on July 12, my birthday is the 14th, and the week generally is the half-way mark of my stay out here. So it's a celebration. I'll be glad when the half-way mark is past—things will go more easily then. I'm not deliriously happy, but I am contented, when the beds aren't buggy, though I dread the maturing of the grasshoppers. I think I'm consolidating my position here all right. I'm not popular—I'm no cowboy—but I think I'm respected, and in some places well liked. They don't tease me as I'm told they did Williams—my manner is importunate in many ways, but it does stop that. I wish they didn't think the Bible was full of prophecies just about to be fulfilled. The Adventists—a stronger force than one would ordinarily realize—are responsible for most of that. It is generally considered heresy not to believe that the Bible refers expressly to the twentieth century. I'll reserve a sermon on that for the later part of September, perhaps.

I have finished *The Fountain*, and have started it again. It is very beautiful and very fine—parts of it I disagree with and dislike, but on the whole as fine a novel as any I know. Someday when war has become an evil dream and economic unrest an obsolete problem our lives will be complicated by all sorts of new problems arising from an advance of knowledge and a transcending of the old crudities of hunger and shelter and the rest. Scientists prepare for such an era; artists assume it is already here, and *The Fountain* is such an anticipation.

Saturday. I rode over to Stone and picked up two of your letters. The earlier one was your reaction to my reaction to the England trip, and a very lovely little letter it was. The second told about George Clarke and Harold's confirmation. I picked up the letter at Meyers' and would have given you a good scolding about it only I read the other at McCraes' and forgot about it. But I must do my duty, painful as it is. Now you won't do George Clarke any harm, I don't suppose, and the affair will probably be all over before this letter gets to you. And I may misunderstand you entirely. But the tone of your letter was too selfish. I don't care if you have read D.H. Lawrence, or that asinine book about him—of course it broadens your point of view, but you don't need to go rushing off to experiment on your friends. No doubt you are "an independent being," "interesting in your own right," "quite mistress of my situation," "almost motherly," and unable to be swept off your feet. But that isn't because you're so all-fired blest, but because you happen to have a man of your own and don't want to start a serious connection with George again. But do you suppose you are the only one to be considered? If it is true that he is still devoted enough to give you a "female triumph" and "could not have found anyone better than me" then most assuredly he will want to come back. What changes have taken place in either of you to prevent it? If he is subtle enough, he may be amused, but it is far more likely that he will be quite seriously hurt. As I say I don't worry much about the situation, though it has its own dangers. It's the spirit in which you meet it that I object to. I love you so much and expect such great things from you, that you mustn't mind if I pull you up with a nervous jerk when you are more adolescent than you should be.

I'm sorry to have worried you. Of course you are going away and will come back and everything will be all right. But you do understand, don't you, dear, that I can't help sometimes feeling a bit imprisoned out here where I can't see you or help you or do all the things I want to do for you? It's a little easier for you, you know. My last Sunday is Sept. 23rd, but I'll cut that last Sunday off if you say so.

I had a hell of a fight with Bessie coming over from Stone and I'm tired out. She was bound she wouldn't go, and kept dashing away from the trail. She knows I'm no experienced rider. Oh, well, another week or so and she'll be all right. She wasn't properly broken to ride.

Lovingly,
Norrie

Shaun R.P., Sask.
[*9 July 1934*]

My sweet pet,

I have another letter of yours now, and I gather that you are beginning to feel the pinch of separation too. We need each other so absolutely that we become disorganized and lost when we aren't together.

Damned if I know what to do about this marriage business. Our careers keep pulling us apart, and yet I sometimes think you won't know whether you are coming or going unless I get hold of you and spank you into shape. But, darling, you've got your work to do, and if you can't see me for a year—well, get your work done in the meantime. But do it easily and coolly, like an adult. Stewing and fretting and rushing won't do. That's adolescence. Do you suppose those ten frosh went under because they worked too hard? They all worked too much, of course, but it was all wasted energy. The various excretory metaphors used by my friends about my first-class exams and A essays were quite in order. Spasmodic strained work means intellectual constipation. If you can't write, it's because you don't want to. Take some time off, read plenty, play the piano till your fingers are numb, do some sketching, walk, loaf around, write to me, and then some night get the damn thesis done. Put some color into it: make it an adventure. That's why I stay up all night writing my essays, going out for coffee and walking the streets at unearthly hours—I don't recommend that to you, but it's fun for me, and romance. Live while you write, and then your writing will be vital accordingly. Writing is an exciting, precise, subtle, difficult business, like a piano recital, but more spontaneous and creative. It's no job for a weakling, but you are not that, unless you weaken yourself by shrinking from its difficulties.

All this doesn't mean much here: it would mean a lot more if I could say it to you, in the flesh. What I was going to try to talk about was whether we are to be married next year or not. Plainly, of course, it's impossible to say, definitely. I won't live on your money. Not that that will be necessary, I hope. Heretical as it sounds I do not see why I couldn't go to Scotland for a year and leave you in Toronto married. The chief difficulty would be the attitude of the Art Gallery. I'm quite sure I shall not go out on another mission field. And living in the same city all winter without marriage would be a risky business for us. Toronto is stuffed with meddlesome fools and busybodies, besides the obvious dangers. And when I am ready to go to Europe I will go. By the way, I suggested in my last letter that I might cut off my last Sunday and leave Sept. 17. If you postpone your trip a day or so we might see each other. Now I'm not urging anything on you, but it is barely possible that twenty-four hours with each other would be refreshing and stimulating rather than purely tantalizing. I understand why you don't like the idea, but wouldn't actually seeing each other, even for a short while, be more comfortable than the thought that we have missed each other by a day or so, you leaving Toronto about the time I was packing up in Stone? The decision is yours, and please tell me what you really think?

Sure I've got some money—collections and so on—more than I can spend. The Mission Board doesn't pay me until it's all over. Sorry if I misled you—I only meant I'd be helpless to go East if anything happened to you. It's just part of the general sense of being held in. I'm doing fairly well here, and I seem to be making some impression, and a few quite good friends. I want to give them, not an abstract set of ideas, or even a new slant on religion, not primarily, but the impress of a personality they'll remember just long enough to consolidate their faith and their liking for religion.

Well, my pet, if I say anything that distresses you, just ignore it. I love you in a boiling, stormy sort of way when I can't see you, and sometimes I say tactless things, or make silly suggestions, just from pure exuberance. Doesn't sound reasonable, but it happens. After all, a bug is a damn poor substitute for you as a sleeping partner, and as my closest female companion, Bessie somehow doesn't seem in it with you. I'll be more normal in Toronto—which is only ten short weeks away.

Norrie

Camp Onawaw, Ont.
[*9? July 1934*]

Written after Kemp had begun her summer job at Camp Onawaw. The chief counsellor at the camp, Margaret Govan, was known as Robin Hood, and the other counsellors took the names of Robin Hood's outlaw companions: Gilbert the Cook, Will Scarlet, Little John, etc. Kemp became Much the Miller.

My darling, I am so very sorry not to have written to you, and now I shall miss your birthday—when I meant to send you something nice. Here I am at Onawaw again, flat broke and very happy, but without anything to send you but a great deal of affection, and this particular amount won't get to you before the thirteenth.

I haven't had any letter from you for almost three weeks, I think. But we must make all due allowance for mail service and for the Blake thesis.

I was busy with mine until the last minute before I came here—finished writing the damn thing at eleven o'clock and left in the afternoon at four. Of course my long-suffering family got me off, or I might not be here now. Daddy recopied the essay, and [Agnes] Beatty will type it. It will reach Ottawa sometime before August 1st. I was going to send it out to you but had to give up the idea for time is getting short, and Daddy has attended to the glaring mistakes—there weren't many—and polished up a lot of the sentences. I wanted your opinion before I handed it in to be read, but that can't be helped now. Anyhow, it should get me across the pond, which is what counts just now.

This summer camp is one of the best things I've done for myself. I *am* having a good time, and enjoying everything. Sometimes I feel a little bit incompetent for five minutes at a time, but not much longer than that, and I am not scared of the youngsters anymore, for the most part. That is the big thing, to get over my small fears of meeting and talking to strange people. I haven't a cabin of my own to look after—I am with Robin in Hilltop. You probably have seen her, Margaret Govan, who took classes with second year Emmanuel last year, and public speaking with McMullen. She *is* a good scout, and I like her very much. It is such a treat to me to be back amongst some of my own people, Vic people, you know. Jean Davey and Margaret Quentin and Molly Sclater and Bea Longley. Jean Evans is coming in August.

I had a letter from Professor Constable which says that the best course for me to enter is the one-year diploma course. To get a B.A. in the University of London would take two years spent *there*. And as yet I can not enter for an M.A. course since I don't know anything about the history of art. The M.A. course takes two years continuously in London. *But* if I pass the exam in June 1935 after this course I shall then be eligible to enter an M.A. course. It seems that one must spend at least two years in any university in order to get a B.A. from it no matter what institution you come from. But it is just a matter of form. Two years study for the B.A. and enough residence fees and the examination fee and you get the M.A. (Oxon.) without further preamble. So it is likely that my best bet is to enter that course, get their diploma and come back to work and save enough money to go over later for two years.

You and I are not going to have a very settled existence for a long time to come. But we have a little more staying power than most. Don't imagine that we can ever grow apart, I am so very sure that we won't. And I don't feel at all green and raw any more. There are many things

I don't know but that is a different matter, for I have my own vantage point from which to view the world, and as soon as I can get over being afraid of meeting people or new situations I shall find out a great deal.

I forgot to say that I am thinking of going to England third class on the *Empress of Britain* on Sept. 15. That would give me enough time to get settled and see a few galleries before the school begins. What do you think of that? Otherwise I should leave Montreal on Sept. 20th or 21st. It won't be possible to see each other before then anyway, I'm afraid. I am just hoping now that nothing has happened to you all this time when I haven't heard what is going on out in southern Saskatchewan.

Your little grown-up on the way,
H.

Piapot, Sask.
[23 *July 1934*]

My darling:

I don't know what's become of my letters; I've been sending them regularly, and I mailed them myself to Fulton Ave. After all, you've been roaming around quite a bit, you know, and you don't tell me where you are, you leave me to infer it from your letters.

If you're leaving in the middle of September, I guess I won't be seeing you. I'll be glad when you're settled in England and I'm off the blasted heath. If these people asked me to come out again, which is highly unlikely, I would be glad to come if they would give me one place to board, preferably Hickmans'.

The Blake thesis is getting under weigh, but the chances of doing anything much with it this summer are pretty slim. If they publish the thesis, I'll buy you an engagement ring with the proceeds, if there are any proceeds. If not, I'll buy you the ring anyway, if at all possible. Every once in a while Toronto looms up like a kind of mirage, and when I get back I think the reaction will be something tremendous. It may even set me to work. Nine more Sundays, and then I start in.

The Bonfoys had their big golden wedding celebration last week in the school. There were at least a hundred and fifty people there, representing as many square miles of territory. The programme was immense, but it went off without a hitch. I played, accompanied three times, spoke at the conclusion, and said grace. That sort of broke up the summer, as it was pleasant to look forward to, back upon, and was nice at the time. It was something of an advertisement for me, too. They had started planning for that thing when I first came.

I hope my letters don't depress you. I keep talking to you—or your ghost—all week. I never talk to myself, you know; I have always talked to some imaginary person, usually a literary hero, but out here you. If I could speak to you face to face, you'd find I was enjoying myself, and not worrying over bugs any more than I worry over exams at college. But when I sit down and try to write, all I can think about is your absence, and how absolutely devoid this country is of any association with you. Primarily, of course, I'm lonesome for Toronto, which means a life I'm used to, intensely interested in, and a life with you. Toronto without you will lack a good deal, of course, but it's still Toronto. Oh, hell, I've said all this before and I never say anything else. And I'm sleepy and hot and bothered and I'm going to bed. Goodnight.

Norrie

Huntsville, Ont.
July 31, 1934

The night letter Kemp refers to, a telegram sent by cheaper rates at night, is missing, as is a telegram from Frye of the same date, in which he talks about taking a "night train" in time to meet her before she leaves for England, to which it was a response.

My poor darling,

Your last letter sounded rather dismal and I am terribly sorry to be such a lazy letter-writer. I keep forgetting that even if I don't send you long ones, I might send short ones a little more regularly.

By this time you will have got my night letter, and I am waiting to hear from you before I book passage. It seems that if you can take that night train we may see each other yet before I go. I do hope so. Oh my dearest, this summer is half over, and this camp is a wonderful place, and I am very happy, but I want to see you so very much.

We have about twenty youngsters making pipes and one learning to play hers. Pipe-playing is great fun—you can arrange all sorts of simple tunes for two or three pipes and tonight Molly Sclater and I have to play a couple of duets.

Well, my dear, I must rush off and arrange the programme for tonight. Hope there is a letter from you on this mail. Oh yes—don't worry about rings—I never wear them anyway! I just want *one* sometime, and I still love you very much!

H.

Piapot, Sask.

Postmarked 13 August 1934; it would appear that this is the letter that the man he gave it to forgot to mail, referred to in Frye's next letter.

Darling, whenever there is an unreasonable length of time between my letters it points to a complete disorganization of work, resulting in my missing one mail after another. Ah, well, even if you are in England I shall be in Toronto where a letter box is just outside, and one doesn't have to ride a horse for five miles in the blazing heat to mail a letter.

I lose a week's salary by leaving the 16th, but so far as I know there will be no other objection from the Mission Board. I will move heaven and earth and several preemptions in hell to get out that night, and think probably I can bribe somebody to take me in, if my trunk goes in some days earlier. The only difficulty will be that my travelling expenses may not come from Toronto in time—they always send them at the last minute—but I can grab the collections and clear out. If I arrive Wednesday morning I'll go to Montreal if I've still got any dough—I have a book of half-fare certificates, you know. That will give us two days, and, what seems equally important just now, two nights, partly in Toronto, partly in Montreal. You may have to sign a Montreal hotel register as my wife, but I leave such things to you. It makes me chew my nails with impatience to sit down and write to you. One kiss is worth all the letters in the world. And when you come back from England, Helen, it will be to a husband. Half of third-year theology last year was married on less prospects than we have. This time next year I sincerely and devoutly hope that you will be my wife and stay that way till one of us dies. I don't see the necessity of dodging around and waiting and talking in terms of an indefinite future. I want you and a few other things like fame and fortune in moderation, which mean nothing without you. Don't worry about an impetuous marriage. I suppose any marriage where the parties aren't over forty, with money in life insurance and bonds, is an impetuous one. I might have been able to enjoy myself this summer, and I have enjoyed myself in a way, but that horrible sick, longing craving for you and sense that any work done this far away from you was a waste of time got me to counting the days.

Hot weather—102 in the shade yesterday. Crops are burning up—they look bleached instead of ripened. It will be a very early harvesting season, with damned little to harvest. What wheat there is, though, will get a fair price. Also the heat seems to be good for bugs. I killed twenty-four at McCraes' last night. I have noticed that it is the original 1910 homesteaders who have them, for the most part—those who came in later are cleaner. *And* I have noticed that families who serve toothpicks at the table, and replace them in the bowls after using them, are quite likely to have them too.

Well, if I am to get this letter off tomorrow I'd better stop it, for now. Six weeks from next Wednesday, forty-two days, if all goes well.

Lovingly,
Norrie

[*Camp Onawaw, Ont.*]
Sunday afternoon [*12 August 1934*]

My dear, I haven't heard from you since your telegram of July 31st but I suppose nothing desperate has happened to you. I am still living a very regular and regimented sort of existence—if regimented isn't a good word, put in your own. I am feeling somewhat disgruntled with life in general but especially with morning worship services, with Jean Evans' solos and ideas of music and Mrs. Turkington's request for "Trees" the second Sunday running, after it has been sung to death by every bawling tenor and sentimental soprano and by Jean Evans at this Camp for about four seasons. Mrs. Turkington has no idea whatever about music and when I came up she as well as some of the youngsters asked for "Regal Echo"—that big bangy piece you played once last year! Which I may explain is the Turk's version of *Rigoletto*. All I'm doing these days is teaching pipe-making, criticizing the small amount of sketching being done, playing piano, swimming—just being generally useful, painting signs, and beginning on a large-sized drawing of camp activities myself which will take the rest of the time to finish. I have not worried about trying to do too much—haven't talked about music or painting or stewed about not having many kids wanting to do sketching when they could do other things more interesting to themselves.

Monday afternoon. I had a very nice letter from Mr. McCurry on Saturday in answer to the one I wrote when I sent the essay. (It was 8,000 words when corrected and didn't look too dull, I think.) He says "I think you can count on a favorable decision by the committee but I will send you formal notification of this before the end of August. Your money will be ready in ample time for your departure on September 21st." So that is a cheerful letter even if there was none from you.

This letter sounds a little goofy but I am not really crabbing. I'm just getting a little tired of the continual round of camp activities, and wanting to see you etc., etc.

Goodbye for this time—mail goes out very soon.

H.

Carnagh, Sask.
[*17 August 1934*]

My dear:

I rather think it will be a long time between letters this time, because I gave the last one to a man to mail who was going into town, and I imagine from the sheepish look on his face and something he dropped that he has forgotten about it. My last letter merely said that it would be all right for me to leave on Sunday the 16th. I will try and see if I can get the communion service changed to that date. On that day I take the field of this pot-bellied jackass up in Tompkins and will hold the seven o'clock service in that dirty little village which is the gateway of freedom. Then all I would have to do is wait for the midnight train.

My work is completely demoralized and disorganized. My visiting is far behind; my reports aren't started; my correspondence is tied up; the thesis is in abeyance, and I don't give a damn about anything: not this close to the end, at any rate. But I've had one break at least. John Bates came up to see me from Robsart, a village fifty miles southwest, and found me at Hickmans'. He has a car: they transferred him at the last minute to what the West would call a town charge. So we went to Eastend together—the only village worth looking at around here—and called on the minister. A Welshman, forced by some insistent call to leave a $4,000 a year job and take up this kind of work, he was a man of broad culture and rich experience—India, Wales, England, United States, and Canada—in the war, and a splendid talker. There is a restaurant in Eastend that serves better food than I ever got in Toronto outside of Eaton's. It seems an eternity since I've propped my elbows on a restaurant table, wrapped my hands around a coffee cup, and talked to somebody like John Bates or Mr. Evans. We got a flat tire coming back. But his visit sure brightened things up for me.

Now, darling, there's not much to tell you that wouldn't be repetition. I'll be in Toronto Wednesday morning as per schedule, the 19th of September.

Lovingly,
Norrie

Triptych. Drawing by S.F.H. Kemp, from *Torontonensis*, 1906
(courtesy of Victoria University Library, Toronto)

The Kemp cottage at Gordon Bay (courtesy of Susan Sydenham)

Frye and Kemp at Gordon Bay (courtesy of Susan Sydenham)

At Gordon Bay. *Back row from left:* Roy Kemp, Gertrude Kemp, Helen; *front row:* Harold Kemp, S.H.F. Kemp, Frye (courtesy of Victoria University Library, Toronto)

Scene at Lake Joseph. Drawing by Helen Kemp, 1936
(courtesy of Victoria University Library, Toronto)

1934–1935

Courtauld Institute of Art
20, Portman Square
London W1, England
[*23 September 1934*]

Written by Kemp on board the Cunard RMS Ausonia *en route to London for her year at the Courtauld Institute. Postmarked from Plymouth, Devon, 29 September 1934; addressed to Frye at* Emmanuel Residence, Charles Street, Toronto.

My darling, it is Sunday night and there is a bishop from somewhere who is going to speak to the assembled company, in the tourist dining room. There was a feeble attempt at a dance last night in the tourist lounge, but there are so few people on board that no one would dance except about five couples. An old boy who is sailing with his sister back to London is the usual "life of the party," and he and I started dancing, and a few others followed. The young student from McGill who sits at our table required some coaching so I started a dancing class. There was another young Englishman amongst the earnest seekers and so Maude Constantine helped him. Maude Constantine is a nice young woman without anything at all to distinguish her from no end of other young women, I suppose—but is quite pleasant and agreeable, and she likes to walk and drags me away from Sinclair Lewis when she considers that I have done enough reading and sitting in a deck chair. Most of the time I read, for I haven't had an opportunity all summer before now to wallow in books. A nurse from Montreal who is going as companion to a sick friend just poked her head in and wants to know what I am doing. Writing letters? Oh yes, she had a lot to do too. Didn't I just hate writing letters? I said no, I really didn't dislike writing letters. (Not to you.) She said a friend gave her a diary and wants a faithful account of her travels written from day to day. I was reminded of Mark Twain and of Jack Oughton asking me if I were keeping a diary. I said no, that writing letters would have to serve. Writing a diary would be quite interesting to read, I suppose, later on. But I have a feeling that for me it would be like going behind a barn and talking to myself. I like to talk to you, because then I feel that I am sharing something with you as I want to do always. But if it is just for myself—there is nothing to that.

It is just the same as ever. Every night I seem to want a little quietness and to know that you are *here*, always. I am afraid that I didn't like leaving you. I cried, just a little, and hid behind a post so that you would not see. But I shook myself and talked to somebody and soon settled down peacefully. For if you are with me it is all right, and I was comforted. And I shall be so glad all year that you did come to Montreal for now my journey has started properly.

I shall stop, I suppose, for tonight, my darling. It is clear moonlight on the water. I shall kiss you soon, to myself.

Helen

7, Taviton Street, Gordon Square
London, W.C. 1
October 12th [*1934*]

My dearest,

I've been feeling all day that I must write you tonight, and in spite of consciously and definitely planning to read my German grammar book, my hand just grasped my pen and decided the affair. Oh my darling, surely I'll never have to leave you again to "complete" my education! I have a feeling that one year of this may be almost enough—I don't think I should like to add a couple more on to this year in order to step out as M.A.

The worst is over now, I think, and it was quite easy—the first lonely week here without friends, I mean. Now I am getting acquainted with people at the Institute and people in the house where I am staying, and I have spent a week with Maysie Roger. Then, of course, Barbara Sturgis gave me lots of letters of introduction which I am sending off as the spirit moves me. You must meet Barbara sometime. She was at St. Hugh's with Kay Coburn and is getting a novel—her first—published by Macmillan. And as I said before, Kay's helpfulness has made me *very* kindly disposed toward her. I think really that she and Barbara gave me the most useful information, and did not bewilder me with tales of how lonely I should be or how seasick, and I have behaved very well on both counts, so far.

After writing notes to each other, Gordon Snelgrove and I at last met, today, and we had lunch together. Oh my dear, I see where I must take that man in hand and try to make something of him. He needs a strong-minded woman, I think, or else one who has a strong will but doesn't show it. And who will make him develop some self-confidence. After a time he might be quite reasonably adequate, but he will never be of great consequence, I am afraid.

I keep thinking of you, and wondering what you are doing and whether you are drinking coffee at Murray's with a kindred spirit and whether you have bought a new suit or not, and does it fit well? Then I hope you are remembering to keep clean handkerchiefs and socks without holes and civilized haircuts! And I wish you would remember to stand up straight and not grow round-shouldered before your time. For I am trying very hard to stand properly and come back to you looking like a female who thinks she owns a good-sized bit of the universe. My dearest dear this is such prim advice from me across a chop~~py sea~~ ocean (no rhyme intended!) but I go walking about the streets thinking about you, and the more I am enjoying what I see, the more I feel a part of you, as if you had quickened all life for me.

I've come to a standstill and the only thing I want to do is to go to a concert and hear a Mozart quartet—with you—and to be able to glance now and then at your profile. And afterwards we would be so happy and I shouldn't be looking at your profile any longer! Then you would say something quite unexpected, just to keep me from being too romantic, and we would both laugh. I have quite a stock of Frygian witticisms up my sleeve to chuckle over at odd moments on the bus and walking down streets, and even in lectures when they're dull.

Do tell me how your lecturing is going to be—what is the course, and will it be much extra work? What you have done and seen? Oh just write to me, and remember that I am loving you more and more.

H.

London
October 17, 1934

My darling, I have a dismal fit on tonight and must talk to you to help clear it up. I am not going to write dismally to anyone at home, but you will forgive me if I explode sometimes to you, won't you? I have a cold, I've got the curse (you might guess that from the date) extra badly this time, and I'm lonely as hell and I don't care whether everybody thinks I am having a hilarious time just by breathing an English atmosphere—the fact still remains. I wrote very cheerfully to Lismer last night and I'm just having a relapse, I suppose.

Tonight I went to a lecture on ancient art by Mr. Ashmole (no end of a specialist, they tell me, but he is rather a dull lecturer with a collar three sizes too large). But I had made a mistake in the time, and had half an hour to wait. So I went downstairs and read the notices on the notice board—S.C.M. meetings, subjects for prize essays, public lectures. Under the last was the notice of the Hibbert Lectures, four of them, to be given by Albert Schweitzer, beginning at that very moment! So I hiked off and left Mr. Ashmole to his digging in Egypt. I'll tell you about this again—my head is aching a little too much—I can hardly see straight.

Next Morning. The air is all clear again, thank heaven. Please don't ever treat a woman unkindly when she is in that condition—of course you never would, and you do understand about such things more than most people. But it seems to me that for a few hours it is just sheer habit and mechanical actions that keep one looking normal. Inside you feel as if you were looking through a thick fog, and all the earth was being swallowed up and there was no friend to help you. Then the last dwindling bit of common sense comes up in a feeble flicker and says firmly, "You know everything is practically as it was yesterday. Just get to bed and have a good sleep. Your tummy will be better tomorrow and you can't decide anything tonight, so stop worrying. And of course Frye hasn't forgotten you even if it is a month since you've seen him. The mail isn't carried across the ocean overnight. Don't be an ass." So one goes to bed. But the potential next generation does make an awful fuss before it passes on into oblivion.

Well, my dear, I was starting to tell you about Schweitzer's lecture. The subject of the four lectures is "The Religious Factor in Modern Civilization" (not exact wording). In this first one he candidly denied that religion has any influence in present-day civilization. It has become separated from our thinking, and the last century in which religion and thought went hand in hand was the eighteenth. He seemed to oppose idealism and realism—the eighteenth being the last age of idealism. He said he had the good fortune of having a father who still lived in the spirit of eighteenth-century idealism and who never could understand the nineteenth. Said it was one of the great glories of Erasmus that he was one of the first of his time to picture a world without wars, an idea which grew in the eighteenth century.

Napoleon was the great force of realism in modern times and the Napoleonic wars were wars in which grew up the spirit of nationalism, which is also identified with realism (surely I should mean materialism? I am writing from memory and my memory is never exact, like yours) for the peoples were now fighting for their very existence as nations. Then he cited Hegel as the first philosopher to formulate the growing spirit. And with him began the modern age. Two great thinkers of modern times derive from Hegel: Karl Marx and Spengler. Well, when he came to Spengler, I sat up and tried to understand. He said Spengler derives from Hegel and his doctrine is that forces work themselves out and we can do nothing. Where Hegel says "forces of progress" work themselves out, Spengler says "forces" work themselves out. He no longer maintains the optimism of Hegel, who says that a higher civilization follows a lower and that eventually a higher civilization is permanent. Spengler compares civilization to a tree. Ours is dying and cannot be saved—as little as a tree that is dying and its leaves faded. Therefore Spengler does not believe we can do anything to influence reality. We must with tragic resignation put up with what happens.

Schweitzer says that when one gives up idealism one must necessarily arrive at such a conclusion. Much of what is now going on on the Continent can be understood only by realizing that men have succumbed to this spirit and feel helpless in the face of events. Each of us as men and women of our own age have something of this feeling of helplessness. All that happens in world history rests on something spiritual. If the spirit is strong it *creates* world history. If weak it puts up with history. Will we *make* world history or will we suffer it passively? Will our thinking again become ethical and religious? That is the great problem.

I must run along now to a lecture on early manuscripts from a German named Freyhan, one of the best we have. The lectures in general are damnably dry and I shall start skipping them very soon, but not until I find out a little more what is expected of one.

October 26. I haven't had much to tell you about since, and could not write anyhow. I have been fighting the blues off and on for the past week. I expected to be quite alone, and heaven knows when some of these Londoners will loosen up! I have never appreciated my friends so much as now when I have no one. But that is not true, really, for there is another girl in the house here who graduated from Exeter [Miss Crowe] and we have been doing things together—we went to see *Richard II* last night and it was beautifully done. And then a very nice thing happened tonight. Miss Wickham who lives next to me invited me in to meet a friend of hers who is taking lessons from Rudolph Dolmetsch. She and I had a big pow-wow, and we are all going to a concert which he and his wife are giving—harpsichord and viol da gamba. When I feel so pitifully grateful to people like that for being just ordinarily kind and friendly, I am somewhat conscience-stricken when I think of some of the people at college who must have needed a little bucking up and I was just as thoughtless as most of the people here. It doesn't occur to the person who casually says "good morning" to you that that may be the only conversation you have had with anyone for a day or two. And while a desert island would not give one much in the way of human companionship, it at least would not mock you with the happiness of families, and mothers taking their little sons to school in the morning, and lovers saying goodnight on the doorstep, and all the ordinary details of everyday life in a world where you have a place and are wanted.

The curious part of all this is that I am enjoying it—like being an actor. I am wrong—it is sometimes like being an actor, and the dull times are when I am forcibly made only a passive spectator. But I am learning many things that are not set down in books. Besides, I have a sort of pig-headed determination to establish myself, to get about on my own and not have it done for me. I want to *know* that I can stand on my feet and take a few knocks without whimpering too much. Except that here I am sending you a long sniffle.

But please, please write to me. I have had no word from you, you know, and it would help. Thank God I have you, or I should feel rudderless. But look, are you getting along, yourself? You must see everyone you can, and meet new people. Theoretically you should be free to do all the things you have been wanting to do—I mean without me to make you do something else. But such theories do not always seem to work out—they don't in my case at any rate. I am very anxious to know how your lecturing is working out. You must not work too hard—leave time for playing about, and take good care of yourself. You looked too thin, or too tired, when I saw you last—I'm living with the shadow of you all year, don't make me come home to find you a shadow indeed. I'm thinking of how good it will be to be back already, even though I can understand how I might like to stay here always. But for the first time I am developing a consciousness of being Canadian, and feeling a tenderness unknown to me before. Just for the freshness and the promise of a young country not bound by tradition—I can't analyse what it is I think of when I think of Canada.

Oh darling, I am an awful bore, I know, but I've told you what is happening to me, and if it is not particularly spectacular, it still is quite true. And you won't be reading this for over a week so don't worry one bit, will you? Miss Crowe told my fortune, reading from my hands, the other night. The only true thing she hit upon without any foreknowledge was that I should marry and live apart from my husband for some time, then live with him again. No quarrel or disagreement, just a separation. ("True" may not be the word to use of something which *may* happen.)

Goodnight,
H.

Toronto, Ont.
[*19 October 1934*]

Darling, it seems almost incredible that this is my first letter to you, when I've been thinking of you so constantly, but your letter took an unconscionable time to get here, and it's taken me a week to find, or rather to make, the time to sit down and tell you any news. Oh, sweetheart, everybody keeps telling me that now is the time for me to settle down and do some work, when my mind can concentrate and my time is my own, and yet they are so absolutely wrong. Everything goes on in the same bunched-up, flustered sort of way with me that it always has. It always will go on that way, until I'm married.

The Blake group as usual is my chief interest. We got started two weeks ago, on a critical bibliography we expect to publish, judging from what Davis said. Next Thursday night I have to read a paper on Blake before the Graduate English Club. Darling, it's my one big chance, and I can't afford to pass up on it, which means I have to work myself blind and deaf over the weekend. It will be the groundwork of the thesis. You see, whenever anybody in the three family colleges does anything really well, the professors always come over and tell U.C. all about it, whereupon

U.C. lays for these white-haired youths in the Graduate English Club. They've been laying for me for two years now. So I've got to smash them and establish myself. I don't want to get a reputation as a monomaniac (Mary Winspear said, "If your name is on the notice what's the use of announcing the subject?"), but I simply haven't time to do anything else. So Blake it is.

I'm eating at the head table now, with DeWitt telling everybody that history is the evolution of the unintended, Barber wanting to know who swiped a book on liberty he left in the common room, Little snorting about Hepburn's policies, Currelly holding forth on all subjects, specializing in tiresome ones, and various high-powered dignitaries eating with their knives. I've won an argument with Dr. Richard Roberts about a passage in Old Testament prophecy, and lost one with [Walter T.] Brown on humanism. At the same time I've found a friend who has moved into the inner circle, my colleague Roy Daniells, back from England, and taking most of Auger's work (Auger has high blood pressure and has temporarily, and probably permanently, retired from his lecture-room pursuit of verbs and adjectives). Roy is a damned good head, doing a Ph.D. thesis on Baroque, depending on me for a music supplement. He likes me, and I certainly like him—we have somewhat similar types of mind. Brought up among the Plymouth Brethren, and bears the scars of some terrific religious experiences. Has an embarrassingly high estimate of my ability.

Teaching hasn't started yet. They don't divide up the work among groups until the first essays come in, which they haven't. I bought a red pencil today (5¢), and will probably start licking it within a day or so. Lane called me into his office the other day and told me that I had definitely established my status as a scholar around here, but the college placed a strong emphasis upon teaching ability and the necessity for getting good instruction across to the undergraduates. That he had a hard time persuading Brown that I would make a good teacher, Brown having a thoroughly American respect for mediocrity and the superstition that mediocrities make the best teachers because they are slow. That it was consequently more or less up to me. That with Edgar retiring within a couple of years and Auger probably out of the picture for good, something big should open up shortly if I produced the stuff. I mustn't miss, of course; go slowly with the kids but keep their interest, and God bless you, it looks pretty bright, darling.

Theology. Nothing new except Macleod in Systematic Theology, who is an unspeakably bad lecturer. In his first lecture he said that faith didn't depend on reason; reason depended on faith. In his second lecture he said that science wasn't purely rational: it assumed certain postulates given by faith. In his third lecture he said that reason didn't explain ultimates, that we had to seek behind it the controlling force of belief. I don't know what he said in the subsequent lectures.

I've started a course on Shelley and Keats with a young man who doesn't particularly like Shelley and Keats. Should be all right.

And I've started to read the *Golden Bough* for my Old Testament, which is all about magic in religion, the development of vegetation rites, the symbolic killing and eating of the god, bewailing the death of the god of fertility in the winter and his resurrection in the spring—the Adonis, Osiris, Dionysus and Demeter cults which all synthesize and coalesce in the Passion from Palm Sunday to Easter. It's a whole new world opening out, particularly as that sort of thing is the very life-blood of art, and the historical basis of art. My ideas are expanding and taking shape so quickly that they frighten me; I get seized with terror sometimes that somebody else will think them out before I do, or that I shan't live long enough to complete anything. I shan't live very long in any case, of course; but that doesn't matter if I make the contribution I seem destined to make. I wish to hell I wouldn't think so much about myself. It wastes time. And I waste a lot of time.

Marg Roseborough and Mary Winspear have an apartment together now, which makes things pretty nice. Last Wednesday after the Blake group they took Charlie and me over and fed us. Mary's promised me a meeting "complete with beer" in the near future.

I've got a new suit—brown, damn you, and it looks fine. Everybody says so.

Well, it's time to quit and get busy on the Blake. Now that the news is off my chest, I can start and think about you for a change. Of course, I do that anyway—your ghost has a habit of floating around. You'd be surprised at the amount of egocentric information I've poured into your astral body since coming here. Oh, my dear, I'd be so sick and miserable if I hadn't seen you in Montreal. But now that I have, why, I have that to think about.

Norrie

[*London*]
October 30th [*1934*]

My darling, your letter came yesterday and changed the look of London, for me—oh my dearest, I have been missing you so much. I love London, but Toronto is still home to me—the university has this place beaten fifty different ways. I don't like the scattered colleges and institutes and branches all over the city. I don't like the utter and absolute isolation of one small group from another. The Courtauld Institute, for instance, runs its own show, and there is hardly any social intercourse amongst the students. So that the picture and conception of university life is a mere mockery. I understand now what you meant when you regarded undergraduate life as religious. I feel that I am one of the few mature students amongst the lot. One of the few, that is, who don't take the place too seriously.

I am so very glad that your career seems to be taking shape in the way that it should. When you wrote to me you were probably in the "before the recital" sort of dither about the Graduate English Club, and I know of course how you feel about it, and how important it is. But darling you must *not* talk about working yourself blind and deaf, and dying before you accomplish anything. It bothers me terribly. I know that you work in fits and starts and when an idea crystallizes nothing can stop you from expressing it. Ordinary things like sleep and meals and having darned socks. But if you won't take care of yourself for yourself, won't you, for me? You are too precious to lose—for so far as I know, death is loss to mortals. Don't burn yourself out. I know that you are great and will do great things, and I feel so scared sometimes. Scared and worried because perhaps the greatest thing and the most valuable work for the wife of a genius is to look after him. And then I think I should run home and marry you and study cookbooks and diets and chase microbes frantically and practically put you in a glass cage and dust it off every hour. But I'm afraid that if I did, I'd feel rather an ass, trying to echo your ideas, and nothing else.

I am glad that Mary Winspear is on hand. Altogether, you will probably have a pretty good time, what with your dignity at the head table and so on. (I don't envy you that in the least. The sight of Currelly across a road makes me uncomfortable, let alone across a table.)

Snelgrove had word from McCurry to go ahead with his Ph.D. and a hint that his scholarship might be renewed next year. Snelgrove and I went out and binged on Saturday, and I talked his ear off, just about. He hoped that mine would be renewed. Just now I don't give a damn.

It is late, and I just meant to write a short note to tell you how much I like you. And how I've spent the whole day wandering about Westminster Abbey, and saw the horse-guards changing at Westminster, and walked along to Trafalgar Square just at twilight—still thinking about dead kings and you and the wonder of the great city bestirring itself after the day's work. I am much more reconciled to the Institute now as Geoffrey Webb, my tutor, a Cambridge man, has told me to cut several courses of lectures and see things for myself. I am going to Canterbury to see the cathedral one day next week. And I am beginning to get a pretty fair idea of the nature of Gothic architecture—I mean, a smattering. For I've just begun to see the beauties of Westminster, although I have been there four times. But it all takes time and work, and I am pretty keen about it. I'm not leading a gay life, though, and that's just as well. I don't know whether to move into College Hall to meet more people, or not. Living alone gives one more room to sprout in silence. Whether silence and peace are better than intercourse with many students from various places, I don't know. I'm not interested in whoopy, but I should like a bit more conversation. What do you think?

One month gone. Goodnight dear.

H.

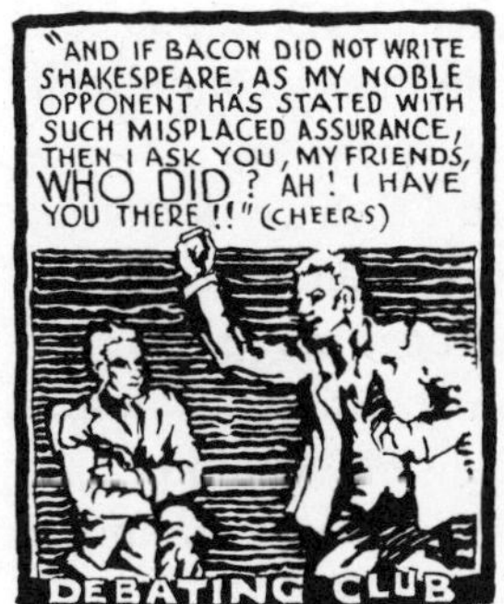

Toronto, Ont.
[*9 November 1934*]

My little girl:

I am nearly going nuts trying to keep abreast with all the work I've got to do and my own physical sluggishness. The reaction from an overtiring summer has finally got me, and I am now in for a session of headaches, burning eyelids, tired and heavy so that I practically never wake up at any decent time in the mornings, rasped nerves, bad dreams and general debility. Also my teeth are being fixed, which doesn't help any. I rather suspect abscesses, and can't help feeling that other things are slowing me up besides tired eyes.

One more bellyache and I'll start being cheerful. Vera [Frye]'s salary is not coming through—she hasn't her last April cheque yet. And Dad's third period—to speak biographically—is drawing to a close. Dad's life consists in settling somewhere, gradually getting into debt, getting behind with rent, owing everybody in sight, ending up as a complete bankrupt and clearing out hastily to start life in a new place. He did that in Lowell, Mass., before I was born; he achieved his Sherbrooke, Que., demise when I was five; he is completing the third one now. He is two years behind in his rent, and was told by his landlord to put up $100 or get out and leave the furniture behind. I rushed $50, which was all I had, down there. I have no idea, of course, what the outcome will be; it may affect our marriage plans to some extent. I've been sort of kidding myself into thinking this wouldn't happen, knowing quite well that it would, subconsciously. Jesus can talk as He likes about it being the duty of a Christian to dismiss his parents as part of an outmoded stage in his development when he really has something to do: it can't always be done like that. Now we'll draw a line under all this and start again.

I haven't been to any concerts yet, except the ones Mme. de Kresz conducts for the Women's Lit. over at Wymilwood. Aside from that I haven't been out much. The Blake group continues to function. The Blake thesis will be good, I think. I read a paper on the subject to the Graduate English group, who were tremendously impressed. They didn't altogether agree, but I shut them up on most counts. Last Monday there was a debate with Osgoode—the stock Church and State subject. I led Emmanuel to a sparse victory, with Earl Lautenslager seconding me. For once, I spoke better than Earl in public.

Saturday morning at nine o'clock I lecture to Frosh on *Tess of the D'Urbervilles*. Saturday morning at ten I lecture to Sophs on *Lycidas*. Needless to say, most of my work goes on *Lycidas*. I have been marking a good many essays, including one by some idiotic woman who told me that Milton wrote his Italian sonnets in Spanish because he could express himself better in that language. I asked Daniells about that, and he thought it was probably her note on his reference to Elizabeth Browning's *Sonnets from the Portuguese*. Daniells I like better all the time.

I found your letter on the notice-board stuck down with five thumbtacks (courtesy Art [Cragg] and George [Birtch]) to prevent me taking it off in too big a hurry. You're a good girl, darling, and the best kind of a sport. Too bad you're lonesome, but I expect you've more or less got that coming to you in England. I rather dreaded it, what with all I had heard about the chilly English and their chilly climate and their chilly houses. Don't get too blue—you seem to be taking exactly the right attitude. You're at a disadvantage not having somebody with you you know and like, and in not, apparently, being in a definitely cosmopolitan centre of culture, such as the universities would provide.

The Schweitzer lecture sounded interesting. You see, for a philosophy of history one has to work with three organic unities, the individual, the historical, and the evolutionary. The first unit is too small, and any attempt to explain history from the hero idea, like Carlyle's, becomes chaotic and irresponsible. The evolutionary unit of the species is too large for history, because it is all one movement; hence the progress theories are also inadequate. Hence there has to be a historical unit in the middle; one double in nature, biological or individual, and at the same time evolutionary to allow for the genuine element of advance. The value of Spengler's work lies in his having realized and defined the former as the culture: a historical growth subject to the organic laws of maturation and decay. The other element was attacked by Hegel from one side, and by Marx from the other, who failed for complementary reasons, at least as far as this particular problem is concerned. Its unit is not the culture but the Incarnation, which permits of a Christian development beyond Spengler, probably the last heretic of the first rank in the modern world. Spengler's own thinking, incidentally, owes very little to either Hegel or Marx.

You are quite right—your absence saves no time or concentration for me at all. I need you to get things working properly, besides wanting you for your own sake. Ever since I first knew you I have been telling you to grow up and find your feet, without bothering very much to define what I meant or exactly how I expected you to attain maturity. Had I tried to do so, I should have wasted time and breath; any impact made by one person on another that is constructive and helpful comes from the loins, not the heart or head. The humbler people, in their deep unconscious wisdom, have expressed this when they speak of teaching as "loining." Well, anyway, the point is that the fullest and most worthwhile life is the happiest, and happiness cannot be egocentric; it has to be common to two people in the deepest kind of sympathy with each other. That is why I can't enjoy anything that has no relation whatever to you, which is why I was so miserable on the mission field. You have the same predicament in London, but where you are you are doing your work as much for me as for yourself. It's the same with me over here, of course. So the year should pass very quickly, my pet.

Well, sweet, this is almost as bleak a letter as the room you will be reading it in, but I'll send it anyway, and compose another shortly. I feel your absence keenly enough, but for all that I occasionally remind myself with a start that you're not right at my elbow after all. What I would be doing now if I hadn't met you at Montreal I shudder to think. Probably shovelling coal on the *Ausonia*, or currycombing cows on an eastbound cattle boat. There's a limit to being short-circuited. Oh, well, you're not here, and that's that. But not forever.

Your letters are beautifully written and a treat to read, and would be if I were a third party instead of the addressee. Women seem to be able to achieve an absolute command of self-expression denied to the more abstract male. Some women, that is, like Katherine Mansfield and Ellen Terry and Helen Kemp. A classification which is more serious than you think.

Lovingly,
Norrie

5, Torrington Square
London W.C. 1
Nov. 27, 1934

My darling, Saturday a big stack of letters came from home, including $1.05 royalty (!) on the map, and a letter from you. Saturday marked a great change for me here. I moved to this house, which is the one Norah recommended. I have a larger room, for which I pay four shillings a week more, but feel that it is money well spent. They serve meals here, and the house is full of students mostly male and medical. And all very friendly and jolly and, for the most part, serious workers. So at last I feel absolutely contented with my house. I can get to work now, which is what I could not do before, but I suppose two months fluttering about is not a dead loss and more or less inevitable in a new city and new course of study. Architecture has been bothering me, but I am working now, and have to produce an essay on thirteenth-century Gothic as seen in Canterbury Cathedral, Westminster Abbey, the Temple Church, Southwark Cathedral, all of which I have visited lately.

I was a little up a tree when I said I was one of the most mature students at the Institute, thank heaven. I have found some very worthwhile people there in addition to the foolish social butterfly ones. I have made friends with a pretty dominant personality—Millicent Rose. She is keen about music and being a strong-minded female, springs to her opinions rapidly and dogmatizes firmly. Cambridge degree in English. 23. Millicent in her way reminds me very much of you as you were when I first knew you, a little less given to acid remarks, but equally positive. And mentally very much alert. She lives next door and envies me in my new room. And truly, I am very happy.

But why else than because you have written to me, and I feel that I am getting a grip on existence once more?

Darling, I knew you should have been seeing a dentist long ago—of course you did too, and had no money. Surely this money-grubbing will end for us sometime? I feel in such a ridiculous position here rolling in wealth and my family worrying along in the same old way, and yours in worse difficulties. If you and I stick to business we shall be able to help out, but how soon? As for our marrying—that should not be much to worry about—when or how it happens. You know that I am not interested in a lot of fuss. Life is wonderful enough from day to day without needing any bang-up festivity or a wedding trip.

There it is again—everything I think about seems to come back some way to you, for I love you so very much, and probably always will. "Probably" is just a reservation to deal with the times when you will be exasperating and your socks will need darning and I shall be too lazy to do it for you.

H.

Toronto, Ont.
[*4 December 1934*]

Juliet:

Oh, dearest, I wish you were back. I can argue with myself as long as I like about this being such a marvellous opportunity for you and so forth and so on, but I can't get around the fact that in the meantime you're not here. And I've got so damned much to do and I haven't been to a lecture for a month and my eyes hurt like hell and I've got to read anyhow and nobody loves me and I'm perpetually tired. It's rather awful, you know, carrying around this lean, hungry, parched body of mine all by myself, when a touch from you would give it strength to go on again. I have to set my teeth, almost, even to make this anaemic kind of contact with you, because of the way in which you are associated with a choking in my throat and a generally stifled and frustrated sensation. I may sound extravagant, but I don't think I'm exaggerating. Bone of one bone, flesh of one flesh; as long as we are that, how can we be torn apart and function properly? Still, friendship is necessary to love, and that means self-development; that is all that reconciles me to your absence.

Because the last thing I want to do is to possess you. I don't want a subservient female to wipe my nose and bring my slippers and tell me what a fine guy I am and give me beautifully balanced meals. If I required that of you, I should be debasing the subtle, cultured, refined woman I fell in love with. Doubtless there are men for whom the wife is merely a representative of an indiscriminate horde of womankind. But I love you, not because you are a woman, but because you are you. If you are going to be true to me you have to be true to yourself.

Managed to get a paper done for MacGillivray on Shelley's idealism. He was vastly impressed and said I must have done a lot of work on it. I didn't get around to undeceiving him. I like my lecturing fairly well. I've got a swell bunch of Frosh kids. We discuss *Tess of the D'Urbervilles*, and the difficulty is not to get them to talk, but to keep too many from talking at once. The second-year bunch is a bit awful—it's supposed to be a textual study of *Lycidas* and they haven't got any texts. How in hell can you teach a bunch of kids about one of the subtlest poems in English literature when they can't look at it? It's got me down. However, *Lycidas* is over with a couple of extremely bad lectures and has given place to the *Pilgrim's Progress*, which I know something about, I hope. After I get through with *Tess* with the Frosh I start *Erewhon*, a curiously futile and sadly dated book. I don't particularly like teaching it, as it is necessary to get all steamed up over ideas and paradoxes which appeared stimulating and brilliant fifty years ago. The business of being Grampa at twenty-two, of rejoicing in obsolete theories when one is purely out of sympathy with them, has its disadvantages.

I don't know whether it was you or your astral body that I told about

Wyndham Lewis' *Apes of God,* a book I'm busy with at the moment. It's a brilliant satire on literary charlatanism in London, imitates Rabelais particularly, with some Joyce—probably the best English novel since *Ulysses,* if that is in English. Sometimes it doesn't quite come off, but after reading it for half an hour I have to dash over to the library with a list of words a yard long to look up in the dictionary, where they are not always to be found.

Incidentally, I am quite well aware of the fact that I write extraordinarily bad letters to you and very infrequent ones. The reason is, I think, that the man who can pour out reams of love letters is far more in love with himself than with his correspondent. He devotes his energy to utterance, or self-expression, and transfers his affection from the lady to the paper. Denied the supreme satisfaction of bed-sheets, he sublimates himself in letter-sheets. I carried on this literary flirtation with you some years ago, in the first summer I was home and we corresponded. But since I have grown to love you so immeasurably more than I did then, or could then, the ideal lady at the other end of the postal service has become a part of myself, and when I write I am painfully conscious only of your absence. Hence these awkward, stammering, whining, almost illiterate letters.

Besides, I think I am going through a rather critical transitional stage. At present I am excessively morbid, given a great deal to self-loathing almost, certainly self-contempt, engaged in being utterly sick and weary of my apparently inexhaustible capacity to waste time, rush wildly down blind alleys, over-exert myself, do all sorts of fool things. I have a fearful lassitude in me, inherited from both parents (Dad's life consists in letting things slide and Mother's in not doing anything about it) which has been increasing every year of my college life, and is I hope gradually working out. Working out by the simple process of becoming horribly bored by everything except what I ought to be doing. But it means something very like a crisis, and I am waiting for one to pass if it is going to. Perhaps I shall be better fitted to marry you next year than this, which is another thing that reconciles me to your being away. But at present I'm sick, definitely. It may pass—such things often do with me, as you remember—and don't worry about it. I am hanging on till Christmas—after that we shall see.

Del [Martin] has invited me up as usual, but he himself is directly leaving for Mildred's [Mildred Learn's] after Christmas, so I accepted for the weekend and may or may not find polite excuses for that. I'd like to go, but I'd like even more to stay here in the dark and sleep. For the rest, my life is quiet enough. One or two shows with Daniells on Saturdays, the highlight of them being a gorgeous Walt Disney called *Goddess of Spring*, a treatment of the Proserpine story.

Haven't done anything new since I wrote you last. Still working on the Blake—ideas getting vaguer all the time. Vera's salary is gradually, but very slowly, coming through.

Well, George Birtch tells me I only have three or four essays in theology to do instead of eight or ten, so I feel more cheerful. In any case I'd better quit drivelling and send this off before you start wondering if I'm alive.

Lovingly,
Norrie

Toronto, Ont.
[*12 December 1934*]

Forwarded twice, this letter apparently took about three weeks to reach Kemp: it has a London forwarding postmark of 29 December, seventeen days after it was posted.

My dearest, I'm frightfully sorry to have missed Christmas—I can't get used to the idea of your being halfway around the world and the imperative necessity of sending Christmas gifts before Thanksgiving, and birthday greetings at Easter. I'm even more sorry to have sent my last letter, which I fondly hope has gone astray. It's quite true that I've been damnably sick all fall, but that's no reason for my inflicting myself on you to quite such an extent. Not in that way, at least.

The Bell Library opened recently and I went over for the prayers and sandwiches. Pratt told me that my appointment was secure for another year at least. He stopped and then added: "At least." Edgar said he'd try to get me some more money next year. I was talking to him a few days ago and he said he'd talk to Vincent Massey and see if there was any money left, and if so he wanted to ship me across to the B.M. next summer to finish up the Blake. This was to be preparatory to a year across later. This all may come to nothing whatever, but at any rate Edgar seems to be taking a definite interest. Auger, poor old boy, is just about gone. He made a good registrar around here, and he'll be missed.

The scare my family gave me a short time ago is gradually wearing off. I think Vera [Frye] is going to take a hand, for this winter at any rate. You see, dear, I owe this college a lot of money, and I want to pay it off if I possibly can this year, because they'd get after my scalp in short order if I got married, as Little expressed it, "on their money." That was what I meant when I said that if the family drained me of too much money it might affect our marriage plans. Now, dearest, I don't care anything about trousseaux or flower girls, and I shouldn't imagine you would either. But marriage it's got to be. I don't want the ceremony, I want companionship. This town is far too small to hold both of us, unmarried. No other arrangement will work.

The chances of my finishing this year in theology are about even. With such a gap in the English staff, I may have to swing over and devote my whole time to English. Roy Daniells, naturally enough, wants me to, and Edgar wants me to, and as soon as this mourning for Auger is over, I shall get Edgar and Pratt to persuade [Walter T.] Brown to let me chuck theology, if they will. I am getting impatient to get my teeth into the work, collect more degrees (this last more as a symbol of progress than as anything intrinsically valuable) and get some real experience as a teacher. And I don't want to hang on with a mixture of luck, gall, overwork, patronage, and the grace of God, pandering to Brown's pro-divinity prejudices.

Keep your chin up with the people you meet. If you know anything at all about what's being talked about, spill it; if not, pretend you do, bluff through and change the subject as soon as possible. If you can't say anything, look interested, as though you could if you wanted to. Whatever you do, remember that speech is better than silence, and if silence is necessary, never allow yourself to look stupid or sheepish. Avoid making obvious remarks, particularly the accepted generalizations concerning the subject of conversation. Above all, strive to cultivate a sort of immense calmness, which implies, without your speaking, that you are just a bit better than your interlocutor, and are quite ready to tear him apart if he makes a fool of himself. You'll have all England, or any country, eating out of your hand in no time.

My lecturing is improving gradually, I think. I'm getting some idea of how to time lectures, and how to emphasize obvious points properly, and how not to qualify my remarks in a buzzing and unintelligible monotone, and a lot of things like that. I'm at Shaw's *Saint Joan* with the freshmen, and start Bacon's *Essays* with second year next week.

I'm afraid my parcel will be a bit late for Christmas, but it might do for New Year's. I send books again, not because I want you to amass a huge library, but because it's the only thing I can give you without consulting you personally that would be in perfect taste. The wrapping up of the parcel was done by Daniells.

Well, dearest, there are a lot more things to say, but I'd better get this off just now. A Merry Christmas and a Happy New Year, my dear. I kiss you across the ocean. I know now what Blake meant by calling the Atlantic the sea of time and space. I wish you would tell me, if you can, when you are returning next year, in case anything comes of this Massey idea—that is, unless your scholarship is renewed.

Lovingly,
Norrie

[*London*]
December 17th, 1934

My dearest—what can I do for you, away so far from you here in London? You break my heart with longing for you and I want to run and comfort my man who is all that I care about, really. But what can I do? God, what can either of us do, but stick it out for another nine months? If anything should go wrong—I dare not think of that. All there is is a trust in something that must be God—and that is an agony of fear and doubt. I sent you a telegram today, and I wanted to tell you how greatly I love you and yearn for you and wish you were well and happier. But in the end it was a sorry affair, rather noncommittal, though I thought you might read my meaning through the clipped staccato of twenty words. For I could not bear to think of my tenderness going through the hands of callous telegraph operators and reaching you through machines and the peeking of Philistines.

I realized with a start that it is a great length of time since I have written to you. I have been puzzling over an essay, and when I need you most I write such incoherent stuff that I haven't the heart to send it. I finished the other night by crying myself to sleep, but I knew what was the matter, as usual. Someday I shan't be such a little bundle of jitters, and of course there won't be any reason for it when you will be there to make my teeth stop chattering and my nerves stop jumping up and down like the devils in Giotto's tortures of the damned. A few weeks ago I had some idea of trying to get this scholarship renewed. I am beginning not to care about that or anything else but getting home to you. And yet, I've got a lot owing to McCurry and Lismer and my family—and you. I wonder and wonder what I should do, and I don't care much what happens because I realize that Toronto is not a stagnant backwater town by any means. But I know you should get away for a time. Here I find Oxford people who put no stock whatever in higher degrees, and of course the Oxford M.A. just represents so much residence fees paid after graduation. No further work required after a B.A. And they look askance at a Ph.D as an American fetish introduced from Germany. Certainly the sort of degree Gordon Snelgrove will get is not making a greater man of him—but he never will be a great man. Agreeable, pleasant, even useful, but not greatly so.

For Christmas I am going to visit two old ladies with a sense of humour somewhere up in the Lake country for a week. Just found out about it today. It may be a silly thing to do—going there at this time of year when all it does is rain and rain, but I've promised and there is no getting out of it now, I think. I could go to Paris for the same money, but if it is a mistake, it is a mistake. At any rate, it is just for a week. I shall leave this London soot and grime and be with people. Then I shall come back for two weeks of sight-seeing here and Promenade Concerts.

Norrie, my dear, I think seriously that you are living too much alone; you sound as if you are letting yourself down. Don't think I don't understand, for I have to force myself to get out and face the world, and meet people and talk to strangers, and figure out ways of keeping from an introspection which in myself grows morbid and fruitless. I sometimes think that I should become a social creature, and help you that way, for you do need bucking up sometimes when you think you are still that little boy who suffered so intensely in school because of his yellow hair and spectacles and ability to beat the others hands down at work. You need a feeling of security, of belonging to a group of your equals, who respect and love you. Just your wife alone will never be able to satisfy you completely without that other also. Jane Welsh helped Carlyle through the bitter rewriting of the *French Revolution*, but she saw him expand and grow in the circle of cultured friends who gathered round him when it was accomplished. I am your Jane Welsh, but with a difference. For the twentieth century has formed a different type of woman. At least it gives her a chance to work at something which keeps her from becoming embittered at her husband alone having a career.

You have too much work to do, not enough new and stimulating friends, you need me and you need a doctor, and a change of scene. The only thing that makes me reconciled to the situation is that I realize it is the only way out of a good many difficulties. If I get a job we can get married, I can help Roy a little, and you and I may do some work that is worthwhile. Certainly I feel that I am just keeping going, but nothing very noteworthy has come of it so far. I have not met anyone yet who has half as great an influence as Miss Ray, Dr. Locke, Lismer—and the Courtauld Institute is made up of dry specialists—on such things as "arms and armour"!—dear old gentlemen like Constable, showy jokers like Webb—rude young gentlemen like Norris, and exasperated Germans like Freyhan. A good number can't lecture for beans although they are reputed to *know* a great deal.

Darling, I love you, and I love your letters. They never are, they never could be, awkward and whining. It is only spoilt babies who whine, and you are a man. I wish you wouldn't forget that you are a great man. The longer I am here the more I know it.

It *is* getting late and I feel pop-eyed with coffee and tiredness and crying and cheering up and now I shall go to bed and think I am with you.

My own darling,
Goodnight.

Toronto, Ont.
[*1 January 1935*]

Darling, thanks so much for Donne. It's the best edition of him extant, and I needed a Donne badly. And thanks for your cablegram, though I didn't follow its advice, but stayed here and worked. I'm rather glad I did, as I'm beginning to take a new grip on things. If this idea of Edgar amounts to anything at all, you could get your scholarship renewed and I could still see you next year. Sweetheart, don't take my bleatings too seriously when it comes to planning your career. I'd never forgive myself if I robbed you of anything you deserve by pulling a Kinder and Kuchen stunt on you. It's because I know I can trust your discretion absolutely that I trust myself to spill everything to you.

The Christmas rest bucked me up, and I think I shall work quietly and sanely for the rest of the year. Edgar's information shows that somebody cares about my immediate future, my fellowship here will be renewed O.K., and all I have to do is drift with the tide. I arose in my wrath the last week of the Christmas term and smote theology hip and thigh—I had five essays and three term exams to get done in a week. So I wrote two Church History essays Monday, two New Testament essays Tuesday, exams in Systematic Theology and Church History Wednesday, exam in New Testament and essay in Religious Pedagogy Thursday. Then I slept and slept. I got four A's in the essays I got back, and am not afraid of not having passed the exams—my New Testament, of all subjects, was a good paper. I am doing some work in Old Testament for [Richard] Davidson that should knock his eye out—connecting it with Frazer's *Golden Bough*. The Blake is getting organized: the introduction has taken what I hope will be its final shape. Do you know—this sounds either silly or a reflection on me—the amount of work I did in that one week actually rested my eyes.

The Blake group girls rallied around nobly in the holidays. After a very quiet and enjoyable Christmas with your family, I went over to their apartment and joined in a party which was very noisy and very genial. With their aid I have consumed a considerable amount of alcohol in the last week. Mary Winspear I like better all the time—I'll miss her next year. Peggy Roseborough is a sweet child—I really didn't discover her virtues last year. She asked me very humbly if I would take her to the symphony once in a while and expatiate for the benefit of her ignorance. Last year she lived with a dominating mother who censored her reading and taught English at the Bible College, and this year she lives with Mary, so has blossomed out.

Now, dearest, I know it rains all the time in London, but don't get in sympathy with the weather too much. As you yourself remark, you don't have to do any work to get places in England, so that needn't worry you, as you start off anyhow with an initial capital of brains and background, to say nothing of a faculty to write, vastly ahead of most other people. If only you had a young husband who would dance attendance on you and hold your hand in the fever of inspiration, show you where to put commas, initiate you into the unfathomable mysteries of semicolons, lead you gently away from abstract colorless words that crackle to concrete ones that resound, give you some idea of rhythm and teach you to type, you'd be all right. Jean Cameron has become much more cheerful this year, Dot Drever says, because she went up and down so often she finally became aware of the rhythm. It's a good tip. You are quite right about the disastrous results of introversion—during these holidays I have gone with a good many people and it's helped me a great deal. I was at dinner with Dr. Pratt the other night—Roy Daniells, Munro Beattie and three U.C. English professors were in the party, which was very enjoyable. Ned [Pratt] is the world's best host. I think it was an extremely good idea to stay here this year.

This is a rambling and incoherent letter, but you get the idea—that I got the work done that was worrying me, the Blake is straightening out, the career lightens up ahead for a little while further, and I have sat up and taken a bit of notice of other people, as you suggest. I hope you have a good time with your old ladies—if they're the right kind of old ladies, as you seem to think, it's a better idea at the moment than Paris, which you can see when you're feeling more like Paris. Oh, dearest, I hope I see you this summer. Things will work out so beautifully when we have each other. Don't cry any more, unless it rests you to do so.

Lovingly,
Norrie

5, Torrington Square, London
January 3rd, 1935

My darling, I shan't write a very long letter this time, as I am trying to catch up with my letter-writing—I've got some fifteen letters to write today, and I'm trying to finish it in order to get at work again. I love to get letters, but the pleasure brings also the need of answering them, and I have not learned to spare myself—I can't just dash off a note and call it a letter—unfortunately I started off with one to the family, and now here you are, and I can never be brief about either one of you.

I spent Christmas at Windermere with two charming old ladies, and visited Wordsworth's cottage and went tramping about in that wonderful country. Saw Stratford-on-Avon too on the way up. Consequently I feel very much more at home in England and much less the ineffectual creature I described to you before. Your advice is very good—I am putting it into practice—but a contented frame of mind is necessary first, and that was given me by your last letter. For the one before that put me into such low spirits that I felt as if all the fates were against me—not myself, but as a representative of the poverty-stricken multitudes who had no right to all the things that are being given me now—money, friends, congenial work, leisure, and yourself. I was afraid, dreadfully afraid, of something bad happening to you—but it has not happened and you are cheerful and hopeful, and full of fight again, and so am I.

It was nice of you to send me what you did—Diego Rivera is a great change after Giotto which is what I'm busy with just now, and his work makes one tremble in one's bones. And Alexander [Woollcott] is lovely—I am enjoying his breezy essays so much—a delightful man of the world who converses wittily over a cocktail.

But as I was saying, your second last letter certainly did arrive, and made me think that I should hurry home as soon as ever I could and make no effort to stay longer. Then along comes this last with its good news about chances of your coming here in the summer, and so I begin to feel full of ambition again.

It seems dreadful that the loss of Auger is something which may be beneficial to you and me. I hate the idea—it brings home so closely how we all live by the death of someone or something. And yet Auger would not grudge anything—he never spared himself to help all students—he was the first person I had to see when I first came, and he somehow summed up all that Victoria College meant. He was kind, and good, and personally interested in one's particular fate. You must know yourself how much worse a death seems, when an ocean is between and when no one here knows or understands anything about the man who has gone. Then too it is so strange to comprehend an event from reports of others, and have no actual physical evidence at all. The same thing brings with it at some moments a hypochondriac fear that you are so far from me, and I don't know what you are like, and I'm scared to death when I think of being your wife.

And it is time to shake myself and stop being so doleful.

I shall talk to Constable at the beginning of this next term, about my case. If the thing is not renewed I'll be returning sometime late in the summer. Going to Italy at Easter, but don't know what happens after our June exams.

Your Helen (quite cheerful once more.)

5, Torrington Square, London
Saturday (near Sunday) [*12? January 1935*]

My dear Frye—

You *are* a very trying youngster. I breathe an exasperated sigh of relief and at the moment I am uncertain which I should spank first—you or Gordon Snelgrove. For different reasons, of course. But I feel like a mother whose child has just fallen downstairs and come up with a cheeky grin. After I have shrieked and moaned and gone into hysterics—there you are, quite safe and sound, and coolly telling me to take a tip from the rhythm of Jean's ups and downs. Oh, *damn* you anyway! It's enough to make any female start blasting like a fish-wife. Wasting my sympathy on you when here's poor dear little Gordon with his turned out ears, and his girlish giggle, and his need of a big strong woman to make up his mind, tell him what to say, whom to like and whom not to dislike, tell him he'll be all right, not to worry for he isn't *really* as dumb as he thinks he is. He has such a painful desire to get a Ph.D. now—writing a thesis on this guy Jonathan Richardson. Of course I must give him credit for having wanted to study the Impressionists, but Constable said more or less "Oh dear no. Why it's never been *done* before!"

The University of London building is coming on apace, and as it joins Torrington Square, half the square is to come down after March 25th and we must move out. Something will turn up in the meantime, so I shan't worry too much about where I'm to live next. Since I've been placidly visiting the National Gallery, going to Proms, and getting a darned sight more conversational at mealtimes, reading Alexander Woollcott and making some more friends, I'm not worrying about anything. Then of course, you silly old thing, I might conceivably be rather pleased at the idea of your being here next summer.

Eleanor Clements stayed here with me all evening (she's a friend of Dot Drever's, and a cousin of Brad Clements. Studying pottery & weaving at the London Central School of the Arts and Crafts.) She and I did a good deal of gossiping tonight. She tells me that Lawren Harris has left his wife and gone—or come here to live with Bess Housser. That the next rumour is that Fred Housser is rather keen about Yvonne McKague. Etc. Great thing, these rumours.

Oh darling, it *is* so like you to couple Peggy's virtues with her humble request for enlightenment with regard to music! I can just see the way to your heart! What *did* I tell you about needing the respect and admiration of people (other than myself)—*I'm* not being respectful. In five, ten, fifteen years' time, when I feel you are losing your zest for living (with me) and if, like Lawren Harris who is reported to have said he needed new inspiration, you need to get rid of me for awhile, I shall depart on a discreet and prolonged business trip.

Now I've been mean enough to twist several of your meanings and fling them back piece-meal in your face. You did it to me once, after I wrote you a rather silly sort of letter about George [Clarke] and when I can't think of anything worse I dig up that as an excuse to spit like an alley cat. And as I explained in the first place, it is just my reaction to having "taken you too seriously." I should have recognized the usual fall panic but somehow I forgot. You are a naughty boy and you ought to have your ears pulled. Consider it done. Quite disgusting—five essays and three term exams—all A's I suppose. Being proud of you and fond of you and terribly scared of seeming miracles, I should hate to let you know that I am just a little bit—well, uh—fond of you. Dear me, no. I've told you that so often.

But after I've got all this off my chest—I do wish you were here just this minute, longer than that of course. You would laugh and I should too, for no reason at all. I am so glad you have had a nice time with Mary and Peggy and Pratt. And I am glad you stayed in Toronto after all, but when I cabled I was in a panic and pictured you sleeping Christmas away in a dismal sort of fog.

Term starts next week, and I'm all ready for it—happy, full of pep, and rather more than usually glad about you. I shall wink at your photograph and turn in for the night—what is left of it. The weather has turned cold, and the shillings fly in my gas metre.

H.

Toronto, Ont.
[*16 January 1935*]

My dearest:

Your last letter has just come. I could kick myself for writing you such infernal rubbish. Please excuse it, and remember next time that you have to allow for the fact that my state of feelings would be described far more fully and emphatically to you than to anyone else. What I wrote you was all quite true, but just as society can endure the most intolerable evils without collapsing, so an individual can be extremely unhappy and still look all right to a casual friend. A closer one can sympathize without being alarmed.

I am glad you had a good time with your old ladies. Perhaps it was a wiser move than Paris, which might have scared you back into your shell again, and anyway, do England first, as Henry James said. Yes, Daniells worried too about the death of Auger being a help to him, but my satisfaction about having a chance to advance has nothing whatever to do with my feeling about Auger's death, which I regret a great deal, and I think it's a bit morbid to confuse the two emotions. Besides, closing the gap quickly and quietly is the only way to handle death.

I spent New Year's with the Millars in Hamilton, which was very pleasant—Mildred Oldfield was there. Then I pushed on to Welland and stayed with Jean [Cameron] a couple of days. Very soft and sweet is Jean—at her worst a bit too soft and a bit too sweet. I once complained to Ernie [Gould] that I always patronized Jean and treated her like a child—couldn't seem to get away from it. Ernie gravely postulated two reasons; first, her association with young [Laurence] Cragg, second, her alveolar arch. Her upper jaw, said Ernie, extends beyond her lower, preventing her chin from being firm and mature, and continually exposing her front teeth. Hence a childish expression. Funny how our careers depend on such trifles: what makes me Victoria's infant prodigy, my grasp of Blake or my hair? They are essential factors in one personality, but the outward visible symbol is the one most easily grasped.

And so I get round again, in spite of myself, to the adoration of my own manifestation of Beatrice. All the beauty and quiet fostering strength of Helen. All womanhood focused, for the personal reveals the infinite, in any object of love. Oh, darling, if I have strained and longed and suffered for you, it isn't solely because I want our bodies to touch. *That* comes up when I try to write letters; the sense of your physical absence. But I don't feel that you are absent, ordinarily. What really pulls and tears at me is a compulsion to struggle to educate myself, to mature and grow serene and strong, to become too big for irritation and sulkiness, to prepare myself for a glorious and terrible life with you. My words sound inflated, but they are inadequate and not false. To live with another human being on equal terms must be by far the most difficult and subtle of the arts, and yet the most thrilling and satisfying. But love and friendship with you! That delicate interplay of wills in a higher plane of existence, where they unite and don't conflict, on the level that you set, would take a genius to sustain. Perhaps I am a genius, in a sense, but when I think of my gawkiness and tactlessness and the mechanical barrenness of my infernally precocious brain, I shudder. The ministry, with its requirement of almost absolute versatility at an indefinitely high pitch, compelled me and yet finally frightened me away. But you don't frighten me: I feel taut and nervous, with shivers in my stomach, as though before a piano recital, but joyous and ecstatic none the less.

We shall live a divine comedy together, our inferno a boiling torrent of sexual love, our purgatory the perfect peace of repose through the satisfaction of desire. We shall descend hell as lover and mistress, you as my monopolized hetaera, into the chambers of the virtuous heathen and the glib liars, talking, chattering and laughing endlessly of our ambitions, interests and studies. We shall be submerged in devouring flames of passion, swept into a delirium of touch. We shall sink to the depths of the universe and beyond, to the utter quiescent coma of union and surrender. Everything hot and troublesome and individual will fall away and leave us together. Then we shall gradually separate, and, immeasurably strengthened and purified, pass through love to the final paradise of friendship, when each will be in possession of an inward privacy of soul, to be respected because of the other.

Well, I must do now what I have done a good many times—shut up after saying too much.

Norrie

[*London*]
January 24th, 1935

My dear, I haven't heard from you again since your letter marked Jan. 1st but I suppose that can be accounted for by the long interval between my letters. I haven't any particular news this time, except that I have a cold and damnit, I just got over having a bad one last week and was dosed by half the doctors in the house. Besides that, I was as homesick as the dickens last week for some four days, for no very good reason, but that passed too. I read your letters to see whether I could feel that I knew you, and I didn't, and I dissolved in total gloom. Things get pretty bad when I can't even imagine you. But I went to see Millicent [Rose], and bless her heart, she was playing the Mozart Clarinet Quintet on her gramophone, and a man in the house has the Bach D minor Toccata and Fugue, and so everything was happy once more. I went to see John Gielgud's *Hamlet* with Maysie Roger who was with me two days last week. And Millicent and I went to *The Magic Flute* last night.

My work is going much better. We've got bang into the Renaissance at last and I've figured out the ways of this crazy Institute, skip lectures when I can, and go to the galleries. I was at the Victoria and Albert today looking at the Italian sculpture, and had the biggest thrill I've had for weeks when I came to Nicola Pisano. Then there is a lot of Donatello, and reproductions of Ghiberti's bronze doors in the Baptistry of Florence, a cast of Michelangelo's David and Moses—about six rooms of marble and terracotta, and two courts of plaster casts. It is funny—Trajan's column in the V. & A. and part of the Parthenon in the B.M.

Oh darling! would I be the proud little chicken, if I could show *you* how to navigate in London! I haven't seen the Blakes at the Tate Gallery yet, and that is where you would be a great part of the time. There are so many exciting things to see, and it would be so much more satisfactory to see them with you. This going about by oneself is a silly way—I mean living by myself fundamentally, for I've got a few very good friends by now. But the time is going very quickly, and I'm almost afraid of June coming the day after tomorrow, and so much to be done. But all one's life is like that, and if they expect me to have anything more than the mere beginning of a taste for sculpture and painting in eight months, they are indulging in rather fond delusions. In my duller moments I think that another year at the Institute would drive me nutty, but if I had a year in which to work on my own track after this survey of art history from Babylon to Bloomsbury, I could have some fun!

Millicent grows ardent and very talkative about Communism. I am interested, and very fond of her, and delighted with her conversation, and her enthusiasm, but I am a little too busy to become a convert.

I must stop now and go soak my head or something drastic for this cold is rather sniffly. All the lights in the house are being turned off one by one, so it must be late. And I can't even kiss you goodnight because you might catch a cold too. I hope my last two letters didn't sound cranky—I remember rather vaguely that I was annoyed with you a little and forget now what for. But you would forgive me, wouldn't you? I think perhaps you might.

Goodnight,
Helen

Toronto, Ont.
[*25 January 1935*]

My dear:

I have just received your letter. This morning I am taking Edgar's period with Second Year Honour to talk to them about Blake. I think I shall pass around some of Norah's [Norah McCullough's] postcards. Speaking of Blake reminds me. As nearly as I can dope it out the Courtauld Institute likes work to be done on English painters; hence Snelgrove has a big advantage over you because he wants to do some work on a tenth-rate Englishman, and you don't. Now England only *has* one painter, who besides being a painter was a poet and a philosopher, and generally the greatest Englishman this side of Shakespeare. Why couldn't you do him? There's very little work done on him: Figgis and Binyon have made collections of his work, and there is a book on the Job engravings, but anything like a rounded study of his work as an artist has yet to be done. And you happen to have a husband who knows as much about him as any man living. So why not do Blake?

Last night I went down to hear John Strachey on the future of capitalism. Night before last was the symphony. The brasses snuffled and gargled and sobbed and farted all the way through Tschaikowsky's Pathetic. The French horns worked the slop-pail alibi for all they were worth. It was awful. Then Boris Hambourg made a frightful mess of a Haydn cello concerto in D. I think there are two concerti in D, and [Ernest] MacMillan seemed to be in some doubt which one he was playing. Then Dr. Adrian Boult, B.B.C. conductor, went to town on the *Meistersinger* Prelude. Gorgeous showpiece for a visiting conductor.

Of course I couple Peggy's virtues with her desire to be enlightened. Isn't that a virtue? And if the girl finds me useful as a sort of cultural gigolo, she flatters me to that extent, and a response to flattery has to play up the qualities that flattery postulates. A teacher is not necessarily a poseur just because he isn't paid for his teaching and does it informally over coffee. Well, I have to get this off right away, as the lecture is at twelve and it's eleven-thirty now.

Lovingly,
Norrie

[*London*]
February 4th, 1935

My dear man!

You are improving! I've had a letter from you on two successive Mondays, and I like you a lot. I'm sorry if I dragged you across the carpet by the hair, and I won't do it again, until next time. That's what I'm for, you know. And you needn't take my mood very seriously—it's all I can do to keep from gurgling because I'm so happy, and I am now contemplating hooking the bright boy of 3T3 and living with him until Blake do us part. (This last in case you insist that I stick around here for a few years for the purpose.)

But darling, you do frighten me sometimes, and you might as well know it. Just sometimes when I feel tired and depressed and you are not near me to make me see you as a human being, very much alive. At those times I can only think of you as one of the great men of our time, someone so far above me, who will reach his goal in spite of everything. Whereas I diddle about—and find it hard to realize that I *have* actually pulled your ears and will do so a good many times yet. I always feel so damned uncomfortable when I get tired and sleepy and sentimental and put anyone on a pedestal. Because I don't feel it my role exactly, to stand round with my ears flapping and admire what you do—and yet I've got so proud of you, and so anxious to know that everything is right with you. Hang it all, anyway, I *am* getting tired of this pen and ink and having only your picture to talk to when I come home.

I *am* a beast to grumble. I started off happy as could be, and now I'll try to remember what I was going to tell you, when I suddenly started bawling like Tschaikowsky. I am arranging my work much better these days, am working on Renaissance sculpture at present. Not going to any more lectures than I can help—skipping things like ceramics and textiles and Flemish painting. I got into a splutter last week struggling with

German, but I resolutely looked at the exam papers, decided I could manage their French and German translation in a walk, that I knew nothing whatever about the medieval period, that I shall know quite a bit about the Renaissance. Four papers—two on a general outline of art history which would shame any yankee college for scope. The special period is the paper to splurge on. Today I worked on Donatello, and tomorrow I'm going to the Victoria and Albert to look at Ghiberti and Donatello and Verrocchio and probably pay a visit to two of the most amusing spots in the place. One is the lunch room and the other is what follows. The lunch room is decorated with William Morris tiles of seasons—there isn't a square inch that hasn't got some design or other on it. And as for the john—would you believe it, the tiles all around the toilet are marked with the monogram of V. & A.

On Saturday I went to see Carlyle's house. I came away with a strong distaste for such museums. They've got locks of his hair, and locks of Jane Welsh's hair and her scissors and work basket. They've got Carlyle's woollen socks and his dressing gown and his portable desk and unused pen nibs. Endless letters, in a beautiful hand, all set out for the curious to read. Among them were three notes he had written to his wife with Christmas and birthday gifts, such tender intimate notes they were. I felt ashamed to be reading them, for they were never meant to be read by idle passers-by. And even if I did forget who I was for the moment and imagined that I was Jane Carlyle—I looked at her picture on the wall and I was indignant. What right had I to intrude, no matter how sympathetically, into a relationship which was theirs alone? No matter if she herself did write impulsively to half her friends when she was annoyed, and berate him soundly. She was a clever, proud woman, and her portrait was as mute and unperturbed as most of the English I have not met lately. At least all these people could come, but she looked over their heads. But there was one horrible enlarged photograph of Carlyle as an old man. The eyes looked straight into your eyes, and they were moist and rheumy and the lids were loosened. He looked so ill and old, and reminded me of my grandfather when I last saw him. He seemed to tell me that to love someone was given to very few! There are so many lonely people, so very many, as you have seen yourself, and to some the same glorious thing happens, and to many others, it doesn't. Why then do you wish to live apart from the man who will be, who is, your husband? What can you gain of spiritual worth, away from him? You meet many new people and see many things in London, but are you getting your roots in the ground, on strange soil? Go home after this year and begin to work, there is enough to be done at home. You will create something there. Do not stay here amongst a crowd of agreeable fools who have no idea what life is to give them, spending your youth for a couple of letters tacked after your name. That is evading the issue. Do you realize that you are nearly twenty-five, and time is as relentless as ever—I stopped talking to myself long enough to look again at old uncle Thomas and he still seemed of the same opinion.

Of course last week I was so fed up with the Institute and the continual lectures with rows of dates and lantern slides that went off quickly one after another. And fed up with wishing we had one really vital personality about. Now that Roger Fry is gone, that hope is gone too. I'd almost thought I'd have to get back to Lismer to get back some interest in painting. But Mr. [L.C.] Knights came to the rescue, indirectly, this weekend. I read a book of his, written by a friend, a Mrs. [Q.D.] Leavis. It is called *Fiction and the Reading Public* and is the result of her research into what sort of stuff the public reads and wants, the degeneration of the quality of reading material with the greater public demand. She examines what makes the bestseller and the bad effect of the Book of the Month Club sort of selection which gives a stamp of approval to work not of great merit, the cheap magazines and the escape from life. I haven't finished it yet, but it offers food for thought. I haven't quite worked out yet what I can best do at home, but at home it must be. I am not made for the altogether contemplative existence, and to spend two years the way Gordon [Snelgrove] is, on his chasing after Richardson's portraits—I can't see it. I seem to jump around rather oddly, but here's the idea: Mrs. Leavis has rolled up her sleeves and got to work on a practical survey of the present situation of literary England so far as the buying public is concerned. And I think that there are a few little problems with regard to art and the artist's public which could be dealt with to greater advantage than a study of Blake by me. I am not up to it as yet—the trouble is that I haven't thought much about Blake, I suppose.

Next day. I have just written to McCurry asking for money to finish out the summer. I haven't the nerve to ask him for another year here. You see it would really mean two years because one has to be here on the spot two years to get an M.A. An extra year for me would send me home knowing a deuce of a lot more, but with nothing in the way of degrees.

That is why I hesitate, knowing that to ask for a renewal would be creating a precedent, as the scheme is for *two years* and not any more.

Must stop now and run off to old Campbell Dodgson on Dürer.

Love—
Helen

[*London*]
Tuesday night [*12 February 1935*]

Darling! do you know what has happened now? Today I had my long expected talk with Constable. You see his secretary scared me off before and I finally wrote him a letter last week, asking what he thought of my applying for a renewal next year. *And* he said that I had been doing excellent work (!) How the hell he found that out I don't know because Webb has no idea what I'm doing. That he would strongly recommend my application and that I'm to write to McCurry & say that. He thinks that if I clear off the diploma exam in June then I can spend the summer and next year working in galleries and museums under supervision. Since I am to work in a gallery when I go back, that would be preferable to working here on a special subject toward an M.A., because I must be familiar with the actual work, and there isn't much time during the course itself. He certainly bucked me up a good deal, said I was to write my letter first then he would send his. And you know, we might just pull it off! I wrote a note to old Snelgrove this morning and he beamed all over, because the poor man had been disappointed at my giving up the idea altogether, and had been trying to cheer me up on Tuesday when he took me off to lunch. There are times when Gordon is a great help, and that was one of them. He's improving these days because he has much more self-confidence since his work is going better and he knows more people.

I told you I was going to visit Edith Manning Burnett. It was even more successful than I had hoped and her husband is charming while she is one of the most fascinating people I have ever gazed upon for a whole evening all at once.

I'm going off to plan the Italy trip tomorrow. Millicent [Rose] is not working at all systematically these days, as Communism dominates her thoughts—there's nothing I can do as she is a much more dominant person than I am. I'm just plugging along getting a foundation for some better work later on, so that my existence isn't particularly exciting. But my French has improved no end and my German is certainly good enough to pass their sight translation exam. I continually marvel at the truly brilliant conversation of Millicent as she stands at my doorstep and paints Russia with all the fervour of a young idealist.

And so, once more I am reconciled to existence here. I still feel that you are rather far away, but that is almost inevitable and so I must work away and remember that when I finally *do* have you I shall love you so fiercely that you will think it is a young tiger you have and not the quiet dimly lit small person who sits here now. But my dear, as you say, everything will be glorious when we are together—and we *shall* be married, won't we! Did I tell you I had written to Lismer explaining situation, i.e. could I have job and be married to you?

I must close up for the night and get into bed which is comfortable, but not companionable.

Helen

[*London*]
Feb. 28 [*1935*]

My dear, if I don't find a letter from you shortly I shall feel very much the ex-wife. But there is no use enlarging upon that. I know what you felt like out west, and I know what Connie [Griggs] meant when she said letter-writing became more and more difficult. All I do is pack up my feelings so far as you're concerned and try to forget about them. For what else is there to do? But there are terrific gales raging on the Atlantic these days, and that must be holding up letters.

One of the men in the house here—Mr. Knights—and I are becoming quite friendly over breakfasts and dinners. He is the one who is writing a Ph.D. thesis on seventeenth-century English social conditions, lectures, and edits *Scrutiny* with F.R. Leavis (Cambridge). We went around Bloomsbury the other night and discussed Millicent [Rose] over coffee. I've been going to some of her meetings and feel that taking up student Communism as an indoor sport is quite a waste of time.

I've had a letter from McCurry, a very nice one, in which he quite agrees that I need more money to last the summer here—he has not had time to answer the other big question, of course.

I'm still working away, all on my own—the idea here is to have supervision regularly and let students go their own way—but we haven't had any supervision all term and no essays to write as Webb is too busy or too lazy to read them and always postpones his session with us. I had a big talk the other day with the librarian here about starting a seminar system, and several other things that I thought should be done. The whole place is pretty slipshod, the way it is now, and if I'm here next year I can see quite a few changes will be worked in. Just now I'm plugging away too damned hard to get a rudimentary knowledge of European art in general to have much interest in anything beyond that.

And so, there isn't much to talk about. I'm working, feel well, happy, etc. But there's just a dull ache where I wish you could be—oh my dearest, I *must* see you this summer! There—I'm crying again, and you told me not to. Well, I haven't before this, and I'll just run out to the mailbox and wink at the moon and send this on its way.

Helen

Toronto, Ont.
[*11 March 1935*]

Oh, my God, child, is it that long since I've written you? I don't know what dimension I'm working in any more. Nothing has mattered, nothing has even existed, for the past six weeks, but Blake, Blake, Blake: I've spun the man around like a teetotum, I've torn him into tiny shreds and teased and anatomized him with pincers, I've stretched my mind over passages as though it were on a rack, I've plunged into darkness and mist, out again into the clear light—where I started from in the first place—rushed up blind alleys of comparison and sources, broken down completely from sheer inertia, worked all night on a paragraph no better in the morning. At that I've completed, as far as the actual typing out goes, only the preface and the first chapter, which runs to about sixty pages. But what I have done is a masterpiece: finely written, well handled, and the best, clearest and most accurate exposition of Blake's thought yet written. If it's no good I'm no good. There isn't a sentence, and there won't be a sentence, in the whole work that hasn't gone through purgatory. Christ! why was I born with brains? And in the middle of it all there are my infernal lectures and my (no adequate adjective) theology. This morning I went to Pelham [Edgar] with the opus. He was interested, and said that Vincent Massey was back from Bermuda, and that he would give me the money all right if he were allowed to do so under the terms of the Massey bequest. Otherwise—well, Pelham hadn't the nerve to ask him to do it out of his private funds, and so: "Don't count on it, for goodness' sake." I don't quite know what that means, but I assume it means there's about an even, or slightly more than even, chance. So now I have to think up reasons why I have to gather material in the British Museum rather than here. I can talk a good deal about the original manuscripts, which are all in London except the one copy of the *Book of Ahania*, which is in Brooklyn—oh hell, I mean the engraved poems which are not available here except in villainous reproductions. The manuscript of the *Four Zoas* I have to see as well, and that's in the B.M. I doubt if Vincent Massey would be particularly impressed by the real reasons why I want to go to London. But surely the stars in their courses *must* be fighting to bring me across to you.

If I see you this summer, then I hope you get your scholarship renewed. If not—I'll have to shut my teeth and face the prospect of another year like this, of trying to live with your ghost, of going off perpetually half-cocked in a series of frenetic spasms of activity coupled with an inertia and a lethargy so terrible I wonder if I'm losing my mind. Things weren't like that when you were here. If I were just doing routine work, I could do anything, but these ideas that circle and cluster and hag-ride me until they're sloughed off in some sort of formal connection are enough to drive me to drink—they would, of course, drive me to you if you were here. At the present time, what with my tremendous exhilaration over having finally bitten the kernel out of Blake, with being sick at the pit of my stomach when I realize how long it is since I've written you, with feeling so utterly lost because I've just finished something big and I can't come to you with it, I feel as though I had fallen over a precipice and hadn't hit ground yet. I don't expect you to understand all this, because I don't in the least understand it myself, and because I can work more or less normally when you're around. They say that women have an intuition that can dispense with rational processes: I don't believe it, but if you've got such a thing for God's sake use it. I'm all right, of course; once I get some theology done and my exams over with I'll feel better. But your sympathy last fall wasn't wasted, as you seemed to think; I'm not dying, but I'm unhappy, and I do so want that summer with you. I'm not doing any more Blake for the rest of the year, so I'll write again soon, more coherently. God knows

I make the world's worst lover at this distance. Bless you, dear; think over the Blake proposition if your scholarship is renewed. Don't turn Communist: you've got other things to do, and Communism as most people conceive it is merely the stampeding of one's emotional reactions to society. There isn't much news, as you may have gathered; what there is I'll tell you in my next letter.

Lovingly,
Norrie

Rome
March 31, 1935

My dearest, your letter came here a few days ago, and more or less changed the world for me. I've been going about for weeks with a pinched little heart that felt like a stone. All I wanted to do was to throw it away somewhere in a garbage heap and bury myself with it. Week after week I hoped that something would be waiting from you, and there was nothing. And all I could do was to swallow my disappointment and arrange my face stiffly to meet the world as if my world were quite as usual. I wrote a horrid note to you. Left it for a day or so to cool off. Looked at it again, and knew I could never send it, for I knew that you must be working hard, and that whatever happened I could not be cut off from you or you from me. But oh, how hard it is to strain and try to be with you, off here in a strange land, where no one knows you and can talk to me about you. And I had another worry up my sleeve. I have come to Italy for six weeks with Millicent [Rose] who, besides being one of the most delightful people I know, is also one of the most arrogant. And in my grim moments she reminds me of you. Sometimes I can't bear to be with her any longer; sometimes I run away to find a tattered remnant of myself, some bit that has not succumbed to her domination, for she is strong, and unconsciously takes the lead, and speaks loudly and dogmatically whether she is right or wrong. And of course, every thing is Communism. Oh God! if she would only go to Russia, or get a job which would teach her the value and the need for painstaking careful work. Cambridge has given her a great deal, but no idea of doing consistent work at anything but what she wants to do at the moment. But her conversation is brilliant, and when she is good-humoured she is so charming that I can't remember the horrid moments. Don't misunderstand what I mean. I mean that in her brilliance and her self-assurance and her dogmatic way of crushing all beneath her, she reminds me of the Frye who came to see me at Easter so long ago. Millicent has her glorious side, and thank God, so have you. But it is part of my general nightmare to identify certain crushed, hang-dog feelings with what I have felt sometimes because of my inability to cope with you. And then I think, because I would never try to live with Millicent for any length of time, how can I dare to live with you? What a nightmare that is when the fit is on!

Now, my dear, your letter. No, I didn't really think my sympathy was wasted last fall, any more than I really thought that anything was seriously wrong when I had no word from you. I might give you the same advice again as I did before, of course, for the circumstances are more or less the same. That is, you have been overworking, and keeping to it too steadily, and you need to see your friends. It makes me feel such an old maid to sit here and say that so primly, when it is half true, but not all true. For if that is all that is the matter with me right now, then a similar remedy should make me feel quite happy. But it doesn't. On the surface I am quite happy but rather dull, and I don't know quite what to do about it, not caring a deuce of a lot what happens. I keep feeling that you should be here, or I should be there with you. I want to be there when you are working, and I want to help when you need help, and I want to be your wife as a wife should be. Not trotting around Italy, and getting all excited because I'm not a Cambridge graduate with a lot of chatter. But if there is a chance of our being together this summer, then everything will be very different. Here is a snag, of course. I'm supposed to spend the summer on the Continent, not in London. I don't quite know how that will work out. Constable has written to McCurry who has suggested $300 extra for the summer but naturally does not commit himself about next year. I wrote to Lismer—I'm not sure whether I told you that or not—and told him what I wanted to do. That is, marry you and work at the gallery.

The trip to Italy is doing a great deal to dispel the cloud in which I've been working all year. I think I'll manage the examination all right, but there is a terrific amount to do, and it is heartbreaking to have to rush over it all with a smattering of this and that. We've been kicking quite a good deal, and the course will be altered next year. But that doesn't help much this year.

These days I am spending in the Vatican—Raphael and Michelangelo and Giulio Romano and Botticelli and Ghirlandaio. There is a gorgeous Botticelli—*Temptation of Christ*—in the Sistine Chapel. I am really pretty thrilled with it all, in spite of all my tale of woe. By the time I have really looked at paintings from now until the end of the summer, I shall know a good deal more. Reproductions are all very well, but pretty thin as a substitute.

Another day has gone by without my packing this off to you. I have just visited the customs today, to lay claim to a copy of the *Toronto Daily Star* which had to be searched, and which contained two pairs of silk stockings. The English customs don't search newspapers, but the parcel was forwarded to me, and of course this is a Fascist country. But that copy of the *Star* gave me one hell of a shock today. I knew it was a pretty bad paper, and thought so every time I had a look at it in Canada House, but somehow the paper that arrived today was much worse than I thought possible. Absolutely nothing in it but five pages of Eaton's advertisements, and I don't know how many of Simpson's. About a page and a half of reading matter all told, except for sporting gossip and society news and what the fifteenth troop of Girl Guides are doing. The only hint of the situation in Europe is that General Smuts doesn't think there will be a war, and H.G. Wells thinks there will be. It's no wonder that according to young [Stafford] Cripps Canadian young people are ignorant of politics and careless of world conditions. And the present situation is not to be disregarded. Rome has a regular system of lighting alarms as protection against air raids, and regular patrols keep the floodlights in readiness, and they practise using the lights every so often. The place is swarming with soldiers, and everyone is splendid with costly uniforms and gold braid. What happens next, one doesn't know.

After my constant exposure to Millicent's political views I still cling to a faint distrust. Otherwise I have no arguments with which to oppose a system which claims to abolish Christ, then puts Marx in his place, which according to Millicent solves all problems by giving everyone enough to eat. Millicent reviles against the capitalists, but doesn't know who they are or how they got that way. Her theory boils down to a hatred of social evils, a glorification of the WORKER, a declaration against Christianity and any religion as a sickness of the mind and the old familiar opiate of the masses idea. The worker, to most Bloomsburyites, seems to me to be the reincarnation of the noble savage of a few decades ago. I don't know what you mean by "the stampeding of one's emotional reactions to society" but I suppose it is summed up in "My God, we're in a terrible state. We must break it all down and rebuild according to materialist principles. This is the age of reason, and not sentiment. Freedom of the sexes, freedom of work and freedom to develop, no dictatorship, let the arts be subservient to the masses, then they will regain their vigour. Above all, let us discard the past, etc. etc." Well, the past can't be discarded, and I don't think a worship of Marx as a hero can suffice. I don't disagree with a good many of the measures suggested. What I do object to is the attempt to cram every human activity into the class-struggle formula. But to treat religion as the sickness of the mind is all very well if due respect be given to the significance of sickness. The sickness of the oyster produces the pearl, and the swelling of the womb brings forth new life. And it's rather ridiculous to disregard both those events as unnatural and not in the ordinary course of events. If you keep the oyster shell spotlessly clean you won't have the pearl. But perhaps it's not economically desirable to have the pearl, perhaps a pearl is only an unnecessary luxury of the wealthy, and undesirable. Perhaps we should allow nothing but what will allow of a free life on a full stomach. Oh, that is not being fair, but I get so tired of this constant arguing about the evils of the present system and so on. I don't know why I uphold the value of religion. Certainly I am not leading a religious life these days.

I really must stop all this and get to bed. Tomorrow we go to the Vatican. Next day we go to Tivoli and the Villa d'Este. Thursday we push on to Orvieto and Assisi, to Perugia and Arezzo, and then to Florence for three weeks. After that, Paris for a day, and London.

And now, I've spent all this time talking about myself, and haven't mentioned a word about Blake. If I were home with you I should know a hanged sight more about the progress of the thesis. Now it is part of your life which I cannot share, but only guess at. But always I love you, and am happy so. By now you will have got to work on theology, and you'll probably knock it for a row again. How, heaven knows. But there is something uncanny about you. For God's sake, be careful, though, and don't over-tax yourself. You're not made of iron.

Your
H.

Toronto, Ont.
[*23 April 1935*]

My dearest girl:

Another one of these orgasmic nightmares, even worse than the last, this time Theology examinations, which I got through, slightly damaged. Out of eight subjects I got seven firsts and a third, the last from our fat friend [Alfred] Johnston—Homiletics. I got the Church History Scholarship again. I was completely exhausted before the exams ever started, I realize that now, and the let-down afterwards was abysmal. I am supposed to be concentrating what remains of my mind on this infernal Keats and Shelley exam, without much success. I feel immeasurably depressed and disillusioned about everything. This annual exam swindle is so atrociously boring. It's so damned easy, and so damned futile, and it does give you such terrific mental indigestion.

The Transatlantic project is out, sweetheart. Massey's ill-gotten gains are being absorbed in a couple of Cambridge students who are getting their scholarships renewed, and have to live there during the summer. So I have decided to grab all the money I can get hold of and stay tight this summer and get caught up in the work. Roy Daniells lent me some money, and I'm staying in his room all summer for nothing, so it shouldn't be so hard. I'm frightfully disappointed, just the same, but there it is. *And* if I spend four months around here without anything to do but work and no one in particular to see—well, even my incorrigible laziness can't hold out against that indefinitely. There will be a piano stored all summer here in Fifth House. So I ought to be radiant and feel that I'm living in a Lower Paradise, and when I'm not writing to you, I do feel as though I'd got a tremendously lucky break. I shall work through all my courses that I have to teach next year—three of them—and see if I can't give my kids their money's worth instead of spouting at them out of a vast and very empty cavern of ignorance.

It was lovely to get your letter from Rome—I don't know your address, so I keep sending mail to London. And don't spend your time thinking up imaginary caricatures of me as a husband—about how I'm going to spend our marital existence trampling on your bleeding carcass, and so on. Not that I blame you, poor darling. But I'm not a blonde beast, and you mustn't get so frightened of the idea of marriage, as though you were a little girl. You see, it's as much as anything my fear of your fear that makes me hate and dread writing to you so. The very fact that you love me implies that you will have violent spells of hating me, when we're not together—perhaps even when we are—and I'm as nervous and fussy as a maiden aunt about your being so far away, and thinking God knows what, brooding perhaps or misunderstanding; in any case not beside me, not safe and sound. All of which sounds very philoprogenitive and bourgeois, but that's how I feel about you. I love you so, darling, and by going away you have sapped so much of my energy and capacity for loving you that I simply shut my eyes and force myself not to think of you. That doesn't mean that I don't actually think of you, dozens and dozens of times a day: It merely means that thinking of you in purely negative terms, as one absent, is a shocking idea; it's a spiritual and emotional masturbation.

Roy Daniells has sailed for England, and I told him to look after you a bit in case you were there too—I very much want you two to meet. And I hope your scholarship is renewed: you have no idea how I swell and glow when people ask me how you are, and I tell them that the "people" over in England are very well satisfied with your work and may renew your scholarship. It makes me feel as though I had some part in it—perhaps I have. For you certainly have a large part in the Blake, although you speak of it as something you can only guess at, not experience. The text I study from you gave me, your picture is stuck in a particularly tricky section of the *Four Zoas*, and somehow I feel as though I couldn't work on such an absolutely sane, gloriously vital human being as Blake at all unless in some mysterious super-chemical way you belonged. If anything happened to you, I should be fit only for the distorted and broken minds of literature—Wycherley, for instance, or Hopkins; at the most Swift or Webster. That is, in case I survived at all. I think I have been closer to death this year than ever before—no, no, don't get alarmed; there's nothing the matter with me; I only mean that I passed most of it in a curiously self-conscious, introspective way which simply paralysed all activity. I read heavily and widely. I rehashed every problem of the universe eight or ten times, and meanwhile dragged my gaunt and celibate body around to engaging in a positive minimum of activity. This summer I shall contemplate some more, but in comparative freedom, without having to watch a clock.

I propose spending the rest of my life, apart from living with you, on various problems connected with religion and art. Now religion and art are the two most important phenomena in the world; or rather the most important phenomenon, for they are basically the same thing. They constitute, in fact, the only reality of existence. So I must turn a deaf ear to the arguments of your friend Millicent about Communism. I quite recognize the challenge; in a possibly quibbling and dishonest way I recognize the necessity for and importance of Communism. But it just won't do, not for me. Obviously the world is entering a prodigious change, but the new morality will have to be something better than a rehash of the vague deistic and utilitarian sentimentalism of the very capitalistic system the Communists are most concerned to attack. There will have to be something better, for me, than the Communistic exploiting of emotion by intellect. Atheism is an impossible religious position for me, just as materialism is an impossible philosophical position, and I am unable to solve the problems of religion and art by ignoring the first and distorting the second. Read Blake or go to hell: that's my message to the modern world.

And I am very tired, and I've forgotten how to write, and I don't know what to say when all there is demanding to be expressed is a vacant feeling inside. In the natural world there is no such thing as a vacuum; in the spiritual world there is nothing else. Davis said what I gave him of the Blake was extraordinarily good—would set a new standard in M.A. theses. Hell—does he think I'm doing all this work for a wretched M.A. thesis?

Dearest, please don't get the impression, from these letters, that I shall spend my whole life in endless complainings. I'm not in the least like that: I've got immense reserves of power and vitality. But I'm only twenty-two, and I've been more or less sick all year, and I've got growing pains, and I feel maladjusted because you're not here, and depressed for more specific reasons like exams. But I love you—so much, so much: and that's all I can say, as anything else sounds trite and irrelevant. And when you finally do come back to me, all this love I've been painfully choking and damming up will pour over you, not tempestuously but soothingly in a genuine release of the spirit. Oh Hell! I knew I couldn't talk to you in this strain without going Swedenborgian. My next letter will see my work over and a less frenetic era of existence ushered in.

Lovingly,
Norrie

Florence. April 27, '35

My dearest, I've just had a letter from Daddy. He says you are not coming. That you will be in the city all summer, and that you are looking ill. Oh my dear, I *am* so sorry to have written such a letter to you, when I should have realized that you would get it in the middle of theology exams, and heaven knows you must have enough to worry you without listening to my growing pains. I don't know what to say about the summer. What *can* I say? I was counting on it so much, and now I must take a deep breath and go on. For my work I hope I get the renewal of money, for I'm terribly raw—but there is a pretty violent pull against my desire to stay. There isn't any use kicking, of course, for if I were home, without a job, it would be intolerable. This way we both have hope, and if we can stick it out together, the time will soon pass. What I worry about most is your health, for you have had a fearful year of it. Surely the powers that be will not leave you stranded, and I hope to God they don't send you to some bug-ridden town in the west again. This theology business is all very well, but old [Walter T.] Brown needn't wear you to a tattered rag in order to satisfy some whim of his own. There is no telling what the Victorian parental attitude may suggest for you. If it were a genuine paternal feeling he might realize you need a rest. They can run a delicate machine at top speed, and they expect something superhuman. If they have any bowels of mercy as well as common sense, they'll stop before they wreck you altogether. My darling, take care of yourself—*don't* work all night, *don't* overtax your strength, for I am afraid of what will happen if you keep on.

Sunday. Today Millicent left Florence according to her plan. Originally we were to leave together and spend a little time in Paris, but she pined so for her Communist friends that she decided to return earlier, and I firmly resolved to get myself home on my own steam and exert my independence. Besides, Millicent wants to march with thousands of her comrades on May Day and I need not indulge in that form of exercise, so that I am staying a few days longer. Helen Lowenthal goes back with me on Wednesday. This morning I went to the train and said goodbye to my companion and when I came back to the house I felt so sad that when the Signora asked me about Millicent I began to cry. I don't know why, except that I do hate saying goodbye to people. Signora understood all about it, and folded me up on her bosom and began to comfort me like the kind motherly soul she is. I cannot tell you how wonderful she seemed to me at that moment. I was feeling like the lost sheep and she gathered me in. She soothed me with kind words, as a mother would do with a homesick child. Seeing Millicent go, suddenly I felt once more a wanderer, all alone, and the realization came over me in a flood—you were not coming, and the time was so long. But after I cried, and Arnoldo came in suddenly in the midst of it and looked sympathetic as if it were the most natural thing in the world—an Englishman would have been awkward with embarrassment—I went off and read Mark Twain. *Eve's Diary*. John Erskine improved upon that in his *Adam and Eve*. Then I started on *Helen of Troy* and the air was clear. Arnoldo has a good selection of books in four languages, and he is generous about lending them.

Back in London.

Came third class all the way, and I'll never go any other way again, I think. Am settled at 90 Guilford Street—house full of men, some very nice. The damn town is so full of people that you can hardly move. About one and a half million more people in London for the Jubilee. You should see Oxford Street! I thought Toronto was vulgar enough when it comes to Centennial celebrations, but London takes the cake.

Had a note from Roy Daniells, and I shall be seeing him soon, probably, and will ask him all about you. I wish to God you'd write to me sometimes these days—my exam is six weeks away, and I don't know much, but expect to wield a pen to fair purpose.

I can't write to you much in the next few weeks as I shall be working pretty hard. But you know how it is. Do let me know what you are doing. Had a long letter from Lismer—marvellous letter. Tells me my marrying would make no difference to him or to McCurry, he thought. The only thing to consider was not to have a family at inconvenient times, as it wouldn't do to have to postpone a gallery talk because of urgent domestic troubles of the lecturer. He *is* an angel!

I must go look at some architecture.

Helen

Toronto, Ont.
[*3 May 1935*]

Sweetheart:

Everything is all over now, in the way of exams, and when I think of you now, all the cloudy veils that have hung around you drop away. When I have nothing to do by the clock, I can love you buoyantly, because you are so definitely in the picture when I'm doing what I like.

In spite of Massey's failure to come through with money, I'm fairly content. I'll see you sometime at all events; if not this year, then next year. In the meantime, I can set about making it more or less worth your while to come back to me. I know perfectly well that essentially I'm still a great yowling infant, having more or less gone through a process described by our mutual friend Mr. Blake:

I strove to seize the inmost form
With ardor fierce and hands of flame,
But burst the crystal cabinet,
And like a weeping babe became—

A weeping babe upon the wild,
And weeping woman pale reclined,
And in the outward air again
I filled with woes the passing wind.

—but I'm growing up, don't you think I'm not. I've got tremendous ideas, but they're like the myths in primitive religions, huge but monstrous, not consolidated, disciplined or defined. Only the Blake—I know Blake as no man has ever known him—of that I'm quite sure. But I lack so woefully in the way of subtlety. I haven't got a subtle mind—only a pounding, driving bourgeois intellect. I don't insinuate myself between two factors of a distinction—I push them aside: if I meet a recalcitrant fact, I knock it down; which doesn't get rid of it, but puts it in a different position. Consequently I'm damnably lonesome, intellectually. I resent criticism, because I don't know, in most cases, what the hell I mean myself, so how should anyone else pretend to do so? Besides, in conversations I take up most of my positions through intellectual arrogance rather than reasoned conviction, and consequently won't back out of them. And besides, there are only two people in Toronto who have the remotest idea what I'm talking about, Roy Daniells and Wilson Knight; and Knight won't read Spengler, Roy won't read Shakespeare, and neither one will read Blake. But the real trouble is that all this work is basically critical, and purely critical work doesn't satisfy me. Because if I am to rest content with criticism I have to pay attention to all these stupid distinctions made by facts: my criticisms are not, properly speaking, criticisms at all, but synthetic recreations. Professor Davis was kind enough, or ignorant enough, to remark that what he had seen of my theoretical reconstruction of Blake was a damned sight more interesting than the original, as far as the Prophecies are concerned at all events. I can draw blueprints for the loveliest castles in the air, miracles of blending size and grace; this is a work of art, creative in essence. It's silly to object that these castles wouldn't stand up if they were built. Who said anything about their standing up? This is one side of me—the synthetic intellectual. I'm a critical capitalist. The English conquered India, the largest, richest, most complicated empire in the world, with a handful of soldiers. I can sail into Blake or Shakespeare or St. Augustine or the Christian religion or aesthetics with two facts and a thesis, and I can conquer it. I may be baffled and obstructed: I may get stuck in a Black Hole, as I have been more or less for a year now; but I emerge with my territory painted all one colour, anyhow. But if you paint everything one colour you oversimplify. And so I have to reckon with another side to me, the creative artist side: at least I call it that because it sounds so swell—it really doesn't get beyond the criticism of criticism. And this side says: You're not working with realities, but with phenomena: go write a novel. A few years ago the challenge was even more uncompromisingly direct: go preach the gospel. And it goes on and says that all this student life is frightfully artificial and deracinated, mechanical rather than organic: all professoring ends in pedantry, pedantry in social parasitism. If you'd gone into music, says the conscience, or the fiend, whichever it is, you'd be caught up in the rhythm of a genuine art: if you must work with debased coinage, words being simply tones encrusted with various kinds of patina, work with them properly. If you were a woman with Helen's brains, physical appearance, capacity for writing and forming a career, would you throw yourself away on yourself? (no, it must be the fiend: surely even my conscience would have a better prose style). Do you love Helen as she deserves? *can* you do so, you snuffy snivelling pot-bellied hay-haired old friar? And thus I stand more or less paralysed, wanting badly to commit myself to something, Communism, Catholicism, pedantry in any line, and realizing that I can't; that the only thing I can commit myself to is my religion and my wife, one being in the clouds and the other in Europe. So I rush around squealing, like a pig in a fire, or sit around with large ideas and not doing anything about them, like a eunuch with an erection.

All this is extremely silly—I hope it amuses you without annoying you. I'm so fearfully egocentric, which is inevitable to adolescence, of course, but you're the only one who can train me out of that. I hope I'm gradually emerging from this cocoon of rapt egoism, but I dunno.

I've moved into First House into Roy Daniells' room and am to stay here all summer. It's a great room, with plenty of books, and I feel luxurious. Cragg left me the key to his room, with his records of course inside. So I'm fairly well fixed this summer, if I can find a key to the Fifth House Common Room so I can go in and assault the piano.

Lovingly,
Norrie

[*London*]
May 13th, 1935

My dear, I've just had a letter today, and one last week, and it does feel so luxurious that I've spent the last half hour reading your last one and laughing more than I've done for some months! You sound quite your usual self—and while I'm not gurgling at your seriousness—some of your similes were a little too much for the chaste purity of the Adam room at the Courtauld Institute. Some of its ghosts must have scuttled into corners if they were looking over my shoulder. Serves them right anyway, proper old girls, they should keep their noses out of things. Though why they should, I don't quite know, for I'm curious enough about them, and would feel no misgivings whatever in poking into their affairs, if I thought I was the only one doing it. I remember telling you how indecent I thought it was to look at Carlyle's love notes to his wife.

I'm back at work, of course, not going to any lectures, tucking in a fair amount of information in a quiet way, not worrying, because I can't be bothered, and not doing very much that could be called exciting.

I had tea with Roy Daniells last week, and I liked him very much.

We met in front of the B.M. and I didn't know what he looked like, of course, and was just about to go up to a man reading a newspaper, who looked rather a likely choice, when up came R.D. We talked about an awful lot of things—I've forgotten what all—about living on two planes of existence, one being unhappy and lonely and the other of quite simultaneous enjoyment of life about one. He does admire you a good deal, and he seems to be very diffident himself. I was terribly glad to see him and almost made him late for his train.

If you see Norah [McCullough], tell her that I have enjoyed being with Edith and Stephen [Burnett] very much. They have just spent ten days in Cornwall. This for your private ear. Stephen keeps correcting Edith, very tenderly and mildly, but with persistence, about such little things. It is just a little trying being the tactful guest. And by Jove, if you try that on me, hay hair my boy, I'll not put up with it at all! It has always been a rule of my parents not to correct their children in front of strangers, and it always seemed rather good taste, to me. I don't quite know why young husbands try to reform their women, but they all do. I'm not quite sure what deep-laid scheme I've got working subconsciously toward your improvement; according to rule there must be something. All I can think of now is that you must keep your socks intact. And then there *are* those intolerable rags you carry as handkerchiefs. But such things can be arranged by any competent housekeeper.

Of course, you must remember, think twice, etc., that there is an awful lot of your territory quite unknown to me, and that I am incapable of understanding (or at least don't, at any rate) a good deal of what you think about! Still, I dare say you have a fair idea of my mental makeup—although some of your pictures of me are not the grim thing I look to myself. I'm just developing a Jane Austen streak, and warning you to look me over in the cold grey light and consider well etc. But of course, don't take me seriously or I *should* feel sad!

Heavens, I must hop into bed. Thank goodness I have one here, and don't have to parade the streets at night like the women outside. Guilford Street and Southampton Row are favorite tempting grounds. Goodnight, and please do write to me now that you have more time.

Your
Helen

Toronto, Ont.
[22 *May 1935*]

Sweet:

Dearest, I'm sorry if you haven't got my letters, but what can you expect when you go vagabonding? I suppose some of them, or all of them, have gone permanently astray. There were three, I think, written between your two letters, of which two whined and one was moderately cheerful. Because I feel ever so much better now that the incubus of work has been removed. And your last Italian letter came this morning, so that I can write without talking into a vacuum.

At the present time I'm more or less waiting around for my eyes to clear up before starting much sustained work. Fortunately, I can type without using my eyes unduly. At present I'm doing the annotations to the Blake extracts in the new issue of *Representative Poetry*. Dull job, but I don't mind doing it. I sent in a list to Davis, who altered it materially for the worse, sent it in to the committee and got it accepted. We worked over it again and I gently pointed out why I thought my original suggestions in the way of extracts were superior to his own, and got him to agree to most of them. I don't know what the committee, or ex-committee, will say, but I don't think they'd have let the accepted list go through intact if they had read any of the poems in it anyway.

I went down one Saturday afternoon to look at a Lismer one-man show: quite the best I ever thought him capable of doing, and the only one of his I've seen. He has a great capacity for getting his drawing clear and his rhythms organized, even if the gaily irresponsible way he lathers on the primary colours gets my goat a bit. After that—I had a little talk with Lismer but not much—I went up to [Herbert J.] Davis' and poured the usual cup of tea over my trousers. Huxley says somewhere that the things that happen to people are the things that are like them, but I don't see what there is about us that impels Providence to soak our haunches with tea at such frequent intervals.

I think I am giving birth to a novel, but maybe that's only because of the relief of exams being over, as one might think he was travelling through interstellar space because his bedclothes slipped off. I don't know anything about it, except that it's going to be a dead secret between us for a long while. And it's NOT going to be about a young misunderstood genius who finally wins through to fame and success through the inspiration of a pure woman. I am going to avoid a writer-hero like a venereal disease. But it'll be a long time before anything exciting happens. I shall never write a novel until I reach maturity, which will be whenever the summation of my past experiences takes on a significant unity.

I think I must have walked fifty or sixty miles in the past week. Spring fever, plus restless people like [Ernie] Gould and [Jerry] Riddell who are supposed to be spending their time marking papers. Also shows. I've been to a lot of shows: they seem to rest my eyes. A week ago I went for a long walk with Arnold of the German department here. After we had discussed Christianity, Nazism, racial temperament, Spengler and the Victoria College faculty, he told me I had an essentially German mind, that I thought of Christianity in a way intelligible only to Germans, and that he would like to read Goethe with me as soon as I knew enough of the language. So I have to go and explain to him tomorrow that *Der Schnee ist immer kalt und nie warm*.

It's been beautiful spring weather, cool and bright. For a long time I've been wondering why Canadian painting irritated me slightly, and didn't seem, even at its best, to ring true to actual Canadian conditions. It seems to me that the trouble is that it's all been consolidated on French impressionism, or at least on some kind of exotic painting which depends on diffusion of light, on analysis of colour, on blending of tones. But when that's done here, and it's done with amazing skill and technique, it gives a theoretical, academic effect, because, in spite of it, Canada doesn't really look like that. This country is glowing in a hard, cold light that cuts out pattern with an edged tool; there is no compromise of outline, no blending or slurring of any sort, nothing but solid hard blocks of shape. The ultimate problem is to organize rhythms, not to analyse coloring.

When I get time to read anything I read Rabelais. Swell guy. There's a novel I should like to write, but I'm not yet old enough. Something about two people, man and woman, as courteous, intelligent, and altogether ideal as I can make them, deeply in love, tremendous mutual respect, common cultural interests. One consolidates on a religious tradition and the other on Communism and the theme of the book would be the struggle between them. A child would grow up, and as neither parent would force his or her ideals down its throat, it would be interesting to see what it would make of the situation. Sometime I shall go to bed with Henry James and spawn it.

Good luck with the exam, sweetheart—perhaps you'll have written it by the time this gets to you. And stay another year if you can, my darling. I want all of Helen I can get. The fascination of watching you grow is over now, and while I shall never get over feeling protective—the physical link in our connection will keep that permanent—you're a wife now, and you can never be anything like a little girl again, except at odd moments. You've gained an immense amount of social maturity, social and emotional too, I think, which is most important; it remains to integrate your intellectual advancement with it. Learning things is linear; growth is a curve, and learning has to be bent into that curve before it's part of a personality. Otherwise the personality is flattened out to fit the inhuman straight line of the intellect. You've got the curve first. This isn't patronizing you; I'd talk to any intimate friend in the same terms, more or less. But I have to struggle to be objective; otherwise I'd be bawling for you to come back at once, which would violate everything our marriage stands for.

Norrie

[*London*]
June 3rd, 1935

Well, my dear, since it seems you don't write to me unless you've just received a letter, and I don't write to you unless *I've* just received a letter, it is time either one of us wrote a little oftener. Your letter (May 22nd) just came today, and so here we are. Yes, I've had all your others. It seems so long ago since I was in Italy that it is rather odd to have you answering the one from Florence.

My examinations are on June 17th & 18th (four of them). There's a German and French translation exam on the 14th, and I have to hike all the way back from wherever I may be on July 16 for a viva voce—they'll probably gas away for fifteen minutes and it will cost me three pounds. Damn them. I mean if I have to come back from France.

Laugh this off: I'm going to the annual conference of the British Museums Association, representing the Art Gallery of Toronto. McCurry thought it would be a good thing, and as Eric Brown said: "You have to represent *something*, so it may as well be Toronto!" That is on July 1st, at Brussels and the Universal Exhibition (probably like the Chicago World's

Fair) is being held there too. So I must get to Paris before then to see the Italian Exhibition at the Louvre, as it ends somewhere about that time. This won't be a long letter as I'm working quite patiently and steadily these days—never felt more sensible in my life. Yeah, I suppose I'm growing up—a few grey hairs and an increased hip line.

I'm sorry about your eyes. You must take care of them, you know. I don't want to have to be Milton's daughter to you yet.

I agree with you about Canadian paintings—but that is exactly what the Seven tried to do, and what all the little people who copied them don't realize. The work of [J.E.H.] MacDonald and [Arthur] Lismer and [Tom] Thomson and [A.Y.] Jackson is a definite contribution to painting, of a large order. But for the rest, I think a new impulse is needed, and how it is to come, I'm not quite certain.

I don't know what I said to Daddy in one or two of my letters about the men in the house and the people I was meeting but he wrote back telling me to be careful if I were contemplating a sort of affair. To which my reply was that I'm not at all interested—not this side of the Atlantic. Which is quite true. There is a great steadying influence in living in a house full of men, and talking to them on equal terms. But that's as far as it goes. It is queer, being in love with so many people all at once in so many different ways, with you at the back of me all the time as my end and my beginning. I can't explain to Millicent [Rose]—I don't try—how glorious it is to have found you. She thinks that she'll try one man for a few months and then go off with someone else when she's tired of him. It is a horrid idea I think.

Now, my dear, just be very nice and write to me straightaway. I am about to trail off to bed once more. I work downstairs in the common room these days with one or two medical students steaming over a nervous system. Their exams are right at hand too. They've all left me, and all I can do is wander off and sleep in my solitary bed and cuss gently.

I'm at last getting some idea of what this course is about. Aside from wanting to come to you, I *do* want to stay here longer and really learn a little about painting. At present you could just about wither me up with any of your various discourses. But withered or not, I'm the leaf and you're the branch—and I'm an evergreen! And so to bed.

H.

[*London*]
June 20th [*1935*]

My dear Frye—

The exams are over, and I didn't do very well, and I hope you aren't ashamed. I don't think I am. I wandered along the Institute yesterday idly considering whether to kick myself severely, go into hysterics and a delicate decline, or just to keep on viewing the world with a cheerful eye and let it go at that. So far I'm doing just that. Anyway, the exam was a very good thing to clear the air and show me what I didn't know—and they managed that nicely. Now I can work away a little less apprehensively and more to the point. I suppose I've passed, but I haven't the foggiest notion really. Sure enough, half an hour before the first exam my lower regions began to kick and I to curse, and once more the moon . . . So what with a pain in the gizzard and six hours of writing a lot of guff to the examiners over a field so wide that it looked like the course in classics when the University of Toronto was founded. And I forgot a lot of things I'd read a month before and didn't read the night before on account of the curse and being tired. And so it goes. I haven't your sporting sense, I think—I don't stick to an exam and get the stuff in my head—well I do, but this time I was a little beaten. Still, it's over now except for the viva voce exam on July 16th and by then I shall have a good many things much straighter in my mind. By the post mortems lately I feel more cheerful, as I am the only one who attempted the exam this time in one year, and next year it is billed as a two year course. And I didn't go blatting around my feelings about the papers—all year I've followed your Chesterfieldian tactics more or less, and seem to get away with something or other.

McCurry has written saying that the committee decided to spread the money as widely as possible and so I come back next fall. But he sent $350 today, and that should last for several months. So now I go to Paris for five days, then to Brussels to the conference, then to The Hague and Amsterdam. I come back to London July 15th, and have another tea date with Roy then.

I shall be so glad to come home—I can't tell you just now. I'm sorry to leave here, naturally, now that I've got my roots in the ground. But I've a habit of doing that wherever I go and there's always a bit of a tearing up leaving one place and going to another. And there has been such a pull all year—naturally it slows up things if one main root is across the Atlantic.

Love,
Helen

Toronto, Ont.
[*28 June 1935*]

Dearest:

I've got two recurring attacks at the moment: sore eyes and Blake fever. The combination doesn't work out so well; it results, as a matter of fact, in a sort of lethargic paralysis. I have just heard from your mother that you will be home this fall. That partly makes up for my not going across to meet you; the summer will go pretty fast now, and I can get down to my work without these horrible stretches of loneliness where I can't do anything constructive, least of all write to you. I had more or less got myself resigned to the idea that you would be over there another year, and never realized until the news came how much I wanted you home as soon as you could come. I feel an immense sense of relief and serenity. Of course, you're still raw, as you say, but you have a big start on most people in Canada. You write with an extraordinary vitality and delicacy, and that faculty of yours won't lose by contact with a more abstract and constructive mind. Men and women think differently, and they have to cross-fertilize each other. A man talks about general principles, and if he is not open to feminine influences he develops a crusty bachelor mind, trying to flatten everything into formulas, make individuals into tendencies, and turn every generalized statement into a ferocious snorting epigram. A woman talks about her reactions to specific people and their work, and if she remains intellectually a virgin she does what all virgins do—gasps and flutters and exclaims and gurgles in the attempt to keep up with her instinct, which, like a spoiled dog on a leash, rushes blindly around in every direction but the right one, leaving her breathless and staggering over obstacles of facts. That's one of the many reasons why we have to get married—to save our brains as well as our souls. Nothing under God's sun could stop me from the procedure of the usual academic bulldog—hold on to one piece of fact and growl—if

I married the usual cooing female, or anybody but you; and nothing could save you from this shrieking, jerking, whirling-dervish Dance of the Spinsters but marriage to me. But that means, of course, the wedding of two minds, to which all physical intercourse and domestication are only preliminary, though necessary. Perhaps I could do as much for you as another year in England: I could save you a lot of work anyway.

I'm doing a frightful amount of work this summer, if I can finish it. The fact that I don't attend lectures is a genuine incubus to me in the academic term, with the amount of work I have to do, and if I don't have things a bit better next year I'll crack up in so many pieces Victoria College will be digging splinters of a promising student out of their anatomies for months. So I'm finishing the Blake, which, considering that I should read everything he read, is no small job, I'm reading everything on the courses I have to lecture in, and getting them organized, which, considering my profound ignorance of English literature and total ignorance of any other literature, is no small job either, and I'm going to write a paper on Calvin and do some work on Arminius which should put me in good enough shape for Theology. That amount of preparation, combined with your coming back, will, I think, save me from a very serious setback. Within about two years a lot of things will have clicked, and I shall be established, if nothing happens.

I know that, and yet there remains this horror of insecurity, the humiliation of feeling dependent on other peoples' good nature, the dread of what a social error, a serious illness, a change in someone else's attitude toward me, might mean; together with the panic of what I don't know, haven't thought through, haven't read, and the desperate struggle to get some sort of balance, some sort of self-possession. If this were nothing but the self-pity incident to such a situation I might kid myself out of it: I've tried hard enough. But I don't think it is, altogether; it isn't my concern over my own fortunes that drives me to work, but the compulsion, which I think is both internal and external, to hammer out my ideas and get them expressed. But you need the conditions controlled for that, and I haven't got them controlled. So I get into some funny states of mind: states in which any simple routine act, like sending out my laundry or getting a cheque cashed, takes on a huge significance; all my energy absorbed in finally doing what all my inertia rebels against because it's an irrelevant act, unconnected with my work. States in which the doing of some supremely silly or disgusting action at the wrong time suggests itself until I have to yell out to put it out of my mind. And so on. Silly enough, but that's the way I acted a good deal of last term, and it felt as though I were definitely headed for breakdown. Getting this summer free solved half the problem very nicely; if I had spent another summer fuming and fretting over the waste of time I'd have been running amuck with a hatchet before now. Having you back is solving the other half, and all that means to me I won't go into, just now.

I write you some funny letters, don't I, for a lover? All convention and tradition is against me. Everybody thought, up to the last century, and most beyond it, that, as women had brains but no disposition to use them, and resented anything but an emotional reaction, any kind of love that went beyond the caresses and endearments of a union based frankly and brutally on mutual possession of bodies had something unnatural about it. But, oh, Lord, how dead, smelly, worn-out, stale that kind of love is! All men, all women, only react in one way to physical intimacy, which was why people had to be so frightfully monogamous. And so prudish too, because if there were no taboos on sex the race would die out. And it's so hard to get away from that. When D.H. Lawrence started writing, everybody thought he'd be the Messiah of a new, fresh, vigorous kind of loving. Well, he did, until the war got him, or Oedipus, or something: anyway he betrayed his trust and slipped back into all the nineteenth-century drivel with *Lady Chatterley*. A sensitive, intelligent person in love today is a kind of pioneer. The Greeks started the antithesis between cultured, intellectual love and emotional physical love by making the first homosexual and the second heterosexual—or at least the Christian Church completed the antithesis. I think we might resolve that antithesis today, but with economic conditions as primitive and barbaric as they are, it would only work in isolated cases, of which you and I, thank God, are one. A lot of people, including yourself, squawk and squirm and giggle occasionally when talked to like this—but, while I may sound silly in my manner of expression, or pompous or what not—I know all the automatic reactions—to be educated intellectually is so easy, and to be educated emotionally so difficult—I despise a Philistine so much in the arts that I can't be satisfied to be one in love.

You know, of course, that I spent some time up north with Roy last week. There were difficulties: I caught a perfect geyser of a cold before I went up, and it rained every day we were there, which didn't improve it. It was pouring rain the morning I left, and all I could think of doing at the moment was getting to the street car, which was unfortunate, as

I had forgotten I had no money. Roy was cleaned out too, so that when we got there we found we would simply have to eat whatever was there. We were better off than Mother Hubbard: there was a box of oatmeal, your mother's lunch, intended for the train, some coffee that would have disinfected a pest-house, and eggs and milk we got from the Hamers. So we lived off oatmeal, that coffee, and the eggs. Roy's digestion was upset, so he didn't want to eat anything anyhow. We practised a bit, but not much. I'm not sure that I like your ghost that close: you see, I didn't know then that you'd be coming back, and, with the memories I had, and your little red bathing suit hanging in the corner (stand by for a tear-drop) and the lonesomeness and the rain—well, I'm damned glad you're coming back. An extremely good head, incidentally, your prospective brother-in-law—damn it, I mean mine, but there's too much down to erase. We spent most of our energy getting the meals. Roy did the work, and I sat around and watched him. I do that awfully well.

I told you, I think, that I was giving birth to a novel. It's developing, very slowly: I start at the wrong end too, and think of the episodes and scenes and conversations first, and try to figure out their context afterward. I am writing the thing, partly because I can't help myself, partly because there's a strong impulse to creative work inside me which I've never satisfied, partly because I want a bit of money to pay up the college and marry you on, and partly because all my confused impressions about where I stand in life generally are clearing a bit. I rather think it will be either so bad I shan't do anything with it, such as showing it to my friends or rereading it, or good enough to be accepted. Somehow I don't think I'll write an unreadable novel. I've got a fair idea of prose rhythm, a fairly decent literary education (for a novelist), a fairly good eye for caricature, and a fairly good idea of what comedy is about. Anyway, we'll see. Just another experiment.

I had an offer to go to Winnipeg as a lecturer in Wesley College—federated with the University of Manitoba—but of course turned it down. E.K. Brown has just gone there, and I'd sooner work with him than with this Edgar–Pratt–Robins combination, but the chances of your being transferred to Winnipeg are considerably more remote than the chances of your staying here, and as I'm comparatively safe here for next year, and as after that it won't matter much where I am, I didn't consider the offer.

You didn't seem worried much about your examinations—I suppose you've grown out of that by this time. Your father recently pleased me very much by giving me the credit for a bit of straightening up emotionally. Apparently you more or less used to flood the place when you had crises to go through. If the stars in their courses didn't fight against you, the moon did. I think the sending of Marion [Kemp] to South Africa an excellent idea. You know my theory about the necessity of transplanting people at maturity to get the best results, and there was never a girl who needed a change of environment as Marion does.

Well, dearest, I never thought I'd count the summer days as eagerly as I did last summer, when I ticked off each Sunday as it came, and the proportion of time I had covered, and the numbers of weeks and days I had yet to go, but apparently I was wrong. Oh, my dear!

Norrie

Toronto, Ont.
Sunday afternoon [*7 July 1935*]

Sweet:

Nothing has happened during the past week except Blake fever. The news about your coming home has loosened something up in me, I don't know what, of course. But at any rate I seem to be working like the devil on Mr. Blake, the devil's spokesman, at least for a while. The harder I work the shorter it'll be. I have worked, off and on, about four years on Blake, and now I know at last what's going into my M.A. thesis and what into my Ph.D. thesis. I shall finish the former by the end of July, I think, if this working streak keeps up, and after it's submitted in the fall I'm going to move heaven and earth to get it published, somehow. My ideas have never been expressed before, yet they're so damned obvious I'm terrified for fear someone will beat me to it. Barring that, barring various accidents and so on, if I can get this thesis into the hands of the right people, I can pretty well take what I want within a very few years. Davis, who is extremely cautious, told me that the first draft of my opening chapter, which is to be entirely revised and rewritten, would set, the way it was going, a new standard in M.A. theses. The Ph.D. thing will be all about Blake in his context—Romanticism and so forth. But that will be just one more job, not a case of hysteria and religious fanaticism and hypnosis and windmill-tilting, like this one. Of course, there is still the possibility that this will be the Ph.D. and that I shan't bother with my M.A. at all.

I still don't quite know what you'll be doing this summer. Will it be the Continent or London?

I love you,
Norrie

Ghent
July 6[–7], 1935
At the "Chapeau Rouge"

My darling, I'm afraid I've been thoughtless again—and your birthday will be over before this can possibly reach you, and I haven't done one thing about it. Please forgive me, won't you?

I've just finished the family journal—more or less complete account of latest events—so if you want to know about my social existence in the last week, do get hold of that. I feel so damned conference-ish and tired with receptions and talking to people and having every minute filled up, that I am glad to be alone this weekend. I spent this morning seeing off the party from Brussels, then had a quiet day in the Gallery and came here. One church is across the road, and if I lean out my window I see the main tower of St. Bavon, very close. That is where the Van Eyck *Adoration of the Lamb* altarpiece is, in one of the chapels of the ambulatory. I haven't seen it yet, because there was a service on this afternoon. It gives me such a queer feeling going into cathedrals where the people are kneeling and going through their formulae in all sincerity, and I nearly stumble over people in the confessional, it being so dark. I wonder whether they resent people like myself coming through and looking on as if they were so many actors in the religious drama. I went to a service with Maysie [Roger] in New College Chapel, some weeks ago. It was Church of England—choir beautiful beyond words, service extremely formal and allowing congregation only as spectators—except that they knelt at intervals. I felt that it was a glorious work of art, that ritual, and that it appealed as anything fine of the past does, but it certainly was little of the present, and in a strictly religious sense, I don't think it had any appeal to me whatever. But I suppose a religion is a purification of the spirit—and that comes in an infinite number of ways.

The eastern idea of priestesses in the temple, for instance, in some ways may be of great significance—through the satisfaction of physical desires and needs. But I don't know anything about it, of course. Unlike you, I don't trouble about problems of the universe and when my conscience gets in shape I realize that my cardinal sin is laziness, and that's all I can muster by way of an Oxford Group Confession. My roommate at the conference talked a good deal of her religious experiences, and of a vision she had had. I've had a few visions—perhaps—but I'd call them something in the way of aesthetic experience. And that might agree with what you say—that art and religion are the same thing. Herbert Read talks about aesthetic experience being the art of contemplation, and I suppose that if one's religion is not swamped by fear it is contemplation. But Lucy Deakin talked of giving oneself to Christ. What does that mean? In the days when the Church could put up with such ideas as *The Marriage of St. Catherine,* it would have one meaning. I suppose this idea of the Church as Bride goes back to the Song of Solomon. But what *is* marriage anyway? Seems to me that for an organization as professedly ascetic as Roman Catholicism it's a bit illogical. But then of *course* it's illogical, and some things can't be reduced to rules and pure reason. There's a story of Lawrence's which ends with the union between the woman and her husband who died some years before. There's another where a woman returns in spirit because her living body had not been satisfied. It may be nonsense, and it may not. When I have thought of you sometimes I have been so comforted—but you call it mental and emotional masturbation. Well, aside from one's revulsion from the word—what of it? I suppose if I'd been a nun I should have been a very devoted bride of Christ—but they call that religion. And after all, Christ was a man once, and for most people the appeal is physical—through memories of his Passion and suffering. I'm getting sleepy, and I've forgotten what my idea was in the first place.

I've been seeing a good deal of Rubens lately—there's a grand salon in Brussels devoted to him, and also one in the Antwerp Gallery, besides the altarpiece and other work in the Antwerp Cathedral. I've been trying, but I'm afraid I do not appreciate the man—too much flesh and too little spirit. Too broadly exuberant rhythms, an easy good humour and a delight in lusciousness and ripeness and fatness, but a neglect of solid firm geometrical austerity in design. He'll sprinkle cupids everywhere, and make his garments flutter wildly. Of course, most Baroque painters had lots of tricks of that sort. Like Tiepolo who hardly ever painted a ceiling without somebody's behind standing out prominently. Once they got off the earth into the clouds, they could do anything, and the natural laws of solid bodies went by the board. If a man like Rubens will have a wife like Helena Fourment, and will insist on painting her as every saint in the calendar not excepting the Holy Virgin herself—then one must rather gasp at the suspension of gravity. Which reminds me—speaking of suspension. Yesterday in Antwerp Cathedral I saw one of the most baroque pulpits I've ever gazed upon, and at the top was an angel, swooping down from above, garments fluttering with great commotion, bearing palms or some more flamboyant form of plant. The angel was originally one of those creatures without visible means of support, so someone had taken pity and added a sort of pipe which reached up to the top of the clerestory windows. But as it was attached to the highest portion of the angel, the effect of the backside suspension was ludicrous, to say the least.

I'd better just send off this, because I don't know when I'll have time to finish it in the next few days. And I've said so many things I disagree with, that it would take several more pages to properly do it on paper. So I've probably been talking nonsense again. It won't be long now until I'm home again—only a few months.

Helen

[*London*]
July 18, 1935

My dear,

Exam results came out today. I failed. It looks pretty grim, written like that, but there it is. And I'm not doing any howling. I feel like a general after a lost battle, but I'm all ready for the next one. Gordon [Snelgrove] is so up in arms about it that he feels like beating up the place, but I assure him that I just did not know enough to make the grade.

I've spent this afternoon hanging onto my nerves and trying to figure out the next step. Have cabled McCurry. Gordon says to go on with the usual plans and not worry about the money which is here for me anyhow, and he will tell McCurry just how things stand here. I don't feel ashamed or degraded or any damned thing at all, for I haven't time to waste now. But I have wondered what you would think. And that has been my worst disappointment. If this makes any difference to you I shall just fade out of the picture so far as you are concerned. It may be better that way. I will not have you marrying a stupid woman.

I phoned Roy [Daniells]. I want to see him before he goes, as I felt I had to talk to someone near to you. I'll see him tomorrow. Takes it quite calmly, and says Toronto in general need not know. And of course that is true. Four people failed out of the nine who tried—the others had been at this two years.

Roy told me that that offer from Manitoba more or less drew from [Walter T.] Brown a direct statement that they intended to hang onto you around the college, and so hands off! Roy is awfully pleased about it as it means that they do not look upon you as an object of charity but as a coming man whom they need. Roy has a great respect for you.

I have had a job offered me by Lismer. He suggests going after one with Alford, also. This setback makes me hesitate somewhat, but I shall think of something.

In a way my failure will perhaps be a help to the next sufferer who is sent over to be pumped full of information and expected to spew it forth in the required eight months. I think that after this the diploma course will be definitely for two years. I don't think Lismer will take this very seriously, as he knows how things are here, but I feel I've let him down, just the same. If I hadn't a good many reasons for not doing so, I'd get roaring drunk and jump in the Thames. But that is just silly, and tomorrow I'll turn up once more and face all the people who feel sorry for me. Damn it.

Next day: I've had lunch with Roy and we've mapped out the next campaign. Tell no one at home except where absolutely necessary, i.e. McCurry and Lismer, and not let the gossips have anything to chew upon. And I'll work here for the rest of the summer, go home to my job and borrow enough money to get back here next summer and write the exam over again. That means a fair amount of borrowing but I'll manage. Roy thought at first that I should not have cabled McCurry but I'm glad I did. His answer was "suggest you continue your work as long as funds last returning to Canada this fall as originally planned. Can you take supplementary exams please consult director." Exams this fall are not possible, but the registrar thinks the other plan will work. I'll see Constable on Tuesday.

So now I shall be in London for most of the time. Things are not so bad as they might be. Bowsie [Elizabeth Bowser] tells me that the only Americans who have done this course in one year are people who have had training before—she has done enough work to get an M.A. from Harvard in the fall, and the other man who got it a year ago had worked on art history as an undergraduate. Bowsie says she didn't get this exam on any work she's done here, but on her Harvard courses. Thank goodness McCurry was sensible about this. I had visions of taking the Saturday boat home in disgrace. Now life goes on as usual.

It is now Sunday. I am staying with Marion Higgs near Cheltenham. We saw Tewkesbury Abbey and Gloucester Cathedral today. Her family makes me understand what Millicent [Rose] revolts against. Millicent incidentally, is now on top of the world, having got through all right. Every little while the depression sets in and I have a little trouble keeping my chin up—my brain tells me that I can see this through, but my emotional makeup goes rather haywire. The Valley of Despond is not cheerful territory.

I must write the family and tell them to put the lid on the affair.

I am evidently a fool with no judgment, no sense of values, an absolute inability to see further than teatime, and possibly not quite sane. I can't cook and I can't keep house. I would not recommend myself for any job just now, not even cleaning your front doorstep. Although I have enough mechanical ability to black your boots. For God's sake forget about me.

H.

Toronto, Ont.
[*24 July 1935*]

Dearest, I don't know that D.H. Lawrence is particularly good for you —he *does* seem to addle your poor brain so. Of course he addled his own. The subconscious is a badly kept jail from which criminals are continually escaping. Psychology tries to clean up the jail by asphyxiating the criminals. In other words, psychology represents the remorseless, inexorable march of the intelligent consciousness into the inmost recesses of the subconscious, freeing the soul from the unbearable tyranny of the brutal, stampeding instincts. But all the Women's Clubs in the country think it represents the freeing of the criminals and the abandoning of the brain to the government of the belly. Lawrence never fully grasped the fact that Freudian psychology was a complete triumph of an intellectual, deracinated civilization—neither, for that matter, did Freud. I admire the best Lawrence, but at his worst he wallows and slavers and bellows like a hippopotamus in the mud. Compare that sulphurous *Fantasia* of his, the facile chatter of a sentimentalist, with, say, the big brothel scene in *Ulysses*, where the subconscious is organized into clear-cut rhythms by a competent artist, and you will see the difference between the genius who expresses his age and the genius who is merely a symptom of it.

And religion is not a specialized department of life. When people talk about "religious experiences" they usually mean mystical experiences which are usually pseudo-mystical or quasi-mystical at the most, resulting in little more than a more effeminate kind of sentimental wallowing in the emotional than you find even in Lawrence. Which is perhaps the worst sentence I ever composed. Well, anyway, the religious life is simply the positive, constructive life, and any experience which seems to *mean* something, no matter what, is religious. And what is the standard of the positive, constructive action? Well, people of different religions have different standards. One of the most positive and constructive activities you engage in is art, and if a great ritual impresses you as a fine work of art, that's your response—a purely religious one. If you don't get a mystical response, it's simply because you're not a mystical type of mind—very few minds are genuinely mystical. When you analyse yourself, you say, you find that your cardinal sin is laziness. Of course it is. Life is activity and experience; constructive activity and intelligent experience is without exception religious. Laziness means the cessation or digression of activity and experience into irrelevance, and is therefore everybody's cardinal sin—only different people, again, have different ideas about what is energy and what is inertia. Once you start thinking about religion as a specialized activity, or as a retreat from ordinary living, you immediately think of it as mysterious, ghostly, esoteric and so forth. Hence all the sham mysticism. Perhaps all mysticism is a sham—I don't know; I sometimes think so, probably because I don't know anything about it. But when most people say they have given themselves up to Christ what they have really given themselves up to is a rabble of confused and chaotic feelings, mostly memories of adolescence, and the best word for the state they get into is maudlin. Your remark about laziness is very shrewd and perfectly sound—as soon as you start to worry about your soul, you're getting away from religion, and as soon as you get to work, you're being religious. My spiritual advice to you as your father-confessor is, mind your own business and stop yammering. Religious people call that being saved.

And what I described as intellectual and emotional masturbation was not the continued thought of you—I'd be as impotent as a guinea pig by now if that were true—but the continued thought of your absence. I don't suppose I put in fifteen consecutive waking minutes without your floating into my consciousness somewhere, but if you died or couldn't come back, I'd have to shut you straight out of my mind or go on the rocks. And now it's easy to think of you and write to you, where it was so desperately hard when I was getting resigned to another year. When you come back, dear, I don't think you'll quite find the sulky and irascible small boy you left with a lump in his throat at Montreal. I've put in a lot of time meeting older people and teaching younger ones, so I'm less precocious and more complete a personality. However, that remains to be seen. You know the famous story of the species of South American flying condor, which became extinct through its habit of flying in spirals till it vanished up its own rectum. Well, that's the inevitable penalty of subjectivity, and I think I've realized it.

Speaking of growing up reminds me of my birthday. Don't worry about not making the explicit gesture, sweetheart; I was pretty sure you were thinking of me. July 14 came on Sunday. Jerry Riddell and his girlfriend took me to church to hear Dr. T.R. Glover, an S.C.M. man who wrote a (rather bad) book on the *Jesus of History* which I found last summer on my field. Then they took me to lunch. They also took me to a Summer Symphony—Cesar Frank fried in lard. Temperature about a hundred and nine.

Did I tell you I had a job? Marking essays in the summer school. MacGillivray just came in and dropped about fifteen pounds of essays on my chair. I looked at several without marking them—it was hot and I didn't altogether trust myself.

You'll give me a more definite date for your return, won't you, darling, as soon as you can?

Norrie

Toronto, Ont.
[*1 August 1935*]

Sweet:

I'm sorry. But it's just as well. You're an intelligent rather than an intuitive type, and you work systematically rather than spasmodically, which means that an intellectual crisis doesn't mean anything to you. So your mental outlines don't altogether fit those of an exam, which places such a premium on glibness and assumes that brilliance is the most valuable of intellectual qualities. First-rate people don't do things brilliantly, they do them readily; and I think that this will make you much more clear-eyed and self-assured and take a lot more of the flutter and splutter and gawkiness out of your work than the most meteoric examination success could possibly have done. Your plan of campaign is an excellent one—Roy [Daniells] is a pretty good head, isn't he? You've got to get that exam, you know. My own exams were usually accompanied by a good deal of self-hypnosis; I knew that a single headache or bellyache would pluck me as bare as Alouette, so I practically drugged myself into a state of unnatural vitality. If I had been capable of menstruation, however, I probably wouldn't have a B.A. yet. The result was far less of a surprise to me than you imagine. What with the size and scope of your course, your complete lack of any academic or artistic background, English academic standards, the complete newness of everything around you, your lonesomeness and isolation from the people who look after you, the social demands made on you, your overconfidence, the amount of work you seemed not to be doing, your physical crises, my eyebrows had been tangled in my hair for some time. You're a bright little Red Riding Hood, but it just wasn't your grandmother. However, I wanted you to find your feet in England, and I think this will help a lot, even if it is a bit of a bump.

Don't end any more letters with appeals to me to forget you. Of course, I know you're over that now, but don't do it anyhow. If love were what the Elizabethans called it, a quotidian fever, any trifling accident like this might make me cool off. But love isn't like that. Not mine anyway. Its real essence is a little diamond packed in ice away inside me, to keep it away from the heat, which would only injure it. It's cold, and it's hard, and it's got sharp edges, but it's unbreakable. Outside are all the emotions, shifting and variable, worked up over everything and ready to stampede without provocation. Inside is a perfectly dry, impersonal respect which has nothing to do with my feelings. A thing like this, of course, doesn't touch me anywhere: but then the worst thing you could do, the most shameful or horrible thing, while it might hurt on all the burning sensitive places, couldn't get through the ice; it couldn't really touch me. Helen Frye. Write that down in your notebook, as Johnson said to Boswell, and never forget it again.

Norrie

Toronto, Ont.
1935 Aug 2

Telegram addressed to Kemp at 20 Portman Square, Courtauld Institute of Art, London W1.

FORTUNES OF WAR CHEER UP AND SHUT UP LOVE,

NORRIE.

[*Westgate in Weardale,*
County Durham, England]
August 3, 1935

The letter referred to by Kemp is missing from the correspondence files.

My dear Norrie,

I haven't heard from you since July 15th but I expect the Canadian mail will be forwarded here tomorrow or next day. I am in the north of England rusticating for a week—walking and climbing hills and swimming in the stream which they call a river—the Wear, and we'd call a trickle of water. It is all so peaceful and untrodden by the tourist traffic. Then we go to see Durham and York, Peterborough and Lincoln. After that, London, then Normandy and Paris. Then I'm coming home.

I could not face another winter here, in spite of all my plans. It can be managed but it is not worth the struggle. God! how I want to come home! I'm sorry I wrote you the last letter, telling you I was staying, but at that time I had everything decided and had even written to McCurry. By the end of the week I decided I was an idiot and changed over again. I was pretty strongly advised by Miss Whinney to throw up the scheme and take the job at home. Aside from the fact that I highly value her opinion, it so agreed with what I want to do anyway that I was easily persuaded. What I shall say to McCurry, I don't know yet. The problem I mentioned still is there. And it is one to be reckoned with. However, we can talk about that later. At least we can talk, not write. I wonder whether you will like me when I come home, I wonder. I feel just a little strange, writing to you these days, and it is about time to come home. I've seen so many places and people, and made friends, only to leave them. One can't go on this way forever.

I hope there is a letter from you this week, it brings you nearer.

My love to you,
H.

Cambridge
August 20 [*1935*]

My dear, Thanks so much for your cable. I began a letter two weeks ago, but let it slide and went swimming with Madge [Willis]. And last week I was so busy seeing cathedrals that I did not do anything else. After a week at Weardale, we went to Durham and York, Lincoln, Peterborough. Madge left me then as she'd got bitten by a (presumably bed-) bug, which left my hide untouched but made her swell up in an alarming way. So I came to Ely and Cambridge alone. The Fitzwilliam here is the Perfect Museum, and the Cambridge atmosphere is a world all to itself. I expect I should feel one of God's chosen if I'd come from Newnham. That is Millicent's college, you know.

I spent part of this morning reading all the letters that had accumulated during the past week, which were sent on to me here. As they were partly reactions to my exam results, I had to take my medicine, and begin to feel rather ridiculous all over again, after I'd more or less decently interred the skeleton. The letters were of course from you and Daddy, as I have not been broadcasting the affair. Daddy seems to think I went to pieces. I did not. I simply had not done enough work. Raw and green and inexperienced. Tried to stuff in too much, without comprehending it, and I'm not made that way.

Of course I've got to get that exam. And of course I will. I had a subconscious idea of where I stood, all year, but I just would not face it. Now the air is clear, and I know what I've got to do next. And I don't think I've done so badly, anyhow, considering the yawning gulf of ignorance which I had to get through somehow. Haven't got through it, of course, but I do see the way the land lies. And I wish you'd stop talking about my finding my feet—I've been tripping over them for months. If I could just forget myself and think of what I should be doing I'd be much better off. I've got a fatal gift of introspection, which amounts to chewing my own gizzard sometimes, and does not result in anything but leaving me more disgusted than ever with that miserable crawling creature which seems to be me. I can never be sure of turning out a butterfly after a fit of stagnation, and even if I did, I expect I would not live like one, but always be alternating between the tree-tops and a cabbage-leaf.

I feel rather grouchy just now. I wish you were here, and I'd have the grouch over with in half a minute, and then we could walk around Cambridge and you'd love it.

Lismer's cable came today. I have leave to stay here longer. I shall be home by October 15th.

Have just been reading *Babbitt*, and Laski's Conway Lecture 1933—Future of Civilization. And the *Morning Post* getting hysterical about Britain's lack of armaments, and the failure of [Sir Anthony] Eden's attempt to negotiate with Italy. What a mess. English papers give us until October before the game begins. Twelve munition factories are being opened in different parts of England. So that our 'protection' won't all be centred in one place.

Helen Frye. I rather like it.

I bought two postcards for you today, and now they won't fit into the envelope. *Death on the Pale Horse* and *Vision of Queen Catherine*. They are the two most magnificent ones I've seen. The Fitzwilliam has three of Joseph and his Brethren—they are early aren't they? I did not like them nearly as well.

Think I'll go wrap a sheet round my grouch and sleep with it. I'll write to you soon when I'm more cheerful—I am sorry.

August 24. Back at Guilford Street. Saturday night. The heat wave which nearly melted England last week has been succeeded by a heavy rain yesterday and today. Cold and raw and drizzling and miserable. London can be the most heart-breaking place in the world. Outside the wetness of the roads makes all the traffic of the automobiles echo and hiss. Up the street two street musicians are performing and a crowd is gathering, for they are very good . . . now they are doing *Londonderry Air* and it is enough to break one's heart. Bloomsbury on a ghastly, lonely, almost unbearable Saturday evening . . . . I'm the only one in the house. All my friends are away—except Madge Willis and Miss Whinney.

Cheer up. This will not do. The point is that I'm just suffering from reaction—the last two days have been rather anxious. When I returned from Cambridge a letter was waiting from McCurry—he and Baldwin had discussed my situation and heartily approved of a second year if I could manage it. Oh my God—suffer another year in this miserable climate with my brain dissolving in the interminable fog and my wits dulled from the intolerable loneliness, and my initiative just about deadened from routine work in the library. Over and above the fact that the Institute has nothing to offer by way of stimulating personalities except one or two with whom I would have no contact. I cannot face it. And I will not. I must be having hysterics or something. I look as hideous as the maniac in *Jane Eyre*, and I've just done in a dozen handkerchiefs during the storm.

Well, I was about to tell you that I went to Miss Whinney again for encouragement. I had just had a letter from Miss Ray who favours staying. But Miss Whinney sat on the idea so hard that I almost took a boat home then and there. She knows the Institute through and through. Thinks the diploma is worth nothing, that I have got as much good out of the place as I will get by another year. I have written a firm letter to both McCurry and to Lismer, and I shall be back in Toronto parking on the steps of the Art Gallery on October 15th at nine o'clock. And if the Atlantic winds have not cleared my head by then I'll go pack my head in ice. But I think I can come back and I'll write the exam—it is just the money I'm thinking of. In the meantime I'm haunting the B.M.—Byzantine art—and the Elgin Marbles, and manuscripts, Prints and Drawings. And I'm going to Normandy and meeting Stien Koetse in Paris, bless her heart. Then I set my nose for home.

I've got a lot I want you to tell me. About the spread of Christianity in the East, and what is the Manichean doctrine, and Neoplatonism, and

Mithraism, and so forth. Dr. Line gave a course on the subject, but I've forgotten most of it, naturally, sliding over the top the way we did. All my life I've been sliding over the top of scraps of facts. This year I tried to understand what I was doing. But that was not what was wanted—I should have been able not only to slide but to turn double somersaults as well. Just the same, I am getting some work done, and the B.M. is glorious, even if it is filled with people and so musty at times that you wonder if you're not in a mummy case by mistake.

Miss Whinney asked me today what Marian Higgs was to do eventually, and I said I thought she would marry a man she met in Heidelburg, after she finished the course. Miss Whinney said—"Oh, a good idea. Why don't you do that?" I said, "But I have a job." Says she—"Well, what of it!" I don't know what gave her the idea, but I had to admit that I was planning to do just that, sometime. And then! She simply laughed to scorn the thought of my staying here next year, couldn't see how I'd considered it for a moment. Said that we in America were working out our art history along different lines to the English method, and she wasn't sure but that it probably was a whole lot better, at least for us. I gave her Lismer's letter to read, and of course it did sound thrilling. Lismer, with all his unconventionalities, is a lot bigger man than almost anyone I can think of at the Institute—with all their knowledge of dates and facts. Here they're academic and dull, and will hazard an opinion on nothing later than 1875. Lismer is, almost single-handed, doing more toward awakening an interest in art than any other man in Canada.

Miss Whinney, incidentally, if I have not told you before, is a friend of Barbara Sturgis—used to be a teacher of hers. Has a job on the staff of the Institute. Came highest in the list, naturally, this year, in the diploma exam, cleaning up any prizes in sight. And when I crab about the Institute, I am not doing so because I made a mess of the exam—I know exactly where I stand there. And I'm doing things about it.

I wish I did not write such woeful letters to you—I don't mean to, but sometimes I cannot help it. And I do *not* spend my time in the rain barrel, even if I sound as if it's the proper place for me. I'm really quite cheerful most of the time. Only sometimes this great city seems like a huge monster ready to swallow me up unless I'm healthy and strong and full of nails.

And I count on you so much—I can't tell you about that. You know all about it. August 24 to October 15—not so long now.

How are you getting on with the Blake thesis? I do hope you can get some of those debts paid back to the college. It is extremely annoying to feel that your friend Johnston, and Bill Little and a good many others would be giving me sidelong glances, stealthily watching for biological developments, simply because you have some months to put in yet, on their money. Well, it is quite a natural viewpoint, of course, as Lismer reminded me. At any rate, I'll not be Helen Frye for some time to satisfy them, and there won't be any developments.

I am feeling remorseful once more at having written such a lot of wet weather into this letter. Today the sun shone brightly and London smiled once more, and so did I.

Helen Frye
(just for practice)

Toronto, Ont.
[*11 September 1935*]

Addressed to Kemp at 20 Portman Square, c/o Courtauld Institute of Art, London; *forwarded to* Hotel St. Ives, Rue de l'Université, Paris, France.

My dear, you will admit, I suppose, that you are a little hard on the nerves. An extraordinary missive from you telling me that you planned to stay in Europe next year, in an extremely light-hearted, not to say hilarious, tone stunned me so completely that I wandered around for a day or so in such a state that it was extremely fortunate that there were no open manholes nearby; and when I recovered, I began the composition of a rather bitter reply, but some instinct made me hold it over the weekend, and then your second letter came, for which I was duly grateful. My life for the last month has been a lot like that last sentence —endless and formless. I've been working for [Norman J.] Endicott as (what amounts to being) assistant editor of *Representative Poetry*. I've composed the notes on most of the poets between Donne and Blake, apart from what Davis and I did last spring; I did the two indices and typed several of the poems for the second volume. It was a routine but exacting job, consisting of endless research into dusty corners, lasting every morning and every afternoon and a good many of my evenings, through weather that would deepen the tinge of a boiled lobster. I've had several sick spells, and the last one lasted nearly a week—been laid up with a headache and sore eyes and backache and constipation and chills and fever and pessimism. I was in bed only two days, but probably should be there yet. The job with Endicott is all done—I cut it, quite decisively, as it was high time my own work was being completed. Of course, it's all grist to my mill—it's loaded me up with a vast store of miscellaneous and mostly useless information—and it may be profitable, though I have no idea how much, if at all. Endicott is not the world's easiest man to work with—he's very nice and I like him a lot, but temperamentally he's so much like me that we get a bit on each other's nerves. I mean he hits other people in the same shattering way that I do, although his almost fanatical meticulousness is a different quality, of course, and when we come in contact it's invigorating but exhausting. However, I know a lot more about *Representative Poetry* than I did, which will be useful next year.

October 15 is all right I suppose; I had more or less got you associated with the opening of the season three weeks earlier, but what's three weeks in a lifetime? Please tell me what boat you are coming on. Somehow I feel that I wouldn't want you to surprise me. I like your friend Miss Whinney—she sounds like a genuine Houyhnhnm. Don't talk any more nonsense about staying over another year, for heaven's sake. No matter who suggests it. Come back to me for information—you can get atmosphere from Europe any time. If you really want me to take a serious interest in your work I'll stuff you so full of ideas about Neoplatonism and Mithraism and Manicheism that all you'll have to do to write an exam or deliver a lecture will be to squeeze your sides. I know about all those things, girl, and you don't. So come back here, and don't spend any more time at the Courtauld Institute Library. Not that I want to spend my time cramming you—on the contrary, seeing as how you have to do some work anyhow, you may as well do as little of it as possible. And you haven't the background, by yourself, to get anywhere academically yet. And I still think my phrase "finding your feet" fairly accurate. If you're going to get anywhere, you either have to walk there yourself or let me carry you, and I can't carry you everywhere. But I can carry you a lot of places, and you'll never go very far without me.

Florence [Clare] called the other day and asked when you were coming home and I told her and she said, "Oh, well, then, that gives you a little more time." God knows what she meant by that, but as Florence frequently calls you a Bohemian I don't suppose it will bear analysis. I think I'll go up to the Couchiching Conference with Jerry Riddell. I want to hear the leader talk about pessimism. He has on his agenda various attitudes to the present world situation, which is a thing the S.C.M. is very fond of discussing, and starts off with pessimism. He gives Spengler as an example of "absolute pessimism" and H.G. Wells as an example of "relative pessimism." I'd like to go up there and twist a knife in him if I got the chance.

Well, if I felt more like writing you a decent letter I'd write you a decent letter, of course. Not feeling that way, I guess I'll go to bed, and write you a decent letter some other time. The last three weeks will be the hardest—what did you tack them on for?

Lovingly,
Norrie

Hotel St. Yves
4, Rue de l'Université
Paris. Sept. 25, 1935

My dear, your letter arrived here today. I don't know how long it is since I wrote to you—some weeks, I know. But there was nothing from you, and Stien [Koetse] and I spent two very busy weeks here, working all day and spending the evenings planning for the next day. And aside from descriptions of Chartres and the Louvre and what not, I did not have a great deal to write about. We got a pile of work done, and then Stien left me last Friday to go to a friend's wedding. So then I was left here by myself, and being alone I have made friends quickly in the hotel. One Englishwoman, old, a suitable chaperone, has been very kind. I have met a Frenchman who plays the violin very well, and we have been playing together. I am amazed that I can play at all, and much better than I expected. Also, I am managing to make myself understood in French, which is really encouraging. The French are so excited, and so gay and friendly—life here is not the same as in London. I have shaken off the dust of Bloomsbury and settled down happily on the "arty" side of the Seine. The place is full of artists and journalists and singers and dancers. Give Florence Clare a jolly good raspberry for me. There's a great deal more in this world than C.G.I.T. groups. And if she called me a Bohemian when I was living such a stuffy life in London, she'd turn gray probably if she knew the sort of place I'm living in now! But she'll never know. One is not a Bohemian because one looks at pictures, and travels. Half the old-maid population of England does just that, and they hardly ever come under the description. Perhaps it is used in the sense of a wanderer or gypsy. She can jolly well go to hell anyway, and I'll not hurt your work when I get back, if that is what she is concerned about. The world, the flesh and the devil may be returning on the *Empress of Britain*, but you are not St. Anthony.

As for my being hard on the nerves, idiot, how *do* you think I felt at the prospect of scraping along in London next winter on insufficient money and a dull routine job? I'm sorry for writing to you at all about it. I was not light-hearted by any means, and if I had not stayed here long enough to get this work done in Paris I should have felt pretty jaundiced with the summer. But I shall have a very fair knowledge of what is in the Louvre, and I shall have seen French Gothic Architecture, with some Romanesque thrown in for good measure.

I am so sorry that you have been ill. Oh my dear, do be well for me, and I'll soon be home. You've been working too hard again, I suppose, and have not had any change during the hot weather. I do hope you are better now, for by this time it is perhaps two or three weeks since you wrote. I shall be glad to be near enough to cast a critical eye in your direction and keep you in order. If you knew how very misanthropic and patronizing you sound, you'd hurry to send another letter, just to reassure me. At present I half expect to see you waiting for me with an encyclopaedia and a stick. You say I'll never go very far without you, and I picture it. You carrying me around between thumb and forefinger, a broken reed which you hold together until the end of time. I really don't think it is worth all the trouble—one hand would be tied up for life and all you'd have at the end would be the consciousness of having seen your duty etc. etc.

I was in Galignani's the other day and saw a copy of Barbara Sturgis' book, and asked M. Moulder how it was selling. We got into quite a conversation and he told me that his business has had a frightful slump in English books. Anyhow, he gave me Barbara's book, as it was a sample copy. So I sat in the Tuileries Gardens and read about Oxford. I think she had a good deal of courage to publish it, it is so immature in spots. But then young women at Oxford frequently are that, and so it is true enough. But the problem always remains: should one publish a novel before one is thirty? Write it, yes, but to give it to the public is a different matter. Still, life at St. Hugh's is very ably set down, judging from the few weekends I spent with Maysie [Roger]. There is always the feeling of a retreat from life—from the twentieth-century horrors, which is all very well for those in the retreat. There is a great artificiality about it which Barbara only dimly hints at. Perhaps I am not sufficiently over-awed at the life of the mind, perhaps I have not the right sense of proportion. But is there any *right* sense of proportion? Mine is different from [Kathleen] Coburn's, let us say. And because of that I'd never get through an Oxford Literature exam. But a lot of things happen to me which would just not turn up in her young life. I don't mean to compare the Coburn and myself, particularly. I was just thinking of the great swirling throbbing stream of life outside the cloister walls, joyous and magic and terrible. While within the walls they sit down calmly and talk academically of the relations between men and women, or whether art is form or is it significant, or is it significant form, or whether art *is*.

Don't mind what I say, I'm just letting off steam. Your letter smells of the cloister a bit too much, and it rather set me off.

I must run across to the Louvre now, as it is getting late. The mob always goes straight to the *Mona Lisa* as the greatest drawing card. I'm a little annoyed with Leonardo just now. That miserable *Bacchus* and *John the Baptist*—which are of course open to doubt as to their authenticity—with their sickly smiles and their rather cloying chiaroscuro.

I picked up a book on Blake the other day—a general sort of essay, in French. I don't think there is anything original in it, as he seems to have gone to Swinburne and the rest for his information. Bought it on the chance of there being a slightly different French slant on the man, but so far I've found only amazement that a people so proper as the English could give birth to a genius so extraordinary.

Take care of yourself, my dear, and don't be disgruntled with me.

My love to you,
Helen

Street in Ghent. Drawing by Helen Kemp, 1935
(courtesy of Victoria University Library, Toronto)

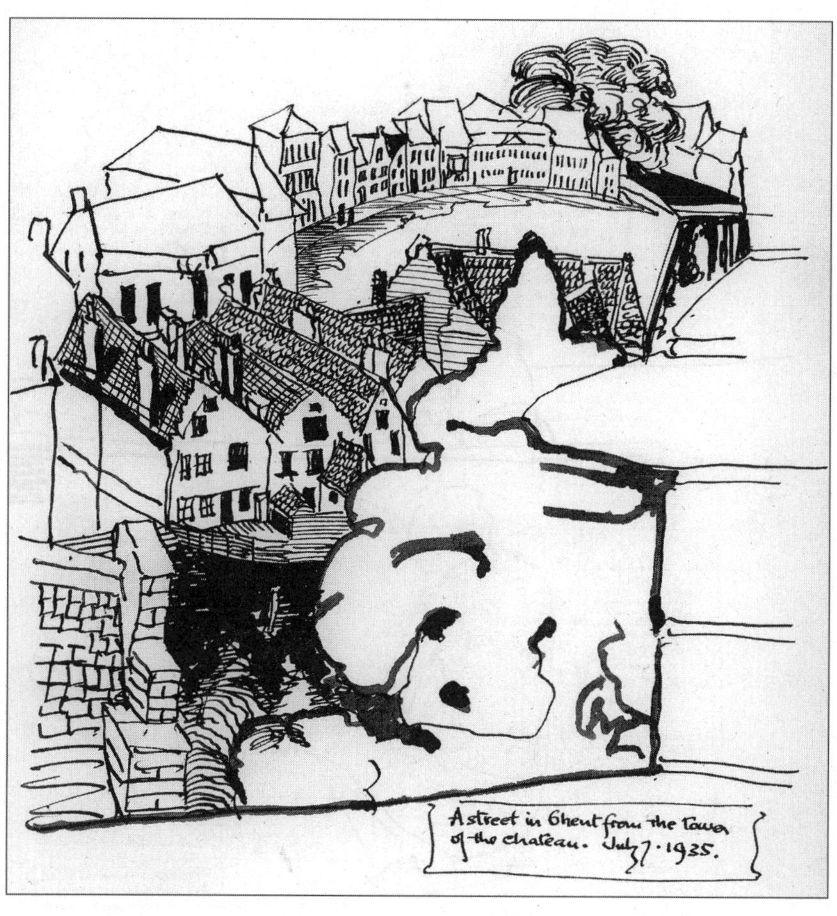

Street scene in Ghent. Drawing by Helen Kemp, 1935
(courtesy of Victoria University Library, Toronto)

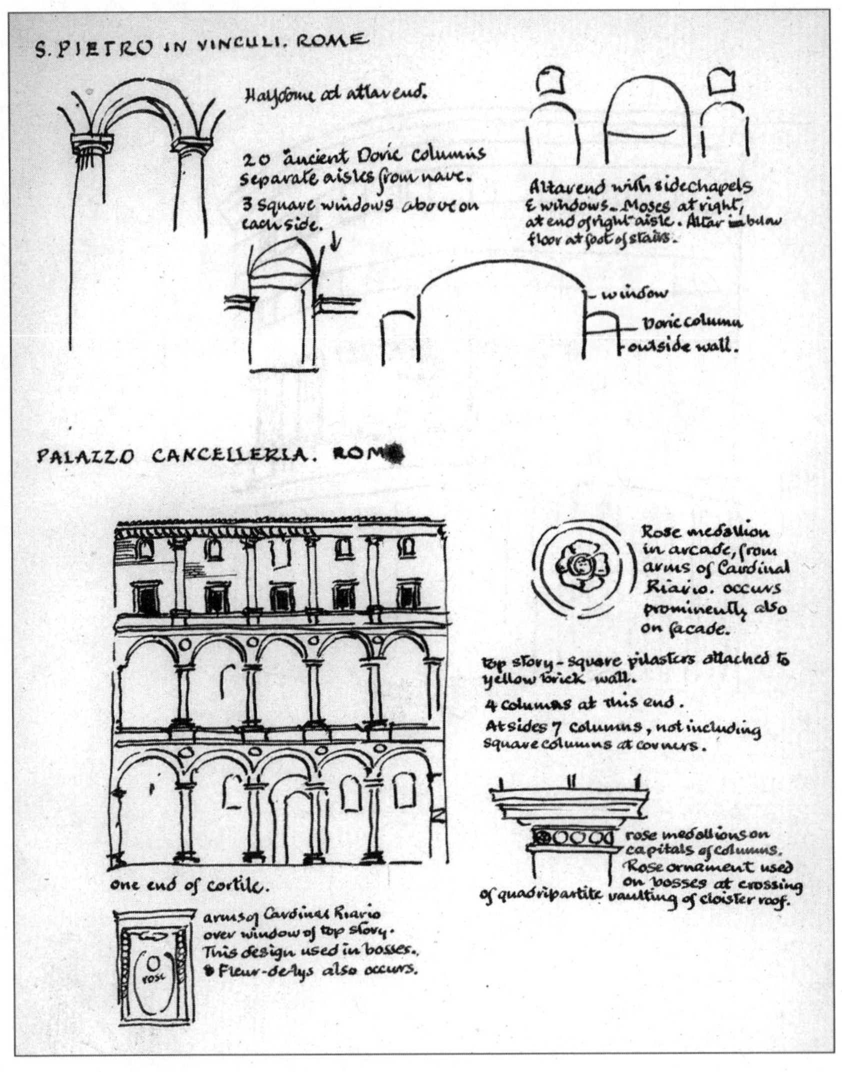

S. Pietro in Vinculi and the Palazzo Cancelleria, Rome. Drawing by Helen Kemp, 1935 (courtesy of Victoria University Library, Toronto)

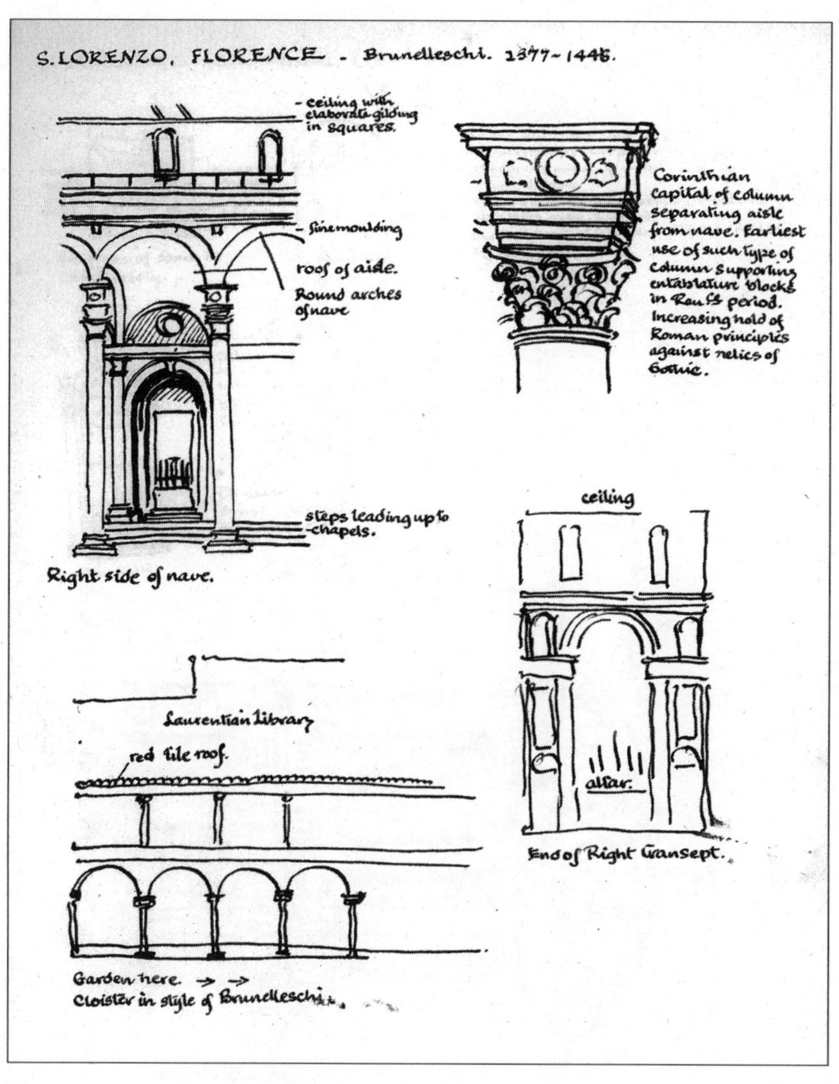

S. Lorenzo, Florence. Drawing by Helen Kemp, 1935
(courtesy of Victoria University Library, Toronto)

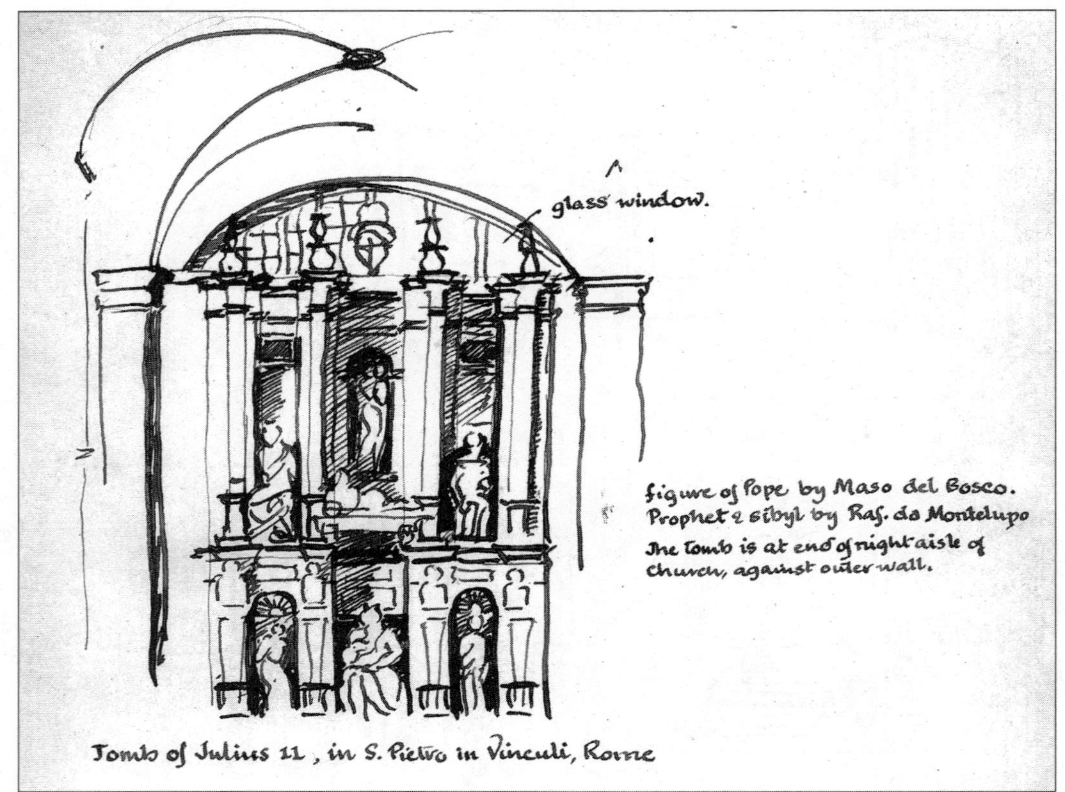

Tomb of Julius, S. Pietro in Vinculi, Rome. Drawing by Helen Kemp, 1935 (courtesy of Victoria University Library, Toronto)

THE

ART GALLERY OF TORONTO

GRANGE PARK

Special series of Five Friday Afternoon Lectures

***With the co-operation of the Dept. of Extension of the* UNIVERSITY OF TORONTO**

"GREAT ARTISTS OF NORTHERN EUROPE"

Friday, February 16th - - at 4.30 p.m.
THE VAN EYCKS—Flemish Painters of the 15th Century (1366-1426) and (1382-1441).
PROF. LESTER G. LONGMAN, McMaster University, Hamilton.

Friday, February 23rd - - at 4.30 p.m.
REMBRANDT (1607-1669)—Dutch Painter.
PROF. J. R. MacCALLUM, Department of Philosophy, University of Toronto.

Friday, March 2nd - - - at 4.30 p.m.
HOLBIEN—German Painter (1487-1543).
MISS HELEN KEMP, B.A., Educational Staff, Art Gallery of Toronto.

Friday, March 9th - - - at 4.30 p.m.
PIETER BREUGEL—Flemish Painter (1525-1569).
ARTHUR LISMER, A.R.C.A., Educational Supervisor, Art Gallery of Toronto.

Friday, March 16th - - - at 4.30 p.m.
INIGO JONES (1573-1652) and the English Renaissance.
MARTIN BALDWIN, Curator, Art Gallery of Toronto.

These lectures are illustrated with lantern slides and free to members and public—students and teachers are specially invited.

Art Gallery of Toronto Lecture series, with drawing on the back, 1936
(courtesy of Victoria University Library, Toronto)

1936–1937

Paddington
Oct. 8 [*1936*]

Frye is in London, England, on his way to study at Merton College, Oxford.

My little girl:

Two days ago it was your birthday, and I wanted very badly to write to you, but I took a warm bath in a cold room, and it's been headache, wretchedly sore eyes and a vacant mind, so no letter got itself written. I think of sending you greetings on your birthday rather than a week or so before it, because naturally celebrating your birthday comes more appropriately from one who gives thanks every day that you got born than from you yourself. Besides, it's as much my birthday as yours. Exactly a year ago—again a delay of two days!—you came back to Toronto, and by doing so made yourself my wife, and by becoming my wife ended my adolescence. I mean by adolescence the period in which I collected materials for building the sort of life I was cut out to build. I had the materials; I knew in a general way I was a pretty froggy sort of tadpole and would never turn into anything different, and I knew I would do the sort of things I had to do no matter what happened. But the point is that a life to be any good has to mean something to the person who lives it as well as to other people, and I couldn't find anything that would give my capacities any value or meaning to *me* until I was sure of you. Now I'm all right—I can go ahead building and planning. You have the power to destroy that building at any time, if it pleases you, but until then at any rate I am secured by knowing that everything I can achieve in contributions to "culture" or "the intellectual life" or whatever abstraction you please, as long as I can keep pouring them out, has another name, and that name its real name, Helen.

So, while I am desperately lonesome for you, I am not lonely. I don't mean only that I have enough people to talk to and enough to occupy me, but also that what I am doing here grows naturally out of my love for you, as well as out of my own urge to advance, the desire of Victoria College to have English-trained professors, or the will of God or the pattern of twentieth-century thought. All these other things are admirable enough, but I shouldn't care to be left alone with them. It's bad enough to have to sleep by myself, without taking a Purpose to bed with me, personal or impersonal. But you're part of the scheme now, and everything that happens, if it fits in with the fact that I love you, is all right.

Why do I protest so much? Partly because I am a little nervous at seeing you holding my happiness in your volatile and temperamental little hands. Partly because I am one of those people who have to give some form of expression to their feeling or burst. And of course I may be simply dramatizing myself, overwhelming you with flatulent words and egotistic emotions over a comparatively simple matter. That is your own opinion—or at least it has been your opinion—so I have gone into it more carefully and from more points of view than you ever did. And what emerged was: it is quite true that I sound like an intolerable prig and am making an abject fool of myself continually. And I don't care; and I shall never care. I don't mind if you laugh at me and say to yourself: "That's Norrie hypnotizing himself again." Because a love which is dignified can never be more than liking or respect: love itself is ridiculous and grotesque, like the sex act itself. I could hardly be a lover without being a clown first. That is because I am blissfully and completely in love with a very real woman. Why do they say "head over heels in love" if they don't mean that a lover will do absurd things, like writing absurd letters to bore his sweetheart with?

I go up to Oxford tomorrow, travelling light because I love you.

Norrie

84 Queen's Park, Toronto
Sept. 30, 1936

Kemp has been appointed don at Wymilwood since Frye's departure for Oxford.

I'm firmly installed here, have had the house meeting tonight and have given out scores of keys. I think I'll be a pretty fair don, feel a little depressed tonight because of too much social activity. We had a tea at the Art Centre yesterday and a big members' tea at the Gallery today; I figure rather largely in this month's bulletin, what with five hundred words of blah on the Soviet show.

I just pulled out one of your letters written in July 1932. It rather gave me a start, the working in and out of your very logical brain in response to my affectionate advances. Poor Norrie! I wish you were here to let me bewilder you again. Oh hell, I can't write to you tonight. I'm so tired I can hardly hold a pen. I had better leave off.

October 10, 1936

Work continues at the gallery—complicated by the curse and constant interruptions and bad management of one kind or another. A crowd of thirty-odd teachers arrived an hour before I expected anyone the other day, and nobody was back from lunch except Baldwin and myself. However, he talked to them. Heaven knows what he said and I'm sure they didn't know, but it was a gallery talk. You see the Soviet show was opening that night; it had just gone on the walls; we were still writing labels for the print room and arranging a showcase full of books and dolls and small pamphlets on modern Russia. The catalogues had not arrived from New York and Aileen Galster was frantically lettering signs to tide over our difficulties. And in came a hundred more teachers, the ones I was expecting. However, all hands went at the pump, Norah and Baldwin talked on the show and I took groups down to the Centre where Gwen Kidd and Dorothy Medhurst looked after them. All this happened yesterday and while there was a formal opening at the gallery there was also this big brass-hat reception at Victoria. They gave me a red badge to wear and dubbed me hostess-at-large, so I felt I had to go. Mother came over and sewed me into Norah's dress, and I finally got there. What a life! The dress was very effective, if you can get the idea from my fashion drawings.

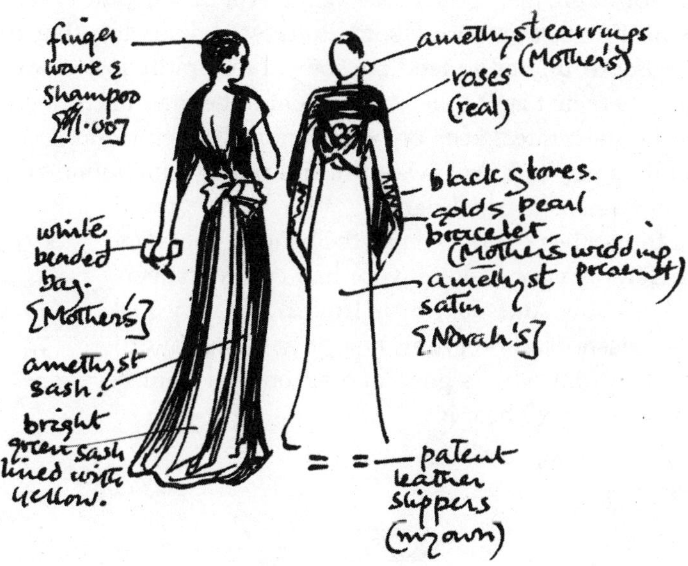

The Governor General was on hand and all the stuffed shirts in town. God, what a bourgeois affair *that* was! There were covered carpets stretched from Vic to Burwash to Emmanuel. Hundreds of people, the crush was pretty stifling. I felt damnably single, I can tell you, what with everyone turning up with husband or wife or fiancé. These Vic family affairs are all very well if your family doesn't happen to be in Merton. However, Miss Ray snapped me out of that by saying "Oh you married women!" and introduced me to Moff Woodside as Norrie's fiancé and I thought the family'd better be well represented. I spent the evening alternately receiving congratulations about the donship and answering questions about you. Roy Daniells suggests that I type out an expurgated edition of your letters for general circulation and Jerry Riddell even offered to edit the collected letters of H.N.F. I do wish you would send a note to Roy and to Art Cragg who seems a bit gloomy in Emmanuel without you there. I ran into George Morrison who stuck to me for the rest of the evening and solved the man problem. I'd forgotten how he danced though, and felt some regret later when he gripped me convulsively and crushed all the roses.

I'm taking on the Women's Lit Art Group, that is, in an advisory capacity. I start on Tuesday with Mrs. Arnold, who is one grand woman. I'm rather appalled when I think of what I've got to get through this year, but I'll do it just the same. *The School* printed my article and gave me 8 bucks for it. I'm just about broke again. Will be for some time.

I think I'll start gathering some interested souls together to listen to records. Art offered to lend me some. I'm rapidly losing my fear of people—there just isn't time. And I seem to be manufacturing conversation at quite a rate. I keep on being amused at being adopted into the Vic family party with you away, I'm still rather dumbfounded, but I'm here and it seems to be all right.

One thing I beg of you—on all the bended knees you like, preferably yours—*do* get your hair cut by someone who knows how. And make them leave it long. One look at your passport photograph nearly gave me hydrophobia. Find out who is good and sit on him until he gets the idea. I can't bear it.

My love to you,
Helen

Oxford
Oct. 11 [*1936*]

Darling:

Sunday in Oxford. I am completely surrounded by shell: I have no curiosity: don't want to go see anybody, or go for a walk: just want to sit in my room, devour books nervously and feverishly, and write to you. I'll get over that, of course. Becoming a freshman again has its temperamental difficulties. Repetition always calls up associations; so I feel the same awkward, coltish seventeen-year-old coming back again. Several reasons—the obvious one that it's all new and I'm lonesome and ill at ease. And I feel a sense of being shut in on the campus. So at Toronto—the first year it was all campus, and I felt haunted by it—then the city grew and the campus faded out, till last year I was a citizen of Toronto, married to you, and only kept the college as a centre of gravity. But there is no Oxford—not for me at least—except the University, and the feeling of moving like a separate disembodied spirit among lights and crowds, which makes me love a city so, will have to remain in abeyance. Where at seventeen I definitely needed the pressure of a social group, here I want to choose my own friends. I shall eventually, of course: but just now I want to be by myself, and open out to others gradually.

Well, I'm beginning at the wrong end as usual. I got up here Friday and was assigned to my room before lunch. It's in the Mob Quad—origin of name unknown, long series of stories invented to explain it—fourteenth century. My room is about the size of the Senior Common Room at Burwash. A chesterfield, two armchairs, seven wooden chairs, a bookcase, two desks, two huge windows with window-seats. Then a bedroom—bed, chair and commode. Also a large central table I eat my meals on. Also a fireplace with an electric grate which stares at me silently and warms up very gradually, a perfect symbol of Oxford. My slender belongings look very meek and deprecating.

Friday afternoon [Douglas] LePan dropped in, and [Joseph] Reid, the only other man on this staircase, from Manitoba. We went for a walk—Oxford has done the secluded academic retreat stuff very well. Curious word, retreat: it seems to imply that the acquisition of knowledge means stepping backward, with one's diffidence and caution increasing at every step. It's a pedant's word: the pedant loves to think that great knowledge is simply the revelation of greater ignorance. Knowledge is power, however. Reid has asked me to breakfast tomorrow morning, and LePan to tea tomorrow afternoon. Reid tells me the ghost of Duns Scotus is supposed to haunt his room: they raised the floor, but the ghost walks at the same level, so maybe I can see his feet and ankles dangling from my ceiling. I hope so, anyway.

Although I have a huge purple pisspot, estimated capacity five quarts, I have to walk over to the New Buildings, several hundred yards away. One wonders how they managed it in the fourteenth century. Out the window, to mortify the flesh of the passers-by? Out in the landing, for the scout to collect? Into the fireplace, to save money?

Blunden seems a very good head and quite prepared to be friendly. Gentle soul on the whole, I should think, but with an unfortunate propensity to assume I know more about the subject than he does. Bryson, the Anglo-Saxon tutor from Balliol, seems to be all right too. And if I say again I shall work this term, it's because this time I have better reasons than an uneasily moaning conscience can provide. I know where I am, working; then I have a certain amount of self-confidence, and there, until I am a little more at home in this grey, misty world of snuffling Englishmen, I shall remain.

I shall not be unhappy here, but neither shall I ever be positively happy; happiness, for me, is only to be found where you are, and I realize as I never have before the fact that there is a certain radiance about you I can never find in anything else I am in contact with—I read over what I wrote on Blake this summer, and can hardly face it—I wince at every paragraph because it calls up some luxuriantly happy scene at Gordon Bay, something in which you figured.

Could I have transferred this feeling to another woman instead of you, if I had met someone else? It's unthinkable: I can't imagine loving anyone else, nor have I met anyone who showed any possibility of meaning what you mean to me. So around my love there is always a mystery: why, in a world that seems to make so little sense otherwise, did something so inevitably right happen apparently by accident? Because it's all right, even the wrongs. I know that now. My religion was, I think, the last thing to centre itself around you.

Oh, my darling! Words and words again. And you so far away.

Norrie

[*Toronto*]
Oct. 14, 1936

My dearest:

Can you hear the hellish row that is going on downstairs? It is the Music Club getting under way. Crawford is trying all the usual tricks, and the chorus is now very nearly in a state of hysteria with exaltation. It is the greatest example of mass hypnotism I know. In two shakes I'll be down there standing on my head too. Crawford uses his musical gifts in a way that I consider just a bit immoral. However, I suppose a musical binge of this sort really does the kids a lot of good.

Roy got his essay on the New Deal off to John Jones, who is typing it for him, last night. I was at Arnolds' having my first German lesson. They seem to be running a sort of pension this year—John helps in the house and Mrs. Arnold is busy with her course in Psychology.

[Barker] Fairley told me that L.C. Knights has a permanent appointment at Manchester now, and he thinks he is married. I'm glad—he needed a job badly, and I hope he has a nice wife. I liked him very much and I'm sure you will too if you ever see him. He came down one night I remember, with an article he'd written on pedantic Shakespearean criticism—called "How Many Children Had Lady Macbeth?"

Did I tell you I'm doing a lecture on The Rococo Spirit in Painting for Ruth Home's museum lectures? Later on I'm doing Late Eighteenth-Century Painting in the same course—the two lectures slated for the Art Gallery of Toronto. Am trying to read some German on the Rococo spirit. Don't know any vocabulary yet, so it is very slow going.

It is a blessing that I am so busy and have other people to think about than myself or how much I miss you. I kept looking over the crowd in Hart House today for a fair head—I always do in that theatre. It is a relic of the days when I first fell in love with you—and the music club is doing a finale that nearly gets me down at this moment. Do you remember the lump in the throat that the final chorus sometimes can give you? And you probably wouldn't remember how I watched you from the other side of the wings the night I was prompting and you were stewing about the pitch of the soloists? I think you went home with me that night. It was about the first time.

Well my darling, I am picturing you in Oxford now and I am so very proud of you. Roy Daniells said the other day that [Pelham] Edgar is due to retire the year after next, just when you are due to come back, "if," he said "you do come back." He seems to expect that you'll get a wonderful job in England. I practised some r's today just in case.

At last the party has broken up. Crawford did the "Theologians" in the minor with the chorus singing it very well. They're all clearing out now. Guess it's time for bed. I wish I could be with you tonight.

Your
Helen

Oxford
Oct. 20 [*1936*]

Darling, I'm sorry to have been so long getting a letter off: I've worked very hard most of the week, on my first paper for Blunden. It was on Chaucer's early poems, which are all in the usual symbolic, visionary form of medieval poetry, and as that happens to be the kind of poetry I know how to read, the paper grew and grew as I worked on it—I spent every working hour of Saturday, Sunday and Monday on it, practically. Blunden said very flattering things about it, but he obviously isn't very fresh on Chaucer. That's the weakness of the tutorial system, I think: the tutor has to pretend to know everything when he doesn't, like a public school teacher. Not that Blunden bothers to pretend much. I think he likes me. However, he absolutely declines to take the initiative in deciding what papers I am to write. Next week I tackle *Troilus and Criseyde,* and may do something with Shakespeare's *Troilus and Cressida* too. I should be rather good on the Shakespeare—I just gave that play a careful reading almost exactly a year ago, and it did something to me—I've never been the same man since.

The rest of life is a bit dull as yet. It's very difficult actually to meet people. Not that I want to meet people much—the freshmen here are nice kids but it's difficult to say anything to them when there's so much to explain, so to speak. I had one in here one afternoon who talked religion and politics at me for three hours. I questioned so many of his assumptions that he was pretty shaken up, but it will do him good, and I think he liked it. The Canadians, Reid and LePan, I see occasionally. The other night a kid came in and asked Reid if he'd ever seen the ghost that is supposed to haunt this particular staircase, as he had, a week ago. I thought he was drunk, but he wasn't, though he admitted he might have been dreaming. There was another man in Reid's room, a Scotchman, and we discussed ghosts, I bringing out my story to show that they existed at a certain level of perception. The Scotchman, who also reads English (Reid is in Mathematics, a Rhodes) was quite overwhelmed by my systematic mind, praised me for about ten minutes on end, and left us at about half-past two, after firing questions at me like "What is your ethic?"

There are three Rhodes men here in first year, two reading English. One from Mississippi—[Rodney] Baine, large, good-humored drawling type, has fed me marvellous coffee in his room twice and is interested in music. I *must* get a piano, although, if I have to pay for it in advance, it will leave me with about one pound for the rest of the term. I'll have to get Blunden to dispatch an S.O.S. to Ottawa around the first of December. It's tying up all my money in this silly deposit (£30) that's left me short. The other Rhodes man is Texas—[Alba] Warren, sawed-off shrimp, all right, but a bit on the bumptious side, I think. We three have a tutorial with Bryson at Balliol for Anglo-Saxon.

Esther [Johnson] and Yvonne [Williams] were in Oxford this week, and we had tea at a place called Kemp Hall. Lovely name. They brought along a girl named Elizabeth Fraser I met at the Art Gallery with Norah [McCullough] one day. She's settled in Oxford as it's a good market for her formal design and illustration work. We parted with expressions of esteem and promises to come together later.

I'm so glad you're having a good time—you should have a marvellous year, and I think of you as filling the breach for the Frye family.

Norrie

[*Toronto*]
October 22, 1936

My dearest, your letters are coming right along now, and it does help the separation a little. I am so glad that LePan came to see you right away, by now you will be feeling a little more at home. The size of your room sounds appalling.

While I think of it: I am dreadfully sorry. I can't send you any money

I'm afraid, because I borrowed $65 for Roy's [Roy Kemp's] fees and won't get it paid back until too late to be of any use to you. I'd ask Roy Daniells for some but think it would be better if you did that yourself. At present I'm living until the end of the month on a dollar that [Agnes] Beatty lent me. The $65 has to be paid back before the end of the year because of the auditors and I'll need a little to come and go on. Perhaps I'd better talk to Roy [Daniells] about it anyhow, because if I wait until you have time to send word back to him you may be penniless before the cheque arrives.

We are terribly busy. I'm always saying that but it is still true. 185 teachers came this morning from ten to twelve for a talk on picture appreciation. Norah and Baldwin had to take them for my members group was at eleven. There aren't many registered, but the group was intensely interesting. I got them talking about what they like in pictures and what they expect to see; showed them Assyrian sculpture and Japanese painting, Frith's *Derby Day* and a fifteenth-century Persian miniature. One realist began to back down and look for something more than accurate representation—she said I'd given her a new idea, and I wound up by asking them for some quality which might be common to primitive art and West European art—shot them Clive Bell's significant form, acknowledging that that was one significant hypothesis. I told them the standpoint of some modern critics exalting the primitive above Renaissance art. They certainly talked and I do think it went across pretty well. I feel ever so much more sure of myself this year for some reason. Next Saturday the children's classes begin and Norah is organizing everything. Marge Boultbee has a stenographer sending out Van Gogh publicity. The bulletin goes to press tomorrow and I've got to turn out 100 more words on Van Gogh, but I seem rather stuck at present.

The Vic Art group is coming to the Art Centre once a week if they get a sufficiently high enrolment, and there are about 25 people coming to me every two weeks for art appreciation at the gallery. And I'm to do a little tutoring if anyone needs it. It is all very good fun and slightly wearing, especially as I've got to work like sixty at German. I seem to be pretty highly organized at present but nothing much has gone wrong so far. We're having a house party on the 21st which I'll have to chaperone. The best thing to do is invite a man and dance too, so I'll have to ask Roy [Daniells] again, in return for that little job I did for him at the hike. But he gets the best of the bargain because this is going to be a good party.

11 P.M. Barbara has been in for the evening and has just left. I had not seen much of her since I moved in here owing to extreme busyness. I read her some of your remarks about Merton. Unfortunately, I have to come to a dead stop now and again, if you *will* talk about purple piss-pots and myself. I do think you ought not to use a purple one. I shouldn't like it myself, but I dare say I couldn't abide their sanitary arrangements anyway. Couldn't you suggest that they partition off one end of the Senior Common Room and install a bathroom? I woke up with a start lately with a nightmare in which I thought I had given one of your last letters to an utter stranger to read, and how I snatched it back when I remembered what you had said in it.

I am awfully tired and must turn in soon. I can not afford to get too exhausted because each day is as strenuous as the one before it. I wish I could hold your hand and go to sleep peacefully. I don't stop to think much of how far away you are, I don't dare. I just go around with you on street cars and go for walks with you along University Crescent in the evening and think of how much you would like it. And I'm always very happy thinking about you and how nice you are. I had a letter from Edith Burnett who was away in Dalmatia when you were in London, and still wants to see you.

My writing seems to be getting smaller all the time, do you think I'm parsimonious?

ANYHOW, I'M SENDING YOU A LOT OF LOVE

I SEEM TO BE GETTING INTO THE WRONG SEASON, BUT THEY'RE ALL THE SAME SO FAR AS YOU'RE CONCERNED. BESIDES, YOU'RE NOT A CLOWN. WHAT IF I SHOULD CABLE THIS—I'M JUST A LITTLE NUTS. HELEN.

Oxford
Oct. 27 [*1936*]

My darling girl:

I should be very happy here if it were not for your absence; but every once in a while some Toronto scene—invariably with you in it— rises in front of me and I realize that I am an exile after all. I love you so. You should be seeing Esther and Yvonne before you get this, so we can see each other at second hand at any rate. Incidentally, I got a very friendly letter from Elizabeth Fraser issuing a general invitation to any sort of meal at any time. I think I shall take her at her word—it's that kind of note—and besides, being able to connect with your circle of friends, even at this distance, means a good deal.

The work is going strong—I keep putting a hell of a lot of work into my papers. I have just finished the *Troilus and Criseyde* thing. I didn't get into the Shakespeare, as there were 8,000 lines of the Chaucer, and I think I worked as hard over it as I ever did over those theological essays that used to bring in such an impressive list of firsts. I think Blunden approves all right, but his main interest is in things like natural imagery of the 19th c. type. I can't write about that intelligently, as I don't think in those terms, and neither did Chaucer. So what Blunden says is that the paper is a very fine piece of work, that Chaucer was quite a poet, that that picture on the wall he bought for ten pounds at an auction, and the catalogue described it as School of Poussin and dated it around 1710: would I give him an opinion on the date? also the next time I pass St. Aldate's Church, would I take a look at the font cover there, which has been varnished out of existence, and which looks medieval, but is, he thinks, sixteenth-century Flemish work done in a medieval tradition, and let him know what I think about it? So I get up and stare solemnly at his bloody picture, and then announce that my opinion on the date of a bastard Poussin is not worth a damn, and that my qualifications for pronouncing on Flemish font covers are exactly nil. Well, no, I let him down easier than that, so that he thinks I know far more about it than I actually do—you know my methods, Watson. I can see where I shall have to marry you and make you live with me at Oxford next year in sheer self-defence.

So far I've gone to two lectures, one by Blunden and one by Abercrombie. They're rather bad, but I may go to some more, as it's a good way of meeting some of the other people in the course. The method of lecturing is very similar to the sort of thing you described at the Courtauld—an endless niggling over minutiae and in hopeless disproportion to the very general scope of the course.

Apparently the tradition I think I mentioned, that the ghost of Duns Scotus haunts this room and the one above it as well as the library (which is really an extension of my staircase) is quite well known and of some standing. HeO±s a long and cold way to come, as he's buried at Cologne, but I can see where the legend of his haunting the library would originate: Merton had the best library in England during the Middle Ages and all of Scotus would be here, being the greatest English scholastic and a Merton man. Then the Reformation came, this library was plundered, the manuscripts torn to pieces and thrown into the quad, and of all authors the one singled out for especial destruction was Scotus. I asked my scout if he had ever sensed a ghost on this staircase, and he said no, but various people have put on surplices and awakened people by putting cold hands on them.

If the music around Oxford doesn't improve I shall grow tone-deaf. Friday night I went to hear Iturbi, who I thought was good. He made a frightful mess of the Mozart (which I heard Schnabel play much better, though God knows he was bad enough) and the rest was tub-thumping virtuoso—Lizst and the galumping Spaniards—i.e., Albeniz and Granados. *When* will pianists learn that the only way to play Mozart is to play him in the completely transparent unaffected way his chamber music is played, and all the querulous barbs and thumps and rushings of time which they think represent expression is all bad taste?

I intended to write this letter last night, but Reid came in and said one of the two university dailies, the *Isis*, had asked him to go to a cinema and write a criticism of it, and would I go with him and write the criticism? So I went to the cinema—the first I had been to since whatever it was we saw last together (ouch!) in Toronto—and wrote it up. The editor seemed very pleased, and said it was much brighter than usual. It was called *Wife vs. Secretary*, one of these how-to-be-sophisticated-though-virtuous pictures. Or at least the picture said that the husband and secretary were virtuous, despite circumstantial evidence, but I couldn't see that the issue would have been affected if they were not, as there was no hint that the wife believed her husband's protestations when she went back to him. It was an interesting example of the way censorship induces hypocrisy.

Well, we're getting close to the end of another month of separation. It really won't be so terribly long—not to look back on it at any rate. But this year is nothing to me compared to two years ago—we're bound together for good now, and I shall love you as long as I live.

Norrie

Wymilwood—
Nov. 2, 1936. 7:30 P.M.

My dearest: I was going to write you a longish account of the doings of the last week or so, but the unforseen happened: yesterday I got an attack of nervous indigestion, fainted, whooped and was put to bed. Fortunately I was at home and everybody was quite solicitous. Roy carried the corpse upstairs, Harold came in from time to time and smoothed the blanket, Daddy came up to see how the patient got on, and Mother sat with me and did her knitting and I enjoyed it immensely. I stayed home from work today and slept all afternoon.

I haven't a great deal to tell except work, work, work. It makes me feel rather worn out by the end of the week, and wishing desperately that you could make some sort of weekend arrangement to come and see me. Perhaps in another decade or so that might come about for people like us. Modern marriage across the oceans with weekends spent together. It would cost a good deal in balloon fares, I suppose, but if you are apt, as Roy Daniells firmly believes, to land a big job in England, I certainly won't be able to do the same.

Barbara has just phoned to say that she has just had a lovely letter from you and that it quite makes her feel that she is back again. She is coming over to see me in a minute or so to tell me all about it. Your last one to me came on Saturday morning. You had just written an essay on Chaucer, had had tea with Esther and Yvonne and Elizabeth Fraser and had £2 in the exchequer. I am awfully glad that you are making friends. I think it will be much easier in Oxford: it is a civilized place, not the bleak jungle that Bloomsbury is at first. I feel rather sorry for the two American Rhodes men coming up against you in a group, and as for the man who told you all about religion! At any rate, I can picture you feeling fairly much in your element writing an essay each week. Roy Daniells was saying on Saturday that he wondered what the university would do if there ever came a really creative person to the faculty, someone who would pour out publication after publication and not be bothered with all the social duties of dons. I expect you will start something when you get back to this comfortable sociable smug little college.

Barbara has come and gone, delighted with your letter. She says that the weakness of the tutorial system may partly be in Blunden's management of it, since her tutor always sent her to specialists in particular subjects, but that arrangement may cause complications financially and some people were stuck with the same tutor all year.

I read part of your letter on Saturday to Roy Daniells who took me out to tea and gave me some help with Baroque & Rococo. He said: "Isn't it just like Norrie to run into someone, e.g. tutor, first off who doesn't know as much as he does about the given subject!" We talk quite a bit about [Kathleen] Coburn and [Florence] Smith. Roy wonders what they'll do with you when you come back, whether they'll put you above those two women, which will break some hearts, or whether they'll put you beneath them, which he says will be ridiculous. I don't care what they do. I want you back here in a hurry. I'll chaperone any number of parties, I'll pour tea like an Amazon, I'll give Sunday teas for Freshmen and listen to their ideas about football, I'll wear a velvet hat with an ostrich plume and grow a front and behind to go with it to show the official prof's wife—I'll do *anything* that's necessary if only you'll come back and marry me and make me the happiest girl in two continents. (The ink has a tendency to clot just where I'm extra emphatic so it must have some sympathy with my views.)

P.S. I sent you 2 bundles of *New Yorker*s last week.

Well, anyway, look what *you're* going to live with!

I'm glad you met Elizabeth Fraser—she is from all accounts a pretty remarkable woman. I met her here in the spring but saw her only for a few minutes. Also, about the money—*could* you get any borrowed from your deposit, or could you get Blunden to wire? I mentioned the fact to Roy [Daniells] on Saturday but he did not offer to help out and I wasn't sure of his mood and did not ask him outright for help. He may be rather hard hit himself as he has been going to an osteopath all fall who charges plenty for his treatments.

Say—*am* I going to talk to you all night?!!

I wish I were. My love to you, my dear,

Helen

Oxford
Nov. 3 [*1936*]

Sweetheart:

The notorious month of November is here at last, and by all appearances I shall not see the sun again until next Easter. A fitting symbol of the dark underworld to which your absence has consigned me. I am imprisoned by rain: my electric light ("all rooms are furnished with the electric light"—quotation from college bulletin, and the subtlest use of the definite article I have ever encountered) burns all day as nature and England are mourning for you outside. I sit indoors like a convict, and look like one. It's easy to say, get yourself a decent haircut. Just you try and get yourself a decent haircut in a strange land. I ask people to recommend me barbers, and they gleefully consign me to some maniac who can't make up his mind whether he wants to produce a Mohammedan saint or a monk out of the object in front of him. The recommendation is based on the fact that the same maniac has cut *their* hair properly, as though that were a valid argument. Darling, there's no use telling the fool what to do: he just doesn't understand what to do. You people with straight turd-colored hair don't appreciate my difficulties. I'll try to find the best barber in Oxford, and that's the best I can do.

Listen, pet, I told you I was short of money because I tell you everything, not because I was hinting for you to send me some. I can live in Oxford all right without cash—everything goes on a bill to be paid next January—all I'm worried about is whether those Ottawa people will come through by the end of this term or not. Don't worry about me: I'll manage somehow. But if you really want to do something for me, my own self-sacrificing little girl—WHEN THE HELL ARE YOU GOING TO COME THROUGH WITH SOME NEW YORKERS?

I've got a piano moved in. I ordered a typewriter, but it didn't come, so I think I'll let it go—Blunden never asks to see my papers, and I can borrow Reid's for any Blake work I may get done. What money I save by scrawling my letters and essays can go on the piano. I went over to Scott's and picked out the best piano they had—which wasn't any too good, as they've been pretty well looked over, so they brought it along, measured the staircase, measured the piano, decided not to argue with the fourteenth century, and took it and me back to the store. Very unwillingly I chose, if you can call it a choice, a wretched little abortion with strings about a foot high and an action like a steam calliope, which eventually filtered through to my room, after getting covered with several pecks of plaster from the ceiling of the staircase. However, all the keys are present, so I started on it. That was Saturday. Sunday Baine came over with a violin and some music—he had told me that he played a violin. He had the Handel Sonata in A, the Beethoven Romance in F, the Mendelssohn Concerto and a book full of a lot of other things. Considering that he's out of practice he's a remarkably good player—very accurate and thorough if not brilliant. I had a swell time, needless to say. In the evening a Freshman named Corder came in with the rest of Roy's repertoire—a book of Beethoven sonatas and the César Franck. Incidentally, Baine is going to leave for Italy directly he leaves Oxford, and wants me to go with him if my money comes through. I don't think I shall, but it's an idea.

Wednesday, I think it was, I dropped in on Elizabeth Fraser and she gave me tea. She's illustrating a book by some maniac of a Greek professor who wanted to excavate Plato's academy and build an international school for the preservation of world peace on the site. The householders living on Plato's Academy told him to clear out, so he sorrowfully returned, shaking his head, and wrote a book in Greek, with an English translation made by someone else, about the swell idea he had. It's full of immense turgid sentences like: "Life did not now present

Illustration for *Plato's Academy* by Elizabeth Fraser, 1936
(courtesy of Oxford University Press)

itself in the guise of alternation between pleasure and pain, but as one great mission and trust, as one great task which it is each man's duty to help carry forward; and as far as the narrow limits of my knowledge allowed I conceived that from the advance of the science of the human mind will emerge an unimaginably great and noble Something of which the least of the immediate results will be the idealization of humanity and the supreme beautification of the life of Man." Now this ungodly tripe appears simply to have swept Elizabeth off her feet: she has been working like mad for a year on illustrations to it—God knows the book could stand a definite image somewhere—her ideas have been gradually developing the way mine have on Blake, into a more and more objective unity all the time, and she regards herself, the publisher, and the translator as initiates into a sort of cult, or at any rate talks that way. I'm afraid that even to please Elizabeth, I can't pretend to like such horseshit; but I think I shall avoid discussing it when I return the book to her.

Blunden improves. He threw flowers at my feet yesterday, I think because my paper was clever, vague and short—*Canterbury Tales*. Told me I'd made a real contribution to criticism, etc. etc., and then talked about Blake for the rest of the hour.

I feel at the moment like shutting myself into the Bodleian and staying there until you come over with the sun. But even in hibernation I should dream of you.

Love,
Norrie

84 Queen's Park, Toronto
November 8, 1936

My dearest: Another Sunday gone, this time a fairly eventful one—the Mozart Requiem at Bloor St. United Church in the afternoon, tea for the Briegers, then a Wymilwood musicale.

Kay Coburn really managed the tea. I just asked the Briegers and they *are* charming. You will like them very much. The Davises, the Arnolds, Kay, Roy (Kemp) were originally invited. Davis had to phone at the last minute that he could not come because Mrs. Davis and Elizabeth Anne were sick. Kay then asked Jerry Riddell and Kay [Riddell] to come and Jessie MacPherson and John Creighton. They all came but J.C. The

Briegers got there right on time and apologized for coming so soon, and suggested that they walk around the park for a few minutes, but I kept them here and showed them the house and they were very much impressed with all the grandeur I'm living in. It was a grand party, with everyone talking intelligently to their neighbours and there were no bad moments—Dr. Brieger and his wife are exceedingly accomplished in the matter of conversation. The Arnolds, I think, had a good time, and I certainly did, for I got a chance to talk to Jerry about you and that's always a help. I met Mr. Davis the other day in the Diet Kitchen and he asked for you—twice—and would like to hear from you. So please be good and write to him—you really should anyway.

I have to postpone activities in German for most of this month because of the Van Gogh show. But after it is over I'm going to make tracks. Brieger asked me how long I was in England tonight, and several things about the Institute, and I had another moment of panic about that *bloody* diploma—I didn't show it of course. I've got to write that off in June or I'll worry about it still, and it isn't worth any more trouble.

Last night Roy K. took me to see Wilson Knight's production of *The Winter's Tale* and it was glorious! I don't know when I have enjoyed anything so much. And I liked to think that Knight is a friend of yours and that he does such good things and I was so glad Shakespeare had written that play.

I forgot to tell you about the Rococo lecture on Wednesday—another group of a dozen old ladies ticked off—I don't know how orthodox on Rococo I was but I think it was interesting and I did not lack words at any rate. I analysed Baroque picture design compared with Renaissance and led from Rubens into Watteau and then the rest was easy. Showed lots of pictures and I think they liked it. My Thursday class is now eleven people and I'll be doing Van Gogh for two weeks.

Monday, Nov. 9. This evening was spent with the dean in council. All evening we talked about smoking, providing smoking rooms and private entertaining rooms for the students and so Jessie Mac is going to bring up the question before the Women's Council and see what can be done. She's a good scout, but very conscious of the position she is in, moving slowly to keep from antagonizing people whose attitude she knows from long acquaintance with Methodism. They're going to fix up the Annesley tea room for entertaining and the women will all be allowed to smoke in their rooms and to entertain men at definite times, in their rooms.

None of this is *law* as yet, but may come about in the near future. Times are certainly changing around here but not any too soon I'd say. We went out for coffee afterwards to the Park Plaza and had *coffee* in the beer parlour and did not smoke because the dean was there. And after the smoking question was gone over the discussion turned to sex relations and F.S. [Florence Smith] said there was a lot of sexual intercourse going on in Toronto, Jessie Mac told me of a case in London, England, which proved that conduct was a good deal less rigid than here, Dorothy Forward talked of couples travelling together in England on their holidays, for the most part platonic arrangements. F.S. said yes, it might be platonic on the woman's side but how long did it remain so with the man? There is no doubt about it, you men are all a little unsafe to be with (bless your hearts, says the widow pro tem). Anyhow, you get the idea. Oh yes, there was one other thing that came up. For the sake of stimulating Conversation we are to think of Interesting People to invite for dinner to come and talk to students afterwards and they can be from the university staff or elsewhere. Then, if university staff, do we invite the wives? Wives are a blight, said Kay [Coburn] and F.S. almost simultaneously. But they'll have to be invited. Various discussions regarding what to do with the dim bulbs, so I said if I were a dumb-egg professor's wife I'd a damned sight sooner stay home than be dragged in because it was the done thing. And then I had to turn the sentence somewhat adroitly to a general sympathy with wives in general realizing that very soon I'd be exactly in that position and mentally noting that refusals are in order to joint invitations to Conversational Orgies in Women's Residences.

I must get this off to the post box. It is really quite thrilling to think of the journey this bit of paper is about to make. I wish I could roll myself up in a carpet like Cleopatra and arrive in Merton and wait in the shadows with Duns Scotus. I wish I could fold myself up in this letter and creep into your waistcoat pocket and stay with you for a long time. I will be your Tinker Bell but I'll not be angry ever and I'll be very quiet and let you read Chaucer and Shakespeare and Blake and Johnson and I'll only tickle your ear occasionally. And I will NOT be a BLIGHT.

Good night my dearest man. I love you so very much.

Helen

Oxford
Nov. 10 [*1936*]

Sweetheart:

There are times when I feel acutely conscious of the minor discomforts of life in England. It is no doubt frightfully vulgar of me to refer to the trivia of daily existence in this venerable and otherworldly seat of learning, but really. Here I am sitting with a whisker half an inch long, waiting for my scout to take away the water I washed my face in out of my wash basin and give me a chance to shave. There's no place I can put the water except into my pisspot, and *that's* full of piss. Meanwhile the hot water he brought me has got cold, and I shall have to heat it up again in an exceedingly temperamental tea kettle. The capacity of said pisspot is considerably less than at first reported. So no doubt you can infer another minor discomfort: waking up with a distended bladder in the middle of the night, staring speculatively at the half-inch or so left at the top, and wondering whether the danger of overflowing it is great enough to make you dress and go your shivering way to the New Buildings. Minor discomfort No. 3: shaving in front of the mirror when the room is so damned cold you cover the mirror with a thick film every time you exhale, and can't see what you're doing.

To switch the subject to civilization for the moment. Thank you very very much for the *New Yorker*s. I spent a marvellous weekend with them. *How* that magazine sustains that incredible prose style the way it does I simply don't know. But for the last three days I've been purring and cooing like a cement mixer, and in the intervals have thought what a swell girl you are.

I had a tutorial again with Blunden last night. Blunden was vague again—obviously doesn't quite know what to do with me but would like to be helpful. I shall have to be careful with that man. I mentioned Skelton, and referred to a very bad editor of Skelton as a congenital idiot. Blunden was tickled—he had written a very unfavorable review of that very edition, and had received a rather abusive letter from the said editor in consequence. It was the right remark, but I could just as easily have made it about one of his friends.

I got a desperate note from Elizabeth the other day, so I went around to see her. That fool who wrote the book she's illustrating has been turning down her designs, which get better as the book gets worse. I can't say I blame the fool, as her drawings have very little to do with his text. He could hardly be expected to realize, however, that the sole merit of his book is in its illustrations.

Charlie Chaplin is here now, but I didn't go—I had the *New Yorkers*. However, I told as many people as brought up the subject to go and see it. Reid goes to Paris for Christmas—I'd like to go, assuming I get some money.

There is no doubt that if I were to try to sacrifice you to my career I should get a very poor exchange. Here I am, in the greatest university in the world, studying the only subject I care a damn for, and still all I can think of is how much I want you, and how much more I want you. Seven months to keep telling you I love you without proving it.

Norrie

Did you know that the word "Kemp" means giant, or athlete or warrior of enormous physical prowess, from the same root as "champion"? Silly name—you really ought to change it, you know.

Oxford
Nov. 17 [*1936*]

My sweetest pet:

I woke up this morning when my scout came in at 7:30 with my subconsciousness registering the fact that I was going to get a letter from you today. Then I went to sleep and dreamed about you for an hour, and woke up and went into my living room and picked up your letter, not even realizing that I ought to be faintly surprised at its presence until later. I love your letters—you wouldn't believe what a physically bracing effect they have on me. I know you love me, but I'm a sort of Shylock in a way—I prefer seeing your name signed to the statement. What my lawyer would do if you decided to run away with some other man! I warn you I'm saving them all carefully. I was amused by your description of life as lived by the presiding spinsters in Wymilwood, particularly at the Smith's [Florence Smith's] remark that a lot of sexual intercourse went on in Toronto. Poor old girl: they should breed a special kind of stud for that sort of female. I've been wrestling with one exactly like her all week—the woman who edited the definitive (I'm afraid) edition of Wyatt, my favorite poet as I think I said. She reduced me to a sort of incoherent splutter when I came to write my paper. Wyatt was a lover of Anne Boleyn's, and was arrested when she was: the spinster's Appendix F is designed to prove that Wyatt never, never actually went to bed with Anne, but that "on the contrary, the relation between them was an agreeable one." Darling, if you think I'm going into Wymilwood to carry on Cultured Conversation, with a lot of Goggle-eyed Gorgons without you there to protect me, you've got a second guess. Now, I must really stop purring and cooing over your letter and pass to the less attractive topic of myself.

Blunden last night. Paper on Wyatt: by no means a bad paper, though not very well organized: I didn't start writing it until ten that morning, and the splutter over addle-headed critics as aforesaid also interfered. Blunden said he had noticed that all his students who really understood what poetry was about liked Wyatt, which was no doubt a compliment. That man must listen to my papers more carefully than I thought. I was listening to a lecture of his on Chesterton last Wednesday in which I suddenly heard a paraphrase of a passage in the last paper I read him, followed by an application of the general principle it embodied to Chesterton. After the lecture he nodded cheerfully at me and said: "I stole from you, but unwillingly: and it was only petty larceny anyhow." I'm just going to take what Blake there is over to him: I want the "favorable half-yearly report" to get to Ottawa before the end of term. I don't want to stay here during the Christmas vac. if I can help.

Tuesday I had Elizabeth in to tea, and she told me all her troubles with her pseudo-Platonist. She's beginning dimly to realize now, I think, that her drawings have nothing to do with his burbling, and is rather depressed about it. She wants to write herself, and illustrate what she writes—she's got all kinds of ability, generalized; how successful she'll be in focusing that ability I don't know. She feels the lack of a systematic training, wanted me to give her something to read, got frightened after I made a few suggestions and said she'd write instead. God knows what one can make of the girl. Her relief at finding someone who wouldn't blush and look the other way when she powdered her nose and who wouldn't think she was a fallen woman if she wanted to go find a bush in the course of the walk suggested that she had been making rather a fool of herself in front of Englishmen recently—I suspect she has a genius for that.

In the course of writing this letter I went to a League of Nations lunch and listened to Gilbert Murray. Magnificent old man, but couldn't say anything except that there's nothing wrong with the League: it's not the fault of the League ideal if the world is being slowly brutalized into a gangland.

I wish you wouldn't get things like intestinal flu, poor child. I do hope you're all right now. Bless you, darling, and keep up the good work. I wish I could have seen Wilson Knight's *Winter's Tale*. My love to everyone you see—I'm giving you enough to supply Toronto with.

Norrie

[*Toronto*]
November 19, 1936

My dearest: I've run out of proper writing paper and I should be in bed, and I've nothing much to say, so I'll just fill ten pages more than likely. Your letter of Nov. 10 came yesterday, and makes me wonder when I wrote to you last. I have been so very busy lately, you can imagine, with the Van Gogh show in full swing. Fortunately we take turns at coming down in the evenings—I was just out two evenings last week and two this week, so it really is not too bad. We have huge mobs of women and children in the afternoons—high schools, technical schools, study clubs etc. etc. Tonight I had to be hostess so to speak, for 200-odd women from the university who came down to listen to a lecture by John Alford. Shades of Lismer! Their idea of integrity is so different—Alford is so painfully insistent on neatly putting Van Gogh in the right category—Lismer's object would be to make people *see* something vital in his work. Alford *ummed* and paused and pawed the air for words and pretty well killed poor Van Gogh so far as that audience went. There isn't too much use in giving people a critical evaluation of a man's work in cold blood: what they want is a warm and glowing appreciation of his work and a clue to what he's getting at. Alford started with a comparison between classicism and romanticism or intellectual and emotional art, and wound up by telling people that Van Gogh was never a first-rate artist because his emotion predominated over his reason and that his later work is marred by too great a subjectivity of approach. Regular wet blanket. A fine way to end a lecture, when you've got two hundred students who are all agog to see a show and you send them away saying it's a second-rate artist anyway but still worth looking at!!! Holy suffering horseshit! I really think that Brieger will outdistance Alford in popularity in no time.

I must go to bed after all that tirade.

My study group turned out with twelve people today and they want a consecutive course—they still continue to talk and I feel much encouraged. I lectured to the Dames Club the other day, expecting to talk to 27 people—there turned out to be forty-five of them with Principal Brown's wife in the front row! So I held forth and a few days later the secretary sent me a note saying that their visit had been the best yet (and they come every year). So that goes into the appreciation file along with the other applesauce.

I'd consider changing my name perhaps—no, I wouldn't consider it at all. I wouldn't need to spend that much time on the question. I'm afraid you're a goner, my boy, or I'm a comer—whatever way it works out, so that we can be together.

Hope there's another letter from you soon—

Love,
H.

Oxford
Nov. 30 [*1936*]

Darling:

I have put off writing you day after day, but no letter has come for two weeks, so I shall have to start this letter to you without one of yours to go on. I got two immense letters last week, one from Barbara and one from Dorothy [Drever], which were a joy to read, though they took me all morning. Dorothy is worried about the challenge of Communism. She's probably in for a bad time, but I don't think permanently. Try to look after her a bit if you can—she's worth it, busy as you are. Barbara is at her best in her letters, I think—she can sustain an amazingly friendly gurgle for page after page.

I have seen a good bit of Elizabeth, off and on—last Saturday we went to the Downs in Berkshire, where she lived last year. We left on the train for Didcot, had breakfast in a pub in a town called Blewbury, walked over to the little village of Aston where she had lived and called on a friend of hers, then walked across the Downs in one of those amazing mists that turn everything into a blue-green grey haze. Elizabeth knows the Downs well, and makes an excellent companion.

There is an organization here called the Bodley Club, named after the founder of the Bodleian, who was a Merton man—apparently it's the only non-athletic group in the college except another beer-swilling outfit. It keeps itself limited to twenty members and is therefore considered awfully exclusive. LePan belongs to it: he brought me along to a meeting last week—an American Rhodes Scholar of German ancestry reading a paper on the dragging of America into the war. The discussion afterwards was fairly bright—a bit forced, but the Club is said to be quite good as College Clubs go. I was elected a member after I left—I'm rather glad, as it's as good a way as any of getting to know the Best People. The mature students have obviously monopolized it.

Reid gave a lunch yesterday to two Canadian Rhodes men and invited me along. He had to read a paper somewhere on Canadian politics and invited our criticisms. It's curious how one has to go away to discover one's own country. At home I should never have said that Canadians had any nationality, and that they consisted of Americans of whom a few imitated the English unsuccessfully and a few Frenchmen tried a rampant jingoism which came off no better. But there definitely is such a thing as a Canadian. The other men were all Westerners, but somehow everything all fell into place immediately—there was a kind of mutual understanding I could not possibly have got with Americans or Englishmen. The political discussion helped (we shared the same prejudices) but it wasn't essential. So you see, blood will tell.

[Rodney] Baine, [Alba] Warren, and a New Zealander named [Mike] Joseph, whom I'm thrown in with a good deal, improve on acquaintance. Baine is about the best chess player in Oxford & Warren about the best golf player, which makes me feel very humble. Warren & Joseph are Catholics, the former the usual muddle-headed reactionary of the Cronin type, Joseph a surprisingly radical one. Joseph is the most intelligent of the three, I think. Baine is very tall and bulky, and can't go out without a huge overcoat and muffler—he's spent the entire term trying to keep warm. He looks funny with me breezing along beside him with my yellow hair & pullover.

I have decided not to write a paper for Blunden tonight. I'm going to go in and twist his neck with my bare hands. I've scared the shit out of him, in the Burwash phrase, and I'm just beginning to realize it, and to comprehend why he gives me that dying-duck reproachful stare every time I finish reading a paper to him. He returned the Blake with the remark that it was pretty stiff going for him, as he wasn't much accustomed to thinking in philosophical terms. I could have told him that there was a little girl in Toronto who could follow it all right, without making any more claims as a philosopher and far less as a student of English literature. So I think I'll start cooing to him.

I was in the English Reading Room of the Bodleian some time ago, looking for Tillyard's book on Wyatt—much the best thing on the subject. I couldn't find it and told the old griffin at the desk. He complained that I was probably just too lazy to get down early enough to get hold of the book in the morning, and I said that was possible, but that it had more likely been lost. So, with much sighing and groaning, he looked it up in the list of lost books, and sure enough it had been stolen for about a year. "Yes," he said, "some dishonest person has taken it," glaring at me as though I were the thief. I suggested it might be replaced. Well, he didn't feel like replacing books: somebody else might take them again (giving me another glare), and he thought it better for the gaps to remain as warnings to other students not to steal the remainder. I said maybe, but it was the business of the Bodleian to see that all books published in England were in it. "Well—how important is Wyatt, anyway? You're the first person who has ever asked for the book, you know. And who is this man Tillyard?" I said important enough for a paper, that I was not surprised if Oxford students knew very little about Wyatt if there were no books on him, and that Tillyard was a Cambridge don who had written a very important book on Milton. "Oh, well, if he's a Cambridge don we wouldn't have heard of him: we haven't got the book on Milton." I said "I know you haven't, and it's a wonder you've ever heard of Milton." (Milton, and incidentally Wyatt, being Cambridge). By that time our exchange of insults was getting fairly good-humored, and after I had told him that the book was published by O.U.P. in spite of its Cambridge lineage and would only cost about seven and six anyhow, he said he'd do something about it, and after several months I might see the book on the shelves. However, he brought the book around to my desk the next day, so he must have been impressed.

I've written an SOS to Ottawa and have asked Blunden to endorse it, and he says he has done so. I shall go back to Guilford Street as soon as I get my money, but expect to be stuck here for a little while anyhow. I've had enough for a little while of this otherworldly paternalism, and would like a big city again and myself all alone in it. From a social point of view I have, in Dr. Spooner's words, tasted the whole worm, but there have been reasons for that, what with the paralysing effect of entering a new country, particularly this country, the work I've been doing, and an invincible shyness which is only gradually wearing off. Also, I've been handicapped by a lack of money. Next term I'll probably expand a bit, take in a few more concerts, and illuminate myself generally.

The term has gone very quickly. Two more terms of the same length, and I'll see you. Oh, darling!

Norrie

[*Toronto*]
Dec. 3, 1936

My dear: I am grabbing a few minutes to send you a line or so as I am told the Christmas mail closes at 5:30 tonight. Van Gogh still going strong: gallery open every evening until Dec. 10 with groups coming and being talked to in one way or another. And now the annual Christmas concert is to be arranged. Victoria continues as before. Last Friday I helped chaperone the Middle House At-Home. It was a beautiful party and I had a very nice time. Saturday I took Roy [Daniells] to see Barbara and Frances Russell—he said that Frances' poem in the latest Poetry Magazine was, to his way of thinking, the best in it. That man is forever having Sunday teas and getting me to come, and of course I enjoy it very well as Wymilwood doesn't tax my powers to any extent. He phoned last night to arrange for this Sunday, and I have seldom heard him in such a hilarious mood—this man [James Holly] Hanford from Cleveland who was lecturing here last week wired him lately offering him a six weeks summer school lecture course in Milton at *ninety* dollars a week! Roy says it is a big joke but he lost no time in answering in the affirmative. He tells me Pratt says that on towards the spring they will send you an outline of courses and will more or less give you your choice so that you'll have another eighteen months to think it over.

Last Monday morning we had a cable from Ernie [Harrison] saying that Marion had done the trick—on Sunday afternoon. A big boy—and we're all now aunts and uncles! He says she is very well too. We didn't expect that to happen until Christmas but you never can tell exactly and Norah says the first one often arrives a little early.

Peggy Kidder is just typing a letter to Zwemmer's about a book I am sending you, 'Masters of the 20th c. Album II'—modern French painters. I haven't the vaguest idea whether it is good or not but it should have some fairly good reproductions and I hope you'll like it. I can hardly think about Christmas—we may get a Botticelli from New York—I mean we certainly will, only it may be a Ghirlandaio instead.

You should see the whoop and holler Toronto's new morning newspaper is making about the King—headline this morning is that he will probably abdicate in a day or so and go into exile with Mrs. Simpson. Percy Bilkey was quite worked up this morning. Told me the King must be nuts, and that woman wasn't any good anyway. She's forty-two, says he, and she's gone through two men already.

I wonder what you are doing for Christmas. I shall be thinking of you, you know how much I think of you. I wish I could have written you a proper letter but there just hasn't been time.

I love you so much, and I hope you will do something very nice at Christmas. Jerry [Riddell] keeps asking for you whenever I see him. So does everyone.

I must stop. The office is in full swing again and I must post this. Bless you, my dear. I shall be home for the holidays.

Helen

Oxford
[*8 December 1936*]

Dear Helen:

Vacation time. Nobody around but a bunch of dispirited youngsters writing Pass Moderations exams. No money, and the Royal Society doesn't care. I'm sending them a cable tomorrow—it may help and it probably won't. I can stay here until the 19th and then I leave for London, money or no money. I'm simply going mad in this place. Dismally cold, wet, clammy, muggy, damp and moist, like a morgue. The room is always as cold as a barn—I can't play the piano because the keys are too cold. The mice are all over everything—they've eaten all my food, and shit all over my dishes. I've got a cold, and I feel like hell. It rains all the time. The sun sets around three o'clock in the afternoon, I think—it's hard to tell. I can't work, I can't think straight, and I've just had a cold dismal lunch in that great bung hole of a dining hall. Ow-oo-oo!

Everybody's cleared out, of course—Baine and Warren have gone to Italy, cursing me for staying around and doing a lot of work. The day we come back—I shall probably be a water baby in the Cherwell by then—we write two exams, one for Bryson on the sixteen hundred lines of *Beowulf* we're expected to read during the Vacation, and one for Blunden on the work we've taken.

Friday. I feel better now, having put in a fairly concentrated dose of Elizabeth since Tuesday, when I wrote the above. Elizabeth *is* a sweet girl—besides, I owe her a pound. I went out and had tea with her Tuesday, after walking around Oxford for two hours trying to keep myself awake, and as it was so foggy I could hardly see where I was going I managed to succeed. Wednesday we went out to a little 14th century church in a place called Northmoor. They had dug several pounds of plaster out of the north transept, revealing a tangled mass of red lines and flakes of gilt Elizabeth said were paintings. So Elizabeth started tracing them and I held her tracing paper for about half an hour. Then we decided it was too cold to work, and went to the local pub to get warm. Yesterday I did absolutely nothing at all—God, I've never been at such a loose end—it's because I feel so helpless without money—except send a cable. I *do* hope the Secretary of the Royal Society isn't too bloody a fool. Your letter of the 3rd came this morning. My congratulations to Marion. Actually, the baby is much the best thing that could have happened—the fuss made about it in July was quite inexcusable. It's true we won't see her for a long time, but that's less important to her than to us.

Yes, we've had Mrs. Simpson too, only our news was later—you being closer to U.S.A. knew all about the abdication weeks before we did. I'm sorry he abdicated, as he seemed to know his job, and definitely had a social conscience compared to this imbecile Parliament—I suppose that was really why they wanted to get rid of him. No doubt he found the pattern of bourgeois rectitude set by his father a bit strenuous. It's probably the death-blow to the prestige of royalty in the country, which is a frightful calamity, I'm afraid, as royalty seems to me to be, or at least to hold together, the most effective opposition to a military despotism. In any other country this would be a paradox: not so here.

The events of the last week of term didn't amount to much. The Bodley Club met again and some depressing individual who didn't know anything about Samuel Butler read a paper on Samuel Butler, and was criticized by someone who knew even less. One of the dons was present, and he and I took the subject in hand. Next night a couple of New Zealanders—[Mike] Joseph I think I mentioned, and a friend of his over in Balliol—dropped in and suggested a pub crawl. The Balliol New Zealander was a good head—one of those unfortunates who are interested in nothing but modern literature, and take classics because they think it will be good for them. He had only one idea at that time—to rush down to London and find a woman to sleep with. He's probably happy now. Both men are Catholics—Catholics seem to suffer acutely from celibacy.

I've been invited to Blackpool for Christmas, but there'd be no point in my going—I should get to London. Several people have offered to lend me money, including Blunden, but I haven't taken it—I may regret that later, of course.

Oh, well, things might be worse. And thanks very very much for the *New Yorker*s—they helped a lot at a critical time. At any other time I'd say they were worth their weight in gold. And I think you're a swell girl and I'm head over heels in love with you and I wish to God you were here or I was there or both of us were together, anywhere.

Norrie

205 Fulton Avenue [*Toronto*]
Dec. 14, 1936

My dearest:

I am sending some letters off tonight on the *Queen Mary*. I had expected a little more time but the mail closes at 7:30 tomorrow morning and no word as yet to you. I am at home but expect to get out on the long trail again presently—Wymilwood is my centre of gravity these days. I shall move home for Christmas and then go back again later.

Such events as Christmas dinners, tea parties, the usual festivities, Burwash carol service last night, formal dinner party at Annesley next Friday, informal one at Wymilwood last Friday, lunch today with Miss Ray at Bienvenu. Discussion: the King, bless his heart—i.e. Edward VIII. Everyone has been in a perfect turmoil here, and the papers have been pretty disgraceful. You have been out of it all and probably can't imagine how bad the American papers can be at times. I mean with this much time at Oxford you may have forgotten some of the vulgarity of the American tabloid. "Wallie meets Eddie,""Wallie in doctor's care," etc. It has been pretty sickening. Now, of course, the *Star* is beginning to turn its machinery to build up a myth around George VI and we see him with his happy family and hear about how different he is from the late King, going to church on Sunday etc. and sitting quietly at home with his wife who has influenza, poor dear. Preachers from all across Canada are quoted re the sanctity of home and family and the great trouble that has been averted. However, I gather that Canterbury is making a howling ass of himself, telling what evil ways Edward has fallen into. The King's speech of farewell was one of the most impressive and heart-rending messages I have ever read. Not only that, beyond its evident sincerity and simplicity, it was a piece of work of the most consummate cleverness, perhaps all unwittingly done. I did not hear it, unfortunately, but Mother says it made Daddy weep, and he was not alone in that. We have heard so much talk, there has been such uncertainty and so many wild reports that one feels completely exhausted by it all. It has been a great victory for the Church, I suppose, and perhaps has done a great deal of good in rousing people to some sense of the solidarity of the empire—that is what Newton Rowell said, something about the empire machinery running smoothly. Hell, I think we let the King down, and that he was railroaded into the whole mess by the slandering yellow-sheet American press. People stand around on street corners and the old girls yell about home and mother—they all scurry for shelter when a question like divorce comes up.

Well, my dear, I did not mean to start on that subject. Here is a bit of news that is rather exciting: Roy won the Lincoln Hutton with his essay on the New Deal, and we all feel pretty happy about it. Kay Coburn was all excited and Barbara phoned to congratulate him and I nearly burst with pride and joy.

It is past midnight and I must post this now and go back to Wymilwood. I do hope you arrange something more pleasant for Christmas than Guilford Street. Write a note to Edith [Burnett], or get Elizabeth to do something for Christmas day if nothing else materializes. But I am sure someone will invite you to spend it with them—I hope so. We are all missing you—Harold wished me to send his greetings, Mother wondered what you'd be doing, Daddy and Roy add their bit to the general message. By the way, Eleanor Caesar tells me that Cameron's got his Ph.D. and sails for home on the 16th. I really must go now, will try to collect my wits in a few days to write you a decent letter.

Tomorrow night Barbara is having a dinner party at the flat. She asked me to come and help her out, the point being that the party is for Wilson Knight. I'll do my best but I do wish you were along. I'm so glad you've got Blunden properly impressed. What about chances of publishing the Blake? Is there any mention of that?

Harold keeps asking me whether I am going up north this summer. How does a summer in Muskoka appeal to you—or shall I come over there as we planned? Where the money is to come from I still don't know, and the rates have gone up, but I can't worry about that.

My love to you,
Helen

Oxford
[*17 December 1936*]

Darling:

The Royal Society came through all right, with fifty pounds. Apparently I have to make a half-yearly report to Pelham [Edgar], he being my Canadian Supervisor. They didn't tell me I *had* a Canadian supervisor, which is one reason for the holdup.

I go down to London Dec. 19. I've been working quietly in my room. My only extravagance when the money came, apart from taking Elizabeth to dinner, was two volumes of Scarlatti—I've been doing a good deal of playing during this vac., as there's no one in the Mob Quad and I can play at any time of the day or night without anyone's hearing me. There are only a few left for meals now—two Australians, two Scotchmen and two Englishmen besides myself.

This letter will probably be late for Christmas—so of course will whatever I send you when I get to London. Thank you for the Zwemmer's book you mentioned you were sending. You rather took the wind out of my sails, as I had more or less assumed that anything I would send you would also come from Zwemmer's. I am getting a bit impatient with having the Atlantic Ocean sitting on all our Christmases—however, it won't be long until being separated from you for months on end will be only a sleeping nightmare instead of a waking one. At present Christmas is nothing but the fag-end of the year for me. Maybe in a few years there'll be so many descendants borrowing your stockings to hang up, the way I used to borrow Mother's, you'll have to spend your Christmases bare-legged.

I was examined last day of term by all the dons and the warden [J.C. Miles], the process being known as a don rag. Said don rag lasted ninety seconds, & consisted of a speech by Blunden and a purr from the warden. I mentioned it in my letter to Barbara, which I filled with the sort of Oxford gossip that doesn't get into my letters to you, on the principle that she'll come around and read it to you.

I don't think Blunden liked my thesis much—he said something vague about all the sentences being the same length—what I think he really resents is the irrefutable proof that Blake had a brain. I am afraid I shall have to ignore him and just go ahead.

This is a filthy letter—please excuse it. I'm at a bit of a loose end—perhaps London will improve matters. I don't think of you any more at Christmas than I do at any other time of year, or I should be quite unable to think of anything else. Don't mind me—it's just that everybody else has gone home to their mammas and left me cursing the Atlantic Ocean.

Norrie

[*Toronto*]
Dec. 24, 1936

My dearest, I have just re-read your letter postmarked Dec. 11 and feel considerably relieved that the end of it was more cheerful than the beginning. I am dreadfully sorry that your money did not come through, and I feel seven different kinds of skinflint for not being able to send you some. I was just paid yesterday or the day before, and I have at last finished paying back what I borrowed for Roy's fees. I'd have cabled you some then but considered that by now you must have borrowed from someone in order to get to London. I do hope you have looked up everyone you know. Roy [Daniells] has just had a card from Harold Taylor at 44 Russell Square, and he sounds a little lonely—living with Saul Rae, Roy says, wondering how that combination is working out.

We are manufacturing the usual Christmas excitement around home, especially Harold who is taking Marion's place as Christmas enthusiast. We have a little tree and I have been out shopping for small things. We are to be alone this year and we will miss you like anything. I sent a card to your mother and said so. I had a sort of fellow feeling, remembering how many Christmases you had been away from home.

I've got a raise—$900 a year instead of $750, beginning last October, but I don't get the benefit of it until January. Let me know whether I can help you then.

Barbara's dinner the other night was very successful from some points of view—Bob Orchard and Wilson Knight talked to each other most of the evening and thus enjoyed themselves. Knight expressed surprise at my knowing you and I affected a casual acquaintance with you which led him to maintain vigorously that you were about to publish the best book on Blake ever written up to the present. He said it was unfortunate that Blunden was your tutor in some ways because his interest is not in Blake—more in little histories like the life of Keats' publisher.

As a mildly academic question: is there any objection to our getting married this summer? Does it matter if an Oxford undergraduate is married? After all, you are not a minor, and I am beginning to pull out white hairs, so your spouse is a pretty hoary female.

The bands and choirs from different churches are singing everywhere tonight. I wonder what you are doing this Christmas Eve. I am so glad that Elizabeth is on hand to cheer you up a bit when necessary, and I've no doubt she is glad to see you too. What about Veronica Wedgwood?

I love you very very much, my dear, and I hope you get my little book before long. I will send you some more *New Yorker*s on Monday.

Helen

Paddington
Dec. 30 [*1936*]

Sweetheart:

I'm staying with Edith and Stephen [Burnett], and I've been here for a week. I like being here, although it isn't the easiest place in the world to work, and Edith and Stephen are very good to me and have made everything very pleasant. The day I came down (Dec. 19) I went to tea at Lady Francis Ryder's—the lady herself has retired, and a number of "hostesses" are there to be maternal. The first time I went it was horrible—the place was full of fat New Zealanders who discussed the weather and Mrs. Simpson. I went back on Wednesday and found a solid mass of Canadians, including Saul Rae, who recognized me and gave me the addresses of all the Canadian colony in Bloomsbury, including Henry Noyes and Harold Taylor. The tea was much better, the hostess being a very intelligent woman and drawing us out for all she was worth. I got an invitation to lunch on Christmas Day which I took rather unwillingly, as I wanted to remain hermetically sealed on Christmas, but saw no good reason for declining. The place was in one of the most complicated parts of Kensington and took a long time to find. Rae was there again and two exotic females—a historian who did most of the talking and a Viennese. Neither very interesting, though the latter was funny. The host was Gladstone's grandson and looked it. However, they were very pleasant and I had a good time. On Boxing Day Elizabeth came down and we went out to dinner and went to see *Murder in the Cathedral* but Elizabeth got sick, almost fainted and had to be brought home in a taxi and sent to bed. Sunday we went out to Hampton Court and exhausted ourselves staring at that *glorious* Mantegna for over an hour. Mantegna must be the very greatest painter who ever lived. Incidentally, the day I came down I went to Zwemmer's and got that book for you. It's a rather pompously pedantic sort of Christmas present, and the paper is the sort you cut your fingers on and I would have liked a few colours, but I was told with some hauteur by the clerk that reproducing processes would only caricature the artist's intentions. It was the only thing they had on Mantegna and I had come in with a sort of *idée fixe* that I'd get something on Mantegna and didn't have the nerve to look a Zwemmer's clerk in the eye and say "And what other painters have you?" So there it is.

Well, anyway, Tuesday we went to see *Murder in the Cathedral* again. It's a wonderful play all right. The chorus of women was full of the loveliest poetry, and as a play it came off very well. Elizabeth left early to get the last train back to Oxford.

I have never missed you more since I went away than I do now—the same physically sick feeling I had two summers ago and never thought I'd have again. Oh, Helen!

Edith sends her love.

Norrie

Surely I've mentioned your Zwemmer book, which I liked very much. I haven't decided whether to leave them there or take them out and frame them—probably the former. Thank you, darling.

[*Toronto*]
Jan. 6, 1937

My dearest: I'm beginning to feel like a pig for not writing to you—work is the only excuse. I worked all through the holidays—the days I had off I spent on mild celebrations like eating turkey and a trip to Guelph for two days. The rest of the time was gallery and Greek sculpture. My study group begins again tomorrow and I'm apt to have a dozen women, and I'm going to give them a dose of Greek sculpture. Thanks so much for the Mantegna, my dear. It is very nice of you, now at last I have a German book of my own to read, and the gallery does not possess the *Klassiker der Kunst Mantegna*, so I'm one up on them. I haven't had more than four German lessons and they were back in October. What I'm to do about it I don't know, everything is so complicated, with our gallery programme as full as usual.

Roy and Harold and I went to hear Stravinsky conduct *Petroushka* and the *Firebird* last night. Stravinsky certainly made the orchestra do things that MacMillan never managed.

My dear, my dear! Your mother sent me a Christmas card and I was so happy! That was awfully sweet of her—at least it was signed Mr. and Mrs. H.E. Frye but I thought it was more likely to be her writing. I was so glad that your money came through at last.

I am so sick of having no time to send you a decent letter. I haven't told you anything about the Tudor Singers' concert at the Gallery or the children's entertainment or Dorothy [Drever], or anything else. And I've *got* to do something about this class tomorrow now.

I feel so strange having all this busy life away from you. The year is going terribly fast, too fast for the amount of work I hoped to get done, but wonderfully fast when I think of you. I'm so glad Elizabeth is there to go walking and exploring those marvellous churches. I love you *very* much, and I hope my accent won't strike you like a meat-axe when next you hear it.

Did I tell you Fred Housser died just before Christmas?

Helen

84 Queens Park, Toronto
January 8? [*10*] 1937

My dear: Back in Wymilwood once more. Yesterday I went with Norah to the Picture Loan Society—did I tell you that it started about three months ago? Gordon Webber, Gordon MacNamara, Norah, Douglas Duncan, Rik Kettle, Pegi Nicol are the committee. They are giving the first one-man show this week—Carl Schaefer. I rented one of Webber's called *Pink Rock*, a lovely thing with green sumacs and blue sky sketched in above great folds of MacGregor Bay stone. Mounted on grey—looks marvellous against my white wall.

I'm going to see Alford on Tuesday, about the exam. We're getting a heavy programme lined up for the February architects' show and I *don't* see how I can do any extra work. German is still a lost cause. We have asked Lescaze to come and give a lecture. If he can't we may try for Lewis Mumford. Dr. Held is giving the Flemish painting series.

Wednesday night. Darling, I've been to Alford, I went yesterday. Yesterday opened gloriously with a letter from you, all about your stay with Edith and Stephen, and I was so glad you were all right. Then I went to see the old mugwump and he advised me not to attempt it this spring—thinks I should enrol as a graduate student and come to his lectures. Well, maybe I should, but *after all*, I have a job in the daytime, and while I could get off for some lectures—well it is impossible. He says, of course if it is a matter of doing it for my job he wouldn't bother, but if it is a case of getting a job somewhere else it would be a good thing to have academic qualification from a recognized institution. He is so discouraging and so pompous and dull and afraid to commit himself. There are times when all I can do is hate him, helplessly. However, Douglas MacAgy turned up last night and we went for a long walk and had some beer. Douglas told me some of his adventures lately with Alford, who is on very shaky ground in aesthetics and laid himself wide open to attack the other day. Anyhow we had a very cheerful time and I felt better.

Here it is, the middle of January. I've done some work on Greek Sculpture. Just how long it would take to organize what I know on the rest of the field (!) I don't know. And there isn't an earthly chance of getting time off before May to work at the stuff consistently. It is all so silly—here I have a wonderful job, full of interest which keeps me hopping all the time, and I'm worrying because I haven't got academic qualifications. Just the same, I feel on devilish thin ice sometimes. Then I go back to work and feel that we are making history in these parts, and devil take the diploma. Look at all the diploma students who have no jobs! Baldwin is quite discouraging about the diploma business—thinks I'm crazy to think about it at all.

I wish I knew what you intend doing next summer. I suppose you will travel on the continent, unless war breaks out all over the place. You should go to Italy in the spring, if you are going, the weather will be glorious. Peggy Kidder talks of going to Europe on a freighter and I may go with her. It's very cheap, but slow. I could meet you in London and I suppose we could go somewhere—I feel so vague at this point, not knowing what your ideas are on the matter, when your term ends, what the financial situation will be next year, what you feel about my last proposition. If only you were here to talk to, but all these bewildering problems have to wait and wait and crawl back and forth across the ocean. I am very tired of the Atlantic. You are not thinking of coming home next summer I suppose? I've got to get something settled soon because I'll have to see about boats, and coronation time is VERY BAD. I could not leave here before May 24th anyway, I suppose, with this don business to think about too. It really is not too bad—in spite of my grumbling I'm enjoying it immensely.

The Annesley At-Home is this Friday. I don't think I will go. As I have a lecture to give to Ruth Home's museum women, I'd better get ready for that. Classicism in France, end of 18th c. I'm going to summarize the first lecture on Rococo for contrast, define classicism—show Greek sculpture etc., then compare it with Greek ideal as understood by Raphael—

in School of Athens for instance. Then dive into Ingres and David and the rest. I think it should be all right. I have learned something this year at any rate, I enjoy painting and sculpture myself a lot more, and that goes a long way.

We've been making out reports to Carnegie, and Baldwin makes wild statements, Norah objects and she and I do the blue pencilling. Wild statement: Mr. Lismer's enthusiasm etc. has been sorely missed this year, but the staff has ably stepped into the breach and the *work has in no way suffered from his absence* (!) (We yanked *that* out!) Continuing my footnote I might add that Norah firmly believes in her dismal moments that Baldwin is trying to oust Lismer. I'm not sure of that but I do say he is *the* most tactless man I know of.

I took the Vic people to see Yvonne Williams' studio today and Yvonne talked about stained glass. She really is remarkable when she is on her own ground, and I was quite thrilled myself. We went to see [A.Y.] Jackson one other day—I don't know what we'll do next time.

Dot [Drever] has joined the Communist Party—last fall—this she told me the other night, in confidence, so don't mention it unless she has already told you. Dot is fairly happy, I think, concerned about her mother who is not well, and also about her place in society when she can not openly state her position because of fear for her job.

Goodness, I *am* grumbling tonight. With Spain in ruins and Hitler about to pounce, and heaven knows what going on in Europe, I go on at this length about my own little world. All I can do is hope, hope, my dearest, lest the world crumble about our heads and everything we care for perish.

Helen

London
Jan. 11 [*1937*]

Sweetheart:

I have been staying with Edith and Stephen ever since my last letter, and will remain here until the end of this week, when I go back to Oxford. I have just put in the dimmest week I've yet had since coming to England—six days of reading 1600 lines of *Beowulf* and being so exhausted when evening came that I could do nothing but go to bed. Christ, what a language. And such a stupid dreary story.

I have wasted more time this vacation even than usual—enough to last me the rest of my life, I should think. The more time I spend with you, the more I seem able to get done. Congratulations on your rise—I never imagined they'd get it into their fat heads you were doing more than $750 worth of work there, especially with Lismer away. Of course I'll marry you next summer, on one very reasonable condition: *Habeas Corpus*. You must produce the body. I can't marry you by correspondence. Perhaps with your rise you will feel more like coming over this summer. I'm not going to rewrite the letters I've already written on this subject, partly because nothing I can say seems to have any effect, partly because I don't want to keep bullying you. I suspect your family of digging at you again. It isn't quite fair to ask me to come back to Canada this summer, but if you ditch your whole scheme of coming over yourself I shall have to, as I can't very well face the prospect of not seeing you for still another year. My heartiest congratulations to Roy: I'd like to see his essay sometime.

God, it takes me a long time to write even a short letter, particularly when there's no news.

Lovingly,
Norrie

Oxford
[*17 January 1937*]

Sweetheart:

I'm back in Oxford now, having spent the whole vacation with Edith and Stephen. I got *Beowulf* read again, by some miracle, and Friday morning came up here. Yesterday I wrote Blunden's term exam—collections they call them here. It was pretty bad—he seemed to have simply opened his Chaucer at random to pick out spotting passages. I wasn't in very good condition for it either—for the last few days I've been vaguely wondering if the flu epidemic is going to catch me—I've been pretty dizzy and even stupider than usual lately.

Sorry if I barked a bit at you in connection with your coming over this summer. Suppose I go to Italy this vacation: then I'll have just enough money, when the final instalment of my scholarship comes in, to buy a ticket home. Oxford is really too expensive to let me do anything with my vacs.—I was pretty lucky this last time. But of course I could ask the College to advance me enough to keep me here this summer, and certainly marriage in England would be a lot less fuss than in Canada—besides, there'd be visiting my parents to consider. This altogether apart from whether or not you want your diploma. The one thing I do know is that I'm going to see you this summer. I see nothing but a possible I.O.D.E. in the way of marriage, and that's hardly enough to set against the advantages of marrying you, as far as your general peace of mind is concerned.

The Mrs. Simpson you gave me was comparatively mild—one paper had "Teddie gets his tart." Another had pictures of her three men with "The Wallace Collection" underneath.

Edith sends her love. When I said to Stephen that you might not, after all, be coming over, he said that *his* house was available if you did come, but I'm afraid that wouldn't do, as they have only one bed, and that a narrow one—one spare bed, that is.

The time should pass quickly now until I see you again. I hope so, anyway.

Norrie

[*Oxford*]
[*19 January 1937*]

I don't know why I'm writing you again so soon, sweet, except that your letter came this morning and the *New Yorker*s. I expect sending those magazines is a bit of a nuisance, but please keep on: silly as it sounds, they mean quite a bit to me. You *do* do them up so well. Thanks for the snapshots: Harold is good, you dimmish, but recognizable enough to make me feel funny inside.

The Oxford Group is a pretty insidious menace—I don't know if I ever told you that you nearly lost your husband to it. One particularly callow infant—in Norm Knight's phrase, just out of the shell and not quite dry yet—at Merton was talking to me at the beginning of the term, at first about music. He wanted to know who were the greatest musical composers, and I said Bach and Mozart. Then about God, man and the world, about which he had ideas. Well, during the first two weeks of the vacation I ran into him again. He'd just joined the Group, and was all starry-eyed: the Oxford Group was going to nip in between Communism and Fascism and save the world—it was just as revolutionary as they were, but better because it believed in God and they were based on a materialistic philosophy. I raised an eyebrow and said that most of the Communists I had known were hopeless idealists, and that Germany had been living off idealism for the last five months, not having food enough to be materialists. Or so they say. Evidently the German newspapers say the same thing about England. Where was I? Oh, yes. This kid walked back home with me and backed me into every corner of Merton College in turn, haranguing me. I ought to join the Group, because the Group needed all the brains it could get. God, it does. After an hour and three-quarters he glanced dubiously at my frozen pan and said: "Of course, I'm just a newcomer to the Group: you can see I haven't had much experience, or you'd have been in flames by now." Word for word.

Your efficient tying-up of *New Yorker*s reminds me of a remark of Stephen's in a particularly sniffish mood—"Why are all Canadians so utterly hopeless at doing up parcels?" Edith: "Because we're not a nation of shopkeepers."

Blunden was very pleased with my exam and said nice things. I was disgusted with it myself. If I can make that impression when half asleep, more than half sick and execrably prepared, I ought to be all right on Schools. I've been fighting off flu and think I'll eventually succeed. This is a dead secret, by which I mean everybody in general and Norah in particular. Elizabeth has been working on a series of imaginative designs, on the borderline of formal design and literary illustration, with a sort of running lyric in free verse as commentary. Not at all publishable: she simply did it and handed it to me. I don't know what to make of it: first time in my life I've ever been absolutely at a loss. It's easy to say it's remarkable, and it's easy to say it's drivel, but neither statement is in the least true. The poem is unquestionably bad in diction, it's hopelessly vague and cloudy, but its rhythms are remarkable, and the drawings, though equally cloudy and over-abstract, are extraordinarily suggestive. The whole is so bafflingly elusive, and yet so disturbing, that I'm absolutely at a loss—knowing Elizabeth doesn't help either. Blunden has asked me to supper this week, and—this being an even deader secret, as Elizabeth would be furious if she knew—I'm going to take them to him. I've *got* to have an intelligent opinion on them. On reading over the above, I find that I seem to be repeating myself, which reflects the confusion of my mind.

Don't let's talk about plans for the summer until the Easter vac. any way. If I haven't any money left, I'll come home. I won't have enough, certainly, to keep me in Europe *all* summer. Trading Europe in for you would be a pretty fair exchange, anyhow.

Norrie

84 Queen's Park, Toronto
January 31, 1937

My dearest, on Saturday there were *two* letters from you, and my whole outlook brightened immediately. I do get a bit fretful sometimes in between letters, and I had not heard from you since January 11th.

There are several sad things to tell you about. For one thing, Dr. George Locke died on Thursday after a month's illness. I think I told you about Housser at Christmas time. It is what makes me so uneasy and so sad—Housser gone, Locke gone, Lismer so far away, you so far away. I am dreadfully afraid of war coming soon, and of something happening to you, of Roy having to go and have his head blown off, and Harold soon being old enough to be eligible for slaughter. There is a feeling here of greater activity, the mines are booming and there is more gaiety in Toronto than for some little time. Everyone said New Year's Eve was the gayest since 1929 and oceans of money was spent. I'm sorry about troubling you with the summer. I know that you are running things pretty close financially—and if there's an I.O.D.E. in the offing I suppose it will be wiser to wait. I wish sometimes *your* peace of mind were slightly troubled, though, so you wouldn't blame me for the idea altogether.

I'm so glad my dear that you did well on the exam. Mary Winspear sends her regards, Peggy [Roseborough] is working on her Ph.D. this spring. Barbara showed me Veronica Wedgwood's very impressive book on Strafford. Your news of Edith and Stephen is refreshing, especially the parcel bit!

What I want to know now is, do you want me to come over for June and July or July and August? Cheaper rates the end of May. I must get reservations in soon and you haven't told me when your term ends. The sailings are pretty crowded and things will be crowded all summer.

It's midnight now and I've got to write a radio talk on Rubens tomorrow. I love you *very* much, and four months to go—

Next day: noon. Daddy earned $8 last week. There's no use my saying I'll put so much aside—there *are* a few demands that I cannot disregard. If you were home you would feel the same way about *your* family, so please don't accuse the family of digging at me again or whatever it was you said. They're not. But if I'm the only one with any money, I can't very well hoard it—you wouldn't if you were in the same position. However, aside from all this doleful stuff, everything is going fairly well. I just meant to tell you how things are with us—family intends to pay back all my loans, but I don't see how they can very well, so why worry.

I'll go off to lunch now. Rubens coming on slowly.

H.

Oxford
[*3 February 1937*]

Sweetheart:

I spent several days staggering around holding on to things, not daring to bend over too quickly for fear I'd stay down, and going through a lot of other antics trying not to get flu, wherein I eventually succeeded. It hasn't been too prevalent among students, although half the scouts are down—mine just got back today, to my great relief. (Damn, I'll have to stop now: one of my tame violinists wants to play with me.)

I have finally persuaded him to try the big fugue in the Mozart sonata in A, so we're happy once more. He's bad in somewhat the same way I am: neither of us can keep time, and we can't learn anything thoroughly. I'm sleepy today, having gone to the O.U.D.S. performance of Shaw's *Caesar and Cleopatra*, a stupid (or at least a tiresome) play badly performed. Their last performance was the *Beggar's Opera*, and in spite of my violent antipathy to that play I enjoyed it—these O.U.D.S. things are only 7 d. on Monday evenings, and worth that, certainly.

Elizabeth keeps well but poor—she owes me £1.10.0 now. She's working on several jobs—one, trying to draw those obliterated paintings in Northmoor I mentioned, and another series of anatomical drawings for a doctor. But of course her book, which she gave to me, took up a lot of time. I showed it to Blunden, who said he liked it, and I think actually he did. He seemed impressed anyway. I couldn't trust my own reaction—at times I thought it was drivel, and yet something in it made me keep coming back to it. The girl has brains, and her poetry shows a genuine feeling for rhythm. If only she weren't so inchoate—I think there's a genuinely mystical quality to her mind, which makes her work over-abstract.

There's a minor Elizabethan poet named Fulke Greville—a great favorite of Roy's [Roy Daniells's] as well as mine, a very intellectual poet and frightfully obscure at times—quite the thing for a Blake student to be interested in. After my first tutorial this term I said: "I shall be reading Sidney and Lyly this week, and will probably bring you a paper on Fulke Greville: is that all right?" He said: "Er—oh, yes—certainly—except that I haven't read much Greville—Aldous Huxley is very much interested in Greville: he started talking about him once, and all I could muster in the way of quotation was"—he quoted two lines—"it wasn't much, but I think I had even that counted to me for righteousness." Blunden and I are definitely going to get along well this term—he's used to me now, and probably my manners are better than they were at first.

Fulke Greville has been keeping me busy—like Blake, his religious, philosophical & political views are all in one piece, and it would take at least a month's solid work to read all of him and tie him all up in a neat little sack. I had only a week—there's no good modern edition (Roy wants to do one, but I'm afraid various people are beating him to it) and there was a baldheaded johnny who had reserved all the books in the Bodleian, so I had to beg all the books from him. I had one of my seizures, and worked every day until my eyes gave out for a week on that paper. Blunden liked it very much, I think. These essays I'm doing are mostly publishable, I should imagine: certainly I've collected a lot of material for future books.

Plans for the summer are still vague—a summer at Gordon Bay is an idea that is beginning to take shape more and more. I don't want to meet people in Canada any more than I can help—just half a dozen—but I do want to live with you and grow for a while. I'm maturing here, and have a feeling that this novel, which has been hanging fire so long, will come off if I can have you beside me. Or something like that. Judging from your account, it would have been physically impossible for you to have done any work towards your exams here—there aren't fifty or sixty hours in a day, and that's that.

Did I tell you that Bryson, the lazy devil, called off our *Beowulf* exam? I must do some *Beowulf* for tomorrow now. Bless you, darling.

Norrie

Oxford
[*9 February 1937*]

Helen, dear, just settle down and be a good girl and wait till I come over—the year ends around June 20. I'm sorry if I've been unjust to your family, but it's hard to see across the Atlantic, and I could hardly avoid thinking in terms of your letters to me in Moncton. But if you aren't ready to try your exams, you certainly won't, and it's no fault of yours—there's no reason for you to come over except that I want to see you, and so it's up to me to make the move now. I won't make your situation, to say nothing of your family's, any more complicated or strained than it is. It was just an idea we couldn't work out. And I have to think of things like the I.O.D.E. So to say that I'm blaming you altogether for the idea of getting married seems rather untrue—I've had that idea a lot longer than you have. But don't worry any more about the summer, or about anything else.

Poor little girl: such a cranky woebegone letter. I do wish I could take you into my arms and quiet your nerves and put you to sleep. Things must be depressing in Toronto with all your friends dying or miserable.

Nothing is happening to me. I had Blunden and Elizabeth in for tea. Elizabeth did just what I thought she'd do: shut up like a clam, and Blunden and I talked shop. It was simply another tutorial. The silly girl—she's in love with one of the biggest men in Oxford—the printer at O.U.P.—and hints darkly of terrible things that have happened, which obviously include the fact that she's managed to make a fool of herself and he won't look at her. She only sees him very rarely, and it plays the very devil with her nerves, which is why she has these spells of shyness. If she could get away from him and from Oxford she'd be all right. I think Blunden liked her, though, and I do think he admired her book. Norah, of course, mustn't get hold of this. Actually, it's a more respectable story than I can make it sound—it's practically been her whole life for two or three years. Her trip back to Canada, when we met at the art gallery, was a reaction from it.

I read my anatomy paper to Blunden last night. He said I had two hundred very saleable pages there, but that Jane Austen's admirers would just read my one sentence on her and conclude that there was a rape afoot. He lives, somewhat like Ned Pratt, in mortal terror of the scholars, including at times me. Anyway, he asked what he should lecture on next term, so I drew up all the harmless names I could think of in the 17th c: he said he was tired of the 18th and 19th and was afraid of the scholars of the 16th.

I've bought myself a lot of typing paper and am going to get a lot of Blake done. I've got to finish my general book on him before the year's out. Give my love to Peggy & Mary when you see them. Does a radio talk on Rubens mean that you are going to talk over the radio? Oh, sweetheart, I love you so: I feel sometimes as though you simply must appear, right here in this room, in front of me, I want you so.

Norrie

[*Toronto*]
Friday. Feb. 19, 1937

My dearest dearest man! I'm starting a new pad and I'm only going to write joyful letters to you from now on. No more cranky sniffling: I've cheered up. The weather has changed and several things have happened in the last week. I've laid a ghost. I've had two letters from you. I have a new dress—and I still think you like me. And no more people died this week except in Spain.

Norah, to begin near the beginning, had lunch one day with the Briegers and they were talking about me, the upshot being that I was to see Brieger about the Courtauld business all over again since Alford couldn't make out what I was talking about. So I phoned Brieger, who immediately asked me up for supper and a French film afterwards at Eaton's with the Haurwitz pair—they're in the Physics department. I had a talk with him before his guests arrived, and I may say that I can hardly wait for you to meet Brieger—he and his wife are pretty well taking Toronto by storm. He got the whole story out of me, i.e. my feeling of obligation to McCurry and my bad conscience in general, and my desire for academic standing in Art History. Then said "But what do you *want* to do? If you could go anywhere, do anything you want—would you go back to Courtauld for the diploma?" I said that I certainly did not regard that of any importance except as a sort of stamp and one that might mean something toward a degree here or somewhere else. He couldn't see it at all—both he and Alford think I should register here as a graduate student next year and take lectures when I can fit them in (which I could do next year fairly well, I think). Brieger talked again exactly as Daddy did—that there was no use becoming a physical wreck trying to work in an examination over and above the gallery job this year. But his final argument was that the disagreement between Constable and his directors was partly over the diploma course which Constable wanted to abolish. Brieger and I pretty well agreed about the waste of time at the Institute and it seems the director had had the same idea for some time. Brieger thinks that the course might be done away with in a few years and—! Brieger sounds here as if he made up his mind that I should not go back. He did not do that of course, he put it up to me and it was the same this time as it was with Miss Whinney. I am taking his advice because it is what I want to do anyway. He and Alford were the people I was worrying about here—I don't think McCurry gives a rap. So I am just going to forget the diploma and start again. It isn't that I'm turning green at the sight of an examination but there just isn't time for it. Norah says I could very likely get off next year to take certain courses and she thinks it's all to the good. At present the German is going slowly and I haven't been able to work at it this week at all.

Tonight we had the Lescaze lecture, last night I was down for the university settlement evening, next Monday there is a lecture by Eric Newton and on Friday the Leo Smith musicale. And so it goes! Lescaze is simply *grand*—you get the idea from the article in the *New Yorker* (Dec. 12) but to hear him talk and to see all the buildings he has designed—! *Now* don't you wish you were in Toronto?

We had a bang-up formal dinner party Thursday night at Annesley Hall when Emmy Heim came to sing. Mrs. Davis was there and she told me H.J. [Herbert J. Davis] is in bed with something. I had to answer an awful lot of questions about you. And if I have not said so before I now most *solemnly urge* you to write to H.J.—he is very keenly interested to know how you are liking everything and how the work is going and I could tell him so little of what he is most interested in hearing. After all, he wrote to Merton for you and surely he isn't difficult to approach.

Oh dear, it's getting terribly late and I must be ready to talk to the combination of the Dean's Council and the Women's Council tomorrow. Should women be allowed any part in the university and if so what and should they compete with men and what is the place of women in community life? And because of their damned luncheon I have to pass up a luncheon at the University Club tomorrow to meet Lescaze—*isn't* it the devil?

I'll not talk about summer or Arnold or anything else until I've had some more sleep. It is nearly one. If I were to imagine *very* hard tonight that I kissed you goodnight do you think it would make any impression on you? Not tonight, I suppose because you wouldn't get this until a week from now and all this will be history by then. Still a sort of thwarted historical kiss is better than nothing at all perhaps, and I'm sending you one all wrapped up in a warm glowing sort of atmosphere, and I wonder where it will land. Now that is a nice idea to play with—I just wonder where it will land—I'll think about that for a long time—or do you think I could send two or three and have a choice?

Sunday. Mother said the other night that January is the family's worst month and that they don't want me to worry any more about money because work will pick up soon and they will try to pay back what I lent them, and by all means to come across if I can manage it, although they would like to have you up north if you come home. I am trying to figure out some sort of itinerary if I do come over to you. It seems a great shame for you to come here when you might be seeing Europe. But I have difficulty picturing just what you want to see and how you want to go if I come with you. It gets so complicated when I think of it —and after a little more experience around Victoria College I begin to see the wisdom, or at least the necessity of bowing to the conventions to a certain extent. I don't want you to be too much indebted to the college—more and more I am anxious about that. I don't want you to have to spend too many years in this college.

Oh well, I'll let it go at that and not worry you any more for a while. Dorothy [Drever] sends her love, and I mine,

Helen

Scout and Scholar (1853)

Oxford
[22 *February* 1937]

Darling: I feel more cheerful now that I've got a note from a bank saying they want to pay me some money—evidently Papa Edgar finally got his letter off to Ottawa. I was afraid the Bursar here would start asking questions.

I'm stiff. I'd spent most of the week trying to write a paper on T.S. Eliot, and for some reason, although I eventually wrote quite a good paper, I took an enormous time writing it—began to worry about the sentence rhythms and echoing vowels and things to the most morbid extent, so I don't think I shall try to write a paper for Blunden this week. Well, I got all soft and feeling as though I needed exercise, so I proposed a walk to Elizabeth on Friday and we started. The first village we struck was named Elsfield, where there was a church stuck on the crest of a hill with two lovely tall windows in the west end evidently designed for clear glass, but had been filled with hideous fussy stained glass—if they'd been clear we could have had a lovely view of Oxford in the valley below the hill. The next village was Wood Eaton, where there's a St. Christopher—a tiny little church with a huge enclosed pew occupied by the lords of the neighboring manor. And a battalion of cows moving along the road with a villager at each end. And no pub. There was nothing for it but to walk to the next village—Marston, about three miles from Oxford. I eventually missed Hall and got to my room about five minutes before the Bodley Club started filing into it. I was footsore and stiff and tired and hungry. The Bodley refreshments—coffee and beer—didn't help at all. However, I got through the paper and a very good discussion followed. About six of them knew their Eliot well—one who knew him personally stayed and talked to me till midnight afterwards. Then I drank all the beer that was left—two bottles, apart from four left for the scout—and went to bed, still hungry. The Bodley Club means a lot of extra work for the scout, cleaning up and so on, and the next morning Reid, upstairs, had the boat club in for breakfast—and they have a terrific breakfast when they're training. About ten o'clock my scout, having fortified himself with four bottles of beer, came stepping into my room. "Finished the breakfast?" I asked. "Yes, er, all but the sweet," gasps Day faintly. "Quite a bit of funk for you, isn't it?" I said. "YES SIR," says Day—the only time I've seen him drop the perfect-servitor mask.

A few days ago I was just going out of the Mob Quad when I saw a scout propping up a square block of stone that I had always taken for a sort of marble cover—in fact, that's what it is—and wondered vaguely about, as there's no plumbing in the Mob Quad. The scout said "Here's a bit of old stuff, sir," and I bent down to look. It's a hole dug in the ground by an anchorite or hermit, over a thousand years old—older than Merton College. Soft, oozy, clammy rock, and no room for him to lie down: he'd have to sleep crouching, or standing like a horse. Ugh! I knew it was around there, but I didn't know just where. They turned it up a few years ago, and it's the oldest building in Oxford, says the librarian, though to what extent a hole in the ground can be called a building I don't know.

I'm damned if I'm going to start a new sheet to tell you I love you.

Norrie

84 Queen's Park
March 3, 1937

I forget when I wrote to you last. I can't seem to remember anything these days, except that there is a great deal to do and time is going very quickly. I spent this evening figuring out how I can afford a summer in Europe. I think I can manage it if there are no accidents. I haven't made any definite plans, except that I'll be taking holidays in July and August if your term ends in June. There is always Gordon Bay of course—Roy intends to go up, and Harold—which makes a perfectly good trio and I *might* even let you play with them sometimes if you're good. Have you written to the I.O.D.E. people? Maysie [Roger] found that they made their awards a long time in advance, so don't put it off too long.

This last week has been a little hectic. Ivor Lewis at last made definite arrangements for the Gallery to go on the air for fifteen minutes each week—Tuesday at 7:15. And I'm in charge—gathering material and choosing subjects and all the rest. We start next week. Baldwin will give the first, Bert Brooker the next, Ivor Lewis and Charlie Band will do one each, and so on. I suppose I'll have to do one from time to time but not at the start. It will be great fun as soon as I learn how to do it, but at present I feel a little anxious. I talk to my group tomorrow, lightly, on Cézanne. These chats are on a pretty low level of erudition, but we have a good time, and perhaps clarify a few ideas.

I've become Jessie Mac's official accompanist, to the joy of all concerned. I am to play for her on Monday at the University Women's Club. The dean just came from a meeting of the Victoria College Council at which they proposed to have a faculty club room which would be limited to men. Jessie Mac blew up and told them she understood their wanting a men's club room but need they call it faculty? I see more and more what a ticklish position women are in around this place. I'll be so glad when you come back and can blow some of those pompous pseudo-scholars to hell. I do so want you to get the Blake published, and a lot more, and hit this college so hard they won't know what's happened.

My dearest, I sound so terribly prosaic. I don't mean to be but I'm hurrying more than I've done since I left high school—here and there, talking to so many people and having to get to bed at a decent time to keep from being cranky, and all this institutional life. I love it of course, I don't know what I should have done without it, and you away, but I can hardly wait until the summer when I can stop for a little while and look at something with you. This noon I stood on a corner for a few minutes and watched the sunshine on the tops of the trees on University Avenue, and a Jew with a fur cap pushing a cart, and another whipping the horse that was harnessed to his rickety wagon. It was so strange and new, I stood there and forgot time and everything else except that I love you, always.

Helen

Mob Quad (1909)

Oxford
[*9 March 1937*]

Darling, Roy [Daniells] has just written to tell me to write [Walter T.] Brown and tell him what my plans for next year are. Now I expect to finish the Blake in Italy, or at least the general outline of it, and when I get back here I want to type three copies and send one to Geoffrey Keynes, one to Edgar, and one to a publisher. If I get a favorable report from Keynes—God knows how long I'd have to wait for a publisher—then the most logical move would be to sit down in the British Museum and proceed to write footnotes on it. I should do that anyhow. So I shall have to tell Brown that if he is willing to send money enough to keep me for the summer I should like to stay here: otherwise I shall return to Canada. If I were only taking Schools, I could easily spend the summer at Gordon Bay; but with this Blake complication it might be suicidal. It all sounds as though I were hedging, but after all your mind isn't made up either, and everything is so much in the air now that you have no definite reason for coming over. I can't tell you anything more definite until I hear from (a) Brown and (b) Keynes. There's no way I can get the Blake ready for publication by the end of next term unless I do not work at all towards Schools, which wouldn't make my chances of a first very bright. I know it's infuriating not to be more definite, but I simply don't know whether I'm going to be here this summer myself or not. In any case I don't know how much money you've got, and how much I should consequently need. If I did come back I should probably have to borrow from you.

This is the fag end of the term, when I feel irritable and depressed. We've had a cold spell lasting several days, and I'm getting sick of the eternal penetrating clammy cold and of this great barn of a room. I have an east and a west window, and consequently get no sun, which stays in the south. There isn't any sun anyhow. And this electric grate never really warms the room—I can't play the piano, I can't work except here in front of the fire, and I have to keep something between the fire and my face or else my eyes get sore. It's very subtle, but the room has me absolutely framed in every direction. Another term of this will be all I can possibly stand. Still, it's a big room, which is why the Bodley Club is having a sherry party in it at six tonight.

Mike [Joseph] and I have been winding up our plans for Italy. I think Mike should be a good man to travel with—he's quiet but has a keen sense of humor, he's a very liberal-minded Catholic, and although he seems to know little of art and music, he's interested in literary symbolism and I'm expecting him to be a big help on the Blake.

Blunden I've stopped writing papers for—we've become quite good friends. He was complaining yesterday that anthologists seemed to be interested only in his very early poems, and said that most people on meeting him expected to see a rustic of sixty-five. He's a shrewd lad: I told him I wanted to write an essay on the Piers Plowman poems after I got through with the Blake, as they were the nearest thing to the Blake Prophecies in English literature. He told me I'd have to lean to edit texts, and said if I could prefix my essay on the Piers Plowman poems to an edition of them, however bad, I might make fifty pounds, but if I just published the essay I'd be "out £3.19.6 and several drinks."

The Senior Tutor [Deane Jones], next to Blunden much the brightest spot in the college, had me over for a sherry party Sunday morning. There was a vast and milling crowd there, but I snitched three glasses of sherry, talked to the Senior Tutor about contemporary German painting, about which I know absolutely nothing. He had one or two rather good things by a completely unknown artist—a Madonna, holding a bright red apple, for one. I made a little speech about contemporary German painting's being able to combine bright colors & get away with it, that German painting showed a vigour and vitality their political ideology only parodied, that the blue of the Virgin's robe & the red of the apple was a case in point, that the apple where one would expect a child carried the mind from the Virgin back to Eve. You should hear me when I have a glass of sherry dangling in front of my nose.

That's all, apart from some phenomenally dull lectures. Mantegna at the Ashmolean by somebody from the Slade. I could have done the Hampton Court lecture better myself.

I love you,
Norrie

Roma
[*24 March 1937*]

Darling:

Still alive, but very tired, with tourist's neck and tourist's feet. We're in Rome and have been in Italy about five days. Term ended in Oxford uneventfully. In London I went to see Stephen and Edith again, and Stephen was quite helpful with addresses of pensions and so on. Then Mike Joseph and I left for Newhaven in the rain, crossed the Channel with a few hours' sunshine, got into Dieppe in more rain, and arrived in Paris about dinner time. We got a bus across Paris, left our bags in a cheap hotel near the Gare de Lyon and went out and had some dinner. Then we went for a walk down the Rue de Rivoli. Early next morning we left for Italy, crossed the border about six, changed trains at Turin, and got into Genoa, dead tired, at about midnight. We fell in with some very friendly Italians, some of whom could speak French, and asked them to recommend us a good cheap hotel. They mentioned the Colombie, which turned out to be the best hotel in Genoa, of course, and it cost us 116 lire to get out of it. Still, the bath we had was worth it. We didn't stop to see Genoa, but left the next morning for Pisa, and spent the afternoon there, seeing the cathedral with the Cimabue mosaic, the Campo Santo with that magnificent *Triumph of Death* and the Gozzolis, and making sure that the Leaning Tower really did lean. We landed in Siena that night, at a pension Stephen had recommended. A little more expensive than we needed, although he said it was very cheap. The management consisted of an old lady, her assistant, and a maid, all very cheerful, extremely friendly, and unable to speak a word of anything but Italian. We had long conversations with the old girl in the evenings, and if we'd stayed there a week we'd have learned some Italian. She was very clever—kept rephrasing her remarks and shrieking at us until the central idea finally penetrated. The house, like everything else in Siena, was an ex-palace, and my room had five enormous pillars with Ionic capitals in a semicircle across the middle of it, with a light shining down from between them. The maid tried to talk to me too, but with less success, perhaps because her points were subtler. She kept saying "Mi bacie," or something: it didn't dawn on me for a long time that she wanted me to kiss her. In the evening she came in and started pulling my hair, got her kiss and departed gurgling. Everybody wants to pull my hair in Italy. In the train to Genoa I caught the words "biondino inglese" and a woman's remark "com'una signorina." Well, Siena is a lovely town—I forget whether you saw it or not. As we got in Saturday night, everything was closed up the next day, but we saw the Town Hall, climbed the tower, saw the Cathedral, went into the little Museum beside the Cathedral where the Duccios are, stood around and looked helpless until the attendant finally let us in and showed us around. Next day we went through the art gallery—the first part of it very good—and left for Orvieto. We spent the afternoon at Orvieto in the Cathedral with a long speech about the Signorellis from a sacristan who seemed to think I could understand Italian, and got into Rome at night. Yesterday we went through the Colosseum, Forum, and Pantheon, and today through churches (Santa Maria Maggiore, San Pietro in Vincoli where the Michelangelo Moses is, San Clemente, probably the most interesting thing in Rome, and Santa Prassede) and the Lateran Museum. Tomorrow to the Thermae Museum, and the Capitoline if we have time. We're leaving the Vatican until after Easter. I don't like Rome much—everything is the biggest and loudest in the world, and the Mussolini mentality is stampeding everything. I wish I hadn't gone to Rome—I'd sooner have stayed in North Italy. Still, it's all very good for me. Of course Mussolini came back from Libya the day we arrived and Rome was a riot of flags and soldiers, which may have prejudiced me. Still, the same sort of mind put up the Colosseum and St. Peter's. And even Rome wasn't as patriotic as Siena, which must have had at least a thousand pictures of his ugly mug on the walls.

Keep on writing to Merton College, of course—I'll get your letters at Florence. I love you very much, stupid as this letter is.

Norrie

Toronto, Ont.
March 30, 1937

My dear: I stayed in Wymilwood during Easter—worked on Good Friday and on Saturday on a radio talk that was given tonight by Judge Denton. On Children at the Art G. of T., the painting of Emily Carr, and events of the week. It was amusing, Baldie delivered the talk to the Judge on Saturday, and on Monday it came back for retyping and all the quotations from Lismer were rearranged and reworded—but in the main the judge seemed to like it.

Norrie, my dear, when you come back here we are going to give little parties for different staff members and we are going to invite the women and anyone who talks about babies and whooping cough won't be asked again. Do you remember what I told you about the *"staff"* Common Room and how the idea was to have a men's sitting room at Burwash and the reason for starting anything different from the Senior Common Room in the first place was because they wanted to get rid of Currelly and a few others. But the women made an issue of it and poor [Joseph] Fisher was having a conference with Jessie Mac about it this afternoon. I was pretty annoyed earlier in the fall when someone said "wives are a blight!" but I see that the Victoria men seem to consider most women as such. Now why is that? Men should always have the companionship of other men just as women need other women, but in a professional way do they need to hate each other so? What a devilish smug place this college is sometimes—I can't figure what is the matter. The men and women surely aren't like this in other coeducational institutions—but perhaps they are, and I just don't know about it.

I spent fifteen cents on a copy of Edmund Blunden's *Undertones of War* yesterday. His picture is in it too. I imagine him to be fairly slight, medium height, slightly stooping and pretty diffident in his manner. I get that impression from his writing too, although I have not got far.

Douglas MacAgy and I went to hear the St. Matthew Passion—it was better than last year, I think, and I took Harold to hear the St. John. The picture committee was considering a Thomson sketch. Mellors have had a very good show of Thomson's work, and Blair Laing gave a radio talk in his inimitable crooning way—well, anyhow, there has been a good deal of interest lately in Tom Thomson. So Blair brought over a pretty feeble sketch and asked $200 for it, and I had to persuade the committee not to get it, Norah reinforcing me in that. Jim Lawson was called in and he advised them to get a Thomson at any price, which doesn't sound very discriminating to me. It was an early sketch—1914, before he had developed that broad sweeping freedom that one expects. This was wiggly and hesitant in its going, though the colour was delicate and very pleasant.

I have been thinking of you in Italy for the last two weeks at least—I was not sure when you were going and you told me nothing of your plans. I hope the man you went with was a good travelling companion, and that Italy was not too hostile to Britishers, although I've been reading some pretty hot shots from Mussolini in the press.

Roy [Daniells] had a tea party on Sunday and it was very nice. I kept counting back to see how long ago it was that you first came to see us and I gave you a raw carrot to eat. It is six years ago, and I'm always a little amazed at how strong-minded I was, my poor dear, you hadn't *much* chance, did you? I remember being sorry for you being so far from home, then scared to ask you to come to tea, then amazed that I had been so bold, and pleased when you were evidently shy and glad to come, and I was vaguely irritated and embarrassed (how many r's) when you made fun of me for playing Goossens, and perplexed at having asked George [Clarke] when I was obviously more interested in what you would do next. Six years. I love you very much and I'd like to tell you so here, tonight, now.

Helen

Florence
[*5 April 1937*]

I forget exactly when or what I wrote last, but I was doubtless in Rome, registering dislike. Rome is horrible. Rome built that Colosseum barn, Rome built St. Peter's with its altar canopy a hundred feet high and its elephantine Cupids in the holy-water basin, Rome produced a long line of tough dictators and brutal army leaders and imbecile Caesars and Mussolini. Romans stare and peer at you hostilely and sulkily in the streets where north Italians are merely interested in you; Rome is full of Germans where Florence is full of English and Americans; Rome stunk; Romans gyp you; Romans break out in a rash of flags the day you arrive and welcome the return of their prodigal son Mussolini. History of Roman art: bastard Etruscan, bastard Greek, stolen Greek, bastard Oriental, bastard North Italian, bastard copies of bastard Greek, bastard Dutch, and various kinds of eclectic bastardy. Its one original art is the circus. By far the most interesting and genuine of the churches was San Clemente, and I liked some of the mosaics—the Cavallinis in Santa Maria Trastevere and the Torritis in Santa Maria Maggiore particularly. The classical museums, the Thermae, the Vatican, the Lateran and the Capitoline being the ones I went to, were huge junk piles, but there were good things in them, and I did get a vague idea of the development of Greek sculpture from superb archaic things like the Ludovisi throne to the Pergamene and Rhodian stuff. As for Rome—well, Rome contributes tons and tons of sarcophagi with the Romans depicted in relief as "conquering the barbarians," i.e., cutting unarmed men to pieces, making their horses step on women's faces, burning houses and stabbing yelling children. There are fine things in Rome, or would be if one didn't have to go to Rome to see them, but some are over-rated. Parts of the Vatican are fine, though one can't forget that one is in the Vatican, what with all their obscene fig leaves. St. Peter's certainly had to be seen to be believed—I knew it was hideous but I didn't think so big a building could be so pitifully unimpressive. But the worst I have not told you. They have a pleasant little trick in this country of "restoring" frescoes: i.e., of removing the whole of the original and substituting a modern copy, or what amounts to one. They are doing that with the Sistine Chapel ceiling at this very moment—when I was there about a third of it was covered up and a great array of scaffolding built under it. They are doing that with the Santa Croce Giottos here in Florence—the death of St. Francis is covered up now, they tell me. They are doing that with the Gozzolis in San Gimignano, a friend tells me who has been there. With that, with the frightful cleaning of pictures in the Uffizi, and with all those sculptures with the head from another statue and an arm from a third, about twenty-five per cent of the things worth looking at are fakes. The rumor that they were putting pants on the Michelangelo figures was denied, but they always deny everything, including the fact that the frescoes are being restored. Still, the tin pants on the Cnidian Aphrodite seem to have temporarily fallen off. I thought the best thing in the Vatican was the little Fra Angelico Chapel. I don't think I like Raphael much—the Logge was terrible—mostly parodies of Michelangelo, with Jehovah scampering around like a scarecrow in a high wind. Of course that had been restored too, and evidently quite recently—my Baedeker was written in 1930, and it was amusing to compare the picture described as "obliterated" with the travel poster leering down at you from the ceiling. The best Raphael I saw was at the Villa Farnesiva, I think—Raphael has a conventional Renaissance mind, and he seems to have no sense of organic form—that is, his pictures are never the exact shape of the conception behind them. Michelangelo was magnificent but Beethovenish—the Adam is incredibly subtle, but I don't think any of him equals the *Triumph of Death* at Pisa as far as impressiveness goes. The trouble with both of them is that they're neither Christians nor pagans: they're just metropolitans—in short, Roman painters. The Vatican picture gallery had two or three fine rooms of early painting, including a Simone Martini head of Christ I liked better than anything else, but most of it was just pure liquid, glutinous shit. So was the Borghese, bar a swell Titian and a copy of a Leonardo; so was the Doria, bar a Velasquez and a Brueghel. The Pantheon was magnificent—inside—one catacomb was thrilling, the other a dismal fake. Well, maybe I was unjust to Rome—there is supposed to be some good relief carving on the Petrified Penis, alias Trajan's Column, which Mike admires because it's sustained its erection so long—but I hated it, and so did Mike, and so did two Americans travelling with us.

I probably told you that we picked up Baine and two Exeter men [Charles Bell and Lou Palmer] in Rome. Baine we left there, and the four of us went to Assisi. We got there at night and spent the next day there. Assisi was glorious. We liked everything there, and would have liked to stay longer. We spent the whole day in San Francesco, apart from a few hours wandering around the town—those Giotto, that Cimabue and what was left of the Cavallini kept us working hard for six hours. The view is gorgeous, and while I know the town is a tourist's museum, it comes off somehow. You were closer to me at Assisi than anywhere else in Italy, I think—I kept you in front of my mind all the time, stuck in so lovely a place with a fool like Millicent [Rose], and wishing you were there with me alone. It was a perfect day, and we made a bad mistake in leaving for Perugia that night. The next morning we went into a place called the Collegio da Cambio and looked at Perugino, some vaguely charming, some sickly. Then the Art Gallery—very valuable historically, I suppose, as it gave the whole Umbrian school, but lousy. Rather a pathetic gallery, in fact. We cleared out of there at noon and went on to Arezzo. I have nothing but pleasant memories of Arezzo—the Piero della Francesca frescoes, which we spent two hours on and which were well worth it, and one of the best dinners we have had in a restaurant just beside it. Well, that night we got into Florence. Florence is frightfully crowded, and for the last two nights we've slept in one corner of a huge lounge room in this pension, but now we've got a room. Yesterday morning we went to the Uffizi. The opening room contained a Cimabue Madonna, a Giotto Madonna, and a Lorenzo Monaco Madonna—three of the very loveliest pictures I have ever seen. I stuck most of the morning in that room. Lorenzo Monaco was a big surprise—he had interested me in the National Gallery but I had no idea that he was in the top rank. There are three of his there, two absolutely perfect, one ruined by cleaning or restoring or something. And I shall return with a profound conviction that Cimabue was the very greatest painter who ever lived, on the strength of two paintings. Well, there was a lot more in the Uffizi—I'm going back tomorrow morning, when it'll be free, to look at the Mantegna and some of the Dutch. In the afternoon—well, the Uffizi took most of the afternoon—we went around and looked at the Cathedral, which was a bitter disappointment—seen in black and white reproductions it's fine, but in its dirty pink and green pristine splendor it's a horror. Today we went to the Pitti Gallery, an experience I am very glad to have put behind me. Fortunately, Italian decadent painting is so bad that it's really extremely funny—we particularly liked the martyrdom of St. Agatha, where a huge blond sow was stripped to the waist and having her breasts worked on with pincers—"Fancy," said Mike, "a female saint's having breasts big enough to get hold of with pincers." Then there was one of a cupid reaching up into the genitals of Hercules. We call them the Teat-Twister and the Testicle-Teaser, and are extremely fond of them. This afternoon we went to the Museo Nazionale—two or three fine Michelangelos, including the Brutus, which I liked better than any sculpture of his I saw in Rome, and a room full of Donatello. I am having a good time. I'm glad I saw Pisa first—I got the impact of the Cathedral and the *Triumph of Death* straight away, and have never seen a better building or fresco since.

There is an amazingly penetrating sweetness about you—I would so much rather see you than the next town in Italy, whatever it is.

Norrie

Toronto, Ont.
April 18 [*19*], 1937

Dearest, your letter came last week, your first from Italy, and I felt quite out of breath with all the sight-seeing you were doing in five days. Your onslaught upon Rome was quite breath-taking. It was very odd, but on the anniversary of the founding of Fascism I kept thinking of you in Italy and remembering all the Fascist songs we had to listen to on that day in Rome, and the weather here was very like Rome. Then for Easter it rained and was cold and I had a radio talk to write and stayed here for much of the time, and the weather did not remind me of Italy.

I am sure Stephen would be helpful for there is *nothing* he likes better to do than messing with railroad maps and keeping track of good pensions. I hope Mike Joseph is as congenial as you hoped. You have already seen Pisa and Siena—neither of which we saw. I hope you walked around Orvieto, but perhaps you wouldn't have time if you left for Rome in the late afternoon. The Signorelli and Fra Angelico chapel is marvellous isn't it? Did you remember all the carvings on the front of the cathedral from the postcards I showed you? They are some of the loveliest things I remember. You evidently did not go to Arezzo, or perhaps you were going to stop there on the way back to Florence—and what about Perugia? At the rate you are travelling you will see a great many places.

I feel as if I have just emerged from a long darkness. I spent all last week in the Infirmary. I have been so tired that I thought I'd never crawl out but I went back to work today, being Monday.

Last Saturday was the Senior Dinner and I managed to get to it more dead than alive. Kay [Coburn] and I were the only dons who went. I had a very nice time, sitting at a table up in the balcony with Les Vipond on my right. He and I got onto a subject dear to us both—H.N. Frye. He said he had learned more from you than from all his other courses put together and was sorry that you were away. As I was leaving with Kay, Dr. Brown stopped to talk to me and asked if I hear from England regularly? I said I had just had one from Italy after an interval of three weeks. Brown wanted to know what your plans are. I said the Blake was nearly finished, but I couldn't very well tell him it all depends on him or on the I.O.D.E. At any rate he was quite affable.

Eric Havelock buttonholed me and asked me whether I am interested in a job on the *Forum*. Pegi Nicol got married and is resigning, and they're looking for an art editor. I'd like the job. I'm afraid it might be a lot of work. I can do a better job than she did, at any rate. As a critic I'm very unsure, but I could farm out a lot of articles. It would be marvellous practice, and I'd meet some very bright people.

I am making plans for coming over and I am not yet sure just when. I'd like to turn up in Oxford and see your rooms before you leave. Would it suit you better if I come then or for July and August, or August and September? I'll have to decide soon. Please let me know as soon as you can what you would like me to do. Barbara will loan me one hundred dollars and I can collect another three hundred or more. That ought to do it if we're careful, but you'd better hurry and write to Brown!

I shall be through here around June 10th. Are you writing exams this year? Or does it matter if I show up a day or so before June 20th? I am getting terribly excited to think that I'm coming to see you soon. My dearest, dearest man. Tell me what you think of the *Forum*—for *me*. Seriously, do you think I should attempt it yet?

Helen

Oxford
[*28 April 1937*]

Sweetheart:

Florence remains the best town in the world. There are foul things in it, though. Santa Croce, for instance. Four of us went there one morning and found the Giotto Chapel full of ladders and scaffolding, so we climbed the ladders and walked over the scaffolding. We were hurriedly informed that we would have to get a permit to do that, but in the meantime ten or twelve other tourists had climbed up after us. Next day Mike and I hopped in again, and as soon as they saw my yellow mop heave in sight they took up the ladders. And no wonder. There was a fat pasty-faced swine there swabbing black paint on the *Death of St. Francis* as though he were painting the side of a barn. In Santa Maria Novella the big Cimabue or Duccio or whatever it is was being carted off while we were there for just one more repainting. It was lying flat on its back with fifteen men all standing around, each with a different theory of how to move it—the only survival of democracy I saw in Italy. The light was shining on it so you could see it hadn't been touched except for the Madonna's robe, which was a sticky black mess. Wait till they improve it and make it all a sticky mess. The big surprise in the Uffizi was 2 Lorenzo Monaco, as I think I mentioned. After four days in Florence, I got a bit stuffed and drunk, mentally—I was taking in so many painting impressions, and I know so little of painting.

We were in Florence for ten days and made two expeditions from there. One was to San Gimignano. It's a gorgeous town, even higher up and more picturesque than Assisi. I went chiefly to see the Gozzolis as I had no idea of what sort of painting was in the Cathedral. Well, I saw the Gozzolis—*Life of St. Augustine*—and they were grand fun. But when I hit that cathedral! We went chiefly for some Ghirlandaios in a locked chapel, but never got anywhere near them. We had noticed at Siena a painter called Bartolo di Fredi, because he seemed to have a passion for horses, and stuck them in everywhere he got a chance. Well, he'd done an enormous series of Old Testament scenes on the left wall—much the most complete we saw in Italy—he finished up with a Job series, for instance, curiously like Blake's in some ways. He's a swell painter, but a completely secular one—his creation of Eve was a lovely floating nude, and his drunkenness of Noah was the funniest I saw, except a mosaic in Venice—Noah was fairly well clothed apart from his huge erect penis that stood up in the middle of the picture, but he managed to look as completely plastered as I've seen anyone look even in Oxford. And, of course, with the Ark or Pharaoh's host drowned in the Red Sea, he just went to town on his horses. He'd obviously never seen a camel, so he just drew more horses, with impossibly long necks. On the entrance wall there was a Last Judgment—the Heaven was pretty perfunctory, but the hell was a Freudian riot—Lechery was a well-built naked woman with a fiend riding on her back and raping her with his tail; somebody else had a ramrod projecting from his mouth and his behind, and Usuria was lying on his back with an enormously distended belly and a devil squatting over his face and dropping a prodigious shower of turds into his mouth. The expression on that devil's face, half grinning and half straining, is something I'd go to Italy again just to see. The New Testament series, by somebody the guide book called Barna da Siena, was a very different matter. The lower row was a Passion sequence, ending with the Crucifixion, which was one of the most profound I ever saw. The man who did it was a genuine revolutionary—in every picture Jesus' enemies, whether Jews or priests or soldiers, were all huddled together in a lowering scowling mass, and the character study of Judas was amazingly subtle. The other expedition was to Prato for the Lippo Lippi frescoes—great stuff, and I should imagine his best work.

Then we went to Ravenna—a swell town, where the mosaics are far better and easier to look at than the ones in Rome. We had a very quiet day there, and went for a long walk under a blistering sun to a church about five miles outside the walls. We got into Padua that night—Bell threw out the wrong bag at the station and my bag, with the Blake thesis in it, went on to Venice. It came back in the morning—Padua is St. Anthony's home town, and St. Anthony is the saint who finds lost things. Padua is an amusing town, with all its narrow streets and its rows of colonnaded loggias where people sit around at cafe tables. The Giotto chapel was magnificent, though I find Giotto, and still more Fra Angelico, don't quite connect as far as my personal likes and dislikes are concerned. Perhaps the next trip will affect me differently. The Mantegna was much the best fresco work of his I saw in Italy, too. We spent a day and a half there and moved on to Venice.

It's a funny town. All the things you read about gondolas and canals and so on actually do happen, and it looks just as it ought to look, except that I didn't realize the "Bridge of Sighs" was bad grammar—it's only about twelve feet long, so there'd only be time for one sigh. Externally, Venice comes off perfectly—even its ugliness—St. Mark's, apart from some howlingly funny mosaics, is as monstrous in its way as the Imperial Hotel in Russell Square, and some of the church façades, which look as though they had been constructed entirely out of pigeon-shit, have a deformed and twisted hideousness that nothing in all the megalomaniac horror of Rome can equal. Still, that all fits in. It's the only real sucker town in Italy. The Italians are on the whole honest, and in Rome only sporadically not so: the only place where one gets systematically gypped and rooked and fleeced and hornswoggled is in Venice. Everybody speaks English there, as it's the place all the Americans go after Paris, and foreigners who speak English are dangerous. Then you go and look at their blasted painting. Huge crammed canvases stewing in an oily morass like the Slough of Despond each jammed all over its hundred square feet with people. And all the pictures express is the fact that they cost a lot of money. Money, money, money. I never came across quite so naive a worship of money before, except in some English eighteenth-century poetry, and I never saw the Communist caricature of the "bourgeois" get so perfectly illustrated. I reread the *Merchant of Venice* on the spot—I had never realized before how much money there was in that play.

I picked up your letter at Venice. As for your coming over, I'm tied hand and foot until I hear from Brown. The one thing I know is that somehow or other we've got to get together this summer—incidentally, I may have to borrow from you if I have to go back to Canada. I stayed in Italy five weeks on twenty pounds counting railway fare, so didn't do badly.

Darling, do you suppose you could make an enquiry or two for me about the I.O.D.E.—find out who I have to write to, and so on?

I didn't learn much Italian. Mike's French is better than mine, and we got along. What surprised me was that one gets further with German than with English in Italy—not that I tried to get anywhere with it, but everybody took me for German and tried to talk it to me. The rapprochement between Italy & Germany is being played up for all it's worth—you see pictures of Hitler everywhere, Italian & German flags beside each other in posters, and anti-Semitic books in bookstores. Of course the Italians made a great fuss over their Empire—Mussolini's title is now "Fondatore dell'Impero," the King is the King-Emperor, and they're frantically jealous of countries with bigger empires. When I got back to France, where Mussolini was allowed to have a mistress, the mistress was said to have had three hundred pictures of Mussolini in her room. She not only loved Mussolini, she understood him.

Where am I? Oh, yes, Venice. We went to Verona, which has a swell Romanesque church—San Zeno, with a lovely Mantegna triptych in it. Not much else in Verona—a sprawling industrialized town. So we made an excursion to Mantua. That was a good idea. The Mantegna Gonzaga series was in desperately bad shape—much worse than the reproductions would indicate—and we were rather disappointed. It was part of a gigantic palace, though, and what with that and Giulio Romano's Palace of T, Mantua put on a superb show. It's full of sixteenth-century Renaissance art at its best, and filled up a gap that had previously been represented only by the Villa Farnesina at Rome. The food at Mantua was ambrosial—about the best we had in Italy, and we had good food there. I'm no champion spaghetti-winder, but I like spaghetti, at least in Italy. Unfortunately, Mantua is way out in the marshes—it's practically an island—it was bitterly cold, and I got the sorest throat I've had since my tonsils came out. I got into Milan that night a very sick man. I was nearly broken-hearted. I had got flu in England at the beginning of last term, it had hung on all term and cut my working efficiency down to about thirty per cent. I had gone to Italy as much for my health as anything else, had struck as rainy and record-breaking cold a spring as there was in England, and here I was in worse shape than ever. Next morning I was better—I couldn't have been worse—but still pretty bad, and I spent a gloomy day in the Brera and Last Supper refectory. That night we climbed into a big clean comfortable Dutch third-class carriage, and woke up in Basel.

We got into Brussels in the afternoon, got a hotel, a bath and some food—my throat was much better. In the evening we went to see *Romeo and Juliet*—in English, with French subtitles. Scene Verona, in front of the church of San Zeno we had just been in. Very good show—Barrymore as Mercutio was superb, though it's an obvious part to steal, and the dialogue was in places surprisingly intact—more so than the stupid little texts my freshies use. The female end sagged a bit—the Nurse wasn't too good and Norma Shearer was a pretty elephantine Juliet, but it's definitely two or three up for Hollywood.

We thought we might see something of the town the next morning, but didn't get up till eleven and just had time to get away on the boat train, which annoyed me, as I wanted to see the fountain with the pissing boy. The Channel crossing was dull and the trip from Dover to London duller. Still, I'm not too sorry to be in England. From Brussels to Brussel sprouts is a let-down, everything in England is bad and expensive, except the few things that are a little better and a lot more expensive; there's not much good about general living comfort in England and nothing distinctively good. Still—one goes to an Italian church to see Giotto or Masaccio and doesn't notice that nine-tenths of the church is insanely ugly—ugly in that shrieking Catholic way that England at its worst doesn't seem to sink to. Sometimes, as in Santa Croce, I felt that the people who ran the place hated the good pictures—damaged them all they could, and if they didn't make money out of them would claw them all off the walls with their nails, tomorrow. I like the Italians, but impersonally—they're not my people—and though Florence, alone of all the towns I saw, struck me as a place one might live, five weeks was all I wanted.

I stayed the night at the Burnetts', and got to Oxford the next day. My sore throat has recurred, but I've been taking things easily and going to bed early. Blunden set us an exam when we got back—he told Warren he would—he didn't tell me. He seemed to like my paper, God knows why—it was written in a pretty bemused state of mind.

Elizabeth, poor child, has moved to the other end of town, and is off to Lincolnshire this week copying wall paintings. I don't know if I give you a favorable impression of Elizabeth or not—the Burnetts don't like her much, but the Burnetts are not very tolerant people. She's a lonely soul with lots of courage, pride and sensitiveness, but she is a swell girl. She hits hard and rubs people the wrong way, in a way I think you understand, after six years of me, but she's more honest and straightforward than I am and has more guts. You'll love her when you meet her. Mother would be very distressed if you went through Moncton without seeing her—please don't do that.

You'd better decide about the *Forum* yourself—your letters sound as though you were just about as busy as you could be, but you know best whether you could make room for it or not. There's no doubt that if you did the job you'd do it very well, and the *Forum* is in many ways a useful magazine to get printed in. Also, I'd like to see you doing the job—actually, I don't think it will hurt you if it does mean overwork—there's always room at the top for things that interest you. Sure, go ahead—if I'm supposed to liven up Canadian music criticism, why not the rest of the family do the rest of the livening?

I'm exhausted with this huge letter, my throat's sore and it's midnight. I want very much to see you; somehow or other, I think I'm going to see you. It's so absolutely necessary. But I must hear from Brown first.

I know what makes my throat sore—it's a lump.

Darling, you do write such lovely letters. And you grow up so fast you scare me.

I shall love you as long as I live.

Very truly yours.

A.G. of T. [*Toronto*]
April 30, 1937

My dear: I am sending you a note in a hurry to catch the boat again. I am trying to get my passage fixed up—at present I am sailing on the *Empress of Britain*, June 12th, and I'm finding out fares in Germany but I can't tell you that yet.

We have just had some trouble with Roy—he had a nervous crack-up and he isn't going to write his exams. We sent him up north to Lake Joseph with La Trobe—the scout master. He's been to Dr. Barnett and to a psychiatrist and he certainly was in bad shape. It has been pretty tough on us all, but he will be better soon I think.

I hope you don't think we're a family of quitters, even though we do seem to have a hell of a nervous system. Poor old Roy thinks all kinds of horrible things of himself—we have to keep him off that, of course. It is damned tough, after all the work he's done on his course this year, and his term marks have been high. [D.J.] McDougall's paper was the one that did it—when he got to work on that he cracked. And McDougall has been giving him firsts on his essays all year. Jerry [Riddell] went to the department and they said he was heading for first-class standing. So what?

I'll write as soon as I make out a list of expenses.

My love to you,
H.

[*Toronto*]
May 10, 1937

My dearest!! Your letter came today, just as I was thinking it was high time that letter promised from Venice arrived. And I nearly had to take a half-holiday to finish reading it. I am terribly pleased that you saw so much of Italy—you covered a great deal more territory than I did, and you had pleasant companions evidently. And heavens above! to have spent only 20 pounds is miraculous. I'm beginning to think I am just a careless spendthrift when it comes to money. Isn't there something that you've forgotten to count—not anything at all?

Now look here, you goose, if you think there is any earthly chance of your getting an I.O.D.E. this late in the season for *next* year, you must be hopeful—they usually award them about a year ahead, or so I have always heard. And they're a little vague, like the rest of these scholarship committees. Now, I'll try to find out—I can't do anything much until tomorrow, too late for this mail. But Brown is coming through, I think. At the baccalaureate sermon he said he'd heard from you, from Italy, but you did not give him your address and would I drop in and give it to him. So I told him it was just Merton College. Perhaps I'd better drop in now anyway and see how the money stands. If I go to see Brown I can give him another opportunity to make me blush as he teases me gently—as his generation rather enjoys doing. That might be a good idea—I'm such a nice quiet shy little thing and engaged to that fire-eater, all quite disarming.

As matters stand at present I'm coming June 12th on the *Empress of Britain*, and I'm working out a scheme for seeing a *lot* of Germany—railway fares will be about $50 from the inquiries I have made. However, I'll probably have to leave the buying of tickets until I see you, since I can't get any reply back in time unless you hurry and write by return mail. If you are coming home after all, would you send a deferred cable or let me know soon and I could send you the money right away. The family would be awfully glad to see you, and it would be especially good if you could be up north this summer with Roy being there. He seems to be better now. We had a cheerful letter from him today.

Please let me know as soon as you can about the money question—I can just get $450 by borrowing $100, and I won't tie up next year any more than that. If you haven't enough then come back here and I'll send you the money—

My love to you,
H.

Oxford
[*18 May 1937*]

Sweet:

I didn't want to write until I'd heard from Brown, and now that I've heard from Brown I still don't feel much like writing. This after he said "Earn as much money as you can so I'll have more left for the others," and "If the worst came to the worst we could put you on the staff and give you a leave of absence." I shall probably go to my grave believing what people say. Honest to God, he told me, in his shuffling official way, that the college would finance my second year. I'm not a complete fool: I know he did say that. Well, I have £30 coming to me from Ottawa: when I get my bills paid out of it I'll have £10.

I see Blunden Thursday night. If he's encouraging, and has some possibilities of a job for the summer up his sleeve, I'll stay here. Otherwise—well, there are two plans. One is to grab Brown's six hundred, trust to God for the I.O.D.E. or something, and hang on. The other is to propose that if he has anything for me next year and will take me without a degree, I'll grab it. I feel nervous now that Brown has started to welsh, and I'd like to have that job cinched. I'm not getting enough out of Oxford to make sacrifices worthwhile to finish my course here.

And sweetheart, I'm fearfully sorry but I *still* haven't been able to decide about the summer. You can see my position. Germany I am afraid is impossible. Besides, travelling on your maiden passport in a Fascist country might be embarrassing. Not that I care. But if I came back to Canada, while I'd have to borrow about $100 from you, still I don't much relish living off the Burnetts until Victoria decided to come through with some of that dough.

Oh, God! I'm sorry to keep you in the air like this, and I hate having to scratch a note like this after keeping you waiting so long. The Blake—or most of it—will be in Geoffrey Keynes' hands in about two weeks, I hope, but it'll take ages before a publisher reports on it. Now you know as much about the situation as I do, what do you think?

I'll write again when I've cooled down.

Norrie

P.S. I'm frightfully sorry about Roy—I do wish he wouldn't worry so over things.

P.P.S. A *New Yorker* would help my state of mind.

Toronto, Ont.
May 19, 1937

My dearest: I do wish your letters did not come in such fits and starts. I'm not complaining really, and I don't suppose you know yet about the money question. Roy Daniells met me the other day and said that Brown or Currelly or someone had dug up another Trick Scholarship for you—$600. They all seem a bit jaundiced because you have not written a word to anyone, and Edgar grumbled that you might be a bit more observant of your social obligations. I think so too, and I'd scold you roundly if you were a little closer. Really—*I* can't write reports to these people about you. If only you'd write them a short note from time to time and keep them mollified. But there you are, and you send Brown a letter at last from Italy, after Roy [Daniells] has tipped you off—to say nothing of what I've poured forth by way of invective. Really, Frye, you *are* an idiot. I hope you will see Roy toward the end of the summer. He might lend you some money, for he seems to have more than he knows what to do with. But for heaven's sake, make arrangements in good time and don't leave it until you starve. Do you feel chastised? There, there, I love you just the same.

Roy [Kemp] has gone to Lake Joseph, and John Harwood-Jones went up last week with him. We had a pretty gloomy report last week, but a better one today. Last week he had a relapse, sleepless nights, and evidently a return of the melancholy and inertia. He was in a devil of a state nervously, but I think he will come round with rest and a good summer.

Norah gave a broadcast last night on children's work: next week I'm doing one on the Permanent Collection. On Coronation day I had a big time looking at parades and paddling at the Island with Douglas [MacAgy]—as I have said, I am very fond of Douglas.

There isn't much news, and besides, someone is waiting here to go to Yonge Street with me to post this. Barbara gave me a cheque tonight for $100, and we'll see her in London.

I hope there is word from you soon. My love to you—

Helen

Oxford
[*21 May 1937*]

Sweetheart:

I'm afraid I shall have to come back to Canada this summer and throw myself on your hands. I've been talking to Blunden: he says the college (here) can raise me about £20 if I write a good exam for him in the fall, and I may raise some more in various prizes and things here. I'll wiggle through somehow if I get Brown's $600, but I can't get through the summer too on that. England is a brutally expensive country, and I would spend all of the $600, counting the £50 I owe here for this term, this summer. I might make my fortune writing, in London, and I might not. Besides, I don't know if I can get the $600 for the summer or not, and it would take me till June 12th to find out. I'm sorry to spoil your trip, but the only excuse I have for staying here—getting the Blake published—would keep my nose in the B.M. all day while you were cooling your heels somewhere else.

This is gently leading you up and letting you down to a touch. Could you lend me £20 ($100) to get home on?

I hate seeing all the people I suppose I shall have to see, and want to avoid Toronto as much as possible. I've got another excellent reason for wanting to come back to Canada which you could trot out to any curious person, and that is my health. It's been frightfully bad all year—I don't know when my vitality has been lower—and I don't think I'd last the second year if I spent the summer freezing my feet in the B.M., or, for that matter, Germany.

I'll try to write you a decent letter as soon as I feel more like it. Still, I'll soon be seeing you.

Until then, I love you inexpressibly.

Norrie

Toronto, Ont.
May 23, 1937

My dearest: Sunday night. I came home for the weekend but the residence is not closed yet, for the O.C.E. people stay on until June 11th, and by that time I shall be in Montreal, probably, seeing your Aunt. Kay Coburn is going across on the *Empress* too, on Carnegie money, for she is getting the Coleridge papers photographed or something. How about a little tea party for the troops? I'm coming especially to see your rooms in Merton, you know, for that was one reason I'm coming so early, to see your palatial retreat. I hope it won't interfere with your plans—if you are writing exams I can keep myself out of the way until you are finished, but I was counting on your not having any until next year.

Last Thursday night I was at a party H.J. Davis gave for Joan Fairley and John Hall, and had a lovely time of course, as one always does. Davis asked me how you are, and I heard to my horror that you have not written to him yet either. When I get to you you can prepare for a long time spent in writing letters, for I'll stand over you with a hair brush until you get them done. I understand how you feel about them of course, but you can't afford to neglect some things, and keeping in touch with the English department here is definitely one thing that must be done. Davis is selling his house. After his year in England he is going to Cornell, for good. That made me feel pretty low, you can imagine. On the other hand, all the more reason for your keeping in touch with him, in case he ever has occasion to recommend some bright younger man for an appointment. All quite aside from considerations of friendliness and gratitude for all that he has done for you already. I hope you are sufficiently bowed low by now, and I'll try not to preach any more. You must be tired of my nagging—two letters of it. It is just anxiety on my part.

I think I will have to get to bed now. I must be on the job in the morning to finish that radio talk.

Love,
Helen

Oxford
[*28 May 1937*]

Darling, I've been sending Edgar four of the 6000-word essays I've been producing every week here—four of my essays, remember—and I've told him my health has been frightfully bad for the last two terms, which is quite true, so that may give him an idea of what I've been doing when I haven't been fulfilling my social obligations. I'm very tired, heartily sick of Oxford, and want to take all your money away from you and come home as soon as possible and rest up. It's getting late—I don't know whether I should cable you or not.

My eyes have been bad since I came back from Italy, and I've slacked off work. I've been overdrawn ten pounds since then too, so have kept quiet. The most depressing event of the term was lunch with the Warden, who is a complete ninny. The Warden doesn't know what to make of the university now that it's gone intellectual on him—he has a vague idea that the Rhodes Scholars are to blame. It was he who more or less began to feed me up with Oxford—he fitted so perfectly into the general pattern. Really, Oxford is incredible.

I've had two outings—one on a picnic to the Chilterns with Elizabeth, which was grand, as we sat in a beechwood with a purple carpet of bluebells all around us. The other was to the Cotswolds with Lou Palmer (one of the Exeter men we met in Italy), Mike and his (Lou's) mother, who has a little car. We saw several very lovely little villages and some wall paintings—the fresco tradition in England is spottier and cruder than in Italy, of course, but they have original ideas about symbolism one could travel all over Italy without seeing.

Some female called Maisie somebody is opening an art gallery, and Elizabeth is putting up some of her drawings. She hopes Maisie may provide a showroom for her. Elizabeth has been the worst possible influence on me because whenever I visit her in a period of spiritual and financial depression, such as occurs frequently, I always find her with just as little money and even more depressed, so we work each other up to the verge of drowning ourselves.

Blunden came back from Germany full of enthusiasm for the Nazis. Poor Oxford always finds itself on the wrong side of a revolution—it gets more Fascist every day. Cromwell nearly wiped it out, and if, as I heard a Communist say recently, the fight in England will be the last and bloodiest in the world, there won't be much left of this place but a tangled mass of barbwire.

Edmund Blunden
(courtesy of Wikipedia)

I'm sorry if I whimper and growl, but I shall keep on whimpering and growling until I get married and get a job. I don't much care what sort of job, at the moment, but it would be too bad if I got the wrong wife—perhaps you could help me pick one. I shall be seeing you shortly, which is really why I am a little impatient with Oxford.

Norrie

Art Gallery of Toronto
Sat. May 29, 1937

My dearest: I suppose I shall soon be hearing from you in answer to my cable, but I'd better tell you what happened here. I went to get the situation clear, straight from the horse's mouth, and had an interview with Brown. He teased me a little about absent-minded professors, which was what I expected. I had to take in his side of the question, and here it is. You have not kept in touch with the English department, you have not made any request for money. The only thing that might have been done, which evidently could have been arranged quite easily, was a renewal of the Royal Society award for a second year. But Pelham Edgar has been very much hurt at your lack of courtesy (Brown) in not keeping in touch with him and has done nothing about it. The word is the same all along the line: you haven't written to any of them but Brown and he knows that that was because Daniells told you to, and then you didn't even drop a line to Daniells. It is a bit thick, you know. So, the only thing Brown can do is get you $600 provided by Currelly for members of the staff—they waive the point that you are a future member of staff—and that on condition that you stay over the second year and find the money somehow. There is a job here for you a year from now. Brown says he's saving it for you, but the condition is that you have two years graduate work at Oxford. There's no use coming home to see about it, he wouldn't take you next fall, not until the next one. And he won't unless you finish the Oxford degree. I cabled because I knew that you'd be needing some money soon. Also the committee which decides on this meets June 8. Brown will get them to agree to forking out the money on condition that you stay the second year, but while that may be passed on June 8, they won't fork out until they hear from you. The Royal Society met here this week, and Brown says he doesn't feel he can ask Edgar to do anything more. There was no mention of the promise he made about a year's leave of absence, and I couldn't drag that in—chicken-livered perhaps. After this we don't believe *anything* until we have it above a signature.

I have cancelled my passage on the *Empress* June 12, and am waiting to hear from you, for the money. I have $165 of my own in the bank and if I don't come over I will pay back Barbara's hundred because we can't afford to run into too much debt. You should stay there this summer, I think. Norah would rather have me here in June, so I am taking July and August off, and can come over then if you find some money. Please let me know—send me a short note *often* so that I can arrange my plans from this end. I leave Wymilwood on June 11, and I am not doing anything about the summer for the time being.

God help us, what a gloomy letter! You have been in worse jams than this before now, or at least about as bad, and we got through them somehow. I do wish you could get a job over there, when I think of how impressed Victoria would be, it seems the important thing to do, rather than coming back here where they know all about your financial troubles, and now and again have a tendency to remember how much money they've spent on you. You must not let me interfere with your plans my dearest, I can leave my feelings in cold storage for another year, that is, if I don't think about it.

The radio talk came off without any difficulties last Tuesday. Had a bad time convincing the family that I did it, Daddy being convinced that it was Norah after all. He thought I must have gone to pieces from nervousness and Norah had to read it for me. Can you beat that! But his faith in his family is pretty badly shaken after Roy's brief excursion off the rails. Walking around with a son casually talking of dropping off bridges is no fun. However, Roy is much better now.

Monday night. Your letter came this morning, saying you were coming home, and I thought that all our difficulties would be settled. Certainly it is the cheapest thing we can do, and probably by far the pleasantest, for the family will be awfully glad to have you. The only thing is—you'll miss seeing Brown. I will send you $100 by the next fast mail after this, as I did not get to the bank today. I'll nose around, and see what else I can do here. Most of my friends are in a curious state about my trip—they still think I leave on June 12th. So I'm having some important changes of plan which make it necessary that I stay here. You don't need to feel afraid to see people—it is quite natural that you should come home this summer and it will be cheaper for both of us. And a lot healthier. I am quite sure we can dig up money from somewhere, so just you write a nice little letter to Brown. And I love you very very much, and want to sit in the sun and watch you get freckled. My dear.

H.

Oxford
1937 May [*June*] 1

Telegram; addressed to Kemp at 84, Queen's Park, Toronto.

MUST COME HOME CAN YOU LEND ME SOME MONEY=

NORRIE.

Oxford
[*8 June 1937*]

Darling, it's perhaps as well that somebody has some idea of how to manage my affairs, as I obviously haven't much idea of it myself. I suppose I have been a complete fool with Edgar, although he talks as though I had never sent him a word. I did write him at Christmas, telling him how I was getting on, how the Blake was going, and something of Elizabeth, who is a close friend of his wife. I also said I would forward some of the Blake in three weeks, and the rest at the end of the following term. Well, in three weeks' time I was down with the flu, and although I slogged and slogged at the Blake for weeks, it just didn't add up to the right answer. However, the first two chapters—half the whole—are getting their final draft now. Blunden has considerable hope of publication, and suggests Faber & Faber as the first move. I have written Edgar, sending him the first chapter of the Blake, and explaining that I'd see him for suggestions when I was in Canada, and that if the book were published I'd want to dedicate it to him. I hated to write and just put him off with more promises—I wanted to deliver the goods. That's the best I can do to mollify him—the book, if it comes out, will be a damned important one, and when Victoria College sees H.N. Frye splashed over the *Times Literary Supplement* they may be less worried about my correspondence. Not that I'm trying to defend myself particularly.

In the meantime the Royal Society has to have his O.K. before they send me the last £30, and they probably won't get it, so I may have to borrow still more money to pay for my piano here. Edgar did nothing whatever about my Christmas letter, and the Royal Society, after a delay of several weeks, finally sent the second instalment without him, so perhaps there is more than one angle to this lack of courtesy business.

As you see, I'm not feeling very well yet, and I'm beginning to feel about you as I feel about the rest: I must get that book out first and listen to complaints about my bad manners afterwards. Bless you, darling. And if you can get a typewriter up to Gordon Bay you really won't have to scramble around cleaning up the messes I make much longer. Don't lose your faith in me.

Norrie

Oxford
[*9 June 1937*]

I'm sorry about my last letter: I don't sound very pleasant at the moment, I know. The point is: the Blake is the only thing I can do now to recoup myself. I am sure it will be published, and that it will attract a lot of attention when it is published. Things will look different then. The whole story looks very different to me than it does to you, but you'll understand much quicker if I don't go into explanations or excuses. I'm damned sorry about spoiling your trip this summer, much more grateful than I can possibly say for what you are doing, and I concede that I have spent the year sleep-walking, oblivious to everything, with my sense of proportion, perspective, good manners and common sense totally atrophied. The only things that can be rescued from this are the dreams that come to me in my sleep.

And, unless sea air can perform miracles, I think that when you see me you will also see why I'm coming to Muskoka, throwing myself on your hands, making no effort to stay over here, and looking pretty ignominious generally. I'm planning to sail from Southampton on June 24 on the *Empress of Australia*.

Blunden says he'll give me an introduction to Faber & Faber. I'm a little afraid of them, though the advantages of having them publish the book are so obvious that it's worth a long chance. Cambridge Press will come next, and I think I should land them all right. Or somebody after them. But I can't start protesting about how much I love you until I have the Blake to point to.

Well, I'm more grateful than I can say for all your work with the College and the money. Your own job, Roy and me must be a terrific combination for your small shoulders. I'm so glad the radio talk came off all right.

[*Toronto*]
June 11, 1937

My dearest: Graduation house party is in progress; I went to the Vic tea party and talked to Pelham [Edgar] and his wife—I didn't mention you, of course. Pelham introduced me as Hazel Kemp again, remembered seeing me in Ottawa and the map etc. Dr. Brown has got the $600 for you from the Board of Regents—he is not sending you a letter because of the lack of time—you leaving there and he being tied up with sitting on platforms while people graduate.

Let me know what boat you're coming on and I'll try to get to Montreal. As it is I don't know when you arrive, when you are leaving or anything. Do let me know, for I want to meet you.

Davis has gone to Chicago but the Wookey [Gladys Wookey Davis] will be here all summer, and we're going up to see her. You are also going to drop in to see Pelham (orders from your business manager!)—the old fossil—I can't understand what is the matter except that a personal note would have interested him probably more than all your brilliant essays. There is just a chance of a very interesting shift here—Peggy Roseborough told me about it. E.K. Brown is coming to Toronto and Roy Daniells may go to take his place. How that affects you I don't know.

Kay leaves on the *Empress* tomorrow—the boat I was going on. Maybe I can come over next year—I hope so. If I think too much of you I feel terribly queer—I'll be so glad to see you, oh my dearest!

Helen

Oxford
[20 *June* 1937]

Thank you, darling. I think I said I was sailing from Southampton on the *Empress of Australia*. I want to get back as soon as possible—I may return to Europe on a freighter. I want to stay in London long enough to look up Geoffrey Keynes. The boat sails June 24 and is supposed to arrive in Quebec 8 A.M. July 1. From there I take something else to Montreal. I've already bought my ticket for Toronto. Please don't bother to come to Montreal unless you really want to—I have a bad conscience about the amount of money you can spend on me. I got the Blake off—the first half—to Faber & Faber today, which is the reason for this type of note. I love you very much—far more than I can attempt to say in my present state of mind.

[*Toronto*]
Friday. June 25, 1937

Addressed to Frye at an unknown location in Montreal.

My dearest: WELCOME HOME! WELCOME HOME! WELC—my typewriter sticks!

I can't find out exactly when the boat-train gets in, sometime in the morning of July 1st, at Windsor Station, Montreal. Very well. I'll be there.

I hope you've had a marvellous crossing. I am sure you will have because the weather here has been perfect for days. But you never can tell about the ocean.

I'll save all my news until I see you.

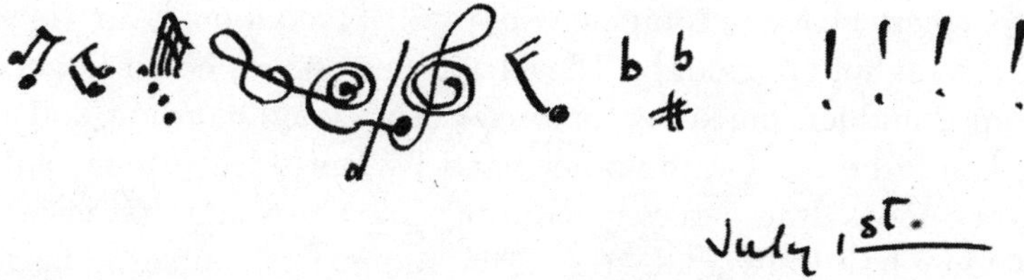

Helen

Toronto
[*21 July 1937*]

After arriving in Toronto from England, Frye joined Helen at the Kemps' cottage in Gordon Bay. In July he took the train to Toronto, where this letter was posted, to discuss his teaching position at Victoria College for the 1937–38 academic year.

Fifteen hundred. At least, I think it'll be that. The Chancellor didn't want to discuss money until the Principal told him how much he could jew me down, but I said I had orders from my fiancée to get more definite information. He said in an injured way, "You're not thinking of getting married, are you?" I said I was. He said "Do you think that's wise?" I said I did. Then he said something about our being separated for the following year, and I said I thought we'd hold out, or words to that effect. He still looked injured—the college could exploit me with less strain on its Nonconformist conscience if I remained celibate. My year at Oxford will be the following one if at all possible, but he can't promise. No leave of absence—I still just get Currelly's $600 for my second year at Oxford and that's all, with what I can save: "the two of you" says the Chancellor with a leer—this year. And of course I can't go on the permanent staff because "for your sake and our sake" I shall have to have at least two years' training abroad, "Principal Brown thinks and I think," and for the same reason I don't get the lecturer's salary of eighteen hundred, but the Chancellor will take the responsibility of saying fifteen hundred. They've got me where they want me and they know it. But I do a lecturer's work, all right. I probably get Roy's three biggest courses—first year 16th c., which I know pretty well, the Milton course, where I have to compete with [A.S.P.] Woodhouse, for 3rd year, and 4th year 19th c. thought. The Chancellor phones Edgar to get that confirmed and lets me know tomorrow (Thursday) morning, so I can't leave before Friday. On the other hand I want to leave then, as John Harwood-Jones' frau moves in Saturday. The Chancellor has visions of my reading frantically all the rest of the summer, of course, and is fussing like blazes to find out exactly what I'm to do. I'll have groups besides that, doubtless. They sure picked up a bargain. I shall remember it when the time comes to discuss my "obligations" to Victoria College.

I told the Chancellor that you would keep your job as there wasn't yet so much prejudice against married women in the Art Gallery as in other places. He winced.

S.H.F. Kemp, Helen, Roy Kemp, Frye, Gertrude Kemp, 1937
(courtesy of Susan Sydenham)

The Fryes, 1937 (courtesy of Victoria University Library, Toronto)

The Fryes on their wedding day (courtesy of Victoria University Library, Toronto)

Portrait of Helen Kemp, 1937 (courtesy of Victoria University Library, Toronto)

The Fryes on their wedding day, 24 August 1937
(courtesy of Victoria University Library, Toronto)

The Fryes at their wedding reception, held at the Guild Inn on the Scarborough Bluffs (courtesy of Susan Sydenham and Victoria University Library, Toronto)

With S.F.H.Kemp at the reception (courtesy of Victoria University Library)

With Roy Kemp at the wedding reception (courtesy of Susan Sydenham)

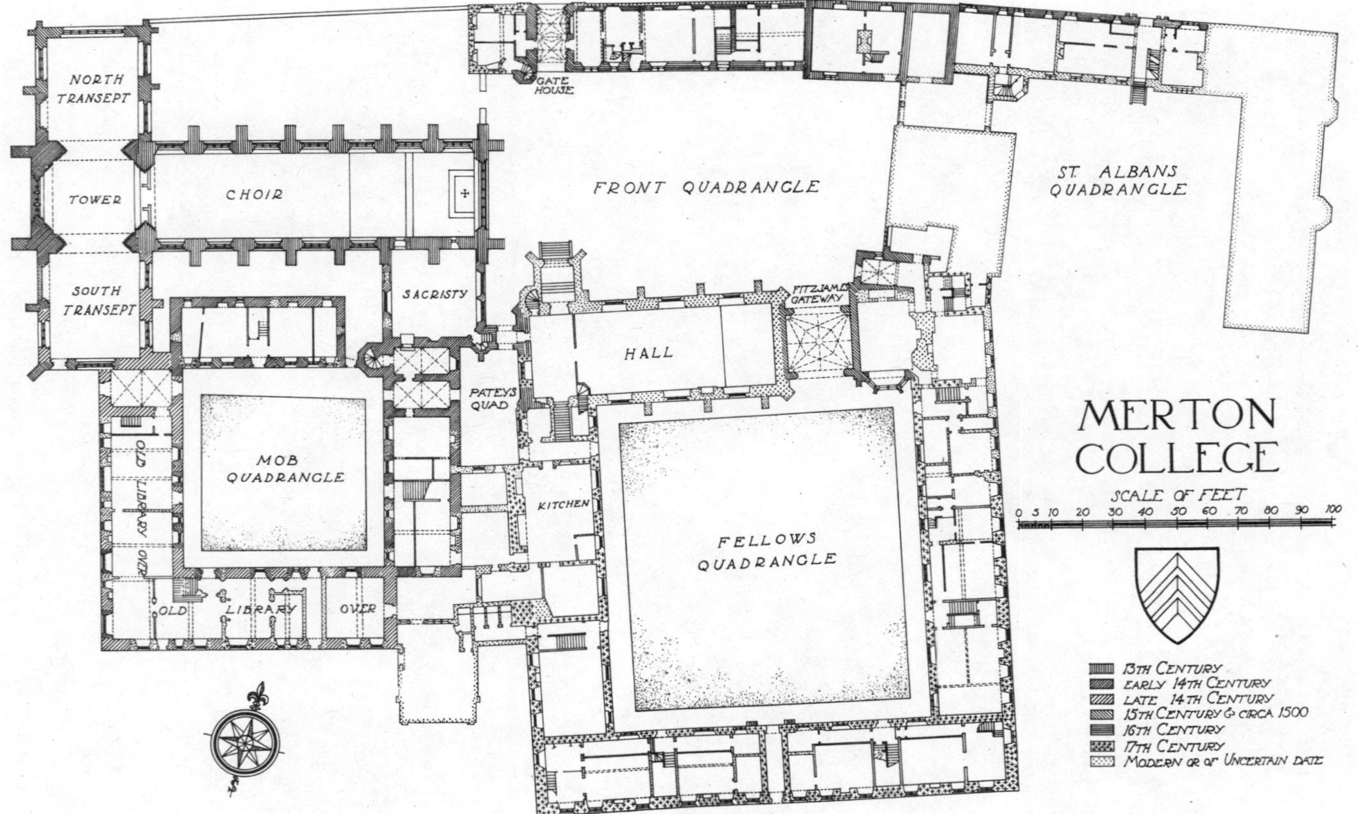

Plan of Merton College (from *An Inventory of the Historical Monuments of the City of Oxford*, 1939)

1938–1939

Southampton

Written on board the Empress of Britain *en route to England. Postmarked 29 September 1938; addressed to Helen Frye,* Art Gallery of Toronto.

My dear:

Well, it's been a bit dull, after all. The food on the *Empress* is bad. English and bad. Or at any rate I can't eat it, and that combined with a cold put me rather off for a day or two.

There are a lot of Rhodes fellows on board—they have two full tables at dinner, though, so I don't eat with them. Of the three men at my table, one is a silly but harmless old buzzard who seems to be a sort of English schoolmaster. Another is a farmer and an M.P. from Alberta—a man somewhat like the Yale man I met on my field. Told me I'd brought back a wonderful accent from Oxford with me. I don't know how often I've been told—by Canadians—that I have a thick English accent—it must be because I have an academic one. The Rhodes men are a bit green. One—Allen—is going to read English at Merton—he's blond and quite naive—I guess Blunden will get along with him all right. He's from Queens, and is a piano player, of the Prelude in C# minor variety. He has a book of 4-hand stuff, and I helped him out one evening with the piano when he seemed to be stuck, so now I'm stuck.

I went to church Sunday morning, and some illiterate ship's officer mumbled the morning prayer. The one thing a religious service, or the reading of the Bible, does to me is to give—sometimes—the emotional intensity that a dream gives an experience, and for the same reason—that your conscious mind is asleep.

I bought a Penguin—Richard Jefferies' *Story of My Heart*—you have the book at home. I'm torn between the desire to save my six pence by reading the book and the utter impossibility of reading it. So I moon around, and occasionally fish it out of my pocket and stare at it.

But Richard Jefferies improves on acquaintance—as a matter of fact I think he's written one of the significant books of his time, which is the later 19th c.

I've just heard Chamberlain's speech. He makes it sound a lot like war—it may be partly bluff, of course, to tell Hitler he means it. I can't understand Germany at all—the Nazis seem absolutely determined to make the rest of the world gang up on them and smash them. By the way, there was a book written in 1912–13, by Norman Angell, which you also have, called *The Great Illusion*, proving that a complete financial breakdown would follow a war. But I still think there's something in it.

Everybody I've talked to seems fairly indifferent to war. They all think it's a bad idea, take support of it by all classes of people to be inevitable, have no conception of any of the underlying motives of war except the immediate political situation, and simply shuffle the countries of Europe around like pawns. There are no strong feelings. They say Hitler's drunk with power, but there's absolutely no smash-the-dirty-buggers feeling—they understand, I think, the distinction between a government's will & what the people want. It's a saner attitude than the 1914 one, if that's any consolation, and however long it lasts.

But in the meantime the passengers are worried, depressed and anxious—there's a gloom over the whole ship. If Germany mobilizes—Russia's air force—Hitler wants the Ukraine—you young men it is who'll have to go—that's what they said in 1914—I guess Dorset will be out of danger—will you go back to Canada—over and over, on and on, round and round. God, I hope it blows over. Everybody seems drifting so helplessly and pitifully, and most of them don't even know it. But there's a 24-hour postponement, which may be the first of a series of stalls designed to save Hitler's face—I hope so.

The crew is practising a blackout drill tonight. The boat has every berth taken for its return voyage. But several people have made tentative arrangements for the next one. If I go back, I'll see you again soon—that would be a very bright silver lining on a very big and black cloud. If you get really scared, cable me saying you're dangerously ill or something. I don't think I'm a coward—I think I'm less of one than people who don't do any agonizing. But war is imbecile, patriotism and duty to the state is a silly idea and will soon look so, and my love for you is very, very real. It's a moral love too, or is so long as morality isn't challenged, but the violent murder of millions of innocent people to support a stupid blunderer against a bullying lunatic so that a few millionaires can become multi-millionaires doesn't strike me as a moral issue.

But if war comes, will it be a Marxist or a Spenglerian one? Will it lead at once to socialist revolutions all over Europe and help destroy capitalism, or will it start brutalizing people to the level at which they accept indefinite series of annihilation wars as part of the scheme of things? Both points of view have so much truth in them.

This morning it begins to look as though Hitler was not only getting the Sudenten territory he asked for, but the four-power pact he wanted. A four-power pact with Italy his stooge, Britain his protesting but effectively bullied fag, and France isolated. If Chamberlain's hatred and fear of Russia is as great as his policy would seem to indicate, I'm very much afraid there's no permanent peace that way, and I shall be going through all these ruminations again in six months.

I'd better finish this before I pack. I love you, I love you, I love you. Nothing else seems permanent in the way of peroration.

Norrie

London
Sept. 30 [*1938*]

My dear:

This is my first day in London. I haven't done anything yet except look around: I can't get at my trunk which has the map which has the streets Elizabeth [Fraser] and Harold Taylor live on, and I'm much too dizzy and stupid to talk to anyone anyhow. Except you, of course.

Well, European politics have entered another phase, I think. I don't know what the phase is, but the four-power capitalist pact is its basis, and it may be the beginning of a transition from national to international Fascism. I got up the Channel seeing war all around me and yet knowing it was all over. Cherbourg first, full of submarines and submarine nets and enormous breakwater walls with round towers at regular intervals, anti-aircraft guns built into the rock of the coast, airplanes roaring overhead, and a general feeling that the *real* defences were being camouflaged. A steward assured me that I couldn't see much. (He explained that Cherbourg was a mawnor nyvol byse.) Then Southampton, with searchlights practising on an airplane—seven of them were trained on it, making a huge star-shaped pattern with a gleaming white plane in the centre. Then London. I stayed at the Imperial Hotel, Russell Square, overnight, and when I got up the agreement had been reached. The newspaper posters carried practically nothing except the word "Peace." Everybody took it very calmly—I was surprised that there were no demonstrations, even when it was a nice sunny day. But there were notices everywhere about issuing gas masks and a long notice about what to do during an air raid—a rather silly document adding up to zero. There isn't anything to do in an air raid, except get off the streets, and leave town if you've got the money. I tried to get a tube to Waterloo for my trunk, and found that a lot of important stations, including it, were closed for "structural alterations," i.e., construction of the only sort of air-raid shelter there is in London. I dropped in to the National Gallery and found a large section of it locked away in a "safe" place, including the first picture I tried to see, Piero's *Baptism*. The parks have been torn to pieces to make trenches. All of which equals forty million pounds. Rather an expensive six months' lease—possibly a year's lease—but cheaper than war, and it gives the taxpayer a healthy idea, if he needs one, of what a war would cost. Of course peace may last indefinitely if Hitler finds the 4-power pact easy to work.

We heard a broadcast on the boat to the effect that Cambridge was postponing opening of term "until further notice," and I heard a rumor from a Rhodes man here that Oxford was doing the same thing, though he later had it contradicted. I'll find out definitely tomorrow, but I'm going up Friday anyhow, as my money won't last two weeks. That means that the Universities will close down altogether in the event of war, which would give me an air-tight excuse to go home .... I wonder if they'd close down for any other reason, not involving so much murder?

I stayed overnight in the Imperial Hotel. Then I got a room on Bernard St., just behind Guilford, for 25 / a week, a room exactly as horrible as that would imply. But I can stand anything for a week. When you're not sleeping in my bed other hardships don't matter much.

It's really true about the Penguin slot machines—each book rests on a chute with a plunger beside it, but as there's only room for one copy of each book, unless they want to stuff the whole machine with two or three, they're all practically empty. Otherwise the bookshops are just what they were. The appetite for books on sex, ranging from historical and semi-erudite studies to Marie Stopes, and from scientific studies of perversions to pornography, is as strong as ever, if not stronger. And Bloomsbury believes just as firmly in the imminent revolution in human imagination as it did two years ago. And Hilaire Belloc is revising an already infamous book on the Jews because of the Spanish war, in which Jewish

Communism is trying to smash the Christian (i.e. Catholic) Church . . . .

I may as well get this off: no use letting it lie around to accumulate more news. I'm tidy about the news litters (no pun) I drop on you.

Norrie

Saturday night. Oct. 1st [*1938*]

Kemp has become a don at Oaklawn, a women's residence at 113 Bloor St. W., since Frye's departure for Oxford.

My dearest: I feel rather queer writing to you. I have just had a long bath and washed my hair (still long!) and climbed into my swanky pajamas, and here I am in the don's sitting room. This week has been hectic. You can imagine, after [Martin] Baldwin left me with the bulletin on my hands, as you saw, and there have been exhibitions and groups to talk to and all sorts of interruptions from people wanting to know about loan material etc. Charlie Comfort and me is friends—he and I went to have our voices tested for radio. I read part of my first radio talk and Mr. Harvey called from the receiving room—give it more *umph!* more from the chest! keep it out of the mud! All of which being translated means: —when the voice is resonant enough it sends a needle vibrating widely and that means it will carry to Vancouver. If it is down in the mud it's flat and the needle hardly moves and the result is a monotone that's very dull and can't be heard very far or even stepped up with their instruments. Anyhow they say I'm all right.

Douglas MacAgy is just back from a flying trip to Cleveland where Thomas Munro offered him a job, but he feels he is obliged to go back for another year to Barnes. However, Munro may hold it over a year for him and is expecting him later, in any case. I had dinner with him and his mother tonight at their apartment, and then he had to go out to Carl Schaefer's where Caven Atkins and Paraskeva [Clark] were going to be. Douglas thinks that there are very few artists anywhere who are doing much these days—civilization rocking with bigger issues than a nationalist art is the general drift.

The papers here had us in a fine state all last week. I went in to see Miss Farrell the milliner, and before I left she was nearly in tears, poor dear. I told her you were on your way over, and then we both got onto the young men we knew etc. It was impossible to keep off the subject and as for Hitler's speech—! Every radio in town carried that screech to a group of scared people. I finally decided after half an hour that I'd spent enough time on that lunatic. Besides, his voice gets into the blood and does queer things to you. I gather they made a few million pounds of mess in Hyde Park and other places. And now, as Charlie Comfort says, we've been sold down the river. Cody, the bloated jackass, got the poor innocent freshmen assembled in Convocation Hall and gave them the usual address of welcome and told them all to go to war and fight for a lot of abstract nouns. As somebody said, Cody is a great fighter—he'd get up and fight to the last undergraduate!

Monday evening. Tomorrow I do an extension lecture on Canadian art to the nurses of St. Michael's Hospital. Thanks to your help I'm getting the hang of this lecture idea, and I'm going to go ahead and talk about what I like. Your Surrealism article looks swell and they're sending you the *Forum* out of good feeling etc. to Merton this year.

They've roped me in on the art group again of course, and I had to talk to two separate seekers after truth tonight—I mapped out the scheme for the study group and then they want also to have a practical group. The bulletin went to press. Don Buchanan told me the result of our voice tests—Comfort is best, Baldwin next, Marg [Boultbee] has good volume but reads badly, I read all right but nature didn't give me much volume. I've put myself down for a talk and D.B. said to go ahead—but I think I'll get some coaching from Sterndale Bennett anyhow. Maybe I'd better keep to writing instead of thinking of radio.

I love you like everything and I hope I'll do you credit with the nurses.

Helen

P.S. I'm at 113 Bloor West. I got your letter and cards after some delay.

Oxford
Oct. 7/38

My dear:

I haven't had a letter from you yet, but perhaps the boats haven't started to come in. I'm at Oxford now, settled in with Rodney [Baine] and Mike [Joseph]. I found out that Mike was across the street from me at Bernard St., so I took him up to the Burnetts' for dinner. They liked him very much, I think. Edith is simply worrying herself into a decline over air-raid precautions and gas masks and the rest of it, and is more interested in the news than she's ever been before.

I spent most of your birthday, I regret to say, reading Middle English, instead of going with Mike to what I gathered was a perfectly swell modern version of *Troilus and Cressida* on the general pattern of the *Julius Caesar* we saw. I had an idea there'd be a lot of exams when I got back. There were, but I deliberately skipped the first (well, I overslept) today, and when I went to see Blunden today he told me that things like collections didn't exist for me. He was very friendly and complimentary all round. I really wasn't ready for anything like a test, so I was relieved in one way, though I'd rather have liked a chance at a £20 scholarship, not that it could have been awarded to me on the strength of what I could write at the moment. Blunden said I'd made a big hit with Geoffrey Keynes, which astounded me—I thought I'd made a complete fool of myself. Then he rambled on to the incredible amount of work some people managed to get done, Hitler being an example . . . the year is going to have its difficulties. Then I went to see Bryson, who ignored exams too, and is getting me to come with a New College scholar, and says he's going to push me ahead rather rapidly, starting with the *Pearl*.

The more I think of Oxford Schools the less I care about a first. The examining board is dominated by two bloody fools, Ridley of Balliol and Fletcher of St. Edmund Hall. Ridley has written a miserable book on Shakespeare and his wife started a B. Litt. thesis on Keats which was simply a writing up of the notes to the definitive edition: Ridley pinched it and produced a perfectly useless book called *Keats' Craftsmanship* as a result. No intelligent student can agree with anything he says, and as he has a childishly bad temper and jumps on anyone who disagrees with him, he's pretty bad. It was he who got Mike his second and Rodney his third: Rodney had defended his hated rival in Shakespearean criticism (Stoll) and Ridley's comment was concerned only with his "ill-mannered" writing. Doug [LePan] very nearly lost his first by disagreeing with him on the viva, but made it up later. As for Fletcher, he thinks he knows something about the 17th c.: he doesn't, but I do. However, I'll work ahead and not worry.

We have a sitting room which is quite comfortable, and a bedroom apiece. My bedroom is quite useless for reading in bed, which is no doubt a good thing. The landlady, Mrs. Grylls, is silly and fussy, but if the others can endure her I suppose I can. We talk so much we haven't done any work yet, but we'll doubtless quiet down.

I think I'll spend the Xmas vac. in Paris with Mike—I want to take a good look at the Louvre, make side trips to Chartres, and live cheaply. Apparently France is cheaper than Italy.

I went to a sherry party Elizabeth was having—she'd invited the Burnetts, but they misunderstood the time. Elizabeth is very nervous and keyed up, and I'm really very glad that she's to be in London this year. It's possible to be friendly with her only on her terms, and while I'm glad I met those terms for a year, I'd just as soon not see her too often this time. I'm very fond of her, and don't want to lose patience with her over trivialities.

When I got here I found a huge pile of sandbags outside the buttery. They were going to turn the colleges into hospitals in event of war—a supremely silly idea—you know what their sanitary facilities are, and we're near railway centres and at the big Morris factory. Besides, as Haldane's book on air raids points out, the moral effect of wiping out Oxford in the early stages of the war would no doubt be considerable.

I love you,
Norrie

113 Bloor St. W.
Oct. 12, 1938

My dearest: The most amazing thing has happened—on Tuesday a letter came from you, written from the boat, and on Wednesday, today, the next one came, written from London. I take it that Oxford opened and that you and Mike are in your flat by now.

Tomorrow night I go to a reception at Browns' to meet the new faculty members. I phoned Henry Noyes but have not seen him yet. He was to be busy all this week, and of course tonight the *male* members of staff are having a dinner to look over the additions.

Roy [Kemp] is going to the opening of the *Paintings of Women* show with me on Friday. I asked Henry Noyes but he has a *two-hour* extension class to give each Friday! He will be making a fair amount at that rate. Sounds quite pathetic about his wife. I guess there's just one thing that would make our situation worse and that is if you were in a sanatorium on the Isle of Wight, with T.B. Poor Henry is trying to get her into the country and put her into a hospital here.

I have been reading Eve Curie's *Madame Curie*, which is charming in spots and the early part especially. Later on she reiterates the wonder of their married happiness and the unique genius of her mother to an extent a little hard to bear.

I'm going upstairs to my single bed now and I guess I'll go to sleep. To tell you the honest truth, I'm not awfully keen about this widow's life. I love you so much.

I kiss you goodnight,
Helen

Oxford
[*21 October 1938*]

My dearest girl:

I suppose I have settled down by this time, but I still feel I haven't. At first I thought I simply couldn't live in this place. Mrs. Grylls is fundamentally all right, but she hasn't a brain in her head, and her stupidity is of the flustered, hen-crossing-a-road variety. However, after one terrific row which was based on the fact that a lawyer had told her she should be getting more than she agreed on for Rodney's room, she's settled down and is quite amiable. I don't spend much time here, except on Sundays. I've finally got used to coming down about nine on the bus and staying down for the day, which means that I do a good deal of work, as about the only place to stay is in the libraries. On this arrangement I seem to be spending more money on lunches than two years ago when I sat in my room more, but you can't work if you're weak inside. But the difficulty of manoeuvring from a home some distance away from one's work is a difficulty I'd better get used to if we get a house in the near future.

I've had one tutorial with Blunden and everything seems O.K. I did so little writing last year that now my sentences creak and groan when I try fitting them together. It takes incessant practice. My handwriting is if possible even worse than usual. But if I write & write & write all this year maybe I'll be able to write schools with fair glibness. Blunden—or did I tell you?—was quite firm on my shelving the Blake and getting to work on schools. I still don't like the idea, but I'm docile. My first paper, on Crashaw & Herbert, was badly written, I thought, but Blunden said he saw no falling off in skill, and that if anything my exegesis had improved. This week I'm slaving away at an epic on Vaughan, Traherne, Herrick, Marvell & Cowley, all people I have ideas about. I got a terrible shock when I saw my *Forum* article, as it's nowhere near my standard of writing, and am getting down to business.

I had tea with Alan Jarvis a few days ago and he looks flourishing: very nice rooms in University College. He had several copies of the *Varsity* there, and they looked as funny as hell: Cody being interviewed about Communism in the University, for instance: "There used to be a few Jews with that idea." And then there was an interview with a certain Mrs. Helen Frye about who's going to carry on after Lismer? "We are," said Mrs. Helen. I suspect that the we is pretty editorial. Anyway, I began to feel homesick, or rather, my homesickness got worse for a bit. Alan had been driving all over Europe with Douglas Duncan. He saw the approved German art show, and showed me an illustrated catalogue. Mostly portraits of Nazi gangsters, sentimental evening-on-the-farm pictures intended to illustrate the romance & dignity of the peasantry, and ripe, juicy, luscious nudes—the coming mothers of the race, you see. One of the lousiest of them was bought by Hitler and became the most popular piece in the show.

I started attending lectures the first week—you know what I am. All pretty awful. Nichol Smith wouldn't be bad for my sort of job: getting one point per lecture hammered home, but to me he's prolix & dull. Then there's Tolkien on *Beowulf*, dealing with a most insanely complicated problem which involves Anglo-Saxon genealogies, early Danish histories, monkish chronicles in Latin, Icelandic Eddas and Swedish folklore. Imagine my delivery at its very worst: top speed, unintelligible burble, great complexity of ideas and endless references to things unknown, mixed in with a lot of Latin and Anglo-Saxon and a lot of difficult proper names which aren't spelled, and you have Tolkien on *Beowulf*.

II. Alan got in touch with me again and we went to Sir Michael Sadler's place to look at his art collection. Sir Michael was former Master of Univ. and Alan had an introduction to him from Bickersteth. He has one of the best collections of modern art there are. A lot of sculpture: things from Sierra Leone and Papua besides Despiau and Maillol and Skeaping and Henry Moore (three lovely things in his garden) and Barbara

Hepworth and two lovely Zadkines. Of paintings, there's a very unusual Matisse, 3 Picassos (one rather messy and one a cubist portrait of a young man, very fine), one Klee (curious), two SUPERB Cézanne watercolours, the best Bouvard I've ever seen, three grand Rouaults, about a dozen David Jones (the man Fairley's interested in). There were a lot of Henry Moore things: drawings of a single theme, like Mother and child, pasted on a larger canvas. Then there were several Kandinskys of the explosive firework period, a good Monet, an early Utrillo and a glorious Marc drawing, and a lot of other things I can't think of just now. Sir M. burbles a bit & his wife is trying, but I had a grand time.

I went down to London Saturday & saw the Canadian show. I'll send the article along as soon as I get some of the intelligent weekly comment on it, if any, and you can see what I've said then. They'd put all the shits in one room—Grier, [Kenneth] Forbes, [George A.] Reid & the rest of it—which I found amusing. Skimpy French carving, good Jobins however, skimpier B.C. totem stuff (better in the B.M.), good Krieghoff, a remarkable 18th c. primitivist "Negro Slave" portrait by some Frenchman, two Kanes. Then a sculpture gallery—Betty Hahn had something in tin which was amusing. Loring & Wyle as usual, Jacobine Jones had a good bull, Mannie Hahn a rather impressive horse's head. Then a room with average Group of 7 stuff, a room with two average Milnes—everybody I could think of was there except Brooker & Muhlstock, & Brooker was in the calendar. And a spotty watercolour room. Will Ogilvie, Prudence Heward, Milne (watercolours especially), Thomson and Varley and Pegi Nicol are our best bets, I think. Fairley wasn't there either. I stayed with the Burnetts as usual & they had Elizabeth to dinner.

You remember young Corder whom I used to do violin with? Well, apparently there's now a cello in the college, and they had a trio with a somewhat inadequate pianist last year. So I've seen Allen (we're all out of residence & have to have a residence piano) and he says it's all right to use his. The pianist in question is also a boy I know quite well, a Lancastrian named [Bunny] Mellor, who had me to tea the other day and whom I asked up later—he was writing a paper on Blake. He said he was tired of getting papers back from Blunden with the note "see H.N. Frye about this" scribbled on them—it's happened twice already.

I love you to the verge of monomania.

Norrie

113 Bloor St. W. Toronto
Saturday. October 22, '38

My dear:

I have never written to you before on a typewriter, and I have no idea how it may turn out. I have been sticking somewhat closely to one lately as I suddenly decided to give Henri Masson a note in the *Forum* and I have been writing letters for future articles—I asked Blunt to do the one on the London show and I am hoping to get Eric Brown to come to life again in the Magazine (that cap was a mistake).

I am sorry that my letters were late in reaching you, I did try to send you news as often as I could, and you will just have to blame it all on the Paintings of Bitches Show. We are getting along fairly well at the A.G. of T. There is certainly enough to do, but I think we will manage nicely. I have Allan Armstrong, the graduate in architecture, to help me with loan exhibitions and to label lantern slides—he looks like a tremendous help, even after one week's trial. I am in the midst of two articles—the one for the *Star* on murals, and my radio talk for Nov. 1. I am trying to get that last one done this weekend because I have to go over it with Sterndale Bennett on Tuesday, and just now my head is so clogged up that I can't think of even a good way to begin. I called it, "Everyman Looks at Art." I am learning how to breathe with my diaphragm and how to talk as if I were in Massey Hall—he says there's hope even if I am only 5'1" with a small chest expansion, that doesn't matter. Anyway he does help my self-confidence. And the voice.

I blew myself to two season tickets to the Music Masters Series at Eaton's Auditorium, the first concert being by Lhévinne. Two groups of Chopin, one of Debussy, and the last was all Liszt. Can you beat it? I phoned Henry Noyes and asked him to go with me. We went out to dinner at the Babloor first and wound up there again afterwards which did a lot toward consoling me of the lack of a better program. Henry tells me that the music group starts this Monday. Mine started last week, with some twenty kids down at the Gallery to see the show.

Last Tuesday at noon, the Faculty Women's Association luncheon was held at Wymilwood, and I went just to keep on keeping the home fires burning. I sat beside Kay Riddell who told me about their difficulties with Gordon Webber who announced to the class that they would not do any drawing or painting this year at all, but that they were going to make constructions in three dimensions out of all sorts of materials. None of the women want to do it, but none of them would tell him so, but just went off in corners, grumbling to themselves. I told Kay to talk to him about it because just because be was hipped on Moholy-Nagy's ideas is no reason why they must all make wind machines etc. for the rest of the year. Magda [Arnold] and I got out after they had introduced the two new wives and left them to the rest of their meeting.

Sunday night. I really don't like writing to you on a typewriter. It doesn't seem like talking to you, not right to you, it is more like giving you an official report on my official life. Norrie, I'm doing a lot of new things this year and getting away with it. I'm developing a voice, for instance. I was practising reading at home this afternoon—booming at Mother from the kitchen to the front room. She is quite interested, and helps me. I have some exercises—aforementioned—which are helping, and I can do them almost anywhere. One month ago today you left, and I am so glad there are only nine more at most—besides I may get there before that. Do you need money? I can send you some if you do. Do you want me to send you your stories submitted to the *Atlantic Monthly*? They were left behind. Do try to start the Blake on its rounds. And although I do understand about the damned Oxford first and those stupid examiners, yet I still think a first a matter of good politics; surely you can put up with the morons for nine months. My best to Mike and Rodney.

Love,
Helen

113 Bloor St. W. [*Toronto*]
[*27 October 1938*]

My dear: It is eleven o'clock and I've been plunking away all evening on my radio talk for next Tuesday, but I've just seen in the paper that the *Bremen* is leaving soon, with this for you, I hope. I get so disgusted: I wrote some of the WORST DRIVEL for that talk and scrapped it, and I now have a fairly straightforward piece of writing but it may have too many ideas in it: I don't know. I read some of the DRIVEL to Mr. Bennett and it sounded pretty lousy to me—I was trying to be chatty about what people think of art and I packed in all the worst clichés I could think of. Now that I have got that off my chest I hope that I *never* start anything that way again. I've been working darned hard—for me. I've got this article still to finish for the *Star*, and the radio talk, and my Thursday lecture on the Devil was today, also a talk to the Vic kids in the college with a lantern. About 25 or 30 turned out, and I think it went off very well—I gave them the "What's Beautiful" talk again.

Pelham Edgar was in the Gallery today talking to Baldwin about the speech he's going to make to open the R.C.A. show next month. I had a chat with him: he said he was glad I was down there, and I was taking Lismer's place wasn't I? I told him I was, at any rate for the time being. He asked me what was the news from you and patted my shoulder when he left. You'd better send him a card—*definitely* one at Christmas. Baldwin thinks my idea for the Chinese show is swell—go ahead. I've got to start on that right away. I've decided to do some talking to a large group too—150 women teachers one evening. No use getting my voice all trained if I don't practise.

Kay Coburn has someone typing her Coleridge ms. in my room during the day on the typewriter I rented. Kay still talks of moving out of residence, so does [Laure] Rièse, a sort of Utopian dream of theirs.

I haven't any news except dinner last night with Agnes Beatty at the Babloor—radio talk all evening then a short walk with Herta [Hartmanshenn]. Guess I'll go to bed. I sometimes dimly imagine that I used to go to bed with you, but maybe I'm dreaming. I don't let myself think of that very often, or else I might get unhinged. It would never do for a don to get the weeps, and my jaw is getting stern. I love you *so* much.

Goodnight my dear,
Helen

Oxford
Oct. 28/38

My sweet pet: I've been working quite hard this week because I got two letters from you Monday morning. I got up feeling restless and not wanting to work, and I knew there'd be a letter for me. I've been here a month now, and there can hardly be more than eight more before I'll be seriously thinking of going back. Oh, my dear! The curious part of it is that I'm lonesome for Toronto as well as you—I hardly expected that, but there it is.

I'm completely disgusted with the way the English mags wrote up the Canadian show. There was some damned good stuff in it as well as a lot of tripe. But nobody seemed energetic enough to get beyond the tripe room. *The New Statesman* was the worst as usual—they made me so furious I wrote them a letter, which they won't publish. They gave it (the two "historical" rooms was of course all they looked at) five sentences and said something about "Morris"—obviously Morrice. I picked that one up and suggested that the critic was wrongly directed by the attendant to the pre-Raphaelite room.

Mike had two New Zealand friends in for the weekend. They're all good-natured Catholics and their conversation is an incredible saga of drunkenness, venereal disease and "affairs." And they have very disreputable relatives, which abashed me, as I haven't any except an uncle who burned his house and tried to burn his wife (dad's sister) for the very sordid rewards of insurance. [Dan] Davin had an aunt who ran a bawdy house, an uncle who was hanged and a grandfather whose handlebar whiskers kept getting in the soup. The last was the only one who really repelled him. The hanged man was subsequently proved innocent, and when I expressed horror and sympathy Davin said: "Oh, well, he deserved to be hanged anyway." New Zealand Irish proletariat, Joyce's material transplanted.

Recital of old music at Brasenose one evening, with some versatile blighter playing the virginals (Byrd, Bull & Handel), the recorder (Handel), the "viola d'amore" (six strings above the bridge and six below), and singing in a choir which did Gibbons, Campion and Byrd. Swell fun. And the trio is really functioning. We did two hours in Allen's rooms and did six Haydns, including the three you did. The more enjoyable the things I do here, the more homesick I get. The cellist is a good lad—has an uncanny ability to count measures.

I think I mentioned Charlie Bell, Mississippi, Rhodes Scholar at Exeter. He's doing a B. Litt.: printing Chaucer's *Knight's Tale* with a translation of the Boccaccio poem Chaucer got it from. As he doesn't know any Italian he's got a job ahead of him. Or at any rate not much. Well, he's not quite living with a very pretty little widow he's engaged to and he has a piano and a collection of records and she's in the Bach choir. She also bought herself a recorder, on my advice. So I think the Bell ménage is likely to be something of a retreat for me this year.

Odi et amo, as Catullus would say. I love you and I hate not being able to. Bless you, darling.

Norrie

[*Toronto*]
Friday. Nov. 4, 1938

My dear: I have meant to write to you all week, but this has been one of those weeks—thank goodness it is about over. The bulletin is about due and I am debating about speakers for the R.C.A. show—I'm putting in the "What Does the Artist See?" series for my talks, which, by the way, need a good deal of pushing again. We haven't done anything about it and I've only had ten people out to each of them so far. We expect Lismer up to do a talk toward the end of the month and I've sent him a telegram as to *when*, but so far, no answer. My radio talk was all right, Baldwin liked it—my voice was a little high was his one criticism, but clear and with more variation. W.G. Constable was here this week and gave a typical Constable lecture on 18th Century British Portraiture—suave and aristocratic and all the rest. It took me back to that year at the Institute with such a smack that I walked home through the park and blew up on the Rièse doorstep. We went off and had some beer and reviled everyone we could think of, quite cheerfully.

I'm getting disgruntled about things lately. There isn't any life in this organization, at least I don't think so. And I get fed up with the residence too, it isn't nearly as tolerable as it was two years ago. I guess I'm getting aged. Sometimes I think I'll clear out, but I know I won't. Here's a compliment for you—Alice Eedy told Elizabeth [Eedy] that you were the best lecturer she had ever had. Elizabeth says she's always coming home and complaining about this guy Maclean. You mustn't mind when I grouse about staying here, it helps me to put it on paper, and you're the only one I know who will take it for what it's worth. Besides, the other night I got so mad because someone asked me AGAIN how it feels to be a grass widow and I said I'm having a grand time etc., and then wished to hell I'd let her have the works and told her. It was Louise Comfort, and Brieger was there in one of his Germanly masculine moods—he said how nice for you—to be in Oxford. So it must be swell.

Tell me if you need any money and I'll send you some—let me know right away or else you may be stranded without anything from Little. Because I may go off on a trip somewhere and spend a lot if you don't warn me. I'm so glad you saw Sir Michael Sadler's collection. Mellors have a good one here just now—French Painting—with two swell Modigliani's, some good Pissarro's etc.

With love,
Helen

Oxford
Nov. 8 [*1938*]

Darling:

It's been a long time since my last letter: I must get down to business and write oftener. I don't miss you so much when I write often, and I'm rather gloomy just now, this being November, the nadir (I hope) of the English year. Christmas cards are already being advertised in the windows. I like thinking of Christmas, because when it's Christmas it's only a week from 1939, and 1939 is the year I see you again. And hear you again. Your voice seems to have been expanding steadily ever since I left, and I'm looking forward rather nervously to my encounter with a blinding glare of purple and a stentorian roar of: "HOW ARE YOU?"

I've been working like hell on my papers for Blunden, who seems delighted with them and suggests a harder one each week. Last week I tied myself in fearful knots over a paper on the character book. That drew a suggestion for exploring 17th c. scientific works, so I'm quitting work for the term, as far as extras are concerned.

The trio goes on merrily. Yesterday we tried to read a Brahms—simple for them, but I couldn't do it at all—and a Ravel, which wasn't simple for anybody. I bought the Haydn minuets. We can play the Haydn C major (the hard one) with quite a flourish now.

I spend quite a bit of time at Charlie Bell's, whose ménage I think I described. Charlie has a lot of good records, including the first five of the *Zauberflöte*, and I think I'll take Alan Jarvis over tomorrow night. He also has a complete set of reproductions of Bellini's sketchbook drawings.

I went to the first meeting of the Bodley Club. A paper on "The English in India" by an Anglo-Indian, breezy and bawdy—a typical Bodley Club paper. Answered by an enormously erudite but rather ponderous and humorless Hindu. Developed into a dog-fight between them. For me who doesn't know a nabob from a cheeroot, pretty dull. I rather rashly volunteered a paper: my idea about *A Short History of the Devil*. I haven't much time, but I've more than I shall have later on.

Now, sweetheart, there's more to write about than that, but I've just dashed this off until I can think of something more. I had a nightmare yesterday morning. I dreamed I was living with you again, and then I woke up.

Thank you, dear, but I don't need any money yet, and I hope I shan't for a few months. I love you.

Norrie

I've just got the new *Forum* and I think your little Henri Masson article is nice. I think you're nice.

Oxford
Nov. 9/38

I don't know why I forgot to tell you in my last note (I remember saying there was more to tell if I could remember what it was) that I went to London with Mike last Saturday to see the Picasso *Bombing of Guernica*. All the studies he'd made for it were there too, studies of bulls, murdered horses, and weeping men and women mostly. The *Weeping Woman* we saw at Toronto was there. I was glad to see those: I couldn't have got much out of the picture itself without them, and they had a vivid impact and a unity I wasn't sure about with the big one. If I'd had more time, though, I think the big pattern would have got hold of me. It's the best contemporary work I've ever seen, I'm quite sure of that. Then we went to a show—one of Hitchcock's, the man who did the *39 Steps*. I liked it even better than that: I think it was called *The Lady Vanishes*. Then we had dinner with Stephen & Edith. They've done so much for me I'd like to get them something for Christmas, but don't know what to get except books, which they have too many of now, unless you could get Edith some silk stockings, which are in great demand in England. Her size is 10, but perhaps you'd better look up her mother.

Joe Reid, the Winnipeg-man-with-the-room-over-mine-two-years-ago-who-made-the-Oxford-Group-confession, dropped into our place on Sunday. He came over on the boat with someone who told him, he thought, that he was going to study geology at Cambridge. He mentioned my name, and the chap said, "Oh, yes, I know Frye: I married Frye." Joe said he didn't look like a sodomite and he didn't think I was one, so he asked again what he was studying at Cambridge and Cragg said "theology."

There's a funny chap in Merton called Mellor, who cultivates me a bit. He's a good example of Mike's remark that all you need to do to become the centre of a cult in Oxford is walk down the High Street with your pants on backward. His particular idiosyncrasy is a beard. He plays the piano, badly, and runs one of the Oxford magazines. Nice kid: my description isn't hostile. He had a 21st birthday last night, and was sent about 30 complimentary pints of beer: his table was a sea of amber. Then we adjourned to his room and really started drinking. A contemporary of LePan's, an enormously erudite philologist and quite good pianist named Brooks, passed out around 10:30, practically disappearing in a fog of puke, which broke up the party. Largely because he kept pouring port into his beer. I went home comparatively ignorant of philology but quite safe inside, knowing more about fruit and grain alcohol.

I love you and I miss you horribly. I keep on dreaming about you and waking up again. I wish I could just stay asleep and wake up in July.

Norrie

113 Bloor Street West
Toronto. Nov. 10, '38

My dearest: I don't know what to do about that fool Canadian show—I wrote to Anthony Blunt for an article and nothing has happened: I've had no answer. I might write to Eric Newton, but in the meantime please send me along yours so that we will have at least one article on it. Probably the best one, but you know how it is with people—an English critic would be a good idea if he had anything worthwhile to say. I met Fritz Brandtner last Saturday at the Picture Loan and got enough for an article on him for this issue. Speaks very well, another of these revolutionary artists—but very full of vitality and pleasantly sure of himself. I liked him very much. Poor old Douglas Duncan has had to carry on practically alone because his committee is away—like Peggy [Kidder] and Norah [McCullough]—or else busy with other things and have just left him holding the bag.

I have had a busy week, but get a holiday tomorrow—Armistice Day—and hope to get caught up on some things. I have a talk to give Marjory King's L.S.R. group on mural painting, and a short article for a school magazine on the value of art to the individual or some damn thing, and this note for the *Forum*. This week I gave various talks in the Gallery—I went to Mr. Bennett on Tuesday for a lesson, at noon, and it was a terribly rainy day. I *was* low, and I couldn't get any pep into a talk at all. I practised making a speech to him—since the radio talk was over we were trying this other thing. He spent all the time making me snap out of that and remembering that I'm top dog in my field so far as those teachers were concerned. Those teachers were the Women Teachers Association that came on Wednesday night. I was scared, for some reason, as I haven't done one of the evening groups so far. Sterndale Bennett worked hard on my ego, though, and by the time I had to talk I made a good job of it, of course. There were 180 people there last night, and they could all hear me, and I talked away about the exhibition and had a good time.

I didn't give the Libido talk today although it was listed for today, because I didn't have time to get new slides. So I talked about pictures in the show, and it went over very well. There were eleven out—my devoted followers! It is getting much easier for me, this talking, but I do get flustered sometimes without you to keep me in good shape. I had to dash up this afternoon and talk to the Vic kids on the Ugly Pictures in the Middle Ages—they seemed quite interested. Sixteen out. It still is not up to your crowd.

Mike's friends sound pretty overwhelming. I'm glad you're a married man. I'm glad you have a trio and Charlie Bell's ménage sounds like a blessing. Betty Mihalko says last year she enjoyed her work but she is bored this year. I don't know whether that has anything to do with you or not. But I know this year lacks something pretty fundamental as far as I'm concerned. Two more weeks and two months are gone. Every day I count it up but the time doesn't go fast enough.

I love you,
H.

Well, here's a long P.S. I've just phoned [George] Grube and he suggests you get in touch with Anthony Blunt and ask him whether he can do the article for us, and if he can't then ask Eric Newton, who is I think art critic on the *Manchester Guardian*. McCurry suggests asking him and I think that is a good scheme. Would you mind? I know it is a nuisance but it takes so long from this end, and to get an article for the January issue we'll have to have it here by Dec. 10th which is the date for going to press. I can't ask for a Newton article if Blunt is doing one, and if you have any luck tracking down Blunt you can find out where we stand. I'll enclose my letter to Blunt which you can send back later.

Again about that article—please send yours along as I said before.

P.S. Had a letter from Barbara: do please look her up next time you're in London. Sturgis: 56 Scarsdale Villas. W8.

113 Bloor West, Toronto
November 21, 1938

My dear: I was terribly sorry to find that I was too late last week to catch a boat, and then I put off writing to you until the end of the week because there was so much to do.

Tuesday: I talked to a group of the L.S.R. on mural painting. There were only about fifteen people there, and they straggled in half an hour late, and the leader of the group was a very nice woman who ran in all out of breath because she attends a dressmaking class that night from six to eight and then has to go to the study group after that.

Wednesday night was the Vic Alumnae dinner in the Round Room at Eaton's, but I didn't go. Mrs. Bennett spoke on Canadian literature—and they said it was a very good evening, but I felt so exhausted that I phoned home and bolted out to Danforth. Harold pulled out his whole bag of tricks and we had a grand time, eating dinner in the kitchen, as it was a cold night, and there were just four of us at home.

Thursday: I went to dinner at the Havelocks'—the Briegers were there and Marcus Tate. We had lots of cocktails and Havelock was quite rude to Brieger and told him he had had too many, and we were all very hilarious and the dinner was excellent. After dinner we drove over in Havelock's ramshackle car to hear Harold King give a lecture on Art and the L.S.R. at the Heliconian Club. I had a swell time. They asked for you, and there was a lot of joking about the fact that Marcus Tate thought I was married to Roy the last time he saw me at the Hart House musicale. I think you and I are very much in the good graces of the L.S.R. I am certainly beginning to feel admitted to a charmed circle.

Friday: completely exhausted and went to bed—not without a good deal of wishing you were on this side of the water. But there, I can't tell you how much I love you and how much I miss you—not on this damned clanking typewriter.

Saturday: Santa Claus Parade, which I went to see, and ran into Alec MacDonald who inquired very kindly about you. In the evening I went to the first meeting of the Artists' Forum which met at Harold King's. He spoke on Daumier and Cézanne, and gave an exceedingly interesting talk. The committee this year is Rik Kettle, Harold King and myself, with Jean [Lennox] as secretary again.

Sunday: slept in until eleven, skipped the Chancellor's sermon at chapel on the present situation, went home for dinner and we had a most hilarious time. Harold and I practised Haydn trios all afternoon while Roy worked at the studio taking a picture of that wonderful dog of Smiths'. Then I went to Fairleys' for the evening and met the Wilkinsons—he is the new medieval history man and his wife is one of the jolliest women I've met. Mrs. Fairley said she'd been wanting to send her love—so she did and she does.

Monday: letters at the gallery—reminding everybody in town to come to Lismer's lecture next Monday. I gather he's going to blow the lid off, but I'm going to have a good audience there for whatever sort of combustion it turns out to be.

I will phone Mrs. Manning re gift for Edith and try to send it off soon.

I'm turning a bright green at all the exhibitions you're seeing—but never mind, I'm developing a VOICE. Tomorrow night I talk to 300 women from the Settlement! Art for the char—in words of one syllable, but loud.

It is queer—tonight I feel all practical and business-like and like covering half-a-dozen more pages to you. And on Friday and Saturday every inch of me was ready to scream that I wanted to touch you and be beside you, and I couldn't put up with this any longer. The psychologists can have it—I don't give a damn. I'm married to you and therefore I can surely admit that I want to be with you so badly that sometimes—Oh well, I expect you know what I mean.

I like your article on the Canadian show and I think we'd better run it along with the other which I do hope you can dig up. And soon.

My love to you,
Helen

[*Toronto*]
Dec. 1, 1938

My dearest: My friend at the Post Office tells me that mail closes for the *Queen Mary* this afternoon so here goes:

Lismer had us all thrilled and up in the air for the weekend—you can imagine. Looking well, but not liking New York, wishing he were back here, but all being friendly with Baldwin etc. He turned up unexpectedly on Saturday—I had been told that he was coming late on Sunday—and was there to staff meeting, and had to be interviewed by the *Star* and the *Telegram* and the *Globe and Mail*. We had a staff party on Monday after his lecture, which increased considerably when we asked others who had not as yet had a chance to speak to A.L. [Arthur Lismer]. Lismer's lecture *Art and Democracy* you can imagine, a summary of world conditions with great energy and highly elaborated, with cracks at fascist dictators and warnings to us to sweep our own doorsteps—then three quarters of an hour, slides rushed through quickly with little comment. The whole thing took an hour and a half and somebody may have got a clear impression, but I doubt it. Baldwin said next morning to me that A.L. gave a fine lecture, but it was a shame that it wasn't written and read better—that he somehow summarized all the things we'd been talking about this year, and that he agreed with all of it. Lismer's coming did not clear up any of our problems and it was just as I expected—that we'd have to carry on with our own ideas and meet new situations as best we can. Lismer doesn't think Norah will be back at all—but then that is just a guess.

Norrie my dear, I'll write you a better letter when I feel better—but I sent you that night letter re *Canadian Forum* article because I would like to get it for January, as well as yours. I hope you can dig it up. I'm trying to find out from Mrs. Manning whether there's anything else beside stockings that Edith would like.

My love to you,
H.

London
[*6 December 1938*]

Sweetheart:

Term's over, and I'm in London. I'm sorry if I was remiss about the *Forum* article: you've got mine by now, of course, but I thought Blunt was your first choice. I didn't know where he was, but took your word for it that Newton was on the *Guardian*. I'll wire again if I get an answer from him. The show lasts here till the end of December, so there's really no hurry.

I stopped work for Blunden this last week, but was kept busy writing this paper on the devil for the Bodley Club. It turned out fairly well, although I didn't get the exact quotations I wanted. It was one of my breathtakingly erudite efforts, and everyone was terrifically impressed. Mike answered it, and was very intelligent: condensed and summarized the whole paper extempore, when he hadn't heard it before. Considering that most of the members were half tight, it being the last night of the term, and considering the terrific speed at which the paper had to be read in order to get the discussion through by midnight, they were quite bright about it.

Barbara dropped into Oxford in course of a hike. She seemed to be quite well: I took her to dinner and to the Playhouse, although of course she would insist on paying her own way. The play was a melodrama by Henry Arthur Jones, quite the best dramatist, except Shaw, of the 1890 period. The play had obviously been doctored to make it a typical melodrama and the actors burlesqued it. The undergraduates, who have got it firmly wedged into their foolish little noodles that no melodrama is to be admired, joined in enthusiastically. I was rather sorry, because the play really had guts, and there were plenty of really bad and much funnier plays of the period they could have done. The next day she came to lunch with Rodney and Mike.

Breakfast with the Chaplain with three other undergraduates. I talked to him about my devil paper afterward and, although I still don't think he's any great shakes, I got a slightly higher opinion of his faculties. I'm told I terrified him so much two years ago he kept saying all last year: "Oh, well, of course, *Frye*—" with a deprecatory smile whenever my assaults on the citadel of Anglican smugness were mentioned.

I seem to be carrying this letter all over London and writing at it everywhere: at the moment I'm the guest of New Zealand House, where I'm to meet Mike. I dropped in on Edith & Stephen but their refugee is still with them.

Look here, I have a bit more to say, but I never seem to be able to get this letter finished, so I'll post it and start on a new one. I love you.

Norrie

Paris
[*11 December 1938*]

Sweetheart:

I think I told you about everything that happened in London except that Mike and I, as usual, went to three art exhibitions. The first was in Tooth's, Epstein's drawings to Baudelaire's *Fleurs du Mal* and some rather indifferent Paul Nash, who I think does landscape and semi-abstract things very well and out-and-out surrealism not nearly so well. The Epstein things I like very much: very sophisticated people were telling each other to go if they liked Epstein but not if they liked Baudelaire, but I thought they were quite swell whatever one thought of Baudelaire. Some of them very Blakean. He'd stressed the symbolism and ignored the cheap sensationalism, and made a very good thing of his subject.

I crossed the Channel without mishap, although it was rough. Our first stop was Rouen. (I'm travelling with both Mike and Rodney.) France is a bit awkward at the moment because all the stained glass has been packed away in boxes during "le moment critique," and we may have to postpone Chartres till after Christmas. We saw the cathedral, though, and St. Ouën, and the Art Gallery.

This is our first day in Paris. We got in last night. We went to see Saint-Chapelle and Notre Dame. That took us till 3, and as everything closes at 4 in the winter time, when it gets dark, there wasn't much to do but poke around in some smaller churches. Then we went to a big bookstore and ran into a couple of Oxford Canadians—Jack Garrett and a Balliol man—and had a drink with them.

I forgot to mention the Art Gallery at Rouen—there was a Despiau show on—mostly heads, and three full-length nudes. It's part of an organized attempt to show Parisian artists in the provinces, and provincial ones in Paris. French art galleries are irritating: you have to go on and on to the very latest Impressionists and the stuff keeps up its quality to the very end, while in Italy you can always quit at the 16th century.

Oh, darling, I want so much to cover all this ground with you: England, France, Italy: I don't care so much about Germany until they throw the Nazis out. Italy's bad enough, but it's so incredibly rich a country. But I want you with me, and the more I see the more homesick I get. And *don't* spend all your money on a trip with Rièse or somebody—not yet. I still have hopes you may come over. I could put in a very pleasant month or so, however much money we may have. No matter what we do, we're no more reckless than Europe itself.

Practically everyone in Paris is English or American.

I love you,
Norrie

Paris
[*11 December 1938*]

Postcard of Picasso's Guernica. *The reference in the first sentence is to the postcard itself.*

I bought this in London, of course: I've carried it around in my pocket till it looks the way it does. Second day in Paris. I've had my first look at the Louvre—painting. Also I've had a Mandarin-Curasol and a Lune-Citron and an Amer-Picon and a Byrrh and a Cointreau and I feel like kissing a policeman and my head spins and I'm quite sozzled and I love you very much. Don't worry: I'll settle down in a day or two and reopen the subject of English Lit.

Norrie

Paris
1938 Dec 19

Telegram; addressed to Helen Frye at the Art Gallery of Toronto.

NEWTON WILL DO ARTICLE MERRY XMAS LOVE=

NORRIE

Paris
[*25 December 1938*]

Sweetheart:

I've neglected you shamefully since I've come to Paris: part of the reason is about ten *New Yorker*s, which I got, and thanks. I also got the *Forum* with your article on Fritz Brandtner, which I liked. Newton sent me a very decent note: I think he'll pan the show, so it'd be just as well if his article and mine about imbecile English critics were printed in separate issues.

Also, Mike, in his quiet way, has kept me going about 24 hours a day. Rodney's been away a week, touring cathedrals in Normandy. We went to the Louvre several times, including one night show: they're too tight to turn the lights on these dark winter afternoons, but they floodlight certain exhibitions at night. So medieval ivories and Limoges enamels really came out where we could see them. And the Musée de Luxembourg, dullish except for the Bourdelle Hercules and a superb Rouault vernicle. And contemporary modern painting at the Jeu de Paume—some lovely Kandinskys and a Klee and a Chagall. Notre Dame of course: the famous gargoyle has had his face lifted. And the huge ethnographical Musée de l'Homme in the Trocadéro: anthropology: primitive and peasant work, beautifully laid out. Two concerts: one a small orchestra playing four Bach piano concerti and a Pergolesi, the other the Pro Arte Quartet playing the Ravel, Franck and Debussy Quartets.

We met Rodney in Chartres. It suddenly turned freezingly cold—about zero weather, and the coldest since 1879, I understood from the papers. As you can imagine, looking at the sculptures outside Chartres was no fun at all. Inside there was a warm register in the north transept we stood on most of the time. But they were taking out a couple of windows beside it and digging in the floor of the nave and kept opening the big west door, so it was pretty barn-like inside too. I'm afraid I thought more about my toes than about the medieval soul, but then I was too short-sighted to see the glass properly anyway. However, I know pretty well what's there to be seen. Darling, we simply must cover Europe ourselves within the next year or two. If we can't make it this summer we'll meet in New York and see it instead, but sometime very soon you and I are going to see everything I've already seen and a lot more too. I don't know why I feel so strongly that I have to see things with you before I feel I've really seen them—probably just because I'm terribly lonesome for you and have never done any travelling with you. But I do, and I'm never really happy no matter what I'm seeing.

This is Christmas night. Last night, the 24th, another month went by. Next week will be 1939, and I think time will go faster then. Last night we went to L'Eau de France, a place the Burnetts had recommended, for dinner: the sort of place where chefs come around with huge alcohol lamp affairs and serve the food on the table. Then we went to Midnight Mass at St. Eustache: a very good choir, with a lot of Bach and several carols. We got home about 2:30.

I hope you found something amusing in the stuff I sent you. That's another reason I want you here: so we can go shopping and I can get you the things you really want.

I gave Rodney and Mike a volume of Émile Mâle apiece, and they gave me a French "History of Contemporary Art"—one of the Cahiers d'Art, and a huge tome, awkward to carry. I was very enthusiastic about it at first, but it follows pretty stock lines: starts with Cézanne, follows with the later impressionists, and from there on is Picasso, Braque, & Matisse, with variations. Still, it will be good fun for me and probably useful to you when the much-wished-for next year rolls around.

Rodney and Mike are fond of movies and drag me around to a lot of them. I've seen the French version of *Snow White*, which gave her a better voice.

I'm quitting now; I'm sleepy. I'll resume in a day or two. Oh, Mike and I spent a day at Versailles. We sort of felt we had to. And when you get in the dead centre of all the algebra and sit down there the sheer monstrosity of the scheme *does* get you, all right, like Hitler's voice.

[*Toronto*]
January 4, 1939

My dear: I've just got back to work, to Oaklawn and to Toronto, not terribly reconciled, after a grand week with Vera in Chicago. I do wish I'd seen Chicago years ago before I ever thought of Europe, then London need not have knocked me flat so completely: It was my first big city, after all, wasn't it! You can imagine all the things we did—we went to the Art Institute and the Oriental Institute, the University, and the Bauhaus, Marshall Fields, the Museum of Science and Industry, the Aquarium. We talked of a great many things, Vera and I, and we got on together beautifully. She said she was glad I thought of coming, and I don't know when I have had such a good time. She took me to *Little Sweden* and we had a drink of glug—their Christmas drink of heated wine. When I got back to Toronto it seemed to have shrunk badly, but now, as usual, it is settling into its normal routine, and so am I.

I wish you'd start thinking about finances after March and let me know what you are planning. I need a new coat just now and if I get it I'll be starting from scratch again by the first of February, so that it will take some time for me to save much. I thought of going to New York and New England if Europe is out of the question, and of course I'm expecting to do it with you, or at least some of it. But *how* are you getting enough to keep you there in the summer, even if I do? Or if I came over in the spring—what then? You figure out something and if you can borrow enough perhaps I can come.

I had a crazy time getting your magazines out of Customs. Thanks so much, Norrie. I liked them very much and I love you very much.

Helen

Paris
[*5 January 1939*]

The letter from Kemp referred to in the first paragraph is missing.

Sweetheart:

Still in Paris. It's now 1939, which is the year I go home. I got a sweet little letter from you at the American Express the other day, and I opened it when I was drinking an apéritif with Mike and a Rhodes Scholar Merton Freshman named Weismiller who has published a book of poems —not bad Robert Frost stuff. But I shut it up quickly because I didn't think I could face both it and the other people at the same time. Any one of your letters can give me a choking feeling that interferes with a Cinzano, but this one seemed to live and breathe you so much that the bottom just dropped out of Paris, and there was I, homesick and miserable. I can't let myself get that way, though, and I don't as a rule. You're so sweet you must be all a dream. Often you are.

New Year's Eve Mike and I went to a Montparnasse cafe full of Americans, and stayed there until six in the morning. Some friends joined us and we had a fair time. But that afternoon I'd drunk several apéritifs on practically no breakfast and no lunch and got a bit unsteady. I was conscious of everything I was doing, including the fact that I was making obscene remarks about Chamberlain at the top of my voice, but I was dizzy. New Year's Eve is fun, with everybody lit and good-natured and trying to sing the *Marseillaise* and *God Save the King* without knowing the words. About four we sobered up and went out for breakfast.

I don't feel that I have enough French for a haircut, so I'll just let it grow. I told the boys it was because I liked being conspicuous: people look at me: it's true that they laugh, but they look. I made this remark in a restaurant, and had barely made it when a whore came over and started stroking it—my hair, I mean, not the remark or the restaurant. Mike and Rodney roared, and the whore, who had missed the context, was quite annoyed. However, she recovered, and said that after she'd seen her "cousin" (the man with her) off at the station she'd meet me in some café or other "pour en faire des bêtises ensembles." Hideous hag. I suppose there are good-looking whores, but heaven knows where they are—they probably don't have to get out of bed.

Well, I seem to have told you all my good stories and here it is two o'clock and I go to Amiens tomorrow. And I've told you about nothing but dissipation, whereas I only dissipated Christmas and New Year's and remained cold sober the rest of the time. So please discount accordingly: the serious part will follow tomorrow night.

Well, now I'm in Amiens. This is the town my brother [Howard Frye] was killed in: only I don't know whether he's buried near here or in the Canadian cemetery at Vimy. Or rather, I don't know where his cross is: I suppose the bomb that hit him did the burying. We went through

Beauvais too, which turned out much better than I expected: it was thrilling with that terrific reaching for height and those superb flying buttresses. We have no guidebook and are probably missing a lot, but we stumbled over another very interesting church in the same town called St. Étienne. In case you didn't see it, there's one thing in it that's been giving me nightmares. Just as we were going out of the church, I saw a big wooden statue of a crucifixion. It caught my eye because that's a very bad and very rare medium for a crucifixion, and as I looked at it it got worse: the lines were all out and the face was awful and everything was all wrong, but wrong in a curiously subtle and direct way. Finally we got a book on the church and found it represented a legend of a Christian betrothed to a pagan who prayed to the Virgin to make her ugly, and woke up the next morning with a beard. Her father was furious and had her crucified. It's one of the most wilfully grotesque things I've ever seen. Amiens is a grand cathedral too: I like the sculpture better in some ways than Chartres: anyway the symbolism is better organized and more completely worked out.

I don't know if I told you about Yves Tinayre's concert. He's a baritone—I heard him in London. He can sing anything, and is a scholar who digs up superb stuff out of manuscripts besides. He gave a long talk to a very small audience and followed it with a programme of 17th c. music. And there was a big fashionable well-attended Ravel concert, on the anniversary of his death. Everybody and everything absolutely first-class—I can't imagine where such extraordinary artists come from. A singer, a violinist, a pianist, a harpist, a conductor, any one of whom would have been a sensation at home or in England.

We made a tour of exhibitions one afternoon, one a grand show with a lot of Klee and some Laurens sculpture. But what's the good of it all when I can't have you? Six months more of my sentence to work out. Oh, darling, I think I'll bust if I don't see you soon. I wish I could fly.

I could fly as straight as an arrow,
To visit my wife over there,
If I could excrete my marrow,
And fill my bones with air.

God bless you, sweetheart,
Norrie

[*Toronto*]
January 29, 1939

Norrie my dear—I've neglected you rather lately, but I'll tell you what has happened since I wrote. I gave a gallery talk on American painting for one thing—that had me worried but I think it turned out rather sensibly. The Wace Lectures in Victoria College were about bits of pottery they'd found in Crete, and proved something or other different about the trade routes of the Greeks. I just went to one and then I drifted over to hear Douglas Bush the following night at Hart House. Humanism in the Renaissance. He's a big brawny square-headed creature with a flat middle-western accent, and he sidles onto the platform and begins a lecture in a monotone which keeps on with no variation except an upward half-tone inflection, or a downward half-tone, at intervals as if he arbitrarily put in a comma every eight inches in his typing. He is swell at witty cracks, and if his manner had been more lively his lectures would have been wonderful. As it was, he held his audience right to the end of the series. They had various entertainments for him, but as Kay [Coburn] said, the women on the staff weren't invited. But if you can't make a better appearance and give as good a lecture as that bird—then I'll take in washing. When you come back I think I'll drag you to see Sterndale Bennett too, so that will take care of some of your machine gun fire. Oh yes, I've got plans for bossing you around, my lad, once I just get hold of you again. However, I think you're going to like it. Hen-pecked husbands complain, but they seem to take it. You've always been fairly docile anyway.

Last Sunday we had tea at Oaklawn with guests and I invited Henry Noyes who is a perfect lamb and one of the best people I know for holding up a limping conversation. Henry told me that he'd been talking to Dr. Brown about possible jobs, and Walter T. told him he'd be glad to give him a recommendation when he wanted it—but as Henry says, that's about all he would give him. Brown met me at one of the Bush lectures (one of the reasons I'd gone, I must confess!) and said he'd just had a letter from Paris. I said, that's funny, so had I. I'm sorry about Henry though. Well, anyway, it sounds to me as if they still mean to have you there next year, and any little thing you happen to er—uh—find out—you might let me know?

Last Monday we had a concert—Tudor Singers—better than ever. Healey Willan has reduced the choir from sixteen to ten and the balance of tone is much more delicate. He has a great nostalgia for the Elizabethans—says they knew how to live, and their music and their social grace is ninety percent forgotten now. It was a grand evening. Tuesday afternoon I gave a talk on modern art to the Vic Alumni—I guess it was all right. It went on just for an hour as they said, but was late because we'd had trouble with the lantern. I went up to see Jack Oughton and Phyllis afterward, and their little Elisabeth. Lovely child—fair and plump and sweet-tempered. I felt like a very unfruitful piece of humanity and didn't know what to do with her, especially when Phyllis let me hold her. You can get the picture.

Last night Earle Birney phoned and I trotted up to see them. I had a swell time, and I told them your story about the whore in the café stroking your hair. Incidentally, I was on the point of cabling FOR GOD'S SAKE GET A HAIRCUT, but just let it pass.

I loved your letters and have been laughing ever since, and wish I could show 'em to some of our more Rabelaisian friends.

I'm glad you took something to the Burnetts. Edith liked the stockings and dropped me a note—please find out if she had to pay duty.

I'm bursting to know what is to happen re finances, as I've written cheques and got *all* my debts paid today and start next month from scratch with about $65. I hope there's a letter from you tomorrow but that's probably too much to ask. I'd love to have heard the Ravel concert and the Yves Tinayre concert, and I love your crazy verse.

Helen

[*Toronto*]
Monday. Jan. 30, '39

The letter from Frye referred to in the first sentence is missing.

Norrie darling! I finished writing to you last night hoping there'd be one from you today—and there was! It is just midnight and I've only now got home from Mimico where I spoke to a study group of friends of Muriel Code—people who had gone to school with her and who meet now as a sort of reading group and review books and occasionally have speakers. I was a bit peeved at being roped in for this but then I was in good form and the girls were nice and some were really keen—so I quite enjoyed it. Sometimes my dominating personality really gets to work and produces something—it seemed to anyway, tonight.

I'm so glad to hear about your financial state, it gives me something to go on. If you aren't able to borrow the 20 pounds then I can send it of course, but if you can then we certainly must arrange a little expedition of some sort. I thought that if you can't afford to stay much longer than the middle of July then I might come about the middle of June when your exams are finishing. Then we could go about a little until you had to be back for the viva. Of course if the college would advance you some money—enough to stay longer—then all would be rosy. We could find out which would be the cheapest country just now with exchanges as they are and that would help too. I think I said that $300 would be about the most I can hope to collect just now.

I wish I could think of three hundred and sixty five different ways of telling you I love you—I hope it doesn't get monotonous.

Helen

Oxford
[2 *February* 1939]

My pet:

It's some time since I've written, but nothing whatever has happened. I wrote a paper on *King Lear* that Blunden seemed to like, but otherwise I've done little work. I don't know exactly what I have done, in fact. That silly bastard Little hasn't sent my money yet, so in the meantime I'm living off overdrafts and borrowed money. That accounts for some of the slackening in activity.

Darling, you'd better make up your mind whether you're coming over here or meeting me in New York. I've told you the financial news: £60 to do me till June. What I think I shall do is not take my degree after my viva, but take it *in absentia* in the fall, when, I hope, I shall be able to pay the fees. That isn't exactly regular, but I think it's legal. That will mean that I can leave the summer term's battels over, as I did two years ago. It depends on how much money you can raise whether you can come or not. If I run short I don't think I'll run too short not to be able to borrow from Mike or Rodney.

I'm expecting Victoria to take me back, of course. I've written to most of the people you mention, but there's no use asking Robins if I'm going back because he doesn't know. There would be only two things preventing my going back. One, they may prefer Henry Noyes so much as to keep him and drop all their connections with me and lose all the money they've invested in me. Two, they may go so broke they won't be able to pay an additional salary, which will mean letting a man go and dropping their standing as a college. See?

On rereading your letter, though, you have a point about the college's advancing money. I'm planning to write the English Department this week. I shall ask my questions of Joe Fisher rather than Robins, though, I think. The difficulty will be putting off the college here and travelling around Europe instead.

Rodney & Mike keep working hard & steadily on their theses. Bryson has switched my tutorial to nine in the morning. I turn up at 9:15, he turns up at 9:40, we quit around 10:50 and leave a girl who was to come at 10, and did, blaspheming in the corridor.

I love you. Write me often. A postcard will do.

Norrie

[*Toronto*]
Monday. Feb 13, 1939

Dear Norrie: Your letter came this afternoon—I was beginning to wonder whether I should send you a night letter to see whether you had pneumonia.

I've just phoned Jerry [Riddell] about the cost of taking your degree *in absentia*—he thinks it will be five pounds extra, otherwise there's no difference, and he said he took his *B. Litt.* after about four years. Only objection is that it comes hard paying the fees later when you're away off from Oxford with other places for your money. Well, if you can't borrow from the college I think you've a good idea there. I think I've answered some of the arguments you put up re the job in Victoria next year—that is—they seem to be expecting you and not Henry.

I'd send you some money now but I suppose by this time Little has come through. As I say, I'll send it at once if you say so, but if you don't give me an SOS then I'll hoard it.

I've been running around at quite a rate. One weekend I spent in the Infirmary with a cold. Then I started out into the world again on Monday full speed ahead. Symphony concert—George Enesco came and swooned over the Beethoven Concerto. They did his Romanian Rhapsody and the *Sorcerer's Apprentice*. Then I took nine kids in the house to dinner at Chinatown—our old friend Charlie Wong looked after us. Played with Roy. Gallery opening on Friday—I went with Yvonne [Williams] and Esther [Johnson] and Gwen [Kidd]. Betty Endicott and I went to hear Poldi Mildner on Saturday night—we had a swell time but Poldi was a great big beautiful Viennese blonde who pounded hell out of Brahms (Variations on a Theme of Handel), Liszt, Chopin, and did the Octave Etude and some Mendelssohn as encores. Complete washout, musically. Sunday morning I took some kids walking in High Park, went home for dinner, went with Roy to a concert at the Granite Club, came here for tea where the kids were discussing original sin and revolting against their parents. Then I went to the Artist Forum meeting—Humphrey Carver on Housing. Excellent discussion. Whew—*that* was a day! The original sin idea, incidentally, came out of the sermon Earl Lautenslager preached in the chapel yesterday. I didn't go, but Jessie Mac was fuming at breakfast time. Earl has evidently gone in for fiery oratory and hell and damnation of the sort that used to go with revival meetings. Kay Coburn said she thought it was almost grounds for divorce if a man developed such ideas. I don't know whether it's Barthian theology or not—they tell me that John Line is spreading some of the same doctrines and that every sermon this year in the chapel has been practically the same to a greater or less degree. When you get time you might tell me about these things. I really don't know what you think and I'd like to, you know. You said you wouldn't force your opinions on me, but I have never thought about it at all. The main impression I got from these reports was that Earl had gone in for a very emotional kind of sermon, and in his talk to the students he kept repeating that he was not one of the clever ones in his year, but that the others—Rhodes scholars and such—were now pagan but he is a Christian.

I'm a bit on edge—I put myself down for a talk on furniture!—and now I've got to tuck in and do it. Really, I don't know how much longer I'll last on the meagre amount of information I have—I've been getting along this year on blarney, mostly. It will be nice to have one person in the family who knows what he is talking about. However, everything's fairly rosy.

I'm not making up my mind about Europe yet, waiting to see about money—and I'll go on a moment's notice if I can. I think I talked about time in my last letter.

I love you very much,
H.

Oxford
Feb. 14 [*1939*]

I don't need St. Valentine's Day to remind me that I love you, but I do need to realize that it's the middle of the middle term, and I'm halfway to Helen. And the sun's coming out, and it's stopped raining, and I got my money from Little this morning. It's because I haven't had that money, and I didn't like borrowing, that I've stayed in Oxford and haven't done much, so there's really no news.

Blunden continues vague and complimentary. He says things like "I wish you'd write these things down, just as you say them: I think there's something to be said for a book of table talk," or "I don't care about a paper: it's enough just to get you talking." But he doesn't seem to remember what I've told him particularly. He gave me a translation of Keats' *Hyperion* into Latin last time: I think it may mean he feels I should be reading more Latin: I actually do think he's oblique enough for that. Neither he nor I have expressed any particular interest in Keats. I haven't done much for him lately: I've been working on a history of language paper I'm worried about, and I think I've broken its back.

The *Forum* didn't send me the issue with my article in it, but they did send me the one with Newton's article in, which I liked: I hadn't realized he'd been in Canada. I think I'll drop him a note and thank him. You've probably done the same.

I got a cool but more or less adequate letter from the Chancellor, answering every point in my letter to him in turn. The Chancellor lacks the gift of torrential spontaneity, I sometimes feel. I still believe he hates me, but probably his brain is too befuddled to remember why.

The trio doesn't function so often now, so I get less practice. We read a Mendelssohn one some time ago in which he burst into the doxology in the last movement. Uplifting man, Mendelssohn. I went to a Dolmetsch concert too, and had a good time. The harpsichordist gave me ideas about Handel and Scarlatti I could never have got from a piano—or from any Toronto harpsichordist. Wanna harpsichord.

Darling, if I get Victoria's appointment for next year in writing, I think I can borrow from anyone here who has the money with a clear conscience. And Victoria should start paying me in July anyway, so a month's advance wouldn't hurt them.

Four months more.

Norrie

Oxford
Feb. 24 [*1939*]

Sweetheart:

Your letter of Feb. 13 just came. I'm sorry if I wrote you a snappish letter a month ago, but I'm apt to take a gloomy view of things during an English winter. I'm badly worried, in that automatic and unreasonable way one does worry, about Victoria: I expect them to take me back, but I've nothing on paper, no replies from anyone (except the Chancellor, who was so noncommittal I could almost hear his boots shuffle) to all my letters, and I just have to sit and wait and hang around until they feel like appointing me. So when you said to write to Robins to see if I was going back I thought Christ, they've got a new idea, and Henry Noyes is trying to grab my job, just as I was afraid he would, and of course he's on the spot and a handsome man. You see, my money hadn't come and I'd caught cold and was getting steadily rained on and was studying initial palatal diphthongization in Old English. And Roy [Daniells] used to keep telling me that the Victorian brass hats were no more rational creatures than the glacier rock in front of S.P.S., and couldn't be trusted as such. So I thought anything might be happening. And I've made no alternative plans. However, I'm hoping for the best. I think I can pile up more concentrated misery in this place than I could in hell. I detest England and I loathe Oxford: I think I always have done. Whether it would be any better with you and some more money I don't know, but I'd like to try it and see.

Assuming I get a job at Victoria next year, my salary would start in July. With that, and with this *in absentia* manoeuvre, which I'll talk to Blunden about, I think we could manage a trip all right. I don't think

I shall have to borrow more than ten pounds, if that, to finish the year with. You'll come, I suppose, as soon as we get some money amassed. I'm not sure I want you before exams: exams to me are rather nerve-racking and humiliating besides, and it'd be difficult to get away from Mrs. Grylls before the end of term. Diarrhea is not a social disease, and I'd sooner empty my pot on my examiners' heads by myself. On the week following exams, however, there'll be a ball it would be nice to display you at. In between exams and ball I may be drunk, but I'll try not to have a drunken and dissolute bum meet you at Southampton or London. According to the plans being bruited about among my friends, you may be met by eight or ten dissolute bums: not at all the sort of thing for a seasick woman. However, come when you like: I'll send you the exact timetable when I get it. But I'd like to give you all my time when you do come, and then again I'd write a better set of papers if I knew you were on the way. I think that little space between exams and ball would be best. Then we'll go somewhere cheap and close to England (with Mike in Paris?) until the viva. Then Germany perhaps, for another month. Then you go back to work and support me, and I come trotting along to keep house. Where shall we live next year? Shall we have a baby? I think I'd be jealous of a baby.

The trio has discovered Schumann, and he's swell. The trio and the dark beer will be the only two things I'll miss next year. Blunden is quite worked up about Kay [Coburn] and her Coleridge: he wasn't very coherent, but the general idea was that she didn't know enough to edit a man like Coleridge, and ought to enlist the aid of some Oxford men. Perhaps he, or his wife, or a friend, had been angling for them and were annoyed at a foreigner's getting them. Or he may simply want to read the stuff within the next five or ten years. Anyway, he seems quite annoyed. I hope she isn't trying to do more than just transcribe them: she'll get massacred by the English reviews if she does. And he's right: she doesn't know enough for any editing: she read a paper to the English Club in which she got Plato mixed with Aristotle and I tore it to pieces in about fifteen seconds. This is private, I need hardly say.

Lent has started. In a few days the calendar will be purged of the last taint of February.

I love you.

[*Toronto*]
March 1st, 1939

My dearest! do you see the date? I am so happy: the weather has changed and we have a sunny day, and I am taking the morning off.

Everyone has been down with the flu—I didn't catch it this time, fortunately. Sunday was an exciting sort of day—it snowed and blew about, a sharp driving sleet that stung you in the face. I went over to breakfast, then went home for dinner. I was to visit the Fairleys but they were all sick too. Lismer came up from New York that morning to see us, and I thought it was a pretty desolate kind of day for him to arrive, but I think he was pleased to be here no matter what the weather. On Monday he was to turn up first thing at the Gallery so I practically ran all the way to the Gallery and then he didn't show up until ten-thirty, and then only for a minute or two. The Centre people were very possessive, as usual. So that I got fifteen minutes talk with him on Tuesday, that was all—about the work we've been doing. But on Monday night there was a meeting of the New Education Fellowship in the Arts and Letters Club. 75 cents for dinner. I nearly wept. There was a very small group made up largely of middle-aged teachers and Art Centre admirers of A.L. [Arthur Lismer]. Lismer was the speaker of course, and although I may have been off-colour after a long day, I think he gave one of the worst rambles I've ever heard him do. Really, Norrie, I feel a little concerned about him—I feel that we are doing quite a good job here and I am seeing the gap close up. And I hate to see him come back and bring out his worst tricks of rambling incoherent sentences, and a talk with no organization, in which if he has ever thought out his central idea, at least he has never defined it. And it is certainly time that he did. On Tuesday we had a chat, but there's so little a man can do about supervising a job from such a distance.

Lismer addressed the teachers' class on Tuesday night—the usual jollying along, and caught his train to New York. Then I went over to the Gallery and talked to two hundred women from the Settlement and had a good time. My voice is much better, and I can be heard quite well in the long Gallery. At noon I'd been to see Sterndale Bennett and he put me through my paces on the opening speech, line by line.

Tonight Harold [Kemp] and I went to hear Piatigorsky who was as marvellous as we had hoped. We worked hard, and managed to get *four* encores!

I must post this now. The girls have been making candy, it's midnight and the place is still noisy. I'll be glad to get back to a certain amount of quiet living one of these days.

I love you,
Helen

Oxford
[*8 March 1939*]

Sweetheart, I have been neglecting you shamefully, but I'll promise to reform and write regularly, or I couldn't expect you to, and I'd get pretty dismal without your letters. I've got your picture, and that along with the coming of spring has lightened my misanthropic soul very considerably. I look and look at it for hours. I never dreamt it would be so fine a picture: all I could think of was your horrible graduation photo and I just assumed no picture could do you justice. Well, it doesn't do you justice, of course, but it's a beautiful picture just the same. It just takes the part of you that will go into a picture: at first I thought it was a bit statuesque and Duchess of Kentish, but I don't think so now. You are a lovely girl, you know: you take my breath away sometimes.

The Merton Dramatic Society, known as the Floats because it goes back to a time when the footlights were chunks of tallow floating on grease, has functioned. There weren't any plays the first year I was up, because somebody always howls about obscenity, and stops them going for a while. Last year they did the *Ascent of F6*, and this year they did a very bad play, badly acted and villainously produced, about witchcraft in a coast town, & a Shaw play about Shakespeare and Queen Elizabeth which was an appeal for a National Theatre. Fortunately they had an extremely good farce sandwiched between them which saved the day—at least that was what everybody said. And even that would have fallen to pieces if one character in it hadn't been so extraordinarily good—at least that was what a lot of people said. The producer enticed me into it by saying I wouldn't have anything to do: once I was in I discovered the Merton Floats have a bigger reputation than the O.U.D.S. itself. Our play was lifted from a Conan Doyle story by a Merton man who wrote it in a sort of Victoria-and-Albert German Romantic style. It was subjected to several layers of modernization and then was all right, except that the Senior Tutor didn't know what the Warden would say about the swearing (the word "bastard," inserted by me). The plot was that a professor (me) is experimenting with mesmerism. He works on a student in front of an audience and they exchange souls. The professor, as the student, goes home and is greeted with rapture by his daughter, who loves the student, & very coolly by his wife, who doesn't. Then I come on, very drunk, as the student. The experiment is repeated & the student & daughter this time exchange souls. Mrs. Blunden was my wife: dons' wives have to take all the female parts. Blunden's respect for me has gone away up, I can see that. If only I knew something about cricket I think Blunden would be quite fond of me. So last week was full of rehearsals and those two performances. I really did make a good professor: you should have seen me.

Can you keep a bag packed, sort of? The minute I get my reappointment at Victoria, or a definite promise of it, in writing, I'll start seeing about an advance and in the meantime will borrow money here. If you're broke now I don't suppose you'll have much. I've heard from Joe [Fisher], but to no purpose, so to speak. Exams here are June 8–14, Commemoration Ball June 19. Hope you can make it.

I'm reading Anglo-Saxon again & finding it fairly straightforward. The time really is going fast now. Term ends this week.

I love you.

[*Toronto*]
March 10, 1939

My dearest: Your letter of Feb. 24 just came this morning. By this time surely you will have had my letters telling you all I know about the situation at Victoria, and you must have received the picture I sent. I am quite sure you are perfectly all right so far as Vic is concerned. I met Joe Fisher one night on my way over to dinner and he said he'd answered your letter. I didn't ask what either of you said but hoped for the best. And Henry Noyes is still looking for a job—I'd like to find him one if there was anything anywhere, not your job, naturally. And Henry is not trying to grab your job, and I know he wouldn't try anything of the sort. The English climate is making you morbid, and a little uncharitable. Believe me, Henry is fine.

I had a grand time on Wednesday, for I had to entertain Robert Davis from Buffalo, who gave a lecture on contemporary painters. I had to gather a gang together for lunch, and then I went to dinner with him at the University Club and then we went to the skating Carnival. Awfully nice, he is, and we had a great time talking about gallery problems and stuff. He tells me that Mussolini has sent over a lot of Renaissance painting including Botticelli's *Birth of Venus* to the San Francisco Fair; that there's to be a showing of contemporary art including Canadian, and of Pacific art—Japanese & Hawaiian and goodness knows what—and North American Indian art. Davis says it will be much better than the New York Fair, which is too huge, and thinks the San Francisco Fair will be one of those things you'd regret having missed—like the Chicago Fair. There's a big Blake show on in Philadelphia now—I'll send you a catalogue perhaps. And in the fall, when the new Museum of Modern Art opens in New York there's to be an exhibition of three hundred Picassos!

Now after your letter comes with mention of a ball at the end of term I'm not sure how the hell I'm going to work in all of these things and it has me quite in a dither, and I realize that my plans are based on an income about the size of Sir Joseph Flavelle's. I think your idea is *really* grand and I'm holding onto the purse strings like everything. I spend my time alternately counting days and counting money—the one side still comes out too much, the other too little, but I'm still hoping.

I love you so much. And sometimes I wonder whether I did live with you. I did, didn't I. Oh Norrie!

Sunday evening. I've got one or two amusing things to tell you and I'd like to be spending this evening sitting beside you by the fire. I'd like you to read to me, and I'd like to be able to kiss you when I wanted to—just about all the time—and that would interfere with the reading. But you might not mind very much, especially since I haven't been very close to you lately. It is just the right sort of night to stay in with you close to the fire. It has been snowing hard all day, and there is a strong wind. Drifts are a foot deep out on Bloor Street, and we are quite surrounded. I am not in Oaklawn at all, but somewhere where you and I are living together. I have a new blouse—a deep mulberry colour which you will like. My new glasses are nice too. And my hair is long enough to wind round my head. I think you'll like that. But I don't know what you're going to think of me underneath the clothes. I'm just a little afraid to take them off, because I'm feeling awfully thin. Sometimes I think I'll go off and do a lot of exercises so that I'll be rounded out more and there'll be a little more of me for you to hold onto. Sometimes I feel thin and small and bloodless and a little apathetic, and I hate being like that—I want to feel warm and strong and I want to love you in a million different ways. When I think of being with you again I do feel hot and cold—you will look at me all over—but I won't be shy any more. I'm too proud of you, and happy because I am married to you.

This morning I came on deck for breakfast and thought I wouldn't go to chapel: Walter T. Brown was preaching. Then I remembered your letter and thought of my wire-pulling schemes, so I dashed over and sat in an aisle seat so he couldn't help but see I was there. I just don't seem to remember sermons, so you'll have to forgive me for that. I met [Wilmot B.] Lane on the way out, so I went over and greeted him gaily. He said he'd had a letter from you in which you'd said you couldn't stand all the Anglicanism around you on every side. I stifled my impulse to say you'd married one. Then we edged over to the wall, and he told me *very* confidentially that you were missing me, too, and that you were just counting the time until THE END. He said, "you know it's *very* hard for a young man to be away from his wife—I know—I've been through it. It's a hard struggle." I made some sort of remark, to which he replied "No, no, it's not likely that he'd tell you about it—but of course I'm different—he would tell *me*." Now look here Frye—none of this man to man stuff with Lane, if I hear any more of this I'm going straight to the Chancellor and have a grandmotherly talk about *my* feelings as a female! I wish I'd stop blushing long enough to insert into Lane the story about the whore who liked your blonde mop.

Norrie, darling, the spring term will be starting soon, the flowers will probably be out even now—where are you going for Easter holidays? As soon as the weather improves I'll go hunting for a place for us to live in next year. I suppose you will agree to any bargain I happen to chance upon? I'll try to get a separate place, *not* in an apartment building, and will keep the rent as low as I can. There is, of course, the possibility of just a room somewhere—but I don't think so. We haven't much furniture for a house—that's the catch.

We'll see—
Helen

Oxford
[*14 March 1939*]

Sweet:

There isn't much to say this time. Term is over, I've moved into residence: Mob Quad again, and I'm staying up a week, reading Old and Middle English. I'm doing three exams a month, and am starting on these two and Chaucer for March. I'd rather like to get £5 worth of books, which I can if I get a first: it would set me up in texts for next year.

I shall be less gloomy with each letter now. March is half over: I can hardly believe that the time really is going, but it is. Next Monday I go to Blackpool with [Bunny] Mellor. I expect to stay until Easter, and perhaps later if I find we get along and I'm doing some work and drinking only a moderate amount (his father runs a brewery). Mellor is young and silly and takes himself far too seriously, but he's a very intelligent kid, and when he gets knocked around a bit more will be all right. I don't know when or how long I'll be in London.

I've heard from Lane and from Cragg. Cragg has "155 families to visit, 3 church services a week, 3 young people's meetings a week, 4 Ladies Aids & 2 W.M.S.'s monthly, besides social evenings, concerts, annual meetings, etc." I ask you! When does he call his soul his own? Lane's letter was rhapsodic: Lane imagines himself to be a poet, and he was trying to match me. Joe Fisher also wrote. Everybody noncommittal. If Brown writes me a noncommittal letter I shall scream. I think it's a good sign that he hasn't.

Darling, you seem to have had a pretty tough winter. Wait till I get back and we'll make things hum in that hick town of ours. My lectures next year will be twenty-five times as good as they were last year, and I can lecture on anything from *Beowulf* to Beverley Nichols at a moment's notice. Once these silly exams are over—but I won't lay plans yet. Reading Latin and Greek, either original or translation, is the next thing I have to do. And then, when I hit a PMLA conference they'll think it's an air raid, or the Martians.

I had a silly don rag, as usual. Bryson reported somewhat vaguely that I was a very competent person doing things in my own way. Blunden said I was Merton's No. 1 chance for an English first. Then the Warden said, "Well, he's a good actor," and I started to leave. Just as I was leaving he said "You musn't laugh when you're acting," Mr. Frye.

I said "I apologize, sir," and walked out. I think he was slightly lit. I had a hangover. I hate people who are facetious when I have a hangover.

I don't know that there's any more news. Very little seems to happen to me these days, which is the way I want it for a bit.

I love you very, very much.

Norrie

London
[*4 April 1939*]

Darling:

I'm back in London again. Somehow I never got to feeling at home in Blackpool: all I wanted to do was sit down and read, and Bunny got fits of trying to entertain me and kept going around seeing people who obviously did not want to see either of us. He's a very nice kid, and I like him a lot, but two weeks among adolescent Englishmen is enough for anybody. Nothing much happened: I did some work, not as much as I should have done, did a lot of beer-drinking, saw some boring movies, played on Bunny's piano (Bunny has an enormous library of exceedingly difficult romantic music, bought after hearing it played by professionals, and which he tackles with disastrous results) and ate my meals. I hope I don't sound too much the ungrateful guest, but you get what I mean. From the money that silly kid spends at Oxford I thought his father was a millionaire, and was quaking for fear my pitiful little bags would be unpacked by a servant, but actually the money represents a lot of parental belt-tightening. It just struck me that I haven't asked my parents for a cent since the spring of 1930.

I got a letter from Robins, which seemed to assume I was coming back: he said he'd be glad when I got the Department "settled down": he spoke of Kay's going away and of having to absorb her work, and generally wrote a reassuring letter.

The English are jittery again: they can't believe Hitler will really back down. They have a superstitious fear of him, I think: they feel he's a man of destiny or something. And nobody, including myself, wants to fight or spend money defending *POLAND*.

I'm awfully tired: slept on a mattress last night that was like a suet pudding. I complained about it this morning, so you can imagine how bad it was. I didn't sleep, as it happens: not a wink. Thrashed around and tried to pacify myself concentrating on you. It wasn't hard to do, at that. Every once in a while I have a horrible claustrophobic feeling as though I were shut up in a cage of air and couldn't even rattle bars. That means I'm missing you again. But it's April. Oh, darling, I'm not much of a hero: I do a lot of whimpering and whining, but I won't dare realize what a nightmare this year has been until it's over. I hope the association between English literature, your absence, and Hitler doesn't remain permanent in my mind. But it won't, of course.

I love you.

"Those Aryans in Germany," says mother's last letter, "are not marching *forward*."

I love you.

All the way from Blackpool to London on the train I saw sheep and little baby lambs, some hardly bigger than squirrels.

I love you.

Norrie

Good old Lane: he reacted just as I wanted him to.

[*Toronto*]
April 5, 1939

My dearest: I've just come from looking at a show of Massons put on for my special benefit. Douglas Duncan brought out all the canvases he'd exhibited some weeks ago. They are amazingly good and I'm certainly going to see him next time I go to Ottawa. André Biéler was in town last Saturday and we had a great sort of chat: I'm invited to stay with them when I go to Kingston. If I weren't saving to come to England I'd make several trips this spring. Mrs. MacAgy is going to New York tomorrow and she asked me to go along. Our summer is going to be good—it must be, after all the temptation I am withstanding!

I don't know what Hitler is doing at the moment: I gather he is just sulking. Papers are running news of Albania. It was also announced today that [H. John] Iliffe was shot and killed by Arabs in Jerusalem. Did I tell you about lunching with him in Brussels? He was a very nice man and very well liked here—he came here from Cambridge and worked in the museum with Currelly. He left here around 1933 and went to Jerusalem as curator of the museum.

The Senior Dinner was a great success and I had a very good time. Didn't get a chance to drop that hint about next year in the right quarter. Robins asked when you'd be back. Joe Fisher said he'd written to you lately again. Fairley told me on Saturday that Henry [Noyes] has been offered a job out west. I hope you have a good time in Blackpool. I don't think I shall be leaving town for Easter at all. I really haven't any plans and I have to be here for another Hart House Quartet concert on Easter Sunday.

I haven't anything to say tonight but I thought I'd better send you a line. Mother and I went to the *St. Matthew Passion* last night. I think it was the best performance I have ever heard. The choirs were splendid. It seemed to me there was a greater precision and greater control everywhere. I wish you'd been there.

Good luck with the work, and enjoy yourself. I don't know whether I'll be seeing you there or here—I simply cannot read what is to happen in the next three months. But take care of yourself, my dear. I am really amazed that it is April, and I love you.

Helen

London
[*8 April 1939*]

The letter from Helen referred to in the second paragraph is missing.

Sweetheart:

Not much news this time. This is Easter, and I'm full of reminiscences. I can remember an extremely pleasant weekend in Hamilton last Easter, with a beautiful woman who somehow seemed to be the very spirit of spring. She went a little dim in the autumn: some of the radiance is missing—but we old men have our memories. Two years ago I can remember standing in Santa Maria Maggiore, listening to a rapid mumble which Mike said was a Paternoster going by in a cloud of dust. Then I got very heavy in the guts, dashed home at a speed the boys said they had never seen equalled, and shat for two hours.

My chief news is a letter from you. I can't imagine where $400 is coming from, but I have great faith in you. Mike is going to be free between Schools and Viva, and I thought we might go to Paris, then to Italy, to see Florence again and take in the Pisa, Siena and Ravenna you missed, then go to Vienna and Munich. Then I could dash off to Oxford and plug for my Viva, leaving you and Mike (whose Viva will be later than mine) to come more slowly up the Rhine, answer my two statutory questions, dash back to Cologne or the Low Countries or wherever you want to be, and go somewhere else. If I take my degree that last week in July I shall have to be in Oxford then too. I don't think Mike would mind going on that trip. As for Rodney—well, I've seen his thesis and I suspect it may be keeping him busy, though I hope not. From Ravenna to Vienna takes us through Padua (Giotto and Mantegna) and Venice (gondolas). Oh, darling, I hope it all works out. But every time I get an idea like that somebody like Mussolini gets a very different sort of idea.

Mike keeps working: yesterday we were stuck with Good Friday and couldn't do anything. We tried to go to Canterbury, but there weren't any trains. We've seen a few movies: a lovely ballet-like French thing, with hardly a word spoken, called *Sous les Toits de Paris*. *Blockade*, which was pretty hard to take, was on the same programme. Then we saw Disney's *Ferdinand*, swell but too short, and a grand piece of Hollywood hokum, so obvious it was really funny: *Gunga Din*. I've been here a week and haven't got in touch with anybody yet. But Henry's mother-in-law sent me a letter and I shall go to see her. I'm very glad Henry is going to Manitoba. Sorry Maclean is a frost: it'll be impossible to fire him now, owing to Brown's shrewdness in giving him a permanent appointment right away. It looks as though Joe [Fisher] (who I think really can teach) and I will have a lot of messes to clear up. Wish Henry was staying.

I love you,
Norrie

[*Toronto*]
April 11, 1939

My dear: It really is grand—about the date, I mean. I think I wrote you a measly sort of letter last week and this may not be much better but I hope you'll forgive it. We're both getting apologetic about letters—

I'm sure it is a sign that we need to get together a little oftener! It is, supposedly, spring at this point, last Sunday being Easter, and *would* you believe it? Last night we had a driving snow storm which messed up traffic everywhere and left the streets slushy and dripping—six inches of water in the gutters. Thursday night Laure Rièse and I went to see a crazy film called *Midnight* with Claudette Colbert wearing lovely gowns and having fantastic adventures in Paris. Friday morning I cast about for something to do and someone at breakfast mentioned Henry Noyes. So I beetled home and phoned him up. I went walking in High Park with him and wound up at his house for lunch. His new job is settled and he is very pleased to be going west. He'll be working under Roy [Daniells] and as he says there is hope for the future since the other members of the department are nearly retiring age. I told him your future was by no measure settled and he said he was sure it was—that when he had gone to see Brown about a job Brown had said they'd like very much to have him here but they were expecting you back. I suppose I should nose around a bit but I'm sure they'll write to you in their own good time. Henry said he thought Maclean a good man, but that he had got off to a bad start this year with the class which was kicking about him, that he is more of a recluse than is understood here, and isn't quite used to the Canadian student. He was doing a number of new courses too. Henry goes to England in May. By the way, you might look up his wife if you can—she is in London now. I think you said you had some sort of address.

You mustn't be alarmed about what I say about rooming houses, I won't do anything rash. I was writing out loud, so to speak, and then the idea sounded crazy. I'm looking for a coach-house apartment or a separate flat or an apartment or a very small house. It certainly will be private for I want privacy! For a few hours a week anyway. I'm beginning to feel that you and I have got ourselves involved in a public career that we'll find hard to kick over. I don't think that I shall want to stop working at the Gallery next year: I'm getting ideas about it. And now that I'm learning to speak to crowds is no time to stop. I'd be home shouting in your poor defenceless ear and driving you crazy. Anyway, I'm thinking of a house to live in.

Let's see. On Saturday I wrote letters to people urging them to come to the children's show tomorrow. I worked until nearly two o'clock and found Mr. Hay still adding up columns so I proposed lunch. We went off gaily together in a pouring rain to Angelo's and had beer and those good omelettes they make. And he talked a lot and we're very good friends. I'm getting on very well this year with the men at the Gallery from Baldwin up and down—feminine wiles etc.! I went off and had my hair curled then, and that brightened me up too. After dinner I was sitting down to a quiet evening when Earl Birney phoned. Said he'd been sick at home with pleurisy and was bothering all his friends. Would I like to come up? So I came up and drank cocktails with him for the evening and we played the piano to each other—very badly. Esther [Birney] was out.

On Sunday afternoon the Hart House Quartet gave its second concert at the Gallery in the Sculpture Court—and we had thirteen hundred and fifty people there!! I was thrilled beyond words. It wasn't overcrowded at all, but people perched on the side of the Court and on the steps and walked in the galleries. Mozart K575, Debussy, Ravel. When the Gallery is crowded the sound carries magnificently. We had people there who'd never heard the Quartet before. Someone asked an old bird how he liked it, and he wrinkled up his owlish old face and growled "Never heard anything like it in my whole life!"

Monday—staff meeting with Lismer who is up to do the lecture tomorrow. He's in very good form and full of ideas. But A.L. [Arthur Lismer] won't be back unless a miracle happens—however, I'm not surprised at anything anymore.

Norrie, my dearest, I hope your work is going well, and I'm glad you're enjoying Blackpool. I've gotten over the Easter holiday now and that is a relief. I'm not miserable, not at all, but I am getting so impatient, sometimes I think I'll burst soon with excitement. There is so much for us to do, to see. I want to kiss you and hold you tight and not let you go. When I finally do come to you I shall probably hold onto you so fast that we'll have a terrible time in buses and undergrounds, knocking people over and looking too newly-wed for anything. I want always to feel young and excited about you. I think I always shall. We'll always be busy and there'll always be so much to tell each other when we have a little quiet space to stop in. I've written all these pages without mention of the Polish border. Damn the Polish border—I hope they hold off until you finish Oxford, and then you come home. I will not think of anything else. Goodnight dearest.

H.

London
[*13 April 1939*]

Sweet:

Somehow or other I keep thinking of you, of how much I want to see you and how little I want to do these asinine exams. You seem to me to be getting pretty close, and the closer you get the more restive and impatient I get. April's half over: that just leaves one month. And if you're really coming across the Atlantic while I'm writing a lot of silly exams it will spread a glow of anticipation over them which perhaps my examiners will mistake for enthusiasm for their questions. June 15 is the day after I finish, so either that or the 16th will be all right.

As soon as Victoria gets around to hiring me they'll presumably start paying me in July, as they did last year, so if you bring all that money over I shan't have to ask for an advance. John Robins tells me I haven't written to Ned [Pratt], which surprises me: I was sure I had. The rape of Albania has changed Mike's mind about travelling to Germany and Italy, but he'll go anywhere in France with us we want him to, and I may persuade him to take the rest of the trip.

Thanks for the *New Yorker*s: the cartoons are a bit feebler, but the stories have more variety: fewer reminiscences about eccentric Aunt Emmas. I've just bought George Moore's *Confessions* in the Penguins. He can't write—lived too long in France to learn English, maybe. The world he lived in, with everybody talking endlessly about Ott [art] and life, is more remote from me than *Beowulf*: it really is.

Mike and I went to Canterbury yesterday. Huge barn of a cathedral: central tower I thought was lovely. I was even more interested in tiny little St. Martin's Church, with its Roman and Saxon and Norman layers. I don't know if you saw it or not: it has a leper squint in the west wall, where they could see the altar, and an excommunicate's squint on the side, where they couldn't. I'm still pretty suspicious of Tristram, but I liked his Canterbury things better.

I met a friend of mine at the B.M. today who is lecturing at Glasgow: he was at Merton two years ago. Said he was just back from France and had no watch because he got home from a party one night and wound his place card and threw his wristwatch in the fire. It gets you that way. He's tied up with a French girl but is rather leery of her because she's Royalist and pro-Nazi. I don't know why men bother with women like that: I certainly wouldn't marry anybody unless she were beautiful and intelligent and accomplished and sensible and virtuous and—what else are you darling?

Norrie

Paddington
[*17 April 1939*]

Dearest:

I sent Miss Whinney a note, and a card came from "A. Duddington" to say she'd gone on her vacation. Apparently A. Duddington didn't recognize my name, as the card was addressed to Miss H.N. Frye. I went to see the Burnetts last night. I can't seem to talk to them on anything but politics these days, and as I don't know anything about politics I doubtless sound pretty green to them. Amy's left them and they have a refugee maid—nice little girl: well, she's a married woman, but she acts a bit kiddish and nearly drives the immaculate Edith crazy with her slack down-at-the-heels Austrian *laissez-faire*. Did I tell you about meeting Jim Arnott, the Merton man now at Glasgow? He told me about a friend of his who had a job during the last war I want for the next one: typing out fancy imaginary menus for the British Army and then releasing them in the trenches when a strong west wind was blowing. I guffawed and said I thought even a German could see through a trick like that, whereupon two Jewish refugees at the next table glared at me.

Don't keep looking at newspapers to see whether it's safe to come to Europe this summer or you'll never get here. It's the newspaper's business to scare you into buying copies. If I have the situation at all figured out, there isn't any danger of war unless somebody loses their head and blunders into it. That may happen, but in the meantime the ruling class of Europe knows that war means revolution. There are national rivalries all right, but the big shots behind the dictatorial and democratic dummies are an international unit and know exactly what they want. And I don't think they want a war: they can sell armaments all right by pretending it's around the corner. Of course eventually it will come, unless Japan collapses in a few months, but not for a bit.

Then I went to see Elizabeth and had quite a good time with her, for once, although as usual I stayed about fifteen minutes too long. We went to see a Rouault show at Zwemmer's and then we went to her room and she showed me two sets of drawings: one to Marvell and one to Plato's *Phaedrus*. Grand stuff they were, too: I'm quite right about her ability, and she's come a long way. She has an uncanny sense of colour and rhythm, and when she brings off a facial expression it's just about perfect. She'd just come from Paris, where she'd spent a couple of days calmly wandering into various people's offices, without appointment, and showing them her drawings. One was Ambroise Vollard. Just like that. Vollard said "but these are very good," quite enthusiastically. The others said "very interesting." The trouble was she hadn't any clear idea why she was showing them to them. But she had a good time, and if she can find an intelligent beautiful-book publisher she may land something.

Well, it's next morning, and I must catch an Oxford train. I love you.

Norrie

[*Toronto*]
April 18th, 1939

My dearest: Two letters came from you today—April 4th and 8th. Also a long one from Lismer who went to Ottawa after leaving us and ran into Alford and all his students who went there to be lectured at in front of the pictures. A.L. is definitely in the dumps: he knows Baldwin doesn't want him back, and I know it. I thought there might be hope but Baldwin sat and lied to me yesterday. He told me how unfair it was to New York for us to ask Lismer to come back etc. He *is* such a yellow-livered cur that sometimes I nearly wonder why I consider staying with the job. I wish you were here to read this letter from A.L. and tell me not to get in a stew. Today has come all in a rush. In the first place it poured as hard as it possibly could. There were your two letters waiting for me at the Gallery and I was jubilant. Then I had to go to the Faculty Women's luncheon at Wymilwood. Mrs. Lane and Mrs. Line and Mrs. Brown all asked for you, and so on. Mrs. Brown said it would be so nice having you back next year—and I asked her whether Dr. Brown had written to you, but of course she didn't know. Perhaps I was wrong to do that but I'm sure it didn't matter much.

Norrie, your trip sounds wonderful and somewhat impossible, unless the war racket dies down. You wrote that last letter the day before Easter—the day after Albania was seized. I don't know where we shall be in two months time, but Italy doesn't sound as if it would be very hospitable to English tourists. With America taking an active part, perhaps Hitler will back down. We evidently have to wait a week for his pleasure. And the *Star* is full of talk of gas masks and the fact that food tickets are all ready in England. And the I.O.D.E. have rushed in and listed what they could do in the way of running ambulances.

Norrie, a while ago I sent your mother a handkerchief which we meant to send long ago—the one you bought at the University Settlement. And I got to talking the way I do, and told her what a great deal I think of you, and the students too—I was feeling a little lonely and the way I love you sort of crept into it. I thought she wouldn't mind—and then I didn't know whether she would. After all, it wouldn't annoy a mother—your mother—to have me tell her how wonderful I think her son is, would it?

I love your letters so, do write when you can.

Helen

[*Toronto*]
May 12, 1939

The PLT (postal telegram) mentioned in the first sentence is missing.

My dear: I sent you a PLT because yesterday I discovered that the *Georgic* was sailing from New York on the 10th and would fit into my plans very well. I'll just wait for your answer, and if all is well I'll come on the *Georgic*. I don't really want to hang around London waiting for you, although if you want me to come earlier—on the *Queen Mary* on the 12th, so as not to hold up your plans for getting to the continent as soon as possible—send me a PLT to that effect. I'll have enough work to do to keep me busy in London for two days anyway: I'm ordering a lot of lantern slides from the Courtauld Institute and I'll have to see Miss Whinney about that. I haven't written much because I'm working like the dickens trying to get away in time. At that, I'm scared that something may turn up to prevent my going. A matter of planning next year's programme ready for the printer earlier than it's ever been done before—it is to be ready before I leave, complete with lectures and class plans etc.

However, I expect to see Lismer in New York for several days—I'll probably go on the bus or drive down with Elizabeth Eedy. I haven't made any arrangements about a flat yet but we may have to leave that until we get back. And I haven't sent you any money, hoping that you could borrow enough until I get there and that the college will do something or other. I said in the PLT to let me know about that—I should hear from you in a few days.

I want to come to Southampton and I'd love you to meet me there, but if you say COME ON THE 12TH I'll be over like a shot. It is whichever is best for you. I am in a state of feverishly counting money and trying to get together three issues of the *Forum* before I go. June is done and I've got some more drawings coming along.

The newspapers are feeding us stuff these days about the royal family, enough to sicken anyone. They'll go past here May 22nd and the term is over early on that account. .

My letters seem to be one long series of travel bulletins these days. It is the winding up of a season for me too. I hope your work is not making you miss the spring—it has been glorious here, suddenly.

If I come on the *Queen Mary* it will be just one month from today. Or else five days later. Which shall it be? We'll have to get our heads together in earnest about France and Germany because I haven't got round to thinking about that part of it.

I hope you simply mop them up at examination time. It sounds like a horrible grind from what I hear. Anyhow, I'm hoping for you, and I'm terribly much in love with you.

Helen

Oxford
[*15 May 1939*]

Sweetheart:

This is Monday morning, and I still haven't heard. Perhaps you'd better drop in and see Robins before you leave, but I think everything will be all right. We could probably live quietly in Paris, seeing what we liked, quite easily on your money alone (I'm quite shameless about living off you, but I always was) until my Viva, even if I couldn't raise any more for a trip later. I'm beginning to wonder if Brown isn't being a subtle statesman and waiting to see whether I pass my exams or not. I think we'd better stay close to Oxford until the Viva and remain either in England or France: I've grown a little more apprehensive about war scares lately. After that, we can collect all the money we can and take the big trip I planned. Of course I'll cable the minute I hear from the College. I think you've got enough money for a month. We're not going to the party: none of my friends are going: only poisonous public-school snobs I've barely spoken to. I admit I don't sound very efficient, but with the College ignoring me my hands are a bit tied. I shall finish this term owing Rodney £20. That's how I stand at present.

I think I did the right thing in writing to Robins rather than Brown, but I shall have to write Brown if I don't hear soon.

What can I say about your coming over? Just a month and I'll be seeing you again. I suspect that those few days between Schools and June 18 I'll be climbing telegraph poles and barking like a dog.

Darling, I want to get a novel written and published. I've got the stuff of an unusually good writer in me, and the sooner I get established as one the better. I don't want to be absolutely dependent on a sycophantic college for my living, or my reputation.

Oh, darling, I want to see you so much.

Norrie

[*Toronto*]
May 16, 1939

My dear: I have been expecting an answer all week to my PLT but it hasn't come—just your letter written May 4th came, but you evidently had not got my last then. As for the rest of my message, I expect you haven't had any news yourself. But tonight I phoned Jerry [Riddell] about dropping in to see them, and as Kay was out I didn't go, but I had a very cheering conversation with him. He says that once a week he lays his ear to Brown's keyhole and hears a few things. At any rate, today he overheard a conversation between Brown and Robins where Johnnie put it up to the Principal in words of one syllable the dilemma you are in about the appointment. I don't know what you wrote him but I gather that your poor wife is debating whether or not she can possibly afford to get over to be with you and it all depends on your appointment. So Brown said of course it was understood that you were coming back but that he couldn't put anything definite yet until the Board meeting or something but on no account was I to hesitate in going to meet you because all would be well. Jerry says that J.D. [Robins] is likely to tell me himself and in that case I'm to look very surprised! There are times when I think I shall have to have twins to keep you right with the Principal!

It's getting late and the *Forum* is being made up a little early this time. Lou Morris trots around bringing me cuts and proofs and stray letters answering all the ones I sent out, and I get some pretty queer drawings sometimes. [A.Y.] Jackson gave us one which Lou seems to feel rather wary about—he's bringing it up now.

Preparations for the King and Queen: In Quebec they had an elaborate meal prepared but the boat is late and the food is late so the reporters are dining off the food of kings. Victoria College is issuing tickets to the staff etc. for window space in the Vic buildings and they are issuing invitations to married couples to move into Gandier House for the night before so they won't have to worry about getting in in the morning. The college grounds will be closed at 10:30 and the procession isn't until 2:30! So we all have to picnic on the premises. The thing that worries us most just now is that perhaps the Americans will design hats like the Queen's and try to make us all wear them.

I love you!
Helen

Oxford
1939 May 16

Telegram addressed to Helen Frye at the Art Gallery of Toronto.

I THINK EVERYTHING ALL RIGHT
YOU'VE ENOUGH MONEY LOVE

NORRIE

Waterloo Station, London
1939 June 17

Telegram addressed to Helen Frye on the SS Georgic.

WELCOME TO ENGLAND I LOVE YOU
WAITING IMPATIENTLY FOR YOU AT WATERLOO STATION
= NORRIE

The Fryes, ca. 1939 (courtesy of Susan Sydenham)

Frye, ca. 1938 (courtesy of Susan Sydenham)

Abbreviations

AGO	Art Gallery of Ontario
AGT	Art Gallery of Toronto
A.L.	Arthur Lismer
Ayre	John Ayre. *Northrop Frye: A Biography.* Toronto: Random House, 1989
BM	British Museum
Bob	the annual skit put on for first-year students at Victoria, named after Cobourg campus custodian Robert Beare
CCF	Cooperative Commonwealth Federation
CGIT	Canadian Girls in Training
CNE	Canadian National Exhibition
CNR	Canadian National Railway
CPR	Canadian Pacific Railway
CW	The Collected Works of Northrop Frye
E	The letter E between two numbers indicates the year of graduation from Emmanuel College (e.g., 3E6)
EC	Emmanuel College
HCM	Hambourg Conservatory of Music
HGK	Helen Gertrude Kemp
HK	Helen Kemp
HKF	Helen Kemp Frye
HNF	Herman Northrop Frye
IODE	Imperial Order Daughters of the Empire
LSR	League of Social Reconstruction
NF	Northrop Frye
NFHK	*The Correspondence of Northrop Frye and Helen Kemp, 1932–1939.* Ed. Robert D. Denham. CW, 1–2. Toronto: University of Toronto Press, 1996.
NGC	National Gallery of Canada
NRA	National Recovery Administration

OCA	Ontario College of Art
OCE	Ontario College of Education
OSA	Ontario Society of Artists
OUDS	Oxford University Drama Society
OUP	Oxford University Press
PLS	Picture Loan Society
PLT	Postal Telegram
PMLA	Proceedings of the Modern Language Association
RAF	Royal Air Force
RCA	Royal Canadian Academy of Arts
RK	Religious Knowledge
ROM	Royal Ontario Museum
SCM	Student Christian Movement
SPS	School of Practical Science, U of T; later the Faculty of Engineering
sup.	supplementary examination
T	The letter T between two numbers indicates the year of graduation from U of T (e.g., 3T3)
TCM	Toronto Conservatory of Music
TSO	Toronto Symphony Orchestra
UBC	University of British Columbia
UC	University College, University of Toronto
UNB	University of New Brunswick
U of T	University of Toronto
V & A	Victoria and Albert Museum
vac.	vacation
VC	Victoria College
VU	Victoria University (Victoria College plus Emmanuel College)
WHO	World Health Organization
WMS	Women's Missionary Society

Directory of People Mentioned in the Correspondence

Abercrombie, Lascelles (1881–1938). Goldsmith's reader in English at Merton College

Adeney, Marcus (1900–98). Cellist in the TSO, 1928–48; teacher at the TCM

Alexander, Howard. VC 3T3

Alford, (Edward) John Gregory (1890–1960). Professor of fine arts, U of T, in the 1930s and '40s; later taught at the Rhode Island School of Design

Allen, Thomas John. Merton College, 1938–40; from Peterborough, Ont.

Anderson, (James) Harold (1901–63). VC 3T3 and EC 3E5; worked in the mission fields before serving the Stone circuit in Saskatchewan

Aristophron, Pan. Author of *Plato's Academy*, illustrated by Elizabeth Fraser

Armstrong, Allan. Architectural student and assistant at the AGT

Arnold, Magda (1903–2002). Ph.D. in psychology, U of T, 1939; later taught at Wellesley College; wife of Robert K. (Bert) Arnold

Arnold, Robert Karl (Bert). Member of the German department at VC

Arnott, James Fullarton (Jim) (1914–82). Classmate of NF at Merton College, 1936–37; became a professor of drama at the University of Glasgow

Ashmole, Bernard (1894–1988). Lecturer on ancient art at the Courtauld Institute

Atkins, Caven Ernest (1907–after 2000). Canadian watercolourist

Auger, C(harles) E(dward) (1877–1935). Registrar and member of the English department at VC

Auger, Wilfred J. (Wilf). Son of C.E. Auger

Aunt Hatty. See Layhew, Harriet Howard

Avison, Ted. VC 3T4; brother of poet Margaret Avison

Baine, Rodney Montgomery (1913–2000). Rhodes scholar from Mississippi at Merton College, 1936–39; later a professor of eighteenth-century English at the University of Georgia

Baker, Noel (1889–1982). Secretary of Robert Cecil

Balbo, Count Italo (1896–1940). Italian aviator and Fascist politician; first minister of aviation in Italy

Baldwin, Martin (1891–1968). Curator, director, and director emeritus of the AGT, 1932–68

Band, Charles S. Member of the council and chair of the educational committee of the AGT

Barbeau, Charles Marcus (1883–1969). Ethnologist; founder of professional folklore studies in Canada

Barber, F(rank) Louis (1877–1945). Bursar and librarian at VC

Barnes, Albert C. (1872–1955). Art collector and educator; owner of the famous Barnes collection in Merion, Pa.

Bates, John (1911–82). VC 3T3 and EC 3E6; brother of Robert Bates

Bates, Robert P. (Bob) (1913–92). VC 3T3 and EC 3E6; brother of John Bates

Beattie, (Alexander) Munro (ca. 1912–2001).VC 3T3; professor of English at Carleton University in Ottawa for his entire career

Beatty, Agnes. Secretary to Martin Baldwin, the curator of the AGT; later Agnes Beatty Hamilton

Bell, Charles Greenleaf (b. 1916). Rhodes scholar from Mississippi at Exeter College, 1936–39; travelled with NF through Italy in 1937

Bennett, E.G. Sterndale (1884–1982). Director of the Toronto Masquers amateur theatre company; adjudicator, teacher, and actor; HKF's speech coach

Bickersteth, (John) Burgon (1888–1979). Warden of Hart House, U of T

Bilkey, Percy. One of the building guards at the AGT

Binning, Joe. VC 3T1; died suddenly on 27 May 1932

Birney, Earle (1904–95). Canadian poet, teacher, novelist, playwright, and editor; taught at UC, 1936–46

Birney, Esther (1907–2006). Wife of Earle Birney

Birtch, George Wellington (1912–88). VC 3T3 and EC 3E6

Bishop, Dorothy (Dot). VC 3T2; worked with HK during the summers at Camp Onawaw

Blunden, Edmund (1896–1974). Poet, autobiographer, critic; NF's tutor at Merton College

Blunt, Anthony (1907–93). Art historian; director of the Courtauld Institute, 1947–74

Bonfoy, Mr. and Mrs. George. Members of the Stone community when NF was a student minister in southwestern Saskatchewan

Boultbee, Margaret (Marge). Public relations secretary at the AGT

Bowles, Richard Pinch (1864–1960). President and chancellor of VU, 1913–30

Bowser, Elizabeth (Bowsie). Student from Massachusetts enrolled at the Courtauld Institute when HK studied there

Brandtner, Fritz (1896–1969). Modernist Canadian painter; introduced German expressionism to Canada

Brieger, Barbara. Wife of Peter Brieger

Brieger, Peter (1898–1933). Lecturer in fine arts, U of T

Brock, Reginald Walter (d. 1935). Dean of geology and geography at UBC; member of the Carnegie committee that studied the problems of museums in Canada

Brooker, Bertram (1888–1955). Painter, writer, illustrator, music critic, and advertising executive; active member of Toronto's cultural and intellectual life

Brooks, Kenneth Robert. Student at Merton College, 1933–40

Brooks, Murray G. General secretary of the SCM, 1927–34

Brown, E(dward) K(illoran) (1905–51). Member of the English department at the University of Manitoba, 1935–37, and at UC, 1937–47

Brown, Eric (1877–1939). Director of the NGC, 1910–39

Brown, Walter T. (1883–1954). Principal of VC, 1932–47; later president and chancellor

Brown, Mrs. Walter T.

Bryson, J.N. NF's tutor in Anglo-Saxon at Balliol College

Buchanan, Donald William (Don) (1908–66). VC 3T0; editor of *Acta Victoriana*; helped to organize the National Film Society in 1936; became associate director of the NGC

Bull, (William) Perkins (1870–1948). Lawyer, author, and businessman; commissioned HK to design the endpapers for several books

Burnett, Edith Manning and Stephen. Friends of Norah McCullough; visited by HK and NF in London on numerous occasions

Bush, Douglas (1896–1983). Harvard professor and literary critic

Cameron, Jean Elizabeth. VC 3T3

Campbell, Lorne. VC 3T4

Carman, Mary. VC 3T3; associate editor, *Acta Victoriana*, 1932–33

Carr, Emily (1871–1945). Canadian artist

Carver, Humphrey Stephen Mumford (1902–95). Landscape architect and town planner; lectured at the School of Architecture, U of T, 1938–41

Case, George. Lived with HK's Uncle Well and Aunt Clara Kemp in Forest, Ont.

Cecil, Robert (1864–1958). English Conservative statesman; was one of the architects of the League of Nations

Chapman, Howard Dennis (b. ca. 1918). Toronto architect

Clare, Florence (b. 1912). VC 3T3; older sister of Ida; attended Toronto Normal School and taught for two years before enrolling in the Pass Course at VC; married Arthur Cragg

Clare, Ida May. VC 3T3; younger sister of Florence; married Bill Conklin

Clark, Paraskeva (1898–1986). Russian artist who came to Toronto in 1931

Clarke, George. Former boyfriend of HK

Clarke, Jack and Alice. Members of the Stonepile community in southwestern Saskatchewan when NF was a student minister there
Clements, Edgar Bradford (Brad). VC 3T4
Clements, Eleanor. Cousin of Brad Clements; friend of Dorothy Drever
Coburn, Kathleen (Kay) (1905–91). Instructor in the English department at VC, assistant to the dean, and women's residence don; became a distinguished Coleridge scholar
Code, Muriel. VC 3T3
Cody, Henry John (1868–1951). Canon of St. Alban's cathedral, 1903–9; chair, board of governors of the U of T, 1923–32; chancellor, 1932–44
Colgrove, Rogers G. (Pete). VC 3T3; often contended with NF at the piano during their student days; taught NF ballroom dancing
Comfort, Charles Fraser (1900–94). Portrait, landscape, and mural painter; director of the department of mural painting at the OCA; taught at the U of T from 1938 until 1960, when he became director of the NGC in Ottawa
Comfort, Louise (1902–98). Wife of Charles Comfort
Conklin, Nora. Sister of Bill Conklin; studied at the Julliard School of Music
Conklin, William D. (Bill). VC 3T3; married Ida May Clare
Constable, William G. (1887–1976). Assistant director of the National Gallery, London, and director of the Courtauld Institute of Art
Constantine, Maud. Young woman HK meets aboard the *Ausonia* in September 1934
Couratin, Rev. Arthur Hubert. Junior chaplain, Merton College, 1936–39
Cox, Lucy. Musician; friend of HK and Roy Kemp
Cragg, Arthur Richard (Art) (1910–97). VC 3T3 and EC 3E7; married Florence Clare; performed NF and HK's wedding ceremony; brother of Laurence H. Cragg
Cragg, Laurence H. (Laurie) (b. 1912). VC 3T4; brother of Art Cragg
Craig, Eleanor. Peggy Craig's younger sister
Craig, Peggy (Peg). Vera Frye's roommate during her years in Chicago
Crawford, Thomas James (Tommy) (1877–1955). Choirmaster, teacher, and composer; conductor of the VC Music Club, 1927–42
Creighton, John. Husband of Sallee Creighton, a reader in the English department at VC
Cronin, Charlotte Boulton. HK's cousin; wife of Patrick Cronin and mother of nine children, including Margaret Cronin
Crowe, Miss. Graduate of Exeter College; lived in the rooming house where HK first stayed when she studied at the Courtauld Institute
Cumberland, John D.W. (Jack). VC 3T2; married Dot Darling
Currelly, Charles Trick (1876–1957). Professor of the history of industrial art at U of T during NF and HK's student days and later professor of archaeology; director of the ROM

Damin, Arnoldo and Signora. Owners of a pension where HK stayed in Italy in March–April 1935

Daniells, Roy (1902–79). Poet, professor, and critic; had a longtime friendship and correspondence with NF; taught at VC, 1934–37; spent most of his teaching career at UBC

Darling, Dorothy (Dot). VC 3T3; married Jack Cumberland

Davey, Jean Flatt. VC 3T3

Davidson, Jean Gertrude (True) (1901–78). VC 2T1

Davidson, Richard (1876–1944). Professor of Old Testament at EC; principal of EC, 1932–44

Davin, Dan (1913–90). Rhodes scholar from New Zealand at Balliol College; later a novelist and an editor at OUP

Davis, Ghent. Wealthy neighbour at the Kemps' summer cottage

Davis, Gladys Wookey. Wife of Herbert J. Davis; gave occasional gallery talks at the AGT

Davis, Herbert J. (1893–1967). Member of the UC English department; taught a graduate seminar in Blake at U of T; left Toronto for Cornell in 1938, and later became president of Smith College; a distinguished Swift scholar

Davis, Robert Tyler (1918–77). Director of education at the Albright Art Gallery, Buffalo, N.Y.

Deakin, Lucy. Friend of HK; they were roommates at the Universal Exhibition in Brussels in 1935

De Kresz, Norah Drewett (1882–1960). Anglo-Canadian pianist; taught at the TCM,1928–35; wife of Hungarian-Canadian violinist Geza de Kresz, with whom she often gave concerts

Dennison, Ruby. Violinist and cellist; taught at the Danard Conservatory; played violin with HK and Marcus Adeney in a 1929 recital at the HCM

Denton, Frank. Member of the council of the AGT

DeWitt, Norman Wentworth (1876–1958). Professor of Latin at VC

Dingman, Ruth Gordon. VC 3T3

Dodgson, Campbell (1867–1948). Keeper of prints and drawings at the BM; an Albrecht Diirer scholar and connoisseur of early prints

Drever, Dorothy (Dot). VC 3T3

Duncan, Douglas M. (1902–68). Toronto art dealer; helped to found the Picture Loan Society in 1936; responsible for the first exhibitions of Carl Schaefer, Will Ogilvie, among others

Edgar, Pelham (1871–1948). Professor of English at VC

Eedy, Alice. VC 3T9; sister of Elizabeth Eedy

Eedy, Elizabeth (d. 1997). VC 3T3; sister of Alice Eedy; married NF on 27 July 1988

Elder, Jean. VC 3T3

Elliott, Ruth. Painter HK met in Ottawa in the summer of 1934
Endicott, Betty. Wife of Norman Endicott
Endicott, James G. (Jim) (1898–1993). VC 2T3; United Church of Canada missionary; called himself a "Christian Marxist"; after the 1949 World Peace Conference in Paris, helped found the Canadian Peace Conference; older brother of Norman J. Endicott
Endicott, Norman J. (1902–76). Member of the English department at UC; younger brother of James G. Endicott
Evans, David Mynydogg (d. 15 November 1934). Minister in Eastend and Waldron, Sask., when NF was a student minister in the summer of 1934; he came to Canada from Wales at the end of World War I
Evans, Jean. VC 3T0; member of the VC library staff during HK's fourth year; worked with HK at Camp Onawaw; married Johnny Copp

Fair, Harold. VC 3T4; editor of *Acta Victoriana*, 1933–34
Fairley, Barker (1887–1986). Member of the German department, U of T, 1915–57; co-founder of the *Canadian Forum* and an early friend of the Group of Seven; a painter himself and an authority on Goethe
Fairley, Joan. Staff lecturer in the Saturday morning classes at the AGT; daughter of Barker Fairley
Fenwick, Kathleen (1901–73). Curator of prints and drawings at the NGC
Fisher, Joseph (Joe) (1907–52). Member of the English department at VC; appointed in 1937, and after a stint in the military, became chair of the department in 1945
Flavelle, Sir Joseph Wesley (1858–1939). Canadian meatpacker, financier, and philanthropist
Fletcher, Ronald F.W.H. Tutor in English at St. Edmund Hall, Oxford
Forbes, Kenneth (1892–1980). Canadian figure and portrait painter
Forward, Dorothy. Don in the women's residences at VC
Fosdick, Harry Emerson (1878–1969). American preacher and author
Fraser, Elizabeth. Canadian book designer living in London; friend of Norah McCullough; befriended NF when he was at Oxford
Freeland, Esther Margaret (Joby). VC 3T3; friend of Lois Hampson
Freyhan, Robert. Young German scholar who emigrated to England in the 1930s; later published on medieval art
Frye, Catharine Mary Maud Howard (Cassie) (1870–1940). NF's mother; the fourth child of Eratus Seth Howard, a Methodist minister, and Harriet Hersey
Frye, (Eratus) Howard (1899–1918). NF's older brother, born on 29 March 1899; killed on 18 August 1918 by artillery fire near Amiens, France
Frye, Herman Edward (1870–1959). NF's father; hardware salesman; born at Windsor Mills, Que., on 30 August 1870 (the same day NF's mother was born), and died on 15 December 1959, at Evergreen Park, Ill.

Frye, Vera (1900–66). NF's sister; taught school in Chicago most of her life
Gabrilowitsch, Ossip (1878–1936). Conductor of the Detroit Symphony Orchestra and distinguished pianist
Garrett, John C. (Jack). Rhodes scholar from Alberta; Merton College, 1937–40
Glaves, Emily. Stenographer in the VU library
Glover, T.R. SCM official
Gordon, Doug. VC 3T3
Gould, Ernie. VC 3T3
Govan, Margaret (Robin) (d. 1987). Extramural student at EC, 1933–34; head counsellor at Camp Onawaw in the mid-1930s; later became director, and eventually owner, of the camp
Green, Gertrude Huntley (1889–1987). Canadian pianist
Grier, Sir Wyly (1862–1957). Canadian portrait painter; knighted in 1935 for his contributions to Canadian arts and letters
Group of Seven. Canadian art movement that drew its inspiration primarily from northern Ontario landscapes; its seven members were Frank Carmichael, Lawren Harris, A.Y. Jackson, Frank Johnston, Arthur Lismer, J.E.H. MacDonald, and F.H. Varley
Grube, George M.A. (1899–1982). Professor of classics at Trinity College, 1931–70; president of the LSR, 1934–35; book review editor and managing editor of the *Canadian Forum*, 1937–41; and a leading member of the CCF

Hahn, Elizabeth Wyn Wood (Betty) (1903–66). Canadian sculptor, muralist, monumentalist, and medallist; married Emanuel Hahn; taught at Central Technical School in Toronto
Hahn, Emanuel Otto (Mannie) (1881–1957). Canadian sculptor and teacher; well known for his realistic commemorative sculptures in the Toronto area and native subjects; married Elizabeth (Betty) Wyn Wood
Haldane, J.B.S. (1892–1964). Biologist; professor of genetics at London University, 1933–37; a committed Marxist
Hall, John. Fiancé of Joan Fairley
Hambourg, Boris (1885–1954). Toronto cellist and founding member of the Hart House String Quartet and the de Kresz–Hambourg Trio
Hampson, (Margaret) Lois. VC 3T3; friend of Joby Freeland; married Gordon Romans
Hand, A.E.R. Cataloguer in the library at VU
Hanford, James Holly (1882–1969). Milton scholar; taught at Case Western Reserve University
Harris, Lawren (1885–1970). Influential Canadian painter; prime mover of the Group of Seven and founding member of the Arts and Letters Club; married Beth Housser
Harrison, Ernie. Friend of Roy Kemp; went to South Africa to work in the mines; HK's sister Marion travelled to Cape Town to marry him in 1936

Harrison, Irwin Hubert (b. December 1936). First child of Ernie Harrison and Marion Kemp Harrison
Harrison, Marion Kemp. *See* Kemp, Marion
Hart House String Quartet. Musical group formed by Vincent and Alice Massey in 1923–24 and sponsored by the Massey Foundation for two decades; members of the quartet during HK and NF's student days were Geza de Kresz, Boris Hambourg, Harry Adaskin, and Milton Blackstone
Hartmanshenn, Herta. Fellow in the German department at VC, 1938–39; don in the women's residences
Harwood-Jones, John. VC 3T6; married Lorna Thompson
Haurwitz, Bernard (1905–86). Honorary special lecturer in physics, U of T
Havelock, Eric (1903–88). Member of the classics department at VC; on the board of editors of the *Canadian Forum*
Hay, W.G. Treasurer of the AGT
Heathcock, Harold. VC 3T3
Heather, Fred. Friend of HK's brother, Roy Kemp
Hebb, Ruth. *See* Dingman, Ruth
Heim, Emmy (1885–1954). Viennese soprano who came to Canada in 1934; formed musical partnership with Ernest MacMillan; taught at the TCM
Held, Julius Samuel (1905–2002). Art historian; came to the U.S. from the National Museum of Berlin in 1934; taught at New York University, 1935–41; lecturer at the NGC, 1936–37, and at the AGT; professor of art history at Barnard College, 1944–71
Hepburn, Mitchell Frederick (1896–1953). Premier of Ontario, 1934–42
Heward, Prudence (1896–1947). Canadian figure and landscape painter
Hickman, Walter and Agnes. Members of the Stone parish in southwestern Saskatchewan; Walter began homesteading on land east of the North Fork School in 1909; Agnes played organ for church services held in the school
Higgs, Marian. Friend of HK and student at the Courtauld Institute in London when HK studied there; HK travelled with her to Paris and spent a weekend at her home near Cheltenham
Holmes, Charles Parson Hartley (Charlie). VC 3T3
Home, Ruth M. (1901–65). Lecturer and guide at the ROM
Hornyansky, Joyce. Toronto musician; wife of Nicholas Hornyansky, the Canadian etcher, printmaker, and painter
Hough, Edna. Along with her sister, Ethel Clower, a friend of HK's parents
Housser, Bess (1890–1969). Wife of Frederick B. Housser; later married Lawren Harris
Housser, Frederick B. (1889–1936). Art historian; married Yvonne McKague
Howard, Catharine Mary Maud (Cassie). *See* Frye, Catharine Maud Howard
Howard, Mary. Second youngest sister of NF's mother; died on 28 July 1932
Huntley, Gertrude. *See* Green, Gertrude Huntley

Iliffe, John Henry (d. 1939). First curator of the Palestine Archaeological Museum, or the Rockefeller Museum, in Jerusalem, opened in 1938

Jackson, A.Y. (1882–1974). Canadian landscape painter and member of the Group of Seven

Jarvis, Alan H. Rhodes scholar from the U of T; studied at Oxford in 1938–39

Jenkins, Annie Lampman (1866–1952). Talented pianist; studied music with Martin Krause in Leipzig; taught at the Krause School of Pianoforte Playing and Singing and at the Canadian Conservatory of Ottawa; organist and choirmistress at St. George's Church in Ottawa. Mother of Dorothy McCurry

Jessie Mac. *See* Macpherson, Jessie

Jobin, Louis (1844–1928). Canadian wood carver; known for his religious carvings for pilgrims and churches

Johnston, Alfred John (1871–1962). Professor of homiletics at EC

Johnstone, Kenneth (Ken). Friend of Norman Knight; he "worked as a meat packer, nursed an ambition to become a writer and eventually became a journalist in Montreal" (Ayre, 408)

Jones, David (1895–1974). Artist and British modernist poet

Jones, (Idris) Deane. Senior tutor at Merton College

Jones, John. See Harwood-Jones, John

Jones, (Phyllis) Jacobine (1897–1976). Canadian sculptor influenced by the art deco movement

Joseph, M(ichael) K(ennedy) (Mike) (1914–81). New Zealander studying at Oxford when NF was at Merton College; later became a distinguished poet and novelist

Judah, E.L. (fl. 1921–34). Curator of the Ethnological Museum at McGill University; secretary of the Canadian museums committee; member of the Carnegie committee that studied the problems of museums in Canada

Kane, Paul (1810–71). Most famous of the Canadian artist-explorers; best known for his paintings of western scenery and native people

Keith, Alexander Murdock. VC 3T4

Kemp, Clara. HK's paternal aunt from Forest, Ont.

Kemp, Daniel. HK's paternal grandfather

Kemp, Gertrude Maidment (1884–1963). HK's mother

Kemp, Harold. HK's younger brother; killed in a bombing raid over Germany in February 1944

Kemp, Hubert R. Professor of political economy, U of T; got undergraduates interested in making bamboo pipes, which they used in a 1939 concert at Hart House

Kemp, Marion (d. 1977). HK's younger sister; went to South Africa in 1936 to marry Ernie Harrison, the first of her three husbands

Kemp, Rebecca Sarah Cronin. HK's paternal grandmother
Kemp, Roy. VC 3T8; HK's younger brother
Kemp, S(tanley) H(eber) F(ranklin) (ca. 1884–1956). HK's father; VC oT6; abandoned his intention to enter the ministry because of deafness; became a commercial artist for Grip Ltd., where early in his career he worked with Arthur Lismer and Tom Thomson; was the chief designer for the Crown Cork and Seal Co.
Kemp, W.W. (Well). HK's paternal uncle from Forest, Ont., where he was the town clerk
Kerley, Annie. Music teacher; daughter of H.H. Kerley
Kerley, Henry Horace (1881–1950). Minister in Tompkins, Sask., 1924–34; NF's supervisory pastor on the Stone mission field in the summer of 1934
Kermode, F. Director of the Provincial Museum, Victoria, B.C., and member of the Carnegie committee that studied the problems of museums in Canada
Kettle, H. Garnard (Rik). Founding member of the PLS, Canada's first art rental; member of the Canadian Society of Painters in Watercolour
Keynes, Sir Geoffrey (1887–1982). Blake editor and scholar
Kidd, Gwendolyn M. (Gwen). Secretary of the children's art centre and public relations secretary at the AGT
Kidder, Margaret (Peggy). Education secretary at the AGT
King, Harold (1904–49). Toronto artist; taught at Northern Vocational School
King, Marjory. Wife of Harold King
Knight, G. Wilson (1897–1985). Professor of English at Trinity College, U of T, in the 1930s; taught at the University of Leeds, 1941–62; his main interest was Shakespeare, many of whose plays he produced and acted in; brother of W.F. Jackson Knight
Knight, Norm. VC 3T4
Knights, L.C. (1906–97). Lived in the same boarding house as HK when she studied at the Courtauld Institute; editor, along with F.R. Leavis, of *Scrutiny*
Koetse, Stien. Friend of HK; studied at the Courtauld Institute in London when HK was enrolled there; they met in Paris in September 1935
Krieghoff, Cornelius (1815–72). Canadian artist; best known for his genre paintings of habitants and Indians, most of which were produced for the tourist market
Krug, Charles Arthur (Charlie) (1906–85). UC 2T6 and EC 2E9; don of Gate House at VC during NF and HK's student days; professor of philosophy and psychology at Mount Allison University, 1931–47

Laing, Blair. VC 3T5
Lane, Wilmot B. (1871–1960). Professor of ethics at VC and EC
Langford, Frederick William (ca. 1880–1970). Professor of religious pedagogy at EC
LaPointe, Jules. U of T student in commerce course; violinist

Lautens(ch)lager, Earl (1906–73). VC 3T1 and EC 3E5; later, principal of EC

Lawson, James Sharp (Jim) (1890–1977). Tutor in the EC residences; became assistant librarian and library tutor at EC in 1935

Layhew, Harriet Howard (Hatty). Youngest sister of NF's mother; in 1917 NF's father moved his family to a farm she ran in Lennoxville, Que.

Learn, Mildred. VC 3T3; married James Delmer Martin

Lennox, Jean. Membership secretary at the AGT

LePan, Douglas (1914–98). UC 3T5; Oxford, 1935–37; taught at Harvard, 1938–41; served in the department of external affairs; appointed principal of UC in 1964

Lescaze, William (1896–1969). Modernist architect, best known for his Philadelphia Savings Fund Society Building

Lewis, Ivor R. Member of the council of the AGT

Lincke, Hans. Friend of Roy Kemp; played cello and studied at the TCM

Line, John (1885–1970). Professor of philosophy and history of religion at EC

Lipsett, Pat. VC 3T3; married Kingsley Joblin

Lismer, Arthur (1885–1969). Painter, art teacher, and member of the Group of Seven; educational supervisor at the AGT, 1927–38; friend of HK's father

Lismer, Marjorie. Daughter of Arthur Lismer; VC 3T5

Little, W.J. (ca. 1901–61). Bursar and senior tutor at VC

Livingston, Doris. VC 3T3; later, Doris Moggridge

Locke, George H. (1870–1937). Chief librarian of the Public Library of Toronto; instructor at the library school, U of T

Longley, Beatrice Bond (Bea). VC 3T4

Loring, Frances Norma (1887–1968). Canadian sculptor and monumentalist; shared a studio with fellow sculptor Florence Wyle

Lowenthal, Helen. Student at the Courtauld Institute when HK studied there; later, guide lecturer at the V & A; travelled with HK in Italy in April 1935

Lyly, John (ca. 1554–1606). English dramatist

MacAgy, Douglas (1913–73). Friend of HK; worked at the Barnes Collection in Merion, Pa., and at museums in Cleveland, San Francisco, and New York

Mrs. MacAgy. Mother of Douglas MacCagy.

MacCallum, Mr. and Mrs. Bob. Members of the Stonepile parish in southwestern Saskatchewan when NF was a student minister there

McCrae, Mr. and Mrs. Frank R. One of the more enterprising farmers in the Stone mission field when NF was a student minister there; he and his wife began homesteading in 1910 and helped to establish the North Fork School; their daughter Edna was the local schoolteacher

McCullough, Norah (1903–93). Assistant educational supervisor at the AGT and close friend of HK; became Arthur Lismer's assistant in 1927 and began work with him at the gallery in 1930

McCurry, Dorothy Lampman Jenkins (1899–1973). Wife of H.O. McCurry

McCurry, H(arry) O(rr) (1889–1964). Assistant director and secretary of the board of the NGC, 1919–39; succeeded Eric Brown as director, 1939–55

McCurry, Margot. Daughter of Dorothy and H.O. McCurry

MacDonald, J.E.H. (1873–1932). Landscape painter, poet, and member of the Group of Seven; began teaching design at OCA in 1921; appointed principal in 1929

McDougall, D.J. (b. 1892). Member of the history department at the U of T

MacGillivray, J.R. (1902–92). Member of the English department at UC

Mackintosh, George A. (Geordie) and Violet Rose. Lived in Stonepile in southwestern Saskatchewan when NF was a student minister; Violet was a schoolteacher at Stonepile when she married George in 1919

Mackintosh, Mr. and Mrs. Hugh. Members of the Stonepile community in southwestern Saskatchewan when NF was a student minister there

McKague, Yvonne (1898–1996). Canadian painter who closely followed the prototypes of the Group of Seven during her early years; taught at the OCA; married Frederick B. Housser in 1935

McKechnie, Egerton (Mac) and Margaret. Members of the Stone community in southwestern Saskatchewan when NF was a student minister there

McLaughlin, Isabel (1903–2002). Early modernist Canadian painter; studied with Arthur Lismer and Yvonne McKague (Housser); influenced by the Group of Seven; exhibited at Hart House in the spring of 1934

Maclean, Kenneth (1908–99). Member of the English department at VC; joined the department in 1938 as Pelham Edgar's replacement

Macleod, John (Jack). Professor of systematic theology at EC

MacMillan, Ernest (1893–1973). Conductor of the TSO, 1931–56

McMullen, George A. Lecturer in public speaking at EC

MacNamara, Gordon R. (1910–2006). U of T 3T4, and Osgoode Hall 3T7; practised law for five years, but then devoted most of his time to painting; owned and painted in the Studio Building, which Lawren Harris had built in the Rosedale Valley for the Group of Seven in 1914, for fifty years

Macphail, Agnes (1890–1954). Canada's first female Member of Parliament and the only woman elected to Parliament in 1921, the first federal election in which women had the vote; active in various political causes, including feminist ones

McPhee, Zene and Fanny. Members of the Stonepile parish is southwestern Saskatchewan when NF was a student minister there

Macpherson, Jessie (1900–69). Dean of women at VC, 1934–63; M.A. and Ph.D. in philosophy; taught ethics at VC

Macoun, Maureen. Member of Sigma Phi, a women's honorary professional and journalistic fraternity at the U of T, of which HK was a member

Martin, James Delmer (Del) (d. 2004). VC 3T3 and EC 3T6; shared a room with NF in Charles House, 1929–30; married Mildred Learn; NF spent several

Christmas holidays with Martin on the family farm in Honeywood, Ont.

Massey, Vincent (1887–1954). Politician and diplomat; Canada's first native-born Governor General; named in 1935 by Mackenzie King as high commissioner to Britain, a position he held until 1946; patron of the arts; served as honorary president of the AGT during HK's years there

Masson, Henri (1907–96). Belgian-born Canadian painter

Mellor, Bernard (Bunny) (ca. 1918–98). One of NF's fellow students at Merton College; B.A. with a second in English, 1939; M.A., 1943

Mellor, Steve and Connie. Members of the Stonepile community in south-western Saskatchewan when NF was a student minister there

Meyer, Walter. Member of the church in Stone, Sask.; accompanied NF on his first Sunday, showing him the way to the churches and introducing him to the congregations; he and Mrs. Meyer, the daughter of the Frank McCraes, had two children, James and Jessie

Michael, John Hugh (1878–1959). Professor of New Testament literature and exegesis at EC

Mihalko, Betty. One of NF's students

Miles, John Charles. Warden, Merton College

Millar, Graham. VC 3T3; married Mildred Oldfield

Milne, David (1882–1953). Canadian painter; influenced by American and French Impressionism, especially Monet, and by Matisse

Moonie, Esmé. Musical and dramatic programmer for Canadian radio, 1929–32; later became a social worker

Moore, Francis John. Leader of the SCM at the U of T until the fall of 1931; secretary of SCM, 1926–31; on the editorial board of the *Canadian Student*

Moorhouse, Hugh Edwin (1912–99). VC 3T3 and EC 3E6

Morrice, James Wilson (1865–1924). Canadian painter; moved to Paris in 1890, where he remained for the rest of his life

Morris, Lou A. (1919–2003). Assistant editor and circulation manager of the *Canadian Forum*; business manager from 1938 into the mid-1950s; proprietor of Old Favourites Bookshop from 1954

Morrison, George (b. 1913). VC 3T3 and EC 3E6

Muhlstock, Louis (1904–2001). Canadian painter of landscape and urban scenes in and around Montreal, especially of Depression subjects, but also known for his figures and animals

Mulliner, Arthur. Student of Harold Sumberg at the TCM; played second viola

Munro, Thomas (1897–1974). Curator at the Cleveland Art Museum; earlier, associate education director of the Barnes Foundation and professor of philosophy at Rutgers

Murray, Gilbert (1866–1957). Australian classical scholar and translator of Greek drama; became Regius professor of Greek at Oxford; six times he stood as an unsuccessful Liberal candidate for Parliament

Neely, Donald and Margaret. Family with whom NF stayed in Carnagh when he was a student minister; Donald Neely was Carnagh postmaster, 1930–68
Neil, John (1853–1928). Minister of Westminster Presbyterian Church, Toronto
Newton, Eric (1893–1965). Art critic for the *Manchester Guardian*
Nichols, Beverley (1899–1983). English essayist, novelist, playwright, and gossip columnist; a number of his books were bestsellers
Nicol, Pegi (1904–49). Canadian artist; later, Pegi Nicol MacLeod; member of the PLS; helped create the first surge of Canadian modernism
Norman, E. Herbert (Herb) (1909–57). VC 3T2; later a distinguished historian and diplomat
Noyes, Gertrude. Wife of Henry Noyes
Noyes, Henry (1910–2005). UC 3T3; M.A., U of T, 1936; Ph.D., University of London, 1938; taught at VC in 1938–39

Ogilvie, Will (1901–89). Canadian painter; the first official Canadian war artist; painted murals for the chapel at Hart House
Oldfield, Mildred (Millie). VC 3T3; married Graham Millar
Orchard, Bob. Poet whose work appeared in the *Canadian Forum* and the *Canadian Poetry Magazine*, among other places
Oughton, Jack. Close friend of HK; lived around the corner from the Kemps at 882 Carlaw St.; assistant in biology at the U of T, 1934–35; became an associate in zoology at the ROM, 1936; later taught at the Ontario Agricultural College and worked for twenty years for the WHO
Oughton, Phyllis. Wife of Jack Oughton; studied biology at UC
Owen, Derwyn Trevor (1876–1947). Elected bishop of Niagara in 1925 and bishop of Toronto in 1932; served as archbishop of Toronto and primate of the Anglican Church of Canada, 1934–47

Palmer, Lou. American student, studying at Exeter College when NF was at Merton in 1936–37; during part of NF's trip to Italy, they travelled together
Paul, James and Minnie. Members of the Carnagh community in southwestern Saskatchewan when NF was a student minister there
Pike, Bill. Friend of Roy Kemp
Pratt, E(dwin) J(ohn) (Ned) (1882–1964). Member of the English department at VC and well-known Canadian poet

Rae, Saul F. UC 3T6; studied economics in England when NF was at Oxford
Raeburn, Sir Henry (1756–1823). Scottish portrait painter
Ray, Margaret V. (Peggy) (1898–1982). VC 2T2; assistant to the librarian at VC; associate librarian, 1935; librarian, 1952; close friend and confidante of HK
Reid, George A. (1860–1947). Canadian painter and muralist; taught at the OCA, 1891–1928

Reid, Joseph B. Canadian Rhodes scholar at Merton College; B.A. in math, 1937; B.Sc., 1939; M.A., 1941

Riddell, Kay. Wife of Jerry Riddell

Riddell, Robert Gerald (Jerry) (1908–51). Senior tutor at VC; later joined the Canadian department of external affairs

Ridley, M.R. Member of the English faculty at Balliol College from 1920

Rièse, Laure (1910–96). VC 3T3 and longtime member of the French department at VC

Roberts, Richard (1874–1945). Minister at Sherbourne United Church, Toronto, 1926–38; part-time lecturer at EC, 1933–34; moderator of the United Church of Canada, 1934–36

Robins, John D. (1884–1952). Professor of English at VC

Roger, Mary Isabel Martha (Maysie). VC 3T4

Rogers, Evelyn. NF's ex-girlfriend in Moncton, N.B.; her father was a railway trade union organizer and active in the CCF

Romans, Robert Gordon (Gordie). VC 3T3; married Lois Hampson

Rose, Millicent. Student at the Courtauld Institute when HK was studying there; a committed Communist; they travelled to Italy together

Roseborough, Margaret (Peggy) (1909–90). Member of H.J. Davis's graduate seminar on Blake, which NF enrolled in during his first year at EC; later Margaret Stobie; went on to a distinguished academic career, ending at the University of Manitoba

Rowell, Newton Wesley (1867–1941). Lawyer, politician, and churchman; helped to develop the work of the League of Nations and was a leading layman in the founding of the United Church of Canada; appointed chief justice of Ontario, 1936

Russell, Dora (1894–1986). Bertrand Russell's second wife; early feminist advocate of more liberal attitudes toward premarital sex, birth control, and planned parenthood

Russell, Frances. VC 3T5; lived with Barbara Sturgis in 1936, taking HK's place in the apartment they had rented after HK became a don at Wymilwood

Rutherford, Gertrude (1893–1962). VC 2T1; associate general secretary of the SCM, 1923–34: principal of the United Church Training School in Toronto, which was affiliated with EC, 1934–46

Ryder, Lady Francis (1888–1965). London resident who befriended a number of scholars and students from Canada and other Commonwealth countries

Sadler, Sir Michael (1861–1943). Helped develop the modern English educational system; art collector

Sanderson, Charles Rupert (1887–1956). Deputy chief librarian at the Toronto Public Library and instructor in the library school, U of T

Sarg, Tony (1882–1942). Illustrator of children's books and humorous stories for the *Saturday Evening Post* and other magazines and proprietor of his own marionette company

Schaefer, Carl (1903–95). Ontario landscape artist; developed rural and social themes in his paintings in the 1930s

Sclater, Mary Lindsay (Molly). VC 3T6; ATCM, 1938; B. Mus., U of T, 1938; became a teacher, author, and organist-choirmaster; daughter of Rev. John Robert Patterson Sclater

Scott, Duncan Campbell (1862–1947). Canadian poet and short-story writer and federal civil servant

Sedgwick, Al. Former boyfriend of HK

Skitch, F.B. (Fred). VC 3T6; music, film, and drama editor for *Acta Victoriana*, 1935–36

Sly, Allan (b. 1907). Organized the men's glee club at Hart House and directed the club in 1933–34; taught at the TCM; became professor of music at Black Mountain College in 1935 and at the College of William and Mary in 1939

Smith, Mrs. Neighbour of the Kemps on Fulton Ave. Mother of Fred Smith

Smith, (David) Nichol (1875–1962). Merton professor of English literature at Oxford, 1929–46

Smith, Florence A. (Smitty). Don in the women's residences at VC and a reader in the English department

Smith, Fred. Friend of the Kemps; his family were neighbours of the Kemps on Fulton Ave.

Smith, Joseph Leopold (Leo) (1881–1952). Composer, writer, and teacher; principal cellist for the TSO, 1932–40; taught at the TCM; professor in the faculty of music, U of T, 1927–50

Smith, (Robert) Home (b. 1877). Architect known for a number of projects in the west end of Toronto, including the Kingsway and Old Mill subdivisions

Smith, Winifred. Proprietor of HK's boarding house in Ottawa

Snelgrove, Gordon. Fellow art student of HK at the Courtauld Institute; from Moose Jaw, Sask.; B.A., University of Saskatchewan; M.A., University of Chicago

Southam, Harry S. (ca. 1876–1954). Publisher of the *Ottawa Citizen*; became chairman of the board of the NGC in 1929; supported the gallery financially and gave it several paintings from his own extensive collection

Stewart, Chester and Martha. Members of the Stonepile community in southwestern Saskatchewan when NF was a student minister there

Stewart, Olga and Preston. Members of the Stonepile community in southwestern Saskatchewan when NF was a student minister there

Strachey, John (1901–63). British socialist writer and labour politician known for his contribution to leftist political thought

Sturgis, (Ellen) Barbara (ca. 1913–2004). Friend of HK and Kay Coburn; briefly rented an apartment with HK before HK became don at Wymilwood

Taylor, Harold. VC 3T5
Thomson, Tom (1877–1917). Canadian painter; began as a commercial artist, but burst onto the Toronto art scene in 1912–13; had first major exhibition at the Arts and Letters Club; friend of HK's father
Thornhill, Reg and Mary. Friends of HK's father and mother; at Reg Thornhill's instigation, S.H.F. Kemp joined the Commercial Artists' Guild
Turkington, Mrs. Edward. Owner-director of Camp Onawaw, a summer camp for teenage girls on a peninsula in Lake Vernon, near Huntsville, Ont.
Turner, W(alter) J(ames) (1889–1946). Music critic for the *New Statesman* and drama critic for the *London Mercury*

Uncle Well. See Kemp, W.W.

Varley, F.H. (1881–1969). Canadian portrait and landscape painter; member of the Group of Seven; taught at art schools in Toronto, Vancouver, and Ottawa
Vipond, Les. VC 3T8; editor of the *Varsity* during his fourth year; later became general secretary of the YMCA of Canada

Wace, A(lan) J(ohn) B(aynard) (1879–1957). Professor of archaeology at Cambridge
Waddington, Geoffrey (1904–66). Musical conductor and administrator; joined the faculty of the TCM and began career as radio musician in 1922; founded the CBC Symphony Orchestra in 1952
Wallace, Edward W. (1880–1941). President and chancellor of VU, 1930–41
Wallace, Robert (1881–1955). President of the University of Alberta and member of the Carnegie committee that studied the problems of museums in Canada
Warren, Alba Houghton (1915–85). Rhodes scholar from Texas at Merton College, 1936–39; B.A., English, Oxford, 1938; B.Litt., 1939; M.A., 1943; began teaching at Princeton, his alma mater, in 1946
Webb, Geoffrey Fairbank (1898–1970). Lecturer in the history of art at the Courtauld Institute, 1934–37; became the Slade professor of fine art at Cambridge, 1938
Webber, Gordon M. (1909–66). Canadian artist; chief assistant of Arthur Lismer at the AGT, beginning work there in 1930; taught at the Children's Art Centre of the AGT, 1935–39
Webster, John Clarence (1863–1950). Chairman of the committee formed by the Carnegie corporation in 1933 to study the problems of museums in Canada
Wedgwood, Veronica (1910–97). Daughter of Sir Ralph Wedgwood; became a distinguished historian
Weismiller, Edward (b. 1915). Rhodes Scholar from Iowa; studied at Merton College

Whinney, Margaret (Dickens) (1894–1974). Friend and confidante of HK; received a first in her studio at the Courtauld Institute in 1935 and was appointed to the staff; former teacher of Barbara Sturgis; became a widely published art historian; great-granddaughter of Charles Dickens

Wickham, Miss. Student who lived in HK's boarding house when she was at the Courtauld Institute

Wilkinson, Bertie (1898–1981). Professor of medieval history, U of T

Willan, James Healey (1880–1968). Composer, organist, choir director, and educator; dominant force in Canadian music for more than fifty years; taught at the TCM, 1913–37, and at the U of T, 1937–50

Williams, Ralph Colin (b. 1909). VC 3T5 and EC 3E7; student minister in the Stone, Sask., parish before NF served there in 1934

Williams, Yvonne (1901–97). Canadian stained-glass artist

Willis, Madge. Friend of Ruby Dennison; was in London when HK studied at the Courtauld Institute; grew up in Weardale, England

Wilson, Alice (1881–1964). VC alumna; distinguished geologist with the geological survey of Canada throughout her career; entered VC in 1901, but, because of health problems, did not complete her degree until 1911

Wilson, Cecil (Cec). VC 3T4; business manager, *Acta Victoriana*, 1933–34

Winfree, Mildred. Fiancée of Charles Bell; NF frequented the Winfree–Bell flat during his second stint at Oxford in 1938–39

Winspear, Mary (d. 1998). Member of Herbert J. Davis's graduate seminar on Blake, which NF took during his first year at EC

Woodhouse, A.S.P. (1895–1964). Member of the English department at UC, 1929–64, and head of the department for twenty years; had an important influence on English studies, especially in Canada, having helped to direct the careers of many university teachers of English

Woollcott, Alexander (1887–1943). New York drama and literary critic and whimsical essayist

Wright, Sherman. Art student on scholarship at the NGC during the time that HK was there in 1934; B.A. in architecture, University of Manitoba; postgraduate work in architecture, Columbia University

Wyle, Florence (1881–1936). Canadian sculptor; first woman to be accorded full membership in the Royal Canadian Academy of Arts; shared a studio with fellow sculptor Frances Loring for more than fifty years